Rage in the Belly

Rage in the Belly

Hunger in the New Testament

LUZIA SUTTER REHMANN
Translated by Monica Buckland
Foreword by H. Martin Rumscheidt

CASCADE *Books* • Eugene, Oregon

RAGE IN THE BELLY
Hunger in the New Testament

Copyright © 2021 Gütersloher Verlagshaus. All rights reserved. Except for brief quotations in critical publications or reviews, no part of this book may be reproduced in any manner without prior written permission from the publisher. Write: Permissions, Wipf and Stock Publishers, 199 W. 8th Ave., Suite 3, Eugene, OR 97401.

Translated from the original, *Wut im Bauch: Hunger im Neuen Testament*. Copyright © 2014 by Gütersloher Verlagshaus, Gütersloh, in der Verlagsgruppe Random House GmbH. Second printing of German edition 2016.
"Salva nos." Hilde Domin, in *Sämtliche Gedichte*, 2009, all rights reserved by S. Fischer Verlag GmbH, Frankfurt am Main. Used with permission.
"Auf einer Friedensversammlung." Dorothy Sölle, in *loben ohne lügen*, 2000. Translation, "At a peace gathering," in *The Mystery of Death*, by Nancy Lukens-Rumscheidt and Martin Lukens-Rumscheidt. Copyright © 2007 by Fortress Press, Minneapolis, MN. Reproduced with permission.
"Gott, du Freundin der Menschen." Dorothee Sölle, in *Träume mich, Gott. Geistliche Texte mit lästigen politischen Fragen*. Copyright © Fulbert Steffensky. Used with permission.
"Wieder II." Rose Ausländer, in *Gedichte*, 2001, all rights reserved by S. Fischer Verlag GmbH, Frankfurt am Main. Used with permission.
"This is how hunger begins." Daniil Kharms, in *The Penguin Book of Russian Poetry*. Translation copyright © Robert Chandler 2013, 2015 published by Penguin Classics 2013, 2015. Reproduced by permission of Penguin Books Ltd. ©

Cascade Books
An Imprint of Wipf and Stock Publishers
199 W. 8th Ave., Suite 3
Eugene, OR 97401

www.wipfandstock.com

PAPERBACK ISBN: 978–1-5326–4224–1
HARDCOVER ISBN: 978–1-5326–4225–8
EBOOK ISBN: 978–1-5326–4226–5

Cataloguing-in-Publication data:

Names: Sutter Rehmann, Luzia (author); Buckland, Monica (translator).

Title: Rage in the Belly: Hunger in the New Testament / Luzia Sutter Rehmann.

Description: Eugene, OR: Cascade Books, 2020 | Includes bibliographical references.

Identifiers: ISBN 978–1-5326–4224–1 (paperback) | ISBN 978–1-5326–4225–8 (hardcover) | ISBN 978–1-5326–4226–5 (ebook)

Subjects: LCSH: Biblical Studies | History and Culture | Feminism | Hunger

Classification: BS 500 (paperback) | BS 500 (ebook)

01/04/21

"Except you're not allowed to talk about hunger when you're hungry."
HERTA MÜLLER[1]

Contents

Foreword by H. Martin Rumscheidt		ix
Preface		xiii
Translator's Note by Monica Buckland		xix
Acknowledgments		xxi
Overview of Chapters		xxiii
List of Abbreviations		xxvii
1.	Bad Times	1
2.	The Poor Preach the Gospel	20
3.	Rage in the Belly	47
4.	The Blind Spot	79
5.	The Geography of Hunger	112
6.	Good Deeds in Times of Hunger	132
7.	Laughing at Table	154
8.	Thirst for More	171
9.	"A Ghost Does Not Have Flesh and Bones"	189
10.	Eating a Transformation	218
Endnotes		247
Bibliography		275

Foreword

In the early summer of 2016, the XII. International Bonhoeffer Congress met in Basel, Switzerland, and my dear friends, Luzia Sutter Rehmann and Christoph Rehmann-Sutter, invited me to stay at their home for the duration of the event. I had studied at the University of Basel in the early 1960s, taking the opportunity to study under Karl Barth in his last semester there, and had fallen in love with the city. Returning to Basel in 2016 was a real homecoming for me.

Luzia and I had met once or twice at the joint annual meetings of the Society for Biblical Studies and the American Academy of Religion. I had already heard of her from her "Doctor Mother," Professor Luise Schottroff, who told me, a professor of historical theology, that I needed to become familiar with a different and important hermeneutic in approaching, reading, and interpreting the Bible. Two major publications became my guide to and in the hermeneutic to which she referred: *Kompendium Feministische Bibelauslegung,* a one-volume commentary to which Luzia Sutter Rehmann had contributed.[2] The second source was a new translation of the Bible into German, *Bibel in gerechter Sprache,*[3] for which Luzia had translated the Gospel of Luke. For me, trained in the classical methods of critical-historical study of the Scriptures as the foundation of the church's doctrines, this was utterly new territory. The idea of *gerechte Sprache* (which I would render in English as the "language of justice") addresses both the centuries-old anti-Judaism of Christian study and interpretation of the Bible and doctrine, and the institutional and intellectual patriarchy and misogyny embedded in them. Karl Barth had remarked that one should read with the Bible in one hand and the newspaper in the other, but this was a novel way to read them simultaneously. In Schottroff's book, *Lydia's Impatient Sisters: A Feminist Social History of Early Christianity,* she calls that interrelated way of reading Scripture "From Life to Scripture—From Scripture to Life."[4] It gave me a new understanding of Bonhoeffer's insistence that in order to discern a truth, both the context in which it was uttered *and* the present interpreter's own context need to be known; there is no such thing as contextless understanding.

My room in Luzia's and Christoph's house was lined with shelves crammed full of books. Every night before falling asleep, I wished fervently that I could absorb all the wisdom on those shelves in my sleep as if by osmosis. When I awoke after the first night and began to peruse now this and then that one, my eyes fell on one with the word "WUT" in large red letters followed by "im Bauch" in small white letters. Then I saw the author's name: it was that of my hostess. It did not take long for me to examine what it was about; the full title was *Wut im Bauch: Hunger im Neuen Testament*, second edition of 2016.[5] Later that evening, as we enjoyed a fine wine on the terrace, I proposed that the book should be translated.

The method of "social-historical interpretation" is not original to this work by Luzia Sutter Rehmann, nor is that of "feminist interpretation." But *Rage in the Belly: Hunger in the New Testament* is a superb application and illustration of what I have described above as Barth's and Bonhoeffer's intention in relation to reading the Bible, but now in a feminist approach.

Let me outline how Luise Schottroff characterizes that perspective in *Lydia's Impatient Sisters*.

> I make the claim that a social-historical interpretation of the Bible that aligns itself in its contents with dominant Western exegesis in fact pursues the maintenance of the social status quo. . . . Since dominant Western scholarship shies away from declaring itself in terms of the aims of historical study and its interests, critical analysis is required for those interests to become manifest. Pursuing such analysis reveals that the term *social history* may, indeed, designate substantially different orientations.[6]

This calls for

> an effort to overcome the split between theory (that is, exegesis) and praxis (that is, Christian conduct of life and liberation work, or—in our context—sermon and meditation on scripture) . . . Interpretation of this kind mirrors both the social contexts of the people who speak in the Bible and the context of the women and men who interpret them today. The orientation and content of this social-historical interpretation of scripture . . . is interested in the *abolition of theory and praxis dualisms;* it wants to declare its own interests. It tries not to hide behind the alleged neutrality of the sciences.[7]

A few pages later, the shortcomings—errors may be a more accurate term—are clearly stated.

> My critique of historical criticism is not that it claims to be critical or that it pursues its work in reflective steps—I do that myself. If only it were critical: less critical in relation to the texts of scripture and more critical concerning today's institutions of domination and their use of the Bible! My critique of historical criticism is that it does not reflect on its own interests and openly declare them. It sides with existing injustices.[8]

Luzia Sutter Rehmann invites the reader to "Come, Read with My Eyes," as Luise Schottroff entitled her chapter in *The Theology of Dorothee Soelle*.[9] As I began to translate Luzia's text, my ordained minister's heart kept wanting to transpose what I read into sermons so that "first world" parishioners and subsequently my seminary students might hear a truly different gospel, which they would not have heard from me even only a few years ago.

Shortly before Dietrich Bonhoeffer was arrested under suspicion of involvement in the plot to overturn the Hitler government, he had composed a reflection on the ten years of Nazi rule. I read his *After Ten Years* now as a document of resistance, but one with a clear recognition of what reading of the Bible was called for in order to halt that regime or, as I now would say more appropriately today, to do *tikkun olam*. What he said in the final section, "The View from Below," is this:

> It remains an experience of incomparable value that we have for once learned to see the great events of world history from below, from the perspective of the outcasts, the suspects, the maltreated, the powerless, the oppressed and reviled, in short, from the perspective of the suffering; . . . that we (have) come to see matters . . . with new eyes; that our sense for greatness, humanness, justice, and mercy has grown clearer, freer, more incorruptible . . . for exploring the meaning of the world in contemplation and action.[10]

From Luzia Sutter Rehmann to Dietrich Bonhoeffer and on to Karl Barth, and circling back through Bonhoeffer to Luzia Sutter Rehmann, is good hermeneutics in my view.

One more word: a hearty and grateful acknowledgment of Monica Buckland. As the work of translation—determined from the outset to be done by her and me—affirmed the wisdom that it would be better for a good translation to be done not out of one's mother tongue into a "foreign" one but from the foreign language into one's "mother tongue." I applaud her good work and assure the readers of this book that you are truly better off with her translation. I am happy with my role as a "theological advisor."

And I gratefully acknowledge the competent shaping of the text in accordance with the *Chicago Manual of Style* by my New Hampshire expert and friend Jeremy Townsend, to whom we could confidently leave the intricate technical matters of scholarly publication.

H. Martin Rumscheidt

Preface

Even though much has been written over the last decades about meals shared in the New Testament, about the table as a place of learning, and the significance of meals from a cultural and symbolic perspective, less attention has been paid to hunger. People not only eat at table, they also learn, celebrate, and experiment there. Social hierarchies are mirrored there just as much as hospitality and compassion. Eating together shapes the structures of a society, its customs, language, and theology. If that is the case, what about hunger?

I began to look at what biblical texts were saying about hunger, and I became aware of how difficult it was even to discover it. While the language about eating is rich with images, the language about hunger is meager; or, more accurately, there is a silence that can easily be overlooked. How can we recognize hunger in the texts, if those who have suffered it do not talk about it? Perhaps it would be better not to mention hunger while we are hungry; perhaps it would be wiser to talk about eating instead. We can find reminiscences of hunger in biblical texts, tiny bones deposited, so to speak, in hidden strata. And this raises the question: How did hunger shape biblical memory?

And so I set out to find the hunger that is so patently absent in the exegetical literature on the New Testament. What does the silence of the interpretation signify? When Mary and Joseph have no roof over their heads (Luke 2:7), and spend the night outside among the animals and the shepherds in the fields, do we wonder whether perhaps they had no bread to eat either? Or does such a question not even occur to us? Mary was certainly thinking of hunger when she sang: "He has filled the hungry with good things, and sent the rich away empty" (Luke 1:53).

While I was researching what biblical texts had to say about eating and hunger, the Arab revolutions broke out in North Africa. And the same question arose here too: Do we think about hunger when we hear of those upheavals? I became aware of how unused we are to seeing the linkages between climate and politics, hunger and uprisings, and to connect what the media publish on different pages and under separate headings. But the connections between mass uprisings, drought, and hunger are actually obvious. The year of hunger, 2008, led to upheavals in many parts of the world, and was a precursor of the Arab revolutions. Environmental factors and climate change cause social stress, impoverishment, and migration of population groups. Middle East expert Thomas Friedman declares the extraordinary drought of 2006–2011 in northeastern Syria to be responsible for the rapid collapse of social structures and the subsequent outbreak of violence.[11] Rural families fled in their thousands from the drought into the cities, but found nothing for their livelihood. They vented their rage in the 2011 protests, which fused with the anti-Assad movement.[12] As I write, millions of refugees are pouring out of Syria, because of the terrible famine that followed the five years of drought.

These events coincided with my research. They began to impact my reading of the Bible. Conversely, my study of hunger made me see connections that I would otherwise have missed. Climatic extremes made for hardships in the population, harsh political systems stoked their rage. Hunger, rage, and uprisings are also found in the Gospels, but we still need to develop a manner of reading them that renders these factors visible.

We, the readers, are at issue here. The texts are circumspect or even silent in relation to hunger. But what is our stance as readers of those texts? Do we suspect hunger when we see the clues for it? The "we" I mean are readers in northern Europe, well-nourished and with full stomachs. What experiences of hunger do we have? Can we read the New Testament writings in such a way that we can see the nexus of poverty, violence, abandonment, and hunger even when the texts do not mention them explicitly?

This raises the question of what sort of hunger we expect to find in the texts. How can we define hunger? When does feeling hungry—having an appetite—turn into hunger? Are we looking for a situation that has been objectively defined as a famine, something that is obvious? How shall we discern a dull, silent hunger that makes no demands? Do we mean hunger in the sense of undernourishment, malnutrition, chronic malnutrition, starvation? Or what about the gnawing, grinding, impatient hunger that makes people flare up and panic?

Narrative texts in the Bible tell of the straw that broke the camel's back, and not of the barely noticed increase, the constant tension of daily privation that never changes. Stories have a focus; they do not recount in monotones the way things have always been; they want to make something very clear. They have an intention that, however verbally reticent, can be emotionally compact. As I searched for texts of hunger in the New Testament I was struck by accounts of rage that can and, in fact, should frighten readers: the rage of Jesus that led to a hunger riot in the forecourts of the temple (Mark 11:15); the rage of John the Baptist, who addressed the crowds and mobilized them—until he was arrested (Matt 3:7; Luke 3:7–20). And the rage of the congregation in the synagogue in little Nazareth, who had such powerful hopes that they nearly exploded with fury (Luke 4:28); the rage of Peter, who was so frightened by his vision that he came to repudiate it energetically and wanted to have nothing to do with it (Acts

10:10–14). Although these texts hardly mention hunger as such, there are sparks of rage throughout them that draw our attention to experiences of privation.

Jesus endeavored to underpin rage about hunger and injustice with solidarity, to channel it and make it productive. The study of hunger thus has implications for how we interpret the Messiah's work (Christology). What was this Messiah actually working on? What took shape in his sight? How did he deal with the masses? The Gospels teem with people who are on their feet. They are part of the picture of the Messiah. Perceiving their hunger helps to liberate these human beings from a role as mere bystanders, as part of the backdrop, or as the audience.

This includes recovering the concepts of "the people" and "the twelve"; they need new historical and theological substance. Today, in the twenty-first century, "the people" has a problematic ring (smacking of ideology or nationalism); in connection with the church, "people of God" has become a formula that signals exclusion rather than inclusion. "The twelve" around Jesus are similarly beset: from a perspective of exclusion (of sexism and clericalism), the term is commonly understood to mean a group of twelve individuals, twelve chosen men.

Perceiving hunger allows these concepts to be fleshed out and opens up a perspective of hope for theology and for the church. The "many," whom we see in the Gospels as straying masses, had not always been the people of Israel, but desperate, disoriented Jewish people under Roman domination. John and Jesus ventured everything, including their own lives, to open up a new future for these masses. They told these crowds to stop fighting and crushing each other, to turn around and start to live with each other. Jesus and John tried to turn the masses into "the people," an extensive family with many branches in the tradition of Jacob, Leah, and Rachel—the house of Israel. They held up before them the collective memory of the exodus tradition, of leaving the house of slavery. With hunger always before them, they knew of the dangers of an uprising that would be followed by bloody reprisal. In the Gospels, Jesus is therefore found where the crowds of people gathered. That was his sphere of action.

The most important result of my research I consider to be the development of a *hermeneutic of hunger*. Hermeneutics thematizes the presuppositions of understanding. The issue is the lens through which we read texts, the assumptions we make in order to "understand" these very old writings. We have frames for reading that function as frames do for pictures: they mask some sections and draw our attention to others; they emphasize, delimit, and turn patterns of color into an interesting or confusing picture. Our own reading-frames rarely contain experiences of hunger. We are not approaching these texts with the expectations of the hungry. We have enough to eat. Our concerns are focused on other things.

Social-historical studies of the supply systems in antiquity, of trade routes, tenancy contracts, tolls and taxes show that Rome took control of the supply of foodstuffs from the provinces and that, when resources were in short supply, the provinces had to look out for themselves. Poverty overtook large sections of the population, not only

PREFACE

the "marginal groups." The question is: How do New Testament texts tell of hunger, about eating in times of scarcity, about the fear of impending famines, and how are their narratives based on the experience of earlier times of hunger?

This is where I want to develop a hermeneutic that traces references to hunger and makes connections visible even when the text does not explicitly mention hunger. This hermeneutic should take account of the fact that people who have enough to eat are susceptible to missing signals that the text sends to the hungry. The hermeneutic has to reflect the blindness of the well-fed readers, to enable them to recognize hunger in the text. I have thus attempted to sketch out an approach that allows hunger in the texts to be perceived. I have identified four text markers to look out for, which assure us that the shadow of hunger is visible in these texts (Chapter 3).

I want this hermeneutic to lead readers into a new reading of familiar texts. This includes developing a new view of theological topics such as the resurrection and the Last Supper. It is important for me, when speaking of resurrection, that we let go of our fixation on the body of Jesus. Questions like, "Did he really physically come back to life? Or was he just somehow spiritualized, as a palpable force?" have to be taken seriously as a starting point. But the executed body of Jesus remains disappeared (clearly so in Luke 24); intensive search notwithstanding, it does not reappear. It is the dispersed disciples of Jesus—both female and male—who are resurrected into a new, collective body of hope. This collective body of the Messiah has to do with the "many" who are hungry. They, the masses, become the "people," and that has implications for the resurrection: those who thirst for community and life are the focus. It is they who laugh out loud at the pranks in the Septuagint's Greek Daniel stories; they who long for home like the poor in Corinth (1 Cor), or the poor in Joppa, together with the soldiers in the house of the centurion Cornelius (Acts 10–12). It is they who shake off death and begin to sing. It is the hungry who want bread *and* life, who are transformed (Mark 6:34–44), and who show us how the power of resurrection works.

In the book of Mark we finally come to see the bread and the cup in the hands of the hungry (Mark 14:17–26). In the hermeneutic of hunger, this observation is the point of departure for interpreting the Last Supper. The basic question is not whether the gathered community believes in the presence of Christ in the bread and the wine, but what a community can do to counter hunger. Is it possible to multiply bread on earth through human solidarity? Is it possible to sit at table and tell subversive stories, about the mighty who could explode with greed? The practice of the Lord's Supper is inspired by the vision of the Twelve, the vision of everyone arising and having enough to eat, a vision of a human family that lives together in respect and affection. Bread is not what is transformed at the table of the Twelve, but those who share it, those who give and take and become learners again and again. The rage of the hungry is stilled in the celebration of the Lord's Supper or, at least, it is interrupted. The supper is changed into a moment of happiness in the shared bread; it is a moment when the Messiah's body becomes visible, palpable, something to be savored, because all at table comprise the body, they are the body.

I rejoice at the multiplicity of translations of the Bible currently available in the English- and German-speaking world. They allow us to see the thinking of translators then and now, and how our system of thinking and understanding functions. Comparing different translations with each other helps readers to see which approach their favorite translation takes. Not only is a diversity of beautiful language to be found in these translations; they also show the diverse theological presuppositions on which they are based, most of which are not explicitly stated. This becomes problematic when readers stop being aware that they are dealing with translations that came out of specific contexts and that speak from a specific perspective. If a reader observes: "But this says something different . . ." this is an important initial observation that helps us to track the differences. What a particular translation says is not necessarily "objectively" correct. Translation is guided by a variety of conditions, which include decisions about what to emphasize and what to neglect. The discourse about this is very recent.

The widely used German translations to which I referred when writing this book included *Luther 1984*, the new *Zürcher Bibel* of 2007, the *Einheitsübersetzung* of 1980 (a joint translation of the Roman Catholic and Protestant churches) and, occasionally, the *Gute Nachricht Bibel*. Their current editions embody long-established traditions of translation that have strongly influenced our conceptions. Most of the time, I have drawn on the translation known as *Bibel in gerechter Sprache* (BigS) [Bible in the language of justice], which—as a voice of liberation theology—places the emphases somewhat differently. The English edition of this book relies mostly on the New Revised Standard Version, or the King James Version. Unless otherwise specified, Bible quotes are from the NRSV.

I have also adopted the rendition in the BigS of the name Yhwh in the running text. The God of the Bible has a name that is inexpressible and should not be rendered using standard orthography. The capital letters should remind us that "God" refers to the biblical God of the exodus, the God of Jesus and the Twelve, whose name remains a mystery and a gift, a commission, and an arcanum. For Christian communities, the rediscovery of this name is still a novelty.

One more point of guidance: I speak of the "Markan" Jesus when I refer to the image of Jesus found in the Gospel of Mark. The same applies to the other Gospels. And when I write "Mark" I refer to the consortium of writers or the authorship designated as "Mark." I do not hold to an individual writer with the name Mark (Matthew, Luke, or John) but speak of a group, a Markan community that wove together the Gospel from the treasure store of their memories (see also note 400).

Luzia Sutter Rehmann

Translator's Note

Many of the points Luzia Sutter Rehmann makes in this book concern the problems of translation. Even when translating simple concepts or descriptions, it is often impossible to render the precise flavor of the original. A different language may use an unfamiliar sentence structure, and have a variety of possible words that approximate, but do not exactly correspond to, a particular phrase or concept. Translation therefore almost always represents a compromise. Decisions have to be made on which words to use and how to arrange them; and these decisions are made by human beings, who exist within a particular context and whose upbringing, education, and personal outlook all influence how and what they decide. By finding out more about the circumstances in which a text was written, we may be able to appreciate why the ancient writers and translators made the decisions they did, and understand better what they may have meant. Luzia Sutter Rehmann comes to the biblical Scriptures with an immense wealth of background knowledge—of Roman and Jewish history, of the Hebrew Bible, of Greek—and in this book addresses points of mistranslation or misinterpretation by the people who translated ancient texts into the vernacular several hundred years after they were first written.

The same principles of compromise and potential misinterpretation apply today, when translating from one modern language to another; but here I have been fortunate to be able to work closely with the author and check exactly what she might mean. I have tried to be as faithful as possible to Luzia Sutter Rehmann's German text, but there are nevertheless some places where this translation diverges from the original publication. Sometimes this is because the decisions made by translators of the Bible into German and into English have been markedly different. These divergences often affect the point Luzia Sutter Rehmann is making; so she and I have had to find a solution, whether that involved rewriting a passage, adding sentences of explanation, or leaving something out altogether.

Some points of divergence also arose out of our discussions of the draft translation. Six years after writing the original book, there were several passages of her German text that she wanted to revise. This has resulted in a few passages that have been moved, cut, or extended.

Translator's Note

Quotations and endnotes are another area of revision. The author and I both agreed that the notes should be more than just a record of her sources: they should also be a practical resource for English-speaking readers who want to find out more. Thus, if a book consulted was a German translation, the original English publication has now been cited; where standard English translations of the German publications consulted are available, these have been given. Online resources were all checked and updated where necessary, or equivalent English-language ones given where possible. Where passages are quoted from German-only sources, I have translated these without giving the original texts as well.

Unless indicated otherwise, Bible verses cited can be assumed to come from the New Revised Standard Version. In some places, to demonstrate the problems of translation, Luzia Sutter Rehmann compares different German versions of Bible verses. Here, we have selected various English versions to make the equivalent point. Sometimes the context or the author's discussion calls for a passage to be translated differently, and occasionally no existing English version quite covers it, in which case I have produced my own translation of the author's German. Other ancient sources are generally cited according to standard English translations. A few typographical and other errors in the original text, almost exclusively in the endnotes, have been corrected without comment.

Although most of the words that appear in this English version of *Rage in the Belly* are mine, Martin Rumscheidt has been an invaluable collaborator, bringing his own wealth of knowledge, and his experience in translating key texts of contemporary feminist and liberation theology. As well as providing draft translations of some chapters early in the project, and commenting on and correcting my own drafts, he remained available for discussion of thorny problems and help in making terminological and other decisions throughout. I am truly grateful for all his support, linguistic, theological, and personal.

Thanks are also due to John Buckland, who translated some of the endnotes; and to Debby Plummer and Clare MacLaren, who patiently responded to my random scriptural questions and provided reassurance.

Working on this book has been an enormously exciting intellectual challenge for me, as well as enjoyable on so many levels, so finally I would like to express my thanks to Luzia Sutter Rehmann for her confidence in entrusting me with the translation of her important work for an English-speaking audience.

Monica Buckland
January 2020
Sydney, Australia, in a time of drought

Acknowledgments

This book emerged out of the research project, "Shared Meals: Location of Religious Identity and Practice in Second Temple Judaism and Early Christianity," which I led at the University of Basel. I would like to thank the Swiss National Science Foundation (SNSF), the Faculty of Theology at the University of Basel, and the Freiwillige Akademische Gesellschaft (FAG) Basel for their financial support. For the diverse stimulation, critique, and support that I have received over the course of the research project, I thank Professor Susanne Plietzsch, Dr. Kathy Ehrensperger, Dr. Peter Altmann, Dr. Nathan MacDonald, Professor Angela Standhartinger, and Professor Ekkehard Stegemann. For the translation of a Latin pillar inscription of Sala [into German], I thank Rolf Coray. I owe special thanks to the late Professor Luise Schottroff, who ignited my interest in the topic of meals and whose social-historical works are the foundation of my research.

I have had the opportunity to present my project in various places. I thank the participants of the conference, "Decisive Meals: Table Politics in Biblical Literature" (at the Castelen estate in 2011) for the discussion of my interpretation of Acts 10–12, as well as at the Bildungshaus St. Virgil in Salzburg, the Summer Academy at Schwanenwerder Berlin, and the Feministische Basisfakultät at the Deutsche Evangelische Kirchentag in Hamburg. In between, I met students and course participants in Basel and Biel, who kept asking unexpected questions and opening up new insights.

I thank my friends Dr. Ursula Rapp and Dr. Ulrike Metternich for counter-checking texts and for extensive exegetical telephone calls that showed me how we journey together in different areas. In particular, I want to thank my spouse, Christoph Rehmann-Sutter, who plumbed the depths and shallows of the topic with me and accompanied me in the tightrope act of formulating thoughts. Numerous other obligations would keep me from writing, but weeks in Vico Equense in the Gulf of Naples were a real oasis. I am grateful to the staff of the hotel who, in spite of linguistic barriers, looked after me with generosity and respect.

I thank my friends for their concern and their enquiries when, year after year, they would hear the same refrain: "I am still working on the book."

ACKNOWLEDGMENTS

And I wish to thank the publisher, Gütersloher Verlagshaus, in particular Diedrich Steen, for their fine cooperation. Thanks also to all who have been waiting for this book and who can now read it with their own eyes.

Luzia Sutter Rehmann
Binningen, March 2014

Many thanks to Marie-Louise Hoyer who with great care and speed checked the manuscript for errors for the second edition.

Luzia Sutter Rehmann
Binningen, February 2016

Overview of Chapters

1. Bad Times

How can we speak about hunger? We start working our way into this problem. The shadow of hunger, which lies over people like a leaden blanket, the shadow of death (Ps 107:10–14; Isa 25:6–8; Rev 21:4), can be discovered. Even if we are unable to see beneath the blanket, since precise information is missing, we can learn how to discern this blanket, this veil, this shadow that hangs over entire regions or groups. Once we know about this shadow, we can challenge the usual translations of Mark 6:31. For example, in Mark 6:34, a crisis becomes visible in the verses about the Feeding of the Five Thousand. "Bad times" reign. The crowds of people wandering about trigger compassion; this moves Jesus to link his fate with the hungry. This compassion constitutes the beginning of his messianic work and of our learning.

2. The Poor Preach the Gospel

What did the poverty of the poor look like? Hunger is part of poverty, just like injustice and violence. When the Gospels refer to the poor, they are not a "marginal group," but large sectors of the population, if not the majority, in Roman cities. How were (or are) the poor perceived—as objects of welfare, as disruptive or rowdy people? When the Bible speaks of the gospel of the poor, what does it mean? The hope of the "many" runs through the ancient Song of Deborah (Judg 5:1–31), as well as the people's outcry in the book of Nehemiah (Neh 5:2–5). But it is also visible in the unrest of the "many" in the Gospels. The gospel of the poor becomes explicit in Luke 7:22—they bring the Gospel (actively), rather than have it preached to them (passively): their jubilation can no longer be ignored. The many begin to stand up.

3. Rage in the Belly

How can we recognize clues to hunger in the texts? Herta Müller calls attention to silence about hunger. Hunger and stomachache produce rage—a rage that drives social movements. I sketch four *text markers*, signals or coloration in the text, that allow the shadow of hunger to be discerned. As an example, we read Luke 3:7–14, in which John the Baptist eats locusts, and rants. Jesus is starving, and battles with the devil (Matt 4:1–11). First, hunger is there; then the battle against it begins, the search for something to counter it. For John and Jesus that something is the Torah, the treasure of experience and wisdom of a people who have always had to battle hunger. Both John and Jesus use their rage to mobilize critical visionary energy. They galvanize others, they take up the rage and start to transform it.

4. The Blind Spot

Discerning hunger helps us not only to criticize the anti-Judaism of the interpretations, but also to circumvent it. We can design new ways of reading, if we read texts as stories of hunger rather than as disputes. As an example, we apply the text markers to three stories. In Mark 2:23–28, Jesus reveals his hermeneutic of hunger. Mark shows how Jesus reads hunger into a text, considering hunger along with David's distress, while the traditional, Christian interpretation speaks of a dispute about the validity of the Sabbath and skips over hunger entirely. The anti-Judaist patterns of thought mean understanding Jesus' anger in Mark 11:17 as being directed against Judaism. We can circumvent this if we read the anger as a critical visionary force, in the context of hunger. The difficult story in Luke 4:16–30 can be read in a new way, if we understand the community in Nazareth as being threatened by hunger.

5. The Geography of Hunger

Acts 11:28 refers to a worldwide famine, which can be verified for the east of the Roman Empire under Claudius. The hermeneutic of hunger places this dramatic fact at the center: we read the literary context of Acts 10–12 in the context of this crisis, which cast its shadows before it.

Where is GOD, when hunger comes? Where do the hungry situate GOD's Spirit and help? Eating together is vital for living, and forms the foundation of a community that threatens to fall apart without food. In Acts 10:1—11:18 we can see how the house of the Roman centurion in a period of food shortage united with the small community in Joppa, and how this was interpreted by Peter as a vision of GOD's good creation (Acts 11:6; cf. Gen 1:24–25, 30).

6. Good Deeds in Times of Hunger

The focus remains on the literary context of Acts 10–12. In the history of exegesis, the encounter between Peter and Cornelius is discussed with regard to conversion, to the crossing of religious boundaries: the Roman centurion was a Gentile who, despite not being circumcised, became a Christian. This reading is no longer convincing. We are searching for hard facts that are less ideological, but better embedded in history. The Jewish tradition of the righteous is a benchmark. Thus, Cornelius is presented as a benefactor, in the tradition of the righteous—which includes the disciple Tabitha. Jesus, too, is viewed as a benefactor. Cornelius decides to help the poor community in Joppa. The congregation in Joppa is already suffering from the famine, and accepts the help offered. This demonstrates how dependent small communities were on good works. But what is crucial is the interpretation; in whose name these good works were performed.

7. Laughing at Table

In the two episodes from the post-biblical era, Daniel battles with Bel and with the dragon, with the greedy, powerful elites, and the systems that devoured everything. Even if laughter is permitted, the analysis is keen. In the end, Daniel himself is thrown to the lions to be eaten. What does it mean, that he survives only thanks to the cooking of the venerable old prophet Habakkuk? Habakkuk embodies the nourishing dimension of the Word, the Torah. What he brings is not just stew, but the opening of a window onto the reality of GOD. The Daniel episodes can be read eschatologically with a view to the fact that they allow the listeners to laugh and take a deep breath, because the stories of power and violence can be interrupted again and again. It becomes evident that eating is of key importance.

8. Thirst for More

First Corinthians poses the question of the bodies that are transformed. With what kind of body will they come? (1 Cor 15:35). Paul speaks of the Spirit that saturates our bodies, thus evoking the thirst for life and belonging. The Spirit is not abstract or transparent, but something invigorating that, like water and like the Torah, is there for everyone. The thirst for more, in Paul, becomes the unifying force that brings the poor in Corinth into the body of hope, of the Messiah. The poor of Corinth lived on the streets, and lodged in gloomy back rooms, but together they were the temple of GOD. For the power of the Spirit was alive in the midst of the synagogue's congregation, when the Torah was read and listened to, and when solidarity was practiced in daily life. When, together with Paul, they resisted poverty, when they helped each other out and shared bread, then together they built a shared house, a space of protection and hope.

Overview of Chapters

9. "A Ghost Does Not Have Flesh and Bones"

In the final chapter of Luke's Gospel, the body of Jesus is sought, but not found. While the Greek text barely mentions Jesus from here on, some translations insert his name in several places. This maintains the idea that it is the body of Jesus that rises again. But if we follow the Lukan text precisely, we can see a different body rising, one that has a heart and eyes, flesh and bones, hands and feet. The students of Jesus are incorporated into a collective body of hope. Their hands and feet become the hands and feet of the Messiah (Luke 24:40). This transformation becomes palpable in the shared discussions of the Torah, when breaking bread in Emmaus, and proclaiming the news in Jerusalem. These events show that the disciples have learned something with which to counter hunger.

10. Eating a Transformation

Jesus' last meal with the twelve plays a defining role in our understanding of the Last Supper. Examining Mark's Gospel, we can see how the reading of the Last Supper changes when we work with the hermeneutic of hunger. The number twelve is part of the vision of people eating their fill; it arises in the context of a shortage of bread (Mark 3:20) and is also indispensable in the Feeding of the Five Thousand (Mark 6:34), where the hungry themselves become food. If the twelve are present at the Last Supper (Mark 14:17), this means that the gathering and healing of the people has taken on form. Those present have become the Twelve, just as the crowds in Mark 6 sat like rows of vegetables, and the disciples in Luke 24 became the hands and feet of the Risen. In Jerusalem those present at the table transformed into a collective body—"This is my body!" (Mark 14:22). And so at the Last Supper it is not that the bread is transformed, nor even the faith of those present: it is about participation, belonging, life and a future.

Endnotes

1. Müller, *The Hunger Angel*, 81.
2. Schottroff and Wacker, *Compendium*.
3. *Bibel in gerechter Sprache*.
4. Schottroff, *Lydia's Impatient Sisters*, 58.
5. Sutter Rehmann, *Wut im Bauch*.
6. Schottroff, *Lydia's Impatient Sisters*, 46–47.
7. Schottroff, *Lydia's Impatient Sisters*, 47.
8. Schottroff, *Lydia's Impatient Sisters*, 49.
9. Schottroff, "Come, Read."
10. Barnett, "After Ten Years," 30.
11. Friedman, "WikiLeaks."
12. Günther, "Der Fluch der Sonne," 35.

List of Abbreviations

1 En.	*1 Enoch*
4 Macc	4 Maccabees
Ann.	Tacitus, *Annals*
Ant.	Josephus, *Jewish Antiquities*
Apoc. Mos.	Apocalypse of Moses
BigS	*Bibel in gerechter Sprache*
Bel	Bel and the Dragon
Dom.	Cicero, *De Domo Sua*
EncJud	*Encyclopaedia Judaica*
FAO	Food and Agriculture Organization of the United Nations
GNB	Good News Bible
Jdt	Judith
JSPSup	Journal for the Study of the Pseudepigrapha: Supplement Series
KJV	King James Version
LB	Living Bible
LSJ	Liddell & Scott, *A Greek-English Lexicon*
m. Sukkah	*Mishnah Sukkah*
m. Ta'an.	*Mishnah Ta'anit*
m. Yoma	*Mishnah Yoma*
Mil.	Cicero, *Pro Milone*
Mur.	Cicero, *Pro Murena*
NA[28]	*Novum Testamentum Graece*, Nestle-Aland, 28th ed.
NASB	New American Standard Bible

LIST OF ABBREVIATIONS

NIV	New International Version
NKJV	New King James Version
NRSV	New Revised Standard Version
Rep.	Sallust, *Epistulae ad Caesarem senem de re publica*
Sib. Or.	*Sibylline Oracles*
Sir	Sirach
T. Levi	*Testament of Levi*
TDNT	*Theological Dictionary of the New Testament*
Tob	Tobit
Ven.	Dio Chrysostom, *Venator (Or. 7)*
War	Josephus, *Wars of the Jews*
Wis	Wisdom of Solomon
ZDF	Zweites Deutsches Fernsehen

1.

Bad Times

AN EXAMINATION OF MARK 6:30-34

1.1 How do we deal with the hunger of countless people—what does their hunger do to us?

When I say I am working on hunger in the New Testament, I encounter two different reactions. Some people are not at all surprised: they know the issue and consider it important; they understand hunger as longing, neediness, as poverty before GOD. This hunger for GOD is widespread in the secularized Western world. Potential resistance against the world of consumption can be located within it, a spirit of resistance against institutionalized religions, and the feeling that everything that can be purchased, consumed, or explained still does not satisfy people's existential needs. But hunger for more than the obvious answers to these longings should not lead to hunger becoming spiritualized, bypassing the grumbling stomachs and empty plates. For GOD is also a GOD of the hungry, and can be recognized in fragrant bread and rice, in clear water, and in justice for all people.

Other people, however, are baffled by my search for hunger. They cannot imagine what hunger could have meant in early Christianity, in the New Testament, in the Gospels, or around Jesus. Where did I get the idea that people were hungry? Where does it say that? And then, when I mention a particular passage in the text, they ask what I'm going to do with it. People may well have been hungry in those times, but what should they make of it now? Should they feel guilty about it? Or do I want them to make more donations to charity?

The force of a hunger that demoralizes, erodes, wears you down is something the younger generation in Europe is unable to imagine. They may have got used to the "blessed are the poor" speech, without associating the poor with the hungry; and they pray, "Give us this day our daily bread," without thinking how necessary this prayer is, even today, for people who are hungry. What I want to do is acknowledge hunger as a theological factor. What theology did the hungry develop? What can we learn from them? Where do we need to correct our own theology, if we want to believe the Beatitude of the Poor?

Hunger in Palestine at the time of Jesus, the time of the great defeat by Rome, has found expression in the texts of the New Testament. But hunger can be found throughout the Bible, an unwelcome, pushy guest that drives people to flee, makes them aggressive—as well as inventive and dogged—and gives them a kind of compass. It is important to avoid hunger, strategies must be developed to counter it, every image of God must be measured against it. Can this image stand up to the shadow of hunger? If we mask the reality of hunger at the time of Jesus and the emergence of the New Testament writings, if we no longer expect hunger, we are reading the texts from the perspective of the well-fed. This has far-reaching consequences—but so does recognizing hunger. This is what this book is about. It attempts to show how we can discover hunger in the ancient texts, and where and how experiences of hunger are given a voice.

It is difficult to talk about hunger. Most of us don't really know hunger, thank God. But even people who have got to know hunger barely speak of it. It is simpler to describe a little incident showing how extraordinary a piece of chocolate was in the post-war period than to put into words the gnawing desolation of daily hunger. A piece of chocolate had to last for the whole family, it was a celebration, it made your mouth water... This allows us to surmise something of the barren presence of hunger, which itself remains unspoken. In essence, hunger exceeds our language skills.

A common method of talking about hunger is to quantify it. "Every five seconds a child under ten starves to death. Every four minutes someone loses their sight due to vitamin A deficiency. In 2008, according to the FAO, 963 million people—almost one in six people on our planet—were severely malnourished."[1] Such figures show the extent of global hunger. They attempt an overview of hunger. But statistics are difficult to interpret, and the figures remain abstract for most people. We can scarcely imagine what they mean.

While in 1990–1992, a billion people were malnourished (19 percent of the global population at that time), in 2010–2012 the number had fallen somewhat, to 868 million (12 percent of the global population).[2] Are hunger and malnourishment the same thing? Which is worse? Where do we get these figures? What are the unreported figures? And what does the "increase" or "decrease of global hunger"[3] actually mean?

We should keep an eye on the hunger graphs when interpreting all these statements. But what should we do with a graph of hunger? What does it do to us?

Probably because I am writing this book, I notice many more news reports about hunger than I used to. It is mostly marginal notes that catch my eye, such as the one about the great famine in North Korea, which claimed almost a million lives in 1994–1996, and the consequences of which are still present.[4] Even today, according to estimates from the United Nations World Food Programme, five million North Koreans are still facing starvation. Did you know that hunger is most widespread in Asia?

Eyewitness reports are better placed than bare figures to make us aware of famines, such as this 2011 interview about the situation in North Korea:

> FOCUS Online: What is the situation outside the orphanages and children's homes? The UN World Food Programme has reported that many people have had to eat grass, herbs, and acorns.
>
> Göken: We have seen many people who are emaciated. They are all looking for something edible alongside the footpath—when they're not having to work in a factory. It's especially old people who look for herbs, as they know where they grow. People are catching little crabs in rivers and lakes. Maize is being eaten very early, before it's ripe. That shows how great the hardship is.[5]

How can you grow, if you only have grass and herbs to chew on? How can you sleep with unripe corn in your belly? What does hunger smell like? How can you work in the factory, if you have slept badly because you're hungry? I am not posing these questions just to show how difficult life must be in times of famine. I really want to know how one can live with hunger. How do you do it? What do you watch out for? What do parents tell their hungry children before they go to sleep? What do people do together, if they can't eat together? How do you celebrate Sunday on an empty stomach?

To develop a sense of the power of hunger, it can be helpful to glance at other cultures. The theologian Meehyun Chung, for example, recounts how the presence of hunger has worked its way into everyday manners in Korean culture:

> For example, every now and then I met with incomprehension when, as is the custom in my culture, I greeted another person by asking whether he or she had already eaten rice. In the best case, people found this funny, but some were affronted. What was completely normal in my cultural context is perceived as inappropriate here. Similarly, there is a Korean cultural tradition, where I offer some of my food to the stranger sitting next to me on the train, before I eat any myself."[6]

Meehyun Chung is indicating something very important: hunger characterizes everyday manners, which is shown by many figures of speech about eating or hunger. But there is also a silence about hunger. Breaking this silence is disconcerting. Some find it funny, being greeted with the question about rice. Others are put out: what's that about? Does she think we don't have enough to eat?

Hunger causes irritation. Like poverty, need, and illness, hunger gives rise to unease. We keep this at arm's length—and not only physically: we don't even want to think that we, too, could be tortured by hunger. This is an understandable reaction on the part of generations of people who have repeatedly had to battle hunger.

Another kind of irritation is a moral issue: hunger sparks a kind of guilt. We are doing too little to combat famine in the world. We know that, but we don't like hearing it; it weighs upon us. We feel powerless in the face of these billions of people. Although we are living in a democracy, in a time of peace, with shelves full in the shops, the mere mention of hunger unsettles us. The fact that there are still so many starving people challenges our world order. This challenge is annoying—as if we didn't already have enough problems . . . Hunger dampens the mood, has something depressing about it. It silences us. And when we don't have the words, we fall back on numbers that make us speechless, or impose moral pressure on ourselves. What else can we say about it?

This is where I begin: discovering hunger in the Bible gives us language. Even stories full of silence can be eloquent. Hunger runs through the Bible like a golden thread, from Genesis to Revelation. It lies in wait for its victims, so to speak, on every page. We can overlook it, turn the page, write it off as unimportant. But it had a tight grip on its victims; they wrestled with it, and they wrestled with theology in the face of a hunger that was always just around the corner. This discovery shook me. Why had the dogged persistence of hunger escaped me?

Most interpretations mention hunger only occasionally, as a side issue, and no more is thought about it. For example, famine is certainly mentioned as the reason for the flight of Abraham and Sarah to Egypt (Gen 12:10). But hunger is not accorded any theological value. This famine stands at the beginning of the stories of the patriarchs, and forms a hermeneutical gateway: entry into the family of Sarah and Abraham, and thus into the history of Israel, takes place via hunger. Everything that follows—the link to the granary of Egypt, the dependency on the fleshpots of Egypt, the exodus from the house of slavery (complete with manna and quails), the longing for a land flowing with milk and honey—all this should be read against the backdrop of Abraham and Sarah's hunger. The theological tradition that developed out of it is an engagement with this fundamental and ever-returning experience of hunger. Hunger is the starting point for what comes next. It strikes again and again, it compels people to move, to revolt, to create alliances, and to fight against a God who blesses some with corn and leaves others to go empty-handed. Hunger for God and hunger for bread are inseparable in Isaiah's vision:

> 6 On this mountain the Lord of hosts will make for all peoples
> a feast of rich food, a feast of well-aged wines,
> of rich food filled with marrow, of well-aged wines strained clear.
> 7 And he will destroy on this mountain
> the shroud that is cast over all peoples,

the sheet that is spread over all nations;

8 he will swallow up death forever.

Then the Lord God will wipe away the tears from all faces,

and the disgrace of his people he will take away from all the earth,

for the Lord has spoken (Isa 25:6–8).

When the last book of the Bible, Revelation, reminds us of Isaiah's vision, of the God who shall wipe away all tears, this also appeals to the God of the hungry. The end of Revelation is about the restoration of Jerusalem after its destruction through war. After a war there is a lack of food, since the fields have lain fallow. The reference in Rev 21:4 to part of Isaiah's vision is linked to a very specific context. These are not any old tears—but tears that come from the hungry, the underfed, those who were malnourished after the Jewish-Roman war, those who would like, finally, to be full for once. The shroud that is cast over all peoples (Isa 25:7) is not a human condition, not a necessary side effect of human existence, not part of our natural not-knowing. I read it as a leaden blanket of shortage, a heavy shadow of hunger that can spread over everyone, every region, time and again—the "shadow of death" (Ps 107:10–14 KJV).

1.2 Hearing the voices of the hungry in the biblical Scriptures

We, the well-fed, are in danger of overlooking the power of hunger. As well-nourished people, we have no idea of its weight, its rage, its effect. How it creeps about and lays its thin, iron hand upon everything. I would like to develop a way of reading that enables us, the well-fed, to perceive hunger, to think about it, and to learn from the people who have wrestled with it.

We have observed that hunger reduces people to silence. This seems to be an important observation, which we make repeatedly when dealing with this topic, and which can lead us further. How can we overcome this silencing, and start to think about it? How can we recognize the hidden hunger in a text—even if it does not clearly state "They were hungry"? What does hunger look like? How does hunger express itself in the text? What are the expressions behind which it tries to hide?

There is hunger in the Gospels, in Paul's Epistles, in the Acts of the Apostles, and in Revelation—sometimes a creeping hunger, sometimes chronic malnutrition, sometimes famine. These texts are of great historical value, because here the voices of the hungry can be heard: most non-biblical source texts from antiquity say nothing about hunger. These texts are where princes and civil servants have their say; but not the hungry. Kings commissioned their own epigraphs, annals, and works of history. It is as if we were searching the TV news or the daily newspaper for hunger today. At most, it is a marginal note, although it affects hundreds of millions of people. It tarnishes the shine of the balance sheets, the feeling of progress, and our sense of security.

Perceiving the voices of the hungry in the New Testament Scriptures is something very special. And it is precisely this that touches me again and again about the Bible: it is not a book of the powerful, presenting the world from their perspective, and glossing over problems. Again and again we can hear the whispering of the forgotten, in the Psalms, for example, in stories that show sudden cracks, that change perspective and allow insertions. Carefully feeling our way along the underside of the texts, so as to hear these voices, is therefore one of the main tasks of reading the Bible through a liberation theological lens. It is important to find voices that are not the leading ones, that are not loud, that do not tell stories in a self-assured way, but that nevertheless refuse to let themselves be written out.

We must use hunger as a starting point, because hunger is a reality that characterizes a whole person and a society. Liberation theology always starts from the experience of the poor, so as to learn from them and with them. Starting out from hunger substantiates references to the poor. Most of the texts in the New Testament were written and handed down by them; the Gospels and the Jesus movement were about them.

Hunger is the hallmark of the poor.[7] The Bible assumes that the hungry are in need of bread and GOD. Those who think that hunger can be quelled by bread alone are making a mistake: first, there is the question of how the bread reaches the hungry. Who grows it, who bakes it, who gives it away? For the poor to get their hands on bread, society requires a minimum level of justice. In times of war and other crises, this is lacking. Bread without justice does not assuage hunger.

> Blessed are those who hunger and thirst for righteousness, for they will be filled (Matt 5:6).

We often encounter this beatitude accompanied by the question of whether it is really about physically hungry people. Even Ulrich Luz, in his commentary on Matthew's Gospel, does not address hunger and thirst, but understands the two verbs metaphorically: they stand, he says, for *sich sehnen* (yearning) and *sich mühen* (laboring).[8] This way, we can replace "hunger and thirst" with other verbs that have nothing to do with hunger and thirst. But isn't this just another reassurance, something to stop hunger approaching us too closely? Isn't the clarity of Matthew's beatitude precisely about the combination of bread *and* justice, water *and* rights?

Separating the material and the spiritual does not get us any further. For the biblical texts it is clear that, "One does not live by bread alone, but by every word that comes from the mouth of God" (Matt 4:4). We have not eaten if we have only had food—nor if all we have had is spiritual nourishment. A good meal consists of material foodstuffs, prepared skillfully, good company, good conversation, and a place where we can rest in safety. This is why precisely this version of Matthew's Gospel—"those who hunger and thirst for righteousness"—is so important: it is about the quenching of hunger and thirst, as much as about the unquenchable hunger for justice.

1.3 Hunger's shadow of death

The hunger for spirituality in the rich, Western world should not be separated from world hunger. They could be two sides of the same coin: material poverty and hunger reign in many places on earth, but in our First World there is a life-threatening hunger for spirituality. We first need to understand this connection, before we prize apart these two shades of hunger. According to Dorothee Sölle, stress, depression, isolation—"spiritual anorexia"—are widespread in the West. It is not just a problem of the rich, but above all of the middle classes, those who no longer have to battle for bread, but who have too little time or opportunity to take a deep breath, to find a shared meaning, to perform meaningful work, and to celebrate life with one another.

> [W]e need to ask what it is that women and men are looking for in their cry for a different spirituality. I try to depict a hermeneutic of hunger. In so doing I adopt what can be learned from the liberation theology of the Third World. The hermeneutics of the poor is one of hunger for bread and liberation. The Bible is read as the answer to what oppression, illness, lack of education, and apathy inflict on human beings.[9]

A hermeneutic of hunger should not be allowed to fragment it, particularly because even spiritual hunger can contain a social vision that strives to steer society and power relationships in the direction of more justice, and redistribution of wealth.

> Real hunger is different. The search for the edible bread of mysticism is not spurred on by dabbling, sniffing now at this and now at that religious tradition. Rather, that search grows with every new defeat of God, with every further destruction of the earth and its inhabitants.[10]

Sölle delineates "real" hunger from escapist snacking, which seeks unknown traditions or texts, or new experiences, but only to pass the time. She emphasizes the necessity of a shared effort. There cannot really be more bread and more liberation for individuals, but only for groups, on a shared path. A hermeneutic of hunger understands hunger in all its deadly meagerness, which cannot be restricted to a material or a spiritual level. Hunger is totalitarian in the sense that it affects all, or at least many, levels. Social isolation, poverty of speech, lack of imagination, black-and-white thinking, a dearth of emotional warmth and gestures that connect us—all these are further levels of the spiritual hunger of many people in Western countries. Their hunger engenders emptiness, which, although it can be plugged or glossed over, cannot easily be filled.

Let me build on this hermeneutic of hunger from liberation theology. Up to now, no *biblical* hermeneutic of hunger has been designed. I would like to show, step by step, how the search for hunger transforms our reading of the Bible. For this, we need social-historical information about the economic, political, and climatic situation of the times as well. But above all we need to relativize our way of reading it as well-nourished people. There are people who have heard the same texts on an empty stomach.

They have surely heard things differently from us. The hermeneutic of hunger aims to undermine the tendency of the well-nourished to ignore the consequences, the devastating effects of hunger, while choosing to understand Biblical references only metaphorically. The starting point of my hermeneutic is hunger in all its diverse dimensions, including the shadow cast before it and dragged behind it, the shadow that silences people. The Bible also calls this shadow of hunger the *shadow of death*, something which can envelop a whole region in darkness.

> 10 Those who sat in darkness and in the shadow of death,
> Bound in affliction and irons . . .
> 13 Then they cried out to the LORD in their trouble,
> And He saved them out of their distresses.
> 14 He brought them out of darkness and the shadow of death,
> And broke their chains in pieces (Ps 107:10–14 NKJV).

The Hebrew wording, "shadow of death," opens up our perception: what we can see is only the grim shadow, not hunger itself. But clearly the "chains" describe the iron hand of its regime. We are no longer blind to its shadow.

> 15 Land of Zebulun, land of Naphtali,
> on the road by the sea, across the Jordan, Galilee of the Gentiles—
> 16 the people who sat in darkness
> have seen a great light,
> and for those who sat in the region and shadow of death
> light has dawned (Matt 4:15–16).

When we add Ps 107:10–14 to our reading of these verses from Matthew's Gospel, we understand where Jesus started his messianic work: in the land of hunger, where poverty and violence reigned. After Jesus had fought a life-and-death battle with the satanic power of hunger (Matt 4:1–11), he went to precisely the place where hunger had spread its leaden shadow. But stop, some may object: what Jesus was battling was not hunger, but the devil. But what makes us so sure that this was not a hunger demon? After all, he did enter the scene once Jesus was totally starving (v. 2). He wrestled with Jesus for bread and stones. At the end, the devil left him—and Jesus went into the gloom, into the land of the shadow of death, and gathered his first disciples around him.

Only a few verses later we hear of people who were suffering from diseases and pain, or shaken by demons and epilepsy (Matt 4:25). And even the beatitude gains another dimension:

> Blessed are those who hunger and thirst for righteousness, for they will be filled (Matt 5:6).

If we try to discern hunger, the texts begin to speak more clearly; the people become more vivid, the image of Jesus gains contours, the dialogues become more understandable. Hunger takes up a key position in the texture that we cannot afford to overlook. When we discern it, many things that were shaky suddenly fall into place, and things that were previously colorless become vivid.

1.4 Learning to read hunger

The ancient sources rarely mention hunger. This is due, among other things, to the nature of the source texts. Peter Garnsey, who has carried out intensive research into food shortage in the ancient world, found that the ancient writers (e.g., Cicero, Polybius, Appian, Cassius Dio) did not have a clear, unambiguous vocabulary for hunger. There are numerous words that indicate scarcity (Greek: *limos/limottein, sitodeia, spanis, aporia, aphoria, endeia, kairos*; Latin: *fames, inopia, penuria, caritas, annona cara/gravis*),[11] yet what precisely they refer to is unclear. *Limos* and *fames* describe endemic hunger. Many other words describe a form of food shortage, the consequence of which is hunger. *Caritas* and *annona cara* describe the high prices, the rising cost of food. *Kairos* stands generally for crisis, including food crisis.

But we lack criteria that establish these terms. For example, poor people have been hungry for some time, while the rich have not. When the prices rise, this can mean a food crisis for some, but a profitable development for others. Food shortage is only a problem for those who have no stocks. It only becomes a crisis when even the seeds have been eaten up or have gone rotten. And even this only becomes a collective crisis if it is also the case in neighboring regions, when no seed can be sown for a longer period, and grain has to be imported from far away. Even then there are profiteers—and very often these are the people who have had themselves immortalized in epigraphs, and who paid for the historians who drew up the annals (the annual chronicles of a city). The poor are always the first to be affected by hunger. Indeed, it almost appears to belong to their lives, if St. John Chrysostom describes them as "people who must hunger and suffer all their lives"[12] (see Chapter 4).

It is not clear whether the terms for hunger describe mere shortage, or starvation that may become fatal. The ancient epigraphs rarely contain any clarifying information on this. They even appear systematically to conceal hunger.[13] Ancient epigraphs avoid suffering in general. They tell of victories, of the brave deeds of individuals, and the wise foresight of the ruling class. But there are no epigraphs about the emperor's personal suffering, and of course there are none about the suffering of the ordinary people.

To find out about hunger, it is therefore necessary to listen, beyond the ambiguous terms, to the narrative context. When in Acts 10:10, Peter feels hungry, and in Acts 11:28, a worldwide famine is announced (*limos*), it makes more sense to connect these two things than to read them quite independently of one another. Peter's explicit hunger is not just having an appetite at lunchtime, but something that becomes a harbinger of what is coming upon the masses of people. Hunger drives Peter to seek allies and to transgress boundaries (see Chapters 5 and 6).

We also need to gather social-historical information about the supply situation, and about the dominant political environment in a particular place at a particular time. Here, too, it is not sufficient to note that people were poor and were repeatedly confronted with epidemic or chronic hunger. The question is whether anything about hunger can be sensed in the specific text, whether it played a role—and what role. How did it influence people's lives and actions? Can we discern something of the despondency that malnutrition can bring about? Unrest, outrage, food riots? And what is the wording, the phrase, which expression is it precisely that gives us signs of hunger's influence, whether as outrage and activity or as subliminal despair? This is where the hermeneutic of hunger takes hold. If we are not attentive to the shadows of hunger, they may elude us. But the texts do send out signals for us to decode. We should pay detailed attention to these *text markers* (see Chapter 3).

Exegetically, this is a challenge. Suspecting hunger is one thing—but how does it reveal itself at this point, what does it say here in black and white? So we have to develop a reading strategy, listen to text signals that well-fed individuals can easily overlook. We, the readers, thus come into play ourselves. We need to become conscious of our reading strategies as well-fed people. This includes the self-critical discernment of anti-Judaism as a way of thinking, something that is often invoked particularly obstinately at points where hunger is overlooked (see Chapter 4).

We can only speak about hunger because we have enough to eat. For otherwise we would be using our time differently; we would need to be getting hold of something to eat, rather than sitting around at the computer. Hungry people don't have the luxury of writing. And if they did, if the hungry started writing—then they would probably rather not write about the hunger that plagues them all, but about times of eating, of flavorsome bowls of food and mother's recipes. How can we extrapolate from flavorsome bowls to the underlying experiences of hunger? Let us try to decode the underlying experiences of hunger: when the texts refer to eating, when they joyfully describe being satisfied (see Chapter 10), perhaps precisely this is about the hunger that would be a known quantity to the readers to whom these texts were addressed.

That the exegetic tradition of interpreting the Bible has not taken on hunger also has to do with hunger being distinctly "unsexy." It is just so pathetic, dusty, dry. You can't win laurels with hunger. The people were poor and sick. Yes, there was certainly hunger, too. But what is the use of engaging with it? That this hermeneutical turn in fact changes things significantly is something I would like to demonstrate, using the example below.

1.5 They were not good times . . .

Immediately preceding the report of the Feeding of the Five Thousand miracle, Mark gives us five verses, which interpreters have said little more about other than that they form an editorial interpolation. These verses connect the dramatic scene of the beheading of John the Baptist (including the banquet at Herod's court, and the family dynamics between Herodias, her daughter, and Herod) with the beautiful feeding story, where thousands of people sit on the grass and are filled.[14]

> 30 The apostles gathered around Jesus, and told him all that they had done and taught. 31 He said to them, "Come away to a deserted place all by yourselves and rest a while." For many were coming and going, and they had no leisure even to eat. 32 And they went away in the boat to a deserted place by themselves. 33 Now many saw them going and recognized them, and they hurried there on foot from all the towns and arrived ahead of them. 34 As he went ashore, he saw a great crowd; and he had compassion for them, because they were like sheep without a shepherd; and he began to teach them many things (Mark 6:30–34).

Five verses to link two scenes? Surely Mark could do this more simply! I will assume that this little, rather unwieldy scene—in which you don't rightly know who's coming and who's going, whether it is the apostles or the "many"—has independent significance as well. In any case, it is no coincidence that the readers are led from the king's court, in which the prophet's head is served up on a silver platter, to the mass picnic. And between these impressive scenes lie these five verses, which are also explicitly about eating.

Most translations render the text of verse 31 to say that the people (whether apostles or the many) *did not have time or leisure* to eat.

> Mark 6:31
>
> . . . for there were many coming and going, and they had no leisure so much as to eat. (KJV)
>
> For there were many coming and going, and they did not even have time to eat. (NKJV)
>
> For many were coming and going, and they had no leisure even to eat. (NRSV)
>
> There were so many people coming and going that Jesus and his disciples didn't even have time to eat. (GNB)

This translation poses no problems of comprehension. Sometimes we too work through lunch and forget to eat, i.e., we put it off till later. The very busy apostles also had to skip lunch—this is what we read—and Jesus noticed, and wanted to give them a rest break. This is why they went away in a boat, away from the people. But the plan failed, because many people also hurried there on foot. Then Jesus had compassion with them (in this case with the many), gave up his well-intentioned plan, and strode over to feed the crowd.

The question is: what is going on here? Why are the people hurrying aimlessly to and fro (v. 31)? Why, in any case, are so many out and about ("from all the towns," v. 33)? What are they looking for? What do they lack?

The Greek text of verse 31 is: *oude phagein eukairoun*. In English: "And the times were not good for eating," or "They were bad times in which to eat."

Peter Garnsey has drawn our attention to the fact that *kairos* is one of the words that describes a crisis.[15] The Greek verb *eukairoun* literally means: the times are good. The negative *oude* reverses this: the times are not good, but bad. So what are bad times for eating? While harvest-time is a period of abundance, where something to eat can be obtained everywhere, winter is a hard time in terms of eating. Nothing more can be found outside; the vines and the fields have been reaped, and stand empty.

The idea that the apostles did not find time to eat, and had to postpone their lunch, appears barely plausible. It does not really fit into the Greek sentence structure (which leaves open who is unable to eat: "they"—more likely the many than the apostles). The drama of the immediate context does not fit such an anodyne interpretation either.

Let us remind ourselves once again of what has just happened in the previous verses. Mark 6:17–28 tells us that, at a banquet to celebrate his birthday, Herod had had John the Baptist arrested and then murdered. There is much of interest in this tale; for example, beheading as the punishment for an insurgent. The punishment thus qualifies the crime: John is murdered as the leader of an uprising, a political prisoner, and the uprising thus loses its head. John's head is served up on a platter during the meal (v. 25), a barbarity that is used to taunt Herod's opponents. Narratively, Mark thus creates a great discrepancy: the wealthy eat at fully laden tables, while times are hard for the people, and thousands are hungry. The rich have the head of the popular movement served up, so that the people stray about heedlessly.

Now the crisis, as introduced by the context, is sketched out. After John's murder, the people panic. They rush about to and fro. Both the poor food situation and the king's political severity provide an outline for the crisis.

Let us proceed to the next problem: who are the apostles (v. 30)? The noun *apostoloi* is formed from the Greek verb *apostellein* ("to send out"). In the immediate literary context we have two very different occurrences of this verb:

- In Mark 6:7 Jesus sent people out two by two (*apostellein*), to heal people and call upon them to turn their lives around.

- In Mark 6:17 Herod sent people out (*apostellein*), to find and arrest John.

So the immediately preceding text contains the verb *apostellein* twice, but applying to two completely opposing groups: the envoys of Jesus, who were to bring peace (healing and conversion) to the people, and the envoys of Herod, who were to undermine and spy on the popular movement. Using the same verb *apostellein* in both verse 7 and 17 causes disorientation, which mirrors the disoriented rushing to and fro of the many people. Who is bringing peace and healing? Who is spying, and bringing danger?

The disciples of John had to go to Herod's palace to fetch the body of their teacher (v. 29). This also made them identifiable to the royal security police:[16] they were very close to the murdered man, and their actions meant they risked being recognized and registered as potential new heads of the popular uprising. Jesus advised them to "go off secretly" (*kat'idian*, v. 31), and "they went secretly" (*kat'idian*, v. 32).[17] The king should not be able to serve up their heads as well. With so many coming and going, the king's security personnel could also be among them, or informers who could spy on the people flocking together. Here, Jesus is not trying to help his apostles to have lunch, but to protect those who are politically in danger. He has them go underground, and creates an opportunity for these people, who could potentially be persecuted, to withdraw from observation.

These considerations now feed into my translation of the five verses:

> 30 The apostles went together to Jesus, and told him all that they had done and taught. 31 He said to them, "Come away secretly to a deserted place and rest a while." For many were out and about, coming and going, and the times were not good for eating. 32 And they went away in the boat, secretly, to a deserted place. 33 And the many saw them going and recognized them, and they hurried there on foot from all the towns and came to them. 34 As he (Jesus) went ashore, he saw a great crowd; and compassion for them spread within him, because they were like sheep without a shepherd (Mark 6:30–34, author's translation).

The murder of the political prisoner at a royal banquet is one side of this drama—bad times for eating are the other. If we merge together these two pieces of information, they do make sense: hard times reigned. The people do not know how they will feed their children, while the upper crust and the wealthy feast at a royal banquet. The prophet John appeared in this crisis as a leadership figure, someone who was able to mobilize the masses (Mark 1:5). The royal house of Herod did not organize any feeding of the poor or shiploads of grain,[18] but had the ringleader of the enraged people locked away (Mark 1:14). Finally, the prophet was publicly mocked by being served as "dessert" at a banquet, to affirm royal power and quash any criticism of the king.

Political injustice, coupled with the fear of famine, has always brought people out onto the streets.[19] Hunger and violence radicalized those who had not yet affiliated themselves with the popular movement around John. In Mark it becomes apparent how the people reacted with panic to the news of John's death. They hurried heedlessly from everywhere; there was great coming and going. Panicking, hungry people tried to gather everything possible and impossible in terms of food to set before their children.

The second book of Kings tells us what this gathering could look like. At the time of a great famine in Samaria (eighth century BCE), Elisha was at his wits' end and had anything outdoors that appeared edible gathered up. But this could have dangerous consequences:

> 38 When Elisha returned to Gilgal, there was a famine in the land. As the company of prophets was sitting before him, he said to his servant, "Put the large pot on, and make some stew for the company of prophets."
>
> 39 One of them went out into the field to gather herbs; he found a wild vine and gathered from it a lapful of wild gourds, and came and cut them up into the pot of stew, not knowing what they were.
>
> 40 They served some for the men to eat. But while they were eating the stew, they cried out, "O man of God, there is death in the pot!" They could not eat it (2 Kgs 4:38–40).

In bad times, the hungry gather everything they can find (see note 5). This behavior has barely changed throughout history. In the book of Job as well (fifth to third century BCE), we see people traipsing, exhausted, through the fields, gnawing on anything that grows:

> All their vigor is gone. 3 Through want and hard hunger they gnaw the dry and desolate ground, 4 they pick mallow and the leaves of bushes, and to warm themselves the roots of broom (Job 30:2–4).

Groups of starving people, who indiscriminately collect up anything edible, fit well into the comparison Jesus made with a flock of sheep (v. 34) that haphazardly graze away everything, even if it is indigestible for them. As well as exhaustion, Isaiah adds another element that can occur in hungry people: anger.

> 21 They will pass through the land, greatly distressed and hungry; when they are hungry, they will be enraged and will curse their king and their gods. They will turn their faces upward,
>
> 22 or they will look to the earth, but will see only distress and darkness, the gloom of anguish; and they will be thrust into thick darkness (Isa 8:21–22).

Jürgen Kegler rightly points out that Isaiah is sketching the real experience of a hungry people.[20] They look upwards—are they searching for a raincloud that could bring redeeming moisture for their crops? Or, seeking help, are they looking to God or to Jerusalem, to the powerful?—and when they look down there is only barren earth, emptiness, stones. Hunger engenders blind rage against the king and against God, against the government, and all those who abandon them.

We can therefore interpret the hurrying to and fro of the many (Mark 6:31) during bad times in two ways. The people are either, like a flock of sheep, searching the land for edible things (as in 2 Kgs 4:38–39 and Job 30:3), or they are up on their feet out of sheer anger and outrage at their political leaders, who hold banquets and murder their beloved chief, but do not remedy their hunger (as in Isa 8:21).

In any case, Mark 6:31f is not about the apostles putting off their lunch—it is not that they lack the time to eat, but that the many people are hungry for bread and for justice.

1.6 Discerning hunger

I have discussed this scene in Mark 6:30–34 in order to show how everything transforms before our very eyes. The *hermeneutic of hunger* does more than just establish that people were starving. The hermeneutic of hunger shows previous readings of this verse—that the apostles did not find the time to eat their well-earned meal—to be an apolitical trivialization that takes no account of either context or precise wording.

Translators who do not discern in *oude eukairoun* the shadow of hunger (see Isa 8:21, "greatly distressed and hungry"; Ps 107:10–14, "the shadow of death") and do not perceive the outrage of the hungry, can produce "they did not even have time to eat." (Although "even" cannot be located in the Greek text.) They do not recognize the connection between the murder of the prophet and his mockery during a banquet and the bad times in which it was difficult for people to find food. But for us, it is important to discern this shadow of hunger—the enraged masses of people, the king's attempt to intimidate the crowds, their scurrying about.

Hunger casts its shadow over families, villages, regions. Even if the texts avoid referring directly to shortage, hunger can be seen in the form of fear, rage, commotion. This shadow makes the text more plastic; the worries of the people and their survival strategies become perceptible. Hungry people do everything they can to get hold of food in bad times.

Discerning hunger helps us to see the people as people; it allows their plight to become physically palpable. This changes the reader's perspective. Those who hurry to and fro (Mark 6:31) are not extras in the scene, people we could by definition overlook as being unimportant. The people in their unrest and helplessness are at the focal point of Mark's Gospel: it is about them. They starve, they suffer from the king's repressions. But they do not give in. They are on their feet, they attempt the seemingly impossible. We could learn from them today about how to battle against the power and domination to which people are brutally exposed.

This also has theological consequences. The text does not direct our gaze towards Jesus, but from Jesus, towards the people. It is important to me that we move away from the idea that the crowds were out and about in order to hear Jesus. At this point in the sixth chapter of Mark's Gospel, Jesus is not the great figure that he later became for Christianity. That thousands of people hurried to hear Jesus preach corresponds rather to the wishful thinking of a later generation of interpreters; in their eyes the many people are just an audience, extras in a scene of divine salvation. They are only "garnishes"; the important figure was Christ, not these people.

> 30 The apostles went together to Jesus, and told him all that they had done and taught. 31 He said to them, "Come away secretly to a deserted place and rest a while." For many were out and about, coming and going, and the times were not good for eating (Mark 6:30–31, author's translation).

The text situates Jesus in the middle of these crowds, who were perhaps looking to gather food and were fleeing from further violence, because John had been beheaded. In the middle of these distraught crowds we hear the voice of Jesus, who is offering shelter to those who have supported John.

> 33 And the many saw them going and recognized them, and they hurried there on foot from all the towns and came to them. 34 As he (Jesus) went ashore, he saw a great crowd; and compassion for them spread within him, because they were like sheep without a shepherd (Mark 6:33–34, author's translation).

Now something surprising takes place. Great crowds of people hurry towards those who wish to hide. The people recognize the envoys of John; they know what has happened. They know the brutal force of Herod. A great show of solidarity begins: many people hurry to those who need protection. They do not abandon them. They choose the orphaned prophetic movement of John. Now more than ever, seems to be the motto. They do not allow Herod to gag them. Herod has achieved the opposite of what he wanted. The crowd is in solidarity; perhaps they too have become radicalized. Their ringleader, their good shepherd, has been killed. They do not scatter but rally, gather together around those who brought the last news of John. The next verse expresses this as well. Now Jesus sees in them a flock without a shepherd, something that triggers deep compassion in him (v. 34).

After Mark 6:31–34 there follows probably the most beautiful story in the Gospels: five thousand hungry people are able to eat until they are full (see Chapter 10)! The four Gospels recount this story a total of six times.[21] The bad times of verse 31 are the starting point for the Feeding of the Five Thousand story. Thousands of people are on their feet, coming and going, and staying hungry. They clutch at any straw that moves, they would be ready to eat grass, but there is no grass, just dry, desolate land (*topos eremos*, v. 31).

1.7 Compassion spreads . . .

I want now to make one final point that is important for understanding the hermeneutic of hunger. When Jesus saw this crowd of people, he was moved with compassion

(Mark 6:34). This compassion unites the political-ethical and spiritual sides of Bible reading.[22] In Greek there is a verbal construction for "compassion": *esplanchnisthe*. This verb is in the passive voice. It does not mean "he had compassion"—the subject suffers compassion, is filled or moved with compassion. The subject thus becomes the object of the compassion. This passive voice cannot be rendered simply in English. Here are a few examples of modern translations:

Mark 6:34

As he went ashore, he saw a great crowd; and he had compassion for them, because they were like sheep without a shepherd; and he began to teach them many things. (NRSV)

When Jesus arrived and saw a large crowd, he had compassion on them because they were like sheep without a shepherd. Then he began to teach them many things. (CEB)

When Jesus got out of the boat, he saw this large crowd, and his heart was filled with pity for them, because they were like sheep without a shepherd. So he began to teach them many things. (GNB)

So the usual vast crowd was there as he stepped from the boat; and he had pity on them because they were like sheep without a shepherd, and he taught them many things they needed to know. (LB)

The passive voice needs to be expressed in a way that compassion is an active force: "his heart was filled" (GNB) reflects the character of the verb. The translation "he had pity on them" flies in the face of the text, which does not present Jesus as the subject in relation to pity. Jesus was "moved, stricken, shaken, inundated"—this would surely reflect the passive voice much better.

While English locates emotions in the heart, the Greek verb contains the expression for "viscera, the innermost (bowels) of the body." The belly as the place for compassion accords with the Hebraic cultural tradition, which allocates affects and passions to different regions of the body. The ancient priests and sages knew about psychosomatic connections.[23]

My eyes are spent with weeping;
my stomach churns;
my bile is poured out on the ground
because of the destruction of my people (Lam 2:11).

The womb—that most internal of abdominal organs—*rechem* in Hebrew, signifies the seat of empathy, of compassion. In Arabic, *rechem* is one of the most common names for God: God is compassionate and merciful. In Mark's Gospel the Greek verb appears four times, twice for healings (Mark 1:41; 9:22) and twice when referring to the starving people (Mark 6:34; 8:2).[24]

The following things should also be considered: in the Gospels, no other person feels compassion towards the sick and hungry. But the name of Jesus is not mentioned in connection with the verb. This indicates that, with its Old Testament background, the verb has a strongly divine, messianic color. The passive voice seems to express this; the active force, the subject of the verb, remains concealed in the *passivum divinum*. This active force of compassion, which has the power to shake people up and change them, comes from GOD; it is wrought by GOD. But those who must act are human beings.

Verse 34 shows that this compassion starts with acknowledging the hungry. Jesus saw the crowds of people wandering about, was seized by a profound compassion, and began to teach them many things. What does he teach them, after seeing how disoriented and hungry they were? Jesus not only recognizes the needs of the people, but also associates this need with the Torah. He describes the suffering people in the same way as the prophets, who time and again criticized the kings' lack of political leadership, by calling the neglected population a "flock without a shepherd" (Ezra 34:2, 8; Jer 10:21; 23:1–2; 50:6; Zech 10:2–3). He teaches them that *they* are the poor of Israel; they are not just insurgent masses, at the mercy of the rage and the contempt of the powerful. They are the people whom ADONAI, their God, loves. GOD will show them a pathway out of the bad times.

Verse 34 thus also incorporates prophetic criticism of the king, through Jesus, when he views the people as a poorly shepherded flock. The house of Herod did not exercise its duty to feed its people. Herod was anything but a good shepherd. His administrators were like shepherds who beat their flocks, neglect them, or lead them astray. But the hungry are the flock of whom the Torah's Prophetic Scriptures write that they need a good shepherd. Thus, recognizing hunger leads to compassion: Jesus calls the times bad because hunger and violence prevail. Jesus discerns in the wandering crowds the people who are searching for a shepherd. The wandering people show him that something has to happen. This can't go on. They all need shelter, help, food, direction.

In these few verses, we can see how the hermeneutic of hunger works: first, hunger and violence have to be recognized. The people are not bustling to and fro out of pure busyness, but it is hunger, it is the bad times, that drives them. Mark's Jesus names this for us, for the readers. Taking this finding as a starting point, the events begin to reassemble differently. The envoys need shelter because the times are so bad and Herod's men are reacting to the people's outcry with repression. A political reading of this verse is recommended: it is about criticism of the king and the prophet's murder, it is about the people who have no future. Ultimately, it changes our perspective of the people and of Jesus: the people take John's side, they stop rushing to and fro, and go to the place where John's disciples are. Jesus is in the middle of his people, the distraught crowd, the endangered movement of John. A deep compassion spreads, in the face of such defenselessness and the way the people side overwhelmingly with John.

It is this compassionate gaze I mean when I say: We have to start with hunger. Discovering the hungry transforms us. The people who call for bread and justice—in North Africa, in Ukraine, in Southern Europe—they are our brothers and sisters. That they exist, that they existed, makes the story more human. The grace of God, the miracle, doesn't begin where everyone is well-fed and there are leftovers (Mark 6:43). The miracle begins earlier, where compassion comes into view, where recognizing and loving come together.

2.

The Poor Preach the Gospel

> The blind see, the lame walk,
> the lepers are cleansed, the deaf hear,
> the dead arise—the poor bring good news.
> Luke 7:22

2.1 How do we picture the poor?

In this chapter I want to look into the question of whom we have in mind when we speak of "the poor." It goes hand in hand with the self-critical question of whether we think of "the poor" as decent people, or as beggars who just get on our nerves; or do we look upon them as politically enraged troublemakers, frustrated recalcitrants? And what comes to mind when we speak of the poor, for theirs is the kingdom of God (Matt 5:3; Luke 6:20)? The beatitudes in Luke picture the poor as hungry, weeping, hated, excluded, reviled (Luke 6:21–22).

I will first look for the Bible's definitions of poverty and the contexts in which poverty is mentioned. For the rich are not hungry. The hungry are the poor—whether temporarily on account of failed harvests, or structurally due to the absence of any social mechanism to deal with times of deprivation. It also matters whether the poor are a few paupers in a village or a city (a "marginal group"), or whether they comprise whole impoverished sections of a region (a majority). If they were many—whole impoverished classes under particular political powers—hunger-driven rebellions need to be taken into consideration.

As I write, in 2013, people are protesting in the cities of Brazil.[25] We hear of unrest in different places all over the world; what started as unrest in Syria has turned into a brutal war. What does such news evoke in us? Are we somehow relieved that the young protesters have such courage, and that there is a rise in solidarity? Do we see "the poor" on the streets in contemporary uprisings, standing up and calling for justice? Or are we afraid for our own peace? Do we fear for the stability of these countries? Where are the poor in these crowds? Can we set them apart at all, or should they be understood as the motor of the uprisings? We have to face the poor and clarify our relationship to them. Just as there are diverse forms of protests, so the poor should also be understood in a more nuanced way. This is the task we ought to take up so that we may recognize and distinguish the faces of poverty and take them seriously.

In this chapter we will also look at how Luke 7:22 has been translated. The German *Bibel in gerechter Sprache* translates that verse with the poor as subjects, while in all the other translations I am familiar with—both German and English—they are objects to whom sermons or proclamations are addressed. Why is that? This new translation has more than just grammatical merit. It is based on the option for the poor that Luke himself formulates in the Beatitudes (6:20) and which I am attempting to trace.

And, finally, we will reflect on the christological implications resulting from the decision to translate the poor as subjects.

2.2 People who must hunger all their lives

Let us begin with the definition of poverty. Does our image of "the poor" also include the hungry? Or only "non-rich" people, who have little money or who do not earn enough? Some current definitions are formulated in terms of income,[26] while others refer to basic human needs.[27] But reference to hunger as a threat to the poor is often an afterthought. The concept of "subsistence level" does not make it sufficiently clear when or whether bread, rice, and clean water are safeguarded. If hunger is not mentioned explicitly, readers may not be able to bring it into the picture; they forget it.

But poverty and hunger go hand in hand. Food security has to do with reserves—with sufficient supplies for the family to get through the long winter; with stores of seeds in time for the next sowing season; with the body's need for vitamins so that it can resist infectious diseases. The poor have little chance to lay in stocks of that kind. Without them they are easy prey for insidious hunger, malnutrition, for the craving of food at winter's end, during adverse climatic conditions or politically insecure times.

When they come across the word "the poor" in modern translations of the Bible, many readers do not know how they should be imagining poverty. Nor do many think of the poor as the majority of the population, as the people. But in a world where there was no middle class, and only a few rich or very rich, most people had barely enough to live on. This also signifies that the poor were not those on the edges of society, outsiders; they were the ordinary people. It might lead some readers to ask themselves whether people then were generally more modest, more frugal, and satisfied with less. That may well have been the case as long as basic needs were met. But where daily bread is the issue, we have to ask what it means that so many people were poor. What are we to understand when biblical texts speak of "the poor"? What did they lack?

The online *King James Dictionary* defines "[t]he poor, collectively, used as a noun; those who are destitute of property; the indigent; the needy; in a legal sense, those who depend on charity or maintenance by the public."[28] This definition leaves readers in the dark about the social structures in New Testament times, under the Roman occupation. What are we to understand "maintenance by the public" to mean? Who were "the public"? What was the relationship of "the poor" to "the public"? Without this frame of reference, without knowing anything about the social and economic changes that took place when land was increasingly transferred by royal decree to the aristocracy and the administrators, we cannot picture the poor. And yet as their lands were taken away and they fell into debt slavery, "the poor" came to mean the majority of the peasants.

The dictionary definition also leaves open whether the conditions in Roman-occupied Palestine were like those of earlier times (up to the fourth or third century BCE) or whether things had improved for the ordinary people. It would be most useful to include information for the period of the New Testament (first century CE) because Matthew's phrasing "the poor in spirit" (Matt 5:3) has given rise again and again to spiritualizing interpretations.

The glossary of the *Bibel in gerechter Sprache*[29] also focuses on the scope of the Hebrew concepts *dal, ani, evyon*. The Greek concept of *tapeinos* is explained with reference to violent oppression, to humiliation, which also includes sexual violence. The meaning of these concepts varies between "weak, wretched, cowered, humiliated, impoverished, of little value": these people are the paupers, the helpless who cannot pay their rents or "levies of grain" (Amos 5:11). *Ani* refers to socially humiliated and oppressed people; impoverished day laborers or landless peasants threatened with the fate of debt slavery. This would be another place to mention hunger and the hungry explicitly, since it is precisely they who were among the wretched.

There are different concepts in Greek for "poor" that may be clearly distinguished from one another. *Ptochoi* generally refers to the poor on the margins or below the minimum levels of existence, while *penes* is the term for those who can still somehow earn a living. Although this differentiation originated in the fourth century BCE, it was valid for centuries. There is a similar differentiation in Hebrew: "[T]he absolutely poor person is frequently called *ebion*, whereas the usual designation for the relatively poor is *ani* . . . More equivocal, however, . . . are the Latin expressions for *poor*."[30]

Stegemann and Stegemann emphasize that there was no unitary class of poor people, but that we should in any case distinguish between the poor and the relatively poor. "This distinction is to be expressed basically in terms of elementary human needs, which in antiquity included nourishment (food and drink), clothing, and lodging . . . And we may presume that the great majority of the people of antiquity hardly got beyond a modest realization of these basic needs."[31] They quote a passage from John Chrysostom (fourth century CE) describing the miserable situation of the rural population, who were completely beholden to large-scale landowners. John Chrysostom speaks of people "who must hunger all their lives." This shows that hunger was a constant companion of the poor even when there was no particular famine.

> Could there be more unjust people [than the owners of land who draw their wealth from the earth]? For when we examine how they treat the *poor and miserable* country people, we reach the conclusion that they are more inhumane than barbarians. On the people who *must hunger and suffer all their lives* they constantly lay impossible levies, burden them with toilsome duties, and use them like donkeys and mules, and even stones; they do not grant them even the least bit of rest but, whether or not the earth produces a yield, suck them dry and give them no consideration whatever. Is there anyone more worthy of compassion than these people when they worry themselves the whole winter, worn down by cold, rain, and night watches, and now stand there with empty hands, still deep in debt, when they then shiver and quake not just from hunger and failure but also from the tormenting of the overseer, from the warrants, the arrests, the calling to account, the foreclosure of the lease, and from the unrelenting demands? Who can enumerate all the things that are done to them, all the advantage that is taken of them? From their work, from their sweat, storage bins and cellars are filled, but they are not allowed to take home even a little bit; rather, [the landowner] hoards the whole harvest in his own chests and throws them a trifling sum as a wage.[32]

Poverty was very widespread during the reign of imperial Rome. Large sections of both the urban and rural population of the Empire belonged to the underclasses; estimates range from 96 percent to 99 percent. There was no real middle class.[33] According to Steven J. Friesen, this was due to the Roman economy being driven by a rural agriculture that was in the hands of a small elite.[34] This economic system imposed domination by the few and pauperization of the majority. Friesen demonstrates the immeasurable poverty using a table of poverty-levels, with seven categories of economic resources; this would apply to the population of a typical large city in the Roman Empire.

Poverty Scale for a Large City in the Roman Empire

Percent of Population	Poverty Scale Categories
0.04%	1. *Imperial elites*: imperial dynasty, Roman senatorial families, a few retainers, local royalty, a few freedpersons.
1%	2. *Regional or provincial elites*: equestrian families, provincial officials, some retainers, some decurial families, some freedpersons, some retired military officers.

1.76%	3. *Municipal elites:* most decurial families, wealthy men and women who do not hold office, some freedpersons, some retainers, some veterans, some merchants.
(7%?)	4. *Moderate surplus resources:* some merchants, some traders, some freedpersons, some artisans (especially those who employ others), and military veterans.
(22%?)	5. *Stable near subsistence level* (with reasonable hope of remaining above the minimum level to sustain life): many merchants and traders, regular wage earners, artisans, large shop owners, freedpersons, some farm families.
40%	6. *At subsistence level* and often below minimum level to sustain life: small farm families, laborers (skilled and unskilled), artisans (especially those employed by others), wage earners, most merchants and traders, small shop/tavern owners.
28%	7. *Below subsistence level:* some farm families, unattached widows, orphans, beggars, disabled people, unskilled day laborers, prisoners.[35]

This impoverished majority—according to Friesen it made up 90 percent of the population (levels 5–7)—was essentially at the mercy of those with possessions, just as John Chrysostom describes. They are people who must hunger all their lives because they are poor, not because there had been an extraordinary drought. Additionally, there was the oppression of the slaves, who were defenseless against arbitrary law.

2.3 Gender-specific conditions of poverty

Many studies of poverty in the Bible consist primarily of analyses of words.[36] It was Phyllis Bird who called attention to the fact that, for a long time, female poverty in biblical times was not taken into account.[37] It is all the more important therefore that the working and living conditions of women and men be examined, as well as gender-specific dependencies. If we look only at small-scale farmers, day laborers, construction workers, and debt slaves[38] without addressing the gender-specific conditions of poverty, we create an image of past history that leaves out women.

This is why I consider it significant that the *Bibel in gerechter Sprache* explicitly makes women visible, even when the ancient texts do not mention them explicitly although it is historically realistic to assume their presence:

> Because they sell the righteous for silver, and the needy [*evyon*] for a pair of sandals—
> they who trample the head of the poor [*dal*] into the dust of the earth, and push the afflicted [*ani*] out of the way;
> father and son go in to the same girl, so that my holy name is profaned;
> they lay themselves down beside every altar garments taken in pledge;
> and in the house of their God they drink wine bought with fines they imposed (Amos 2:6-8).

Poor people had to sell themselves for a pair of sandals. Humiliated as a result, they were exposed to violence. The Hebrew text refers unequivocally to young women (girls) in verse 7 because their situation cries out to heaven. It is both legitimate and important consciously to include the realities of female life when speaking about the needy, the poor, the afflicted—and not to think of women only when the word "girl" appears.

Later, in Amos 8:4–6, we again meet the poor (*evyon*) who are trampled on, and the needy who are afflicted, in that scales are falsified and measuring cups reduced in size. Then the helpless (*dal*) and the poor (*evyon*) can be bought for a pittance or for a pair of sandals. Amos exposes the owners' greed that stops at nothing. Grain is weighed wrongly and oversold—even the "sweepings of the wheat" (Amos 8:7). People who have no land of their own and those who have lost their harvest through drought, debts, and lease payments, have no means of defending themselves. Since they need grain, they are entirely at their landlords' mercy. Such fate befell fathers and mothers, daughters and sons, old and young equally.

2.4 Poor people or troublemakers?

The language gives away who it is we are thinking about. The term "the poor" sounds relatively neutral, or at least unalarming; "the masses, the mob," on the other hand, has something dynamic about it, something that threatens to start moving, like a mound of rocks that begins to slide or a mud avalanche that can't be stopped once it has tilted too far. The masses easily get out of control—as in the riots in England[39] or those in the Paris *banlieues*.[40] But should we equate "hooligans" with "the poor?" Are they not just hooligans who lack good manners and shrink from nothing, and are just plain bored?

When a head of state has to give reasons for such excesses it is highly likely that he or she will rely on this pattern. Those who set cars on fire were "hooligans"; what they did was "violence" pure and simple. Some seek to portray these excesses as acts of violent, irresponsible youths. Others hold governments responsible for them. But actually we should ask what these young people are trying to say. What is going on to make them lash out like this? What do they need?

When the financial crisis struck Europe in 2008 and governments reacted with austerity measures (*austeritas*: Latin for harshness, stringency, discipline), hundreds of thousands of people, young and old, took to the streets together. They were forced to bear the states' costs for saving the banks. Outraged masses of people protested in Spain and Italy, as well as in Portugal, Greece, and Israel.[41] The middle classes, students, young people, pensioners, home owners—the poor of Europe look like you and me. They are not people on the margins, not misfits, not uneducated. The protesters articulate precisely what they need. But in the face of these protests, governments are helpless or obdurate.

In addition to these new mass protests I would like to call attention to two further phenomena that can help bring our picture of "the poor" into sharper focus. The poor are not only male. There are also "rampaging women," such as those in the activist group Femen. Femen is an organization that advocates for self-determination, in particular for women. It became known for "topless protests" against election fraud, sex tourism, Islamism, Vladimir Putin, Silvio Berlusconi, and many others. After the Prime Minister of Ukraine declared in March 2010 that implementing reforms was not women's business, Femen called on the wives and girlfriends of members of the cabinet to participate in a sex boycott. They also declared that the humiliation of women and the curtailment of their social roles in Ukraine "displayed a dangerous tendency."[42] Many of their actions made the headlines because they were carried out topless. The organization reminds us that when we think of "the poor" we need to think about women too. The poverty of women includes structural inequality, discrimination and disregard, as well as material poverty.

The unrest of the immigrants in Rosarno, Italy, is another example of contemporary uprisings.[43] In January 2010, African workers in the orange groves of Calabria protested against exploitation and discrimination. The riots broke out when shots were fired on a group of immigrants and one African was injured. Witnesses to the event then set several cars on fire, smashed the windows of shops, and shouted, "We are not animals." They accused the local population of racism. Seven protesters were arrested for acts of violence, damage to property, and civil disorder. The grove workers lived in barracks without electricity or toilet facilities, or in abandoned factories. They worked fifteen hours a day for a pittance. The population of Rosarno, for their part, felt threatened by the many immigrants and responded to their protests with force.

These and many other reports about social unrest and protest are easy to find on the internet. The choice of words in these reports sets the course of our perceptions. If they refer to hooligans, anarchists, the unemployed, they often mean groups of young people with no career prospects. We are subconsciously led to believe these young men are committing violent acts because of their youth or their elevated testosterone. This makes their protest a matter of biology, and provides a false excuse for it, so that it is no longer taken seriously. Hooligans just want to have fights and destroy things. The choice of words alone suggests that they have no agenda, no political consciousness. It makes a huge difference whether we call them insurgents or hooligans:[44] the word "insurgents" immediately makes us think of a politically motivated protest, and assume that there is an agenda to it, a will.

If we now speak of the *poor of the Bible*, it is also important to reflect critically on our images of them. We should not romanticize the poor,[45] as decent people who have come off badly, who have at last been given a chance and whom we should benevolently allow to carry on. Neither should we despise them as dirty, uneducated, violent mobs who overrun everything. "The poor" are, in moral terms, neither good nor bad; they can be dangerous for the privileged, but mostly they are just annoying and unpleasant.

I place these considerations at the beginning, because while reading or translating biblical texts, it is not only important to know Greek, but also to understand what we associate with "the poor" (*ptochoi*). We have to ask ourselves who were among the poor at the time the texts were written, and who were the poor to whom Jesus was referring. At the same time, it is relevant for our reading which poor we have in view today, and which poor slip out of sight. Who are the poor and what can they do in our imagination, so that we accept them as messengers of joy and preachers of the gospel?

2.5 Contexts of poverty

Who are the poor and what is their gospel? These two questions are closely interlinked. Of course, the gospel of the poor has something to do with them. Or to put it like this: the rich and the poor are probably glad about different things. Hungry people rejoice in bread and rice, which the well-fed barely notice. Rejoicing has to do with what people are waiting for, what they are reaching out for.

In the Greek-speaking world of antiquity, *euangelion* meant news of victory.[46] Those who are threatened by an enemy, who are at war, yearn for the news, "We have won." Then shouts of joy, the women's ululation, and the fanfares mean, "The war is over, the enemy is leaving." The cries of jubilation are the news, and whoever listens to the trilling will instantly hear and understand the news of peace (Isa 52:7).

But *euangelion* can also be a piece of bread or the birth of a son. Whatever brings deliverance becomes *euangelion*, the good news. What are the poor hoping for, what is it they need, what do they reach out for? What is deliverance for them?

> 12 For he delivers the needy [*evyon*] when they call,
> the poor [*ani*] and those who have no helper.
> 13 He has pity on the weak [*dal*] and the needy [*evyon*],
> and saves the lives of the needy.
> 14 From oppression and violence he redeems their life;
> and precious is their blood in his sight (Ps 72:12–14).

In this psalm the poor cry out for deliverance; they need help, since oppression and violence dominate their lives. Their blood is being spilled. Their deliverance has to do with justice and the dignity of life; they need someone to fight for them.

The poor of those times and of today are united in their demand for bread, justice, and freedom. This longing for a government that protects the poor against the greed for profit and power of the rich, as phrased in Psalm 72, still drives people onto the streets.

All these protests have their own history and their own development. I found out little by little that people were protesting in Egypt long before the winter of 2010. When in 1977 the then president Anwar al-Sadat tried to cancel the state subsidies for some foodstuffs, he triggered a wave of protest that forced him to cancel his plan.[47] Bread is highly subsidized by the Egyptian state to this day.[48]

In 2008, I read about the effects of rising costs on the Egyptian people for the first time.[49] *Le Monde diplomatique* reported it extensively. "Muhammad al-Attar told *Al-Ahram Weekly*: 'The city is burning. Thousands of demonstrators are out on the street, throwing stones, chanting anti-government slogans and defying the batons of the riot police, tear gas and bullets.' Al-Attar is a member of the elected strike committee of the 25,000 workers at the gigantic Misr Spinning and Weaving Co, a public-sector textile conglomerate and the largest industrial enterprise in Egypt."[50]

There were also food price riots in Bangladesh in April 2008, when 20,000 textile workers engaged in street battles with police. They were protesting against the low wages that did not allow them to buy enough food. In India, there was a 135 percent increase in the price of onions in the summer of 2010. The price of onions is an indication of crisis: Indian food is almost unimaginable without onions. In 1998, the municipal government of Delhi fell because it urged the poor to cook without onions in order to save money.[51]

When the price of grain exploded worldwide in the spring of 2008, riots erupted in Cairo. The United Nations also warned that a famine was looming in Somalia, as the rising costs of food put a huge burden on the people because drought and civil war had made them highly dependent on imports. Three years later, in 2011, famine broke out in Somalia. At the same time, people in Cairo were calling for revolution. It is hardly a coincidence that the global price of grain was higher than ever before. When grain prices, stoked by speculation, rise until they explode, there will be consequences. There is a connection between riots and the price of bread.

What would have been *euangelion*, news of deliverance, for people in Egypt, Bangladesh and Somalia?

2.6 Food riots

One of the oldest references to food riots comes from Egypt in the twelfth century BCE. The Pharaohs built the pyramids as massive tombs, which would of course have to be tended by subsequent generations. Hordes of workers were required to guard the pyramids, do necessary repairs, and protect them against storms and heat. Ramses III paid the workmen at the necropolis of his predecessor Ramses II in natural produce, which he had delivered to them four times a year. In 1159 BCE these workers protested, and told the authorities: "We have been driven here by hunger and thirst; we have no clothes, we have no oil, we have no [fish]."[52] There was looting and violence until an overseer was dismissed and the workers got what they needed.

Fish was to the ancient Egyptians what potatoes were in nineteenth-century Europe. The Great Famine ravaged Ireland from 1845, when the potato crops failed through potato blight. But the Irish tenants were abandoned to their fate by the English landlords, who even exported Irish grain for their own needs. The landlords used the dramatic depopulation of the Irish countryside to enlarge their properties. They emerged from that catastrophe even more powerful. But the Irish population was depleted and weakened in every respect. At least a million Irish people died of starvation. Another million emigrated.[53]

George Bernard Shaw's description in *Man and Superman* (1903) of how people were left to starve is impressive. There was no famine in 1847, but English rule ensured that the Irish population starved:

> Malone: My father died of starvation in Ireland in the black 47. Maybe you've heard of it?
>
> Violet: The Famine!
>
> Malone [with smoldering passion]: No, the starvation. When a country is full of food, and exporting it, there can be no famine. My father was starved dead; and I was starved out to America in my mother's arms. English rule drove me and mine out of Ireland.[54]

How does a famine come to a country? Lack of rainfall, flooding, swarms of locusts, infestations—the crucial question is not what causes crop failures but how communities deal with a shortage of foodstuffs. When dramatic climatic conditions cause harvests to fail, great solidarity is needed on the part of neighboring countries or the world community as a whole, so that social unrest can be avoided. Famines often cause whole regions to destabilize (as in Somalia in 2008 and Syria in 2013). Civil wars impede aid convoys and agriculture, so that local troubles can expand into other regions.

2.7 The Song of Deborah

Just as the protest of the pyramid workers in the twelfth century BCE is the oldest written evidence of a food riot, so the Song of Deborah in the book of Judges contains very old traces of similar incidents, in one the oldest sections of the Old Testament.[55] We can recognize processes of impoverishment in it that have remained a threat to this day.[56]

Judges 4–5 describes an ongoing social conflict that finally turned violent. People had been living under tyranny for twenty years (Judg 4:3). For a whole generation they had cowered down and tried their level best to earn a living. But when barley-bread was unavailable and the caravans stopped coming, and people suffered more and more from hunger, their patience ran out and a violent uprising ensued.

During those times Deborah was a prophetess, counselor, and judge. She gave the rioters a voice and led them in their struggle for liberation. One of her songs has been handed down, in which she bewails the distress that besets the land:

> 6 In the days of Shamgar the son of Anath, in the days of Jael, the highways were unoccupied, and the travelers walked through byways.
>
> 7 The inhabitants of the villages ceased, they ceased in Israel, until that I Deborah arose, that I arose a mother in Israel.
>
> 8 They chose new gods; then was war in the gates: was there a shield or spear seen among forty thousand in Israel? (Judg 5:6–8 KJV).

None of the English translations, unfortunately, takes into account that the Hebrew word in verse 8 may actually be *lechem* (bread) rather than *lacham* (war). *Strong's Concordance* does acknowledge the primitive root of *lechem*, *lacham*: "to feed on; figuratively, to consume; by implication, to battle (as destruction):—devour, eat, ever, fighting, overcome, prevail, make war, warring."[57] Yet, starting with the Septuagint, most translators have eliminated this ambiguity, deciding instead to render the word as something associated with war. The German *Bibel in gerechter Sprache*, however, translates verse 8 as:

> They chose new gods; the barley-bread had disappeared. Shields were not seen, nor spears, among 40,000 in Israel.[58]

The context gives this translation a certain weight. The "mother in Israel" arose because there was no bread to eat. New gods were worshipped in the hope that they would bring bread. The army was completely vulnerable without the faithful support of the Israelites' God.

Here, the prophetess describes a cycle of hunger. When *trade routes* have become unsafe so that caravans and traders can no longer travel on them, trade comes to a standstill. That jeopardizes the replenishment of supplies from other regions, such as when there is a grain shortage, or when people even eat next season's seed to still their hunger. Trade and trade routes take on unique importance in times of drought.

When bands of robbers make roads unsafe, *byways* through almost impassable areas must be found in order to avoid them. Byways and the *enslavement of the peasantry* are mentioned together. Debt slavery drives farmers off their lands. The farmers lack means when the harvests are meager and lease payments for their land are high, so that they have to sell their children or even themselves into debt slavery.[59] The robber bands grew in numbers as a consequence: farmers who had lost their fields and yards gathered into groups and went after what they needed. The decline of a free peasantry makes social conflict inevitable.

Another incident, not far removed from the Song of Deborah, should be read in the light of hunger. Sisera, the enemy's commander-in-chief was killed—not by an army in battle, but as he fled and begged for water (Judg 4:17–21). Jael, a "civilian" in whose tent he sought protection, killed him cold-bloodedly and with her own hands. This story too shows that the uprising took place in a time of drought, and that it was an uprising of the hungry. It is worth noting that women are prominently mentioned: it is the people who arose to fight, on their own initiative. These are uprisings resulting from social hardship at a time when the barley-bread had disappeared.

Barley was an important basic commodity for both poor and rich.[60] It was undemanding and highly resistant to arid conditions. Since maize, potatoes, and rice were not yet known, the various grains were the most important source of food. A lack of barley-bread probably stands for additional grave shortages of food. When even barley-bread can no longer be had and a commander-in-chief has to beg for water, then the food situation is precarious. The battle for bread, water, and freedom is already being addressed in the oldest part of the Bible.

2.8 We are many!

The book of Nehemiah tells of noisy protests in relation to debt slavery and hunger in the fifth century BCE:

> For there were those who said, "With our sons and our daughters, we are many; we must get grain, so that we may eat and stay alive." 3 There were also those who said, "We are having to pledge our fields, our vineyards, and our houses in order to get grain during the famine." 4 And there were those who said, "We are having to borrow money on our fields and vineyards to pay the king's tax. 5 Now our flesh is the same as that of our kindred; our children are the same as their children; and yet we are forcing our sons and daughters to be slaves, and some of our daughters have been ravished; we are powerless, and our fields and vineyards now belong to others" (Neh 5:2–5).

The distress described here affects a great many people, the majority of the population. They protest here as "the many." Foremost—the noisiest thing—is the cry of the hungry: "We must get grain, so that we may eat and stay alive." Get grain—even though they sow it and harvest it, they do not own it. Now they want to go and take it so that they may eat and stay alive. Other voices cry out that they have to mortgage their land and houses in order to buy grain. Still others complain that even this is not enough: they have to sell their children, or their wives, into debt slavery. Finally, off the record, so to speak, they tell of their daughters' sexual degradation. The rich take power over the impoverished peasant families, not only their lands and possessions, but also their bodies. And the poor have nothing with which to counter them.

The lack of bread triggers the uprising, but it is the debt slavery as expressed here that is at the heart of the protest. The affected people were not only impoverished, but their families were torn apart. The disintegration of family structures implies destitution, especially if the state has not set up a system of social security. The weaker the state, the more important the webs of family, something that had been true for the people in these regions since the demise of the northern kingdom of Israel and the southern kingdom of Judah (eighth to sixth centuries BCE).[61]

The food riot described in the book of Nehemiah has a surprisingly good ending. The Persian governor Nehemiah, a member of the upper class who has returned from exile in Babylon, hears the cries of the people and decides to join together with the free citizens and the administrators of the city to fight for the people. He declares: "You are all profiteering from your own people!" (Neh 5:7). And he demands that they give back to the people what was rightfully theirs:

> "Restore to them, this very day, their fields, their vineyards, their olive orchards, and their houses, and the interest on money, grain, wine, and oil that you have been exacting from them." 12 Then they said, "We will restore everything and demand nothing more from them. We will do as you say" (Neh 5:11–12).

The protest pays off, like a flash of light in the middle of the book of Nehemiah; a piece of heaven becomes visible, a sign of how the world could be. The government acts wisely and prudently. They give back what they had taken: fields, vineyards, olive groves, and houses—no wonder the people had risen up! What else should they have lived off? The government was compelled to return what usury had yielded, the excesses of what they had taken. The government had given itself the right to impose a tax on the produce of the land (grain, grape juice, olive oil, and all the other fruits of the harvest). But in those days that did not mean building schools and storage facilities, water reservoirs and road networks. The city wall around Jerusalem was constructed through forced labor.

2.9 Seeking the many

After these two examples from Judges and Nehemiah, the question arises as to whether there are accounts of uprisings from the time of Jesus as well,[62] or from the period when the Gospels came into being (between 70 and 90 CE).

Matthew's Gospel depicts the people's hardship very clearly overall, and repeatedly denounces the political leadership (Matt 10:6; 15:24). It shows that the majority of the people came off badly under the self-serving government, comparing the people to a flock of sheep that is badly led and consequently wanders about in vain, not finding any food:

> When he saw the crowds, he had compassion for them, because they were harassed and helpless, like sheep without a shepherd (Matt 9:36).

Now we may legitimately ask whether those poor people, for whom Jesus had compassion, would have dared to riot. They were badly off, they were poor and in debt, and suffered numerous illnesses. But did they consider an uprising? Are there traces of an uprising of the many, as in Nehemiah 5? Is the civilian population enraged, as we heard from Deborah in Judges 4–5? Or does Matthew present these people as victims of the regime? This is also the crucial question about hunger, because hunger should often be understood as the last straw that breaks the camel's back, or the spark that causes smoldering dissatisfaction or social tensions to explode.

The great longing for deliverance, as described in Mark 1 and Luke 1–2, is surely an indicator for the distress and the growing impatience of the crowds. According to Mark 1, all the people were on their feet, people came from everywhere to hear John the Baptist, for him to open up new prospects for them. They were ready to be baptized and to join his movement of repentance and new beginnings.

> And people from the whole Judean countryside and all the people of Jerusalem
> were going out to him, and were baptized by him in the river Jordan (Matt 3:5).

But the reverse perspective is also appealing: did John go to where crowds of people were gathering? Was he courageous enough to give the enraged people a voice? Did he look for crowds and speak to them until they followed him? If a people is suffering, they do not need to be shaken into action, but held back from violent clashes with the ruling powers. It could therefore be that the two prophets John and Jesus made it their business to prevent a violent uprising in Palestine, and sought to convince the crowds not to incite riots but to live by the Torah.

"To live by the Torah" would then mean not being ground down in militant insurgency but to rise up together and look nonviolently for what GOD is doing in their very midst. This should not be equated with political indifference or a search for personal peace of mind.[63] Instead it would mean: The scattered people must be brought together, and be set free from the misery of debt slavery,[64] the sick and injured must be healed, and the righteous path practiced together. Living by the Torah means solidarity with the impoverished—which does not exclude unrest and uprising but gives them a different foundation.

Fear of impending famine, rage about unequal distribution, and yearning for freedom drove people onto the streets in antiquity as well.[65] But how many people did these things affect in Palestine in Jesus' time? I am not looking here for a number that can be documented,[66] but ask whether we can find the same feeling of outrage in the Gospels that we saw among the poor in the book of Nehemiah. In Nehemiah's time the people cried out: "We are many." This call to rise up reflects an outrage that will no longer put up with the misery.

2.10 Seeing the many

In my search for this feeling of outrage I am guided by the word "many." The Greek term *polloi* is most often translated as "many." But it can also mean "great." *Polloi ochloi* can therefore be translated as "great crowd of people" or "many people, many multitudes." Keeping this in mind, we become aware of how many people or large crowds are on the move in Matthew:

> And great crowds followed him from Galilee, the Decapolis, Jerusalem, Judea, and from beyond the Jordan (Matt 4:25).
>
> Great crowds followed him (Matt 8:1).

"Many" are on the move, and restless. They came from all over the place (Matt 4:25). Could those people just take days off and wander about? Who was looking after the livestock and the vegetable plots in the meantime? Could they afford to lay down their work as day laborers, weavers, washerwomen, fishermen, farmworkers? Or was it that they had no work at all to lay down? Did they come from their homes, workshops, and farms, or did they no longer have homes and were therefore on the streets?[67] And finally: Did they assemble where Jesus was, or did Jesus go where the crowds gathered?

> When Jesus saw the crowds, he went up the mountain (Matt 5:1).
>
> Now when Jesus saw great crowds around him . . . (Matt 8:18).
>
> When he saw the crowds, he had compassion for them, because they were harassed and helpless, like sheep without a shepherd (Matt 9:36).
>
> Jesus began to speak to the crowds (Matt 11:7).

Jesus notices the crowds of people and begins to speak to them. It is not he who calls them from their homes; he finds them outside, restless and homeless, in need of something. He heals them (Matt 12:15; 15:30). This sets the multitudes all the more in motion:

> When the crowds saw it, they were filled with awe, and they glorified God, who had given such authority to human beings (Matt 9:8).
>
> Now when Jesus had finished saying these things, the crowds were astounded at his teaching (Matt 7:28).
>
> And the crowds were amazed and said . . . (Matt 9:33).
>
> All the crowds were amazed and said, "Can this be the Son of David?" (Matt 12:23).

How do we imagine enthusiastic crowds? *Polloi* are out and about, filling the town squares. They are restless because they live on the edge of the subsistence level, or below; it takes very little to nudge them below the subsistence level. Many of them are overcome at the words of a rabbi. They drop everything and gather together incessantly (Matt 13:2; 14:13; 19:2; 20:29). What effect would all those gatherings have had on the Roman administrators and the house of Herod? Would the Roman landowners and leaseholders have perhaps considered them hooligans, frustrated and rebellious people, robbers who were jeopardizing their property? In contrast to the fear of the wealthy and powerful, "the many" appears to be a term without negative connotations, describing the momentum of the masses on the move without characterizing them as a threat.

I would like to draw attention to a further point that is important for our understanding of "the many." There are no references in the Gospels to colorful market scenes, to daily or weekly fish sales, or harvest festivals. This is not to suggest that these events did not take place. But we should take the Gospels' silence on that seriously. No idyllic conditions are described there. No Gospel even remotely sketches an amply laid table.

The wedding at Cana (John 2:1–10) may look like an example of the opposite. But careful reading of the Johannine narrative shows that more is going on in our imagination than what is in the text. Apart from Pesach, this wedding is the only large village feast mentioned in the Gospels. But all we find out about the wedding is that it ran out of wine (John 2:3). So this is not a description of abundance either, but of a feast under conditions of scarcity.[68] Other than the lack of wine we are told nothing of a richly set table. John is silent on this, as he is on the feast at Bethany (John 12:1–8). What did the meal look like in the home of Mary and Martha and their brother Lazarus, which they had prepared together? Did they serve wine? Mark does not provide any information about food or menus either, not even when Herod throws a banquet for his courtiers and officers and the leaders of Galilee (Mark 6:21). Luke, too, is silent about what there was to eat at the Sabbath meal in the house of Simon the Pharisee (Luke 7:36–50). Even the final meal of Jesus in Jerusalem is not described in detail. The texts suggest that it was a Passover meal, but we cannot say with certainty what was on the table.

This silence about food is astonishing and persistent. It leaves behind a very restrained image of the people who are eating and celebrating.[69] There are no descriptions of ample meals or culinary arts,[70] nor do we hear people singing[71] or see them dancing.[72] But again and again we encounter many people and their sick. The people who are ill or tormented by demons give us an indication of the overall context of poverty.[73] The gatherings of the multitude are made up of these people, who do not find a table laid with food anywhere, but who search restlessly for help and are unable to go on living as before.

> And great multitudes came unto him, having with them those that were lame, blind, dumb, maimed, and many others, and cast them down at Jesus' feet; and he healed them (Matt 15:30 KJV).
> And great multitudes followed him; and he healed them there (Matt 19:2 KJV).

In connection with the impoverishment of the peasants and the collapse of village structures under the Roman tenancy system, social historian Richard A. Horsley speaks of a population with a tendency to revolt:

> There is simply no solid evidence to support the romantic notion of the last generation that Jesus attracted primarily the marginalized members of society,

> such as "sinners" and prostitutes or rootless individuals who had abandoned their lands and families. Evidence for economic conditions and land tenure in Palestine at the time of Jesus suggests that peasants in the hill country of western Judea had indeed been losing their lands to wealthy Herodian landlords. . . . The frequent attention to debts and their cancellation point to an audience still on the land but unable to make ends meet, given the demands for taxes and tribute. . . . And as studies of peasant revolts have found, it is villagers in just such circumstances who tend to become involved in popular movements and revolts. On the other hand, those who have already lost their land become heavily dependent on wealthy elite families or their agents and hence are less free to join movements.[74]

If we include these reflections and observations in our considerations, we begin to see the "many" who accompany Jesus or seek him, or those with whom he mingled, as a suffering and destitute majority, as people who work hard yet barely make ends meet.

I would like to keep these "many" in view as masses of human beings whose poverty makes them a potential for unrest. Jesus worked with them to stop them engaging in acts of violence and to open up a future for them. When he, like many others, made a pilgrimage to Jerusalem for Passover, he was going where most of them went and where umpteen thousand people[75] gathered. On the way to Jerusalem, he encountered great multitudes of people who also were pilgrims to the capital city. He was surrounded by masses, of *polloi*, in the midst of them (Matt 21:8-9, 10-11; 23:1):

> As they were leaving Jericho, a large crowd followed him. 30 There were two blind men sitting by the roadside. When they heard that Jesus was passing by, they shouted, "Lord, have mercy on us, Son of David!" (Matt 20:29-30).
>
> A very large crowd spread their cloaks on the road, and others cut branches from the trees and spread them on the road. 9 The crowds that went ahead of him and that followed were shouting, "Hosanna to the Son of David!" (Matt 21:8-9).

The people were calling for help. The Romans officials and the Jewish power elite would have heard that cry for help as signal for insurrection. In any case, they were keeping an eye on Jesus as the "leader" of these crowds, and were afraid of him (Matt 21:15, 45-46; 22:15-22; 26:3-5). His execution took place with an eye to the many who cheered him and who were to be rebuked with his death. Matthew interprets his execution as a death for the sake of the many:

> . . . for this is my blood, which is poured out for many (Matt 26:28).

Looking at the "many" in this manner may also open up a new perspective on that sentence. For those who sought to keep the masses under control, executing Jesus was an act of pacification. His blood had to be spilled because the many were disposed to riot. But the friends of Jesus, the Matthean community, saw it differently: his blood was spilled so that the many might have a future. Jesus died on account of Rome's politics of repression; for the many, so that they might live.

Without him, the protests continued violently, and a generation later, under the guidance of nationalistic powers, led to the great uprising against Rome,[76] a devastating war against the then most powerful military superpower (66–70 CE). Jerusalem was besieged and the inhabitants starved, the temple destroyed, and the peasantry dispossessed even more brutally. But only twenty years after the end of the war the Gospels came into being; they remembered "the many," what it was like to live according to the Torah, and to be in solidarity with the impoverished, as Jesus had taught through the Torah.

2.11 The many women

When we read of "the many," we should be aware that they included women. Greek was an androcentric language. A masculine plural gives no indication of whether women were included, or how many women there were; the masculine plural *polloi* does not have to be understood as a strictly masculine term. It can include very few women or very many. It is quite astonishing to what extent these female "many" have been ignored in the history of exegesis. Mark and Luke tell of a few women whose names are known and others whose names are not, but they also talk about multitudes, the many, a large crowd of women followers.[77]

Above all, the word *pollai*, the feminine plural form—"many women"—is used at a very prominent place. At the execution of Jesus, the male disciples are missing in the Synoptic Gospels. But here, under the cross, Mark explicitly identifies three groups of women who are part of the Jesus movement. First, he speaks of women who watched from afar and were eyewitnesses to the crucifixion, including the women of Jerusalem, who had joined the movement only lately in that city.[78] But the eyewitnesses also include women from Galilee, disciples who are remembered by name and who had followed Jesus and served him since his time in Galilee (Mark 15:40). And finally, Mark refers to many more who had gone up to Jerusalem with Jesus:

> There were also women looking on from a distance; among them were Mary Magdalene, and Mary the mother of James the younger and of Joses, and Salome. 41 These used to follow him and provided for him when he was in Galilee; and there were many other women [*allai pollai*] who had come up with him to Jerusalem (Mark 15:40–41).

The verbs *diakonein*—to serve—and *akolouthein*—to follow—can be considered key words that distinguish the named women as disciples.[79]

We learn from these clusters of women watching the crucifixion about the various groups—some from Jerusalem, others from Galilee—among whom the "many others" who had gone up with him stand out. In them we can see the enraged crowds who dropped everything and did not flinch from confronting the powers that be.

Luke, too, adds another large crowd of women to the list of women disciples remembered by name:

> . . . and Joanna, the wife of Herod's steward Chuza, and Susanna, and many others [*heterai pollai*], who provided for them out of their resources (Luke 8:3).

Both of these passages make it clear that, as well as the named female disciples, the Jesus movement included many others, a sizeable crowd of women. Luke 8:4 speaks of a "great crowd" (the non-gender specific *ochlos pollys*) of city people who had gathered together. Jesus taught the Torah in a way that opened their eyes to their own present situation.

2.12 The many as a messianic factor

The same word, *polloi*, which is found in the hungry people's cry of rage (Neh 5:2), runs like a golden thread through the whole of Matthew's Gospel; it also appears repeatedly in Mark and Luke and allows the image of a kind of omnipresent crowd to form. There are substantive implications to this observation.

For a long time, my perspective had been trained in such a way that I did not really see these "many." I thought of them as "extras," who had no purpose other than to listen and to be entertained. I perceived them as being merely incidental. And I always saw Jesus shining out from the background of the many. He was the active one, who spoke, healed, taught. The people were the object to whom he spoke, whom he healed and taught. But our observations reveal something else: Jesus met these crowds everywhere. He accompanied them, and tried to give them the orientation that a rabbi could provide: the Torah.

Christian attention has focused on Jesus, his uniqueness, his preaching, etc. And in Christian theology this uniqueness always had an anti-Judaist flavor, with the general tone of Jesus being different from his Jewish contemporaries. But the more Jesus was set aside from the people around him, the lonelier he became. The Jesus who was isolated from Israel in this way became the Christ of Christians. He was surrounded by uncomprehending—albeit faithful—disciples, as well as by an uncomprehending family and Jews who did not recognize him. That detachment from Israel, from the Torah, from the history, the hopes, and the real people of that period, has had consequences for the image of Christ, and has led more or less directly to an otherworldly and unpolitical Christology. Being worldly was indicative of a suspicious link to the Jewish people.

This anti-Judaist coloration of Christology was associated with a colonialist perception of the many. They could be ignored and were theologically insignificant. These assumptions blocked a clear view of the people who poured out onto the streets, restless and hungry. Today, I am trying to perceive the many, the outraged masses, the protesting crowds. They accompanied Jesus on his path, and he accompanied them. They had already been on the road with John the Baptist (Matt 3:5). They had had enough of this government, of exploitation and poverty. Jesus joined their protest, joined the movement of John (who too was executed). Jesus found his role as a Torah teacher and prophet. But he certainly also learned much from those mothers and fathers, who were prepared to suffer, prepared to stand up for their children (cf. Neh 5:2f).

The Gospel of Matthew portrays Jesus as part of this crowd of people. It is as though Jesus were visible only in the midst of a huge crowd. He is there, where they have gathered. Revising my perspective shows that Jesus is one of the many, or is in the midst of the many. And these many are not merely hundreds or thousands, but people who are ready to protest, people who are no longer able to hold back. Sometimes they come to him, sometimes they are already there and he is one of them.

I read these concentrations of many people as a messianic factor that makes the urgency of deliverance and of bread abundantly clear. In the crowds we find highly diverse population groups from different geographic, political and cultural backgrounds. They come from Galilee, Judah, Perea, from villages and towns. They are tax collectors, civil servants, day laborers; they work on farms, in the salt industry in Tarichea (Migdal), they fish. There are prostitutes, widows, leaders of synagogues, Torah scholars, scribes, Levites, Pharisees, and so on. These people are sometimes differentiated, but are also included among the many. They are initially united by deprivation, not by a common vision for the future, which was yet to be developed. John the Baptist and Jesus worked on it—and the Gospels. They tried to form the diverse multitudes, the masses (*polloi, pollai, ochlos*) into a *laos*[80]—a corporate body.

Here is where I add my hypothesis: The Messiah can be found not only among the poor or by their side. Where people join together in solidarity, where they stand up and shout for joy—this is where the messianic power of the people of Israel awakens to new life. The many are where the Messiah is situated—or, in different words, the messianic power revives the exhausted and the sick (Matt 9:36) and turns "the many" into the people, the gathered, healed, raised up poor of Israel. It can therefore also be said that wherever a healed and united people is raised up out of the many, we can see the Messiah at work.

2.13 Problems of translation (Luke 7:22)

After examining the contexts of poverty and the gospel of the poor, the omnipresence of the many on the streets and the messianic power that invigorates them, I turn now to the translation of Luke 7:22. Translations of that verse makes evident what translators believe the many (*polloi* and *pollai*) to be capable of, and how they understand them.

Luke 7:22 (par Matt 11:5):

> And he answered them, "Go and tell John what you have seen and heard: the blind receive their sight, the lame walk, the lepers are cleansed, the deaf hear, the dead are raised, the poor have good news brought to them." (NRSV)
>
> Then Jesus answering said unto them, Go your way, and tell John what things ye have seen and heard; how that the blind see, the lame walk, the lepers are cleansed, the deaf hear, the dead are raised, to the poor the gospel is preached. (KJV)

English translations render the first four clauses—concerning the blind, the lame, the lepers, and the deaf—almost identically. Notable differences emerge only in the fifth and sixth clauses: the dead and the poor. The dead are mentioned not as agents—subjects—but as objects: they are raised. I will address this further below.

It is not only the translations cited, but all the other English and German versions—indeed, the entire tradition of translation into the vernacular—that render "the poor" in the dative case, turning them into objects to whom the good news is preached or proclaimed, disregarding the fact that, in the Greek text of Luke and in the Vulgate, the poor are the subject of the verb, not its object.[81] As soon as this inversion takes place, the poor stop appearing as active agents; their empowerment to preach the gospel becomes invisible. They are presented as people to be preached at, the only group in this sentence who do nothing. The blind, etc. become active, but not the group of the poor. This sets them apart, isolates them from the others. But in the original, all groups in the verse are in the nominative case, all—the dead and the poor included—are equally subjects that govern a verb.

Turning subject into object has far-reaching christological consequences. This sentence about the poor who preach the gospel should be understood as the climax of Jesus' answer to John's disciples, who asked: "Are you the one who is to come, or are we to wait for another?" (v. 20). Jesus does not point to himself. His reply is not: "Yes, I am the one" or: "No, no I'm not. Wait for another." Luke does not have Jesus reply to their question immediately, but prefaces it with an action and a reference to previous events: it was a time when he had healed many who had suffered from disease, plagues, evil spirits, and blindness.

> Jesus had just then cured many people of diseases, plagues, and evil spirits, and had given sight to many who were blind. 22 And he answered them, "Go and tell John what you have seen and heard: the blind see, the lame walk, the lepers become clean, the deaf hear, the dead arise, the poor preach the good news (Luke 7:21–22, adapted from NRSV).

John's messengers are told to report back to him as witnesses of what they had seen and heard. Verse 21 reports that Jesus had healed many people. But there was something else they were to tell John, couched in the words of verse 22. Their answer should not bring reports about a healer, but about the people's rising and becoming alive. The people are at the center of verse 22; the diverse members of the People come into view, those who begin to see and hear, whose skin becomes healthy, and whose legs strong; and whose dead rise up. The time has come, the poor arise, jubilant!

Only when the poor are jubilant is the answer to John's question complete: the sick members of the People come alive again, and the poor announce the nearness of their GOD, who has turned to them and saved them. This answer sings of the messianic power that Jesus recognizes in the many who rise up. This answer is not the report of a miracle worker but of the Messiah, whose arrival amongst the people is tangible.

Verse 21 uses the word "many" (*polloi*)[82] twice. Here they come into view, the many who have flocked together from all over, because they were hungry, they had lost their lands, their livelihoods. Jesus worked with these people. This is about them. The blind, the lame, the lepers, the deaf, the dead—these are the poor, out of whom Jesus wants to form a *laos*, a people that is healed and gathered, that stands up for itself as one people, rather than battling one another or fighting for individual survival.

Luke 7:21–22 describes the poor according to different physical ailments: it may surprise us that the dead are included, since they do not fit in this list of the suffering or impaired. The dead are no longer suffering but are, in a manner of speaking, blind, lame, and deaf rolled into one. Their senses have died. They cannot be reached through any channel. What all the groups mentioned do have in common is that they cannot make full use of their senses, organs, or bodily functions. That is to say, the poor whom Luke lists are not defined in terms of their different incomes or volumes of debt, nor in terms of their productivity or social status. Luke's list allows the members of an injured people to come into view.

It is also not a random list of sufferings, but is in line with a tradition of describing an injured people:

> Then the eyes of the blind shall be opened, and the ears of the deaf shall be unstopped.
> 6 Then shall the lame man leap as an hart, and the tongue of the dumb sing
> (Isa 35:5–6 KJV).

> 10 My heart throbs, my strength fails me;
> as for the light of my eyes—it also has gone from me. . . .
> 13 But I am like the deaf, I do not hear; like the mute, who cannot speak.
> 14 Truly, I am like one who does not hear,
> and in whose mouth is no retort
> (Ps 38:10, 13–14 NRSV).

> 7 For thus saith the Lord; Sing with gladness for Jacob, and shout among the chief of the nations: publish ye, praise ye, and say, O Lord, save thy people, the remnant of Israel.
>
> 8 Behold, I will bring them from the north country, and gather them from the coasts of the earth, and with them the blind and the lame, the woman with child and her that travaileth with child together: a great company shall return thither (Jer 31:7–8 KJV).

God saves, heals, and gathers the body of the people. Before our very eyes, there is a transformation of the injured members into a jubilant body of the poor. Now, says Luke, the majority of the people begin to rise up out of paralyzing, oppressive poverty. The many become seeing, leaping, cleansed, hearing people, who are alive and jubilant. Here, Luke is describing the resurrection of Israel. The "many," the disoriented crowds, lying on the ground ("sheep" in Matt 9:36), turn into an upright, jubilant people.

2.14 A first-hand experience

Thus, if we want to hear the gospel, the good news, we have to inquire about the poor. It is they who bring the good news—*euangelizontai* ("bring good news, proclaim news of joy"). In Greek, the verb is not in the passive but in the middle voice.[83] They are not the ones to whom something is brought or proclaimed (passive); it is they who bring good news with them.

Since there is no middle voice in English, I must detail the difficulty of translation once again. While translating in the passive voice makes an object out of the subject—"the poor have the good news brought to them"—a translation in the active voice would read: "The poor proclaim the good news." From a grammatical point of view, this would be an acceptable rendition. But a translation of the middle voice would have be reflexive: "The poor bring *themselves* good news."[84] The poor are the agents, the subjects who do the proclaiming; bringing themselves the good news and telling it to one another. They act for one another, not against; no longer for others—the rich and powerful—but for themselves.

This statement—that the poor begin to shout with joy—is found also in the Greek translation of the Septuagint:

> On that day the deaf shall hear the words of a scroll,
> and out of their gloom and darkness the eyes of the blind shall see.
> 19 The meek shall obtain fresh joy in the Lord,
> and the neediest people shall exult in the Holy One of Israel (Isa 29:18–19).

Isa 29:18–19 is thus also about the deaf who hear and the blind who see, and the poor (here: those who are the neediest) who exult and rejoice because of God. The messianic era is characterized here through these rejoicing and healed people. When the people begin to understand, when they are no longer deaf, then joy and hope will be alive among them. The gospel of the poor ululates with joy about the GOD who enables them to arise, and gathers them together.

In addition to the blind and deaf of Isa 29:18–19, further groups of people come into view in Luke and Matthew: the lame and the lepers. This accumulation of afflictions may indicate that the situation of the people had worsened, which makes sense with the reference to the dead in particular. Mentioning the dead brings to the surface the rulers' political capriciousness (Luke 13:1–5) and those they had murdered (Matt 2:16–18).

The Greek middle voice (third person plural) of the verb, *euangelizontai* in Luke 7:22, is also found in the three verbs of Isa 29:18–19 in the Septuagint:

akousontai—they hear

blepsontai—they see

agalliasontai ptochoi—the poor rejoice

It is easy to translate the last verb, "to rejoice," in its middle voice—someone does not cause the poor to rejoice, nor do the poor make someone else rejoice; they themselves are the ones who rejoice. But when we seek to make this reflexive form of the middle voice apparent, we need to find another way of translating "to hear" and "to see."

The Greek middle voice is difficult to render in English. German offers the possibility of a reflexive form, but this does not always work in English, and in any case the reflexive is only one facet of the Greek middle. All forms of the middle voice are a departure from the prototypical transitive event where the subject is the initiator of the action, and an object, distinct from the subject, is the endpoint of the action.[85] In the middle voice, the subject of the verb performs or experiences the action expressed by the verb in such a way that emphasizes the subject's participation; the subject acts on, for or towards itself.[86] The wide variety of subject-focused verbal ideas include self-interest, self-involvement, emotional and mental states, and states or conditions.[87] For a verb like *euangelizomai*, which is derived from the noun *euangelos*, we can conclude that the subject acts as *euangeloi* for themselves, that is: the poor act as *euangeloi* for the poor.

The deaf hear the words of the scroll, the Torah (in the middle voice, *akousontai*, Isa 29:18)—i.e., not only do they hear the words aurally, but they establish a relationship between the written words and their own situation.

The eyes of the blind see (*blepsontai*, Isa 29:18)—i.e., not only do they see, but they grasp what the words of the scroll have to do with their bleak situation. They recognize the meaning of the words for their lives, for themselves.[88]

The poor rejoice (*agalliasontai*, Isa 29:19) about GOD—analogously to the two previous renditions of the middle voice we might translate that as: The poor make a connection between themselves and GOD, they relate GOD to themselves. They recognize that: "What is written in the scroll concerns us. It applies to us. It is about the darkness in which we live. Now! It is about justice for us and for our lives. The name of GOD—justice, life, faithfulness—is our orientation."

This is how the middle voice *euangelizontai*[89] expresses the relationship between the gospel and those who convey it. In no way is a gospel preached to them—instead they, the poor, discern the saving truth that concerns them. It becomes their gospel. That is, they are not just proclaiming the good news actively—which might still mean that it was news they have been told to spread, news that has nothing to do with them, like the way that the mail service delivers messages.[90] The middle voice shows that the blind and lame, the lepers and the dead had at one time or another experienced the power of the Torah for themselves at first hand, and they began to proclaim this power to one another.

> Jesus had just then cured many people of diseases, plagues, and evil spirits, and had given sight to many who were blind. 22 And he answered them, "Go and tell John what you have seen and heard: the blind see, the lame walk, the lepers become clean, the deaf hear, the dead arise, the poor preach the good news (Luke 7:21–22, adapted from NRSV).

Luke 7:22 answers the question in verse 20: "Are you the one who is to come?" Jesus' reply speaks of the healing of the many. They are no longer blind, no longer downcast, no longer isolated, and they begin to understand what the Torah is about. The injured body of the people is gradually recovering.

This can also be seen in connection with the exodus. I refer to a familiar interpretation of the book of Exodus by Rabbi Ishmael; we should not for one moment forget that the Gospels were Jewish writings. For Rabbi Ishmael, too, the power of the Torah can be experienced physically:

Mekhilta de-Rabbi Ishmael, Tractate Bahodesh (Exod 20:18–22)

> Rabbi says: For when they all stood before Mount Sinai to receive the Torah there were—so Scripture tells us—no blind ones among them. For it is said: "And all the people saw" (Exod 20:18). It also tells that there were no dumb ones among them. For it is said: "And all the people answered together soon as they heard it" (Exod 19:8). And it also teaches that there were no deaf ones among them. For it is said: "All that the LORD hath spoken will we do and listen to" (Exod 24:7). And it also teaches that there were no lame ones among them. For it is said: "And they stood at the nether part of the mount" (Exod 19:17). And it also teaches that there were no fools among them. For it is said: "Thou hast been shown to understand" (Deut 4:35).[91]

When the people stood at Mount Sinai to receive the Torah, according to Rabbi Ishmael, there were no more lame people, for all were standing on their feet. There were also no mute people among them since everyone answered. Everyone saw, so there were clearly no blind people.

According to the rabbi, "the people" meant "all"—in the same sense as "many" encompassed the great majority that clearly included the blind, the deaf, etc. It goes without saying that he includes everybody who stood at Sinai and experienced the power of the Torah.

These cures of the blind, mute, and lame so that the whole people can receive the Torah and no one is left behind (not even those left behind when someone dies) do not, for Rabbi Ishmael, have messianic implications. This is not about the person of Moses as a great revelator, not about the uniqueness of the moment, not about medical healing miracles on Sinai. At the focus are the power of the Torah and the people. Everyone can receive the Torah. No one is unable to do so; no one can say: "I am blind and can't read the words," or "I do not have the education," or "I am not so mobile and can't walk there." The Torah is accessible to all, and with regard to the Torah all are equal—it is meant for everyone and its power can be experienced by everyone.

2.15 A messianic chain reaction

Luke's statement about the poor who experience deliverance in their own bodies—whether they are seeing how others began to leap about, or they themselves are able to stand up—is a glimpse of the people who flocked together from everywhere, of the mass gatherings of the "many." Those rallies unsettled the political rulers; that is why Herod had their leaders arrested.[92]

The prophet John's arrest is part of the literary context of that statement. That is to say, we must not ignore his arrest and focus only on the rejoicing and the healing, on good news and the Messiah. All the while, this man is in the dungeons of the fortress Machaerus. He will be beheaded and his head publicly mocked. The kind of execution shows what the king had in mind: the instigator is to be removed and the movement rendered "headless" and ridiculed.

In Luke 7:18 (and par. Matt 11:2), we hear of the prophet John one last time. From the prison, he sent messengers to Jesus. That means that John was not in isolation: he heard what went on outside and kept in touch with events. He wanted to know what was going to happen to the poor, now that Herod had struck. Into whose care could he commit his flock? "Are you the one who is to come?" This question shows how closely he was committed to the many: ultimately, they have to bear the consequences. Who will support these people? Who will rein in their rage and channel their aggression toward solidarity? Who will accompany these people on their path?

> Jesus had just then cured many of diseases, plagues, and evil spirits, and had given sight to many who were blind. 22 And he answered them, "Go and tell John what you have seen and heard" (Luke 7:21–22).

Verse 21 refers to the many people who stood up. The eyes of many were opened; they began to understand connections, and left no one behind—not even the dead.[93] Where members of the people are made whole, that is where messianic deeds occur (cf. Matt 11:2). John's two messengers are to tell John about these deeds. They are to report on what they themselves see and hear; for they are also part of that body of people, and their own eyes and their own ears are astonished by what they see and hear.

The jubilation of the poor sings of a people that stands together, ready to walk out of misery. Such jubilation triggers a messianic chain reaction, which we can see in verse 22, in the various limbs that begin to stir. A people rises up before our very eyes. A people's movement arises and lives—and its different members begin to lift themselves and one another up. "People's movement" was not a term used in Luke's day: instead, his contemporaries would have understood the description of the injured, sick, or dead body of the people that begins to show life again, to leap, and to rejoice.

3.

Rage in the Belly

Anger is loaded
with information and energy.
AUDRE LORDE[94]

RECOGNIZING INDICATORS OF HUNGER

3.1 A guest between the lines

It is difficult to talk about hunger if you know hunger; it leaves you speechless. But this kind of silence can be eloquent, particularly in connection with experiences of hunger.

Still, it makes no sense to presume hunger summarily. Of course, we may experiment with the assumption that the people in the Gospels were familiar with hunger. But the question is how it projects itself into a particular text. *How* does the shadow of hunger color a scene? What are the words, verses and actions that we can attach to indications of hunger? Such questions are even more difficult to answer when we know of people's speechlessness about their experience of hunger. In a sense, hunger can be an invisible *leitmotif* in a text, and easily elude us. To detect its shadow, to ascertain its presence, we need to identify historical clues to malnutrition, food shortages, or impending famine, as well as literary signals.

Since poets too are able to speak about what lies between the lines, it is worthwhile listening to them first. How do they portray experiences of hunger? What words do they find? And what can we learn from them for our engagement with biblical texts? We begin with texts by Daniil Kharms and Herta Müller, both of whom know how to find words for hunger.

In what follows, I seek therefore to find a method that allows people who have not experienced hunger to discern the shadow of hunger at a textual level. I sketch methodological steps for probing biblical texts for signs of hunger, or for bringing the shadow of hunger into view. These steps follow signals that I call *text markers* (see below), which I examine for their suitability.

We begin with an investigation of reports about John the Baptist in the Synoptic Gospels. Can such text markers be found in these reports? The prophet, fasting in the desert, the crowds who go out to him there, his angry speech: nowhere do we find the word "hunger." Yet we encounter hunger between the lines, an uninvited guest. What changes in our reading when we find the presence of hunger?

I also wish to analyze the "temptation of Jesus" in terms of the hermeneutic of hunger. The verb "to be famished" is found in the text where Jesus comes into our gaze (Matt 4:2; Luke 4:2). That is to say, gazing at Jesus makes hunger visible. Making hunger visible thus turns into a political-theological message: Jesus struggles with the satanic face of hunger, the hunger-devil. This existential encounter takes place right at the start of his public activity, meaning that his struggle with hunger (the devil) is programmatic. For readers of Matthew's and Luke's Gospels, hunger acts as a doorway into them. The path of Jesus started out in Galilee. Here, he found his first companions (Matt 4:17–22), and here the departure out of the land of hunger began.

3.2 When you're hungry . . .

When Daniil Kharms was born in December 1905, St. Petersburg was already the scene of revolutions. Following the October Revolution in 1917, famine broke out. Civil war shrank the St. Petersburg population from 2.5 million pre-Revolution to 722,000 in 1920. Daniil Kharms's life was marked by the harsh transition from Czarist past to Soviet future, by waves of arrests and poverty.[95] In 1942, Kharms starved to death in a Soviet prison in Leningrad, while the German army besieged the city.

On 28 September 1937, once again under arrest, Daniil Kharms wrote:

> This is how hunger begins:
> first you wake in good cheer,
> then weakness begins,
> and then boredom,
> and then comes the loss
> of the power of swift reason
> and then comes calm—
> and then the horror.[96]

He describes how hunger begins every morning. In the short span of time after the night-time cramps, bad dreams, and waking up, there are words to depict the beginning of hunger. But the ability to think atrophies quickly; weariness, like lead, blankets everything—and then the poet becomes mute. Horror reigns, and silence.

The Russian poet succeeds in interlacing the physiological effects of hunger with consciousness. Hunger affects the whole person, affects thinking and language. Hunger appears here as an internal bodily awareness, a perception of the world and of one's own person in this world.[97] Hunger invades the body, enters the person, penetrates the center of one's being, and occupies all activity. People who are familiar only with appetite cannot fathom such a horror. It has everything to do with physical pain, with fantasies, extreme weakness, rage, angst and humiliation. Hunger encompasses far more than having an empty stomach.

In her novel *Atemschaukel* [The Hunger Angel] Herta Müller describes this horror as something that takes possession and dominates a human being, even decades after the starvation camps:

> No words are adequate for the suffering caused by hunger. To this day I have to show hunger that I escaped his grasp. Ever since I stopped having to grow hungry, I literally eat life itself. And when I eat, I am locked up inside the taste of eating. For sixty years, ever since I came back from the camp, I have been eating against starvation.[98]

In *The Hunger Angel*, Herta Müller tells of a Russian forced-labor camp for Romanian women and men, who were very badly malnourished. The novel draws on authentic reports from a former inmate of the camp. The situation in such a camp cannot be compared with that of an ancient city or a village in Palestine where hunger reigned.[99] Nevertheless, we can learn much from the author that helps us in reading the Bible: she knows that it is nearly impossible to speak about hunger when one is possessed by it:

> What can be said about chronic hunger. Perhaps that there's a hunger that can make you sick with hunger. That it comes in addition to the hunger you already feel. That there is a hunger which is always new, which grows insatiably, which pounces on the never-ending old hunger that already took such effort to tame. How can you face the world if all you can say about yourself is that you're hungry. If you can't think of anything else.[100]

> Hunger is always there.
> Because it's there, it comes whenever and however it wants to.[101]

> Except you're not allowed to talk about hunger when you're hungry.[102]

> When our hunger is at its peak, we talk about childhood and food. The women at greater length than the men.[103]

These passages evoke the following observations:

1. Hunger may be present in the text before we suspect it, because it is present in a manner that we cannot imagine. It may perhaps even be there long before a story begins. Perhaps it is mentioned only if a fresh hunger is added to the one already there. Perhaps it torments the most vulnerable most of all—and that is considered normal and not worth mentioning. A level of hunger can be constantly present—something we no longer realize. Perhaps only the fear of really great hunger is mentioned. We need to approach the text with a suspicion of hunger: it is not that hunger has to prove its presence, but that we have to learn to read it, to assume it as a prerequisite for the narratives, without it having to announce itself officially in the text. This does not mean reading hunger into the text without reason for doing so: there must be clues in the text. But people who do not know hunger have to learn how to suspect its presence.

2. "What can be said about chronic hunger"? Hunger does not fit well into language. Words shiver in the face of hunger. They hide its vehemence, its cruelty, its brutal ordinariness, and its totality that forces people to their knees and humiliates them because they are at its mercy. Hunger dominates people, their thoughts, their strivings, and their actions. For the famished, this experience of being under such control is an insult. And so with hunger comes shame, rage, humiliation, powerlessness. Language is simply too puny for such liminal experiences. Just as people who have experienced violence are often unable to speak about it, it is often impossible to speak about hunger. ("Except you're not allowed to talk about hunger when you're hungry.") It may even be that speaking about hunger only makes it bigger. This is why it is dangerous to give hunger a platform: it would only upstage everything else. To give it space is risky; it would take over completely and devour everything in its path.

3. Thus, it is important to hear the silence in the text. What can be said about the hunger that is present and weighs heavily, causing havoc, gnawing, devouring, killing . . . ? The silence expresses its presence more clearly than words, which fail us when we are hungry. The silence is the shadow of hunger that gives it away. We, the well-fed, might be curious to find out what it is like when hunger overwhelms people. And we might wax eloquent as though hunger were a cool and novel experience, for we delight in experiences that promise a surge of adrenaline. But hunger has nothing to do with adrenaline kicks. Hunger eats up adrenaline; hunger is tedious, burdensome, suffocating, and if we talk about it, it only grows. Hunger is present without having to be talked about. This is something we readers need to get used to.

4. Hungry ears want to hear stories about eating. ("When our hunger is at its peak, we talk about childhood and food. The women at greater length than the men.")

Stories of eating are less likely to be told at table, but more likely to be told by people with an empty, growling stomach. We can presume that women in particular will be handing down and telling stories about eating, because they knew exactly how to make proper bread, and which condiments they needed to make food tasty. Cooking would be their domain, if they had something to cook. But in times of hunger they still had stories to tell; the knowledge, the memories, and the words that would not assuage hunger but bring a bit of happiness nonetheless. Eating is a good subject to talk about; hunger is not.

3.3 Signals of hunger in the text

There are a great many stories of eating in the Bible, including in the Gospels. There are banquets and parables about banquets, there are conversations at table and after-dinner speeches, the story of the Last Supper, and the prayer for daily bread. The question is why people told so many stories about eating.

If we take the observations in the previous section seriously, we could conclude that the more stories there were about the table the more extraordinary it was to share a meal. We might suspect that the *Sitz im Leben* of those narratives is a time of deprivation, of chronic hunger. Because the narrators had very little bread to share with one another, they relied on memories. They seasoned the little bit of bread with stories of wheat and fish. They pined for bread, for enough to eat, and kept alive the memory of the table as promising a transformation that will take hold of the hungry once they have finally eaten their fill.

But the silence around hunger makes it difficult for exegetes to track it down. How did the texts bridge that silence? The following text markers may signal the *possible* presence of hunger: 1. talking about eating or food; 2. silence about hunger; and 3. Torah quotations that refer to a situation of hunger or describe experiences of it. I regard such intertextual references to be important, particularly in places where language is itself a victim of hunger. Such quotes from the Old Testament Scriptures may be read as eloquent recollection, as signals, particularly where that silence is most dense. Intertextual references can give voice to those whom hunger has rendered speechless, and season a story emptied by famine.

An additional text marker is: 4. the emotional disposition, the sense of body and world that a text communicates. Daniil Kharms's description of horror corresponds to a physiological and psychological strain that may be felt as an aggressive, irritated, and unpredictable tension or panic. The rage of the hungry is eloquent and is often described by outsiders as a rage in the belly,[104] this excruciating stomach pain that can lead to all kinds of protests, unrest, and outbreaks of violence. When tensions run high, when the protagonist appears to be furious, then we can interpret this rage politically as a signal of hunger.

3.4 Rage as a critical-visionary force

People socialized as Christians, in particular, seem to be quite uneasy about the emotion of rage. For them, rage does not accord with the GOD of love, with the selfless Jesus, and the sisters and brothers who greet one another with the kiss of peace. In this scenario, rage is first and foremost a moral problem. It would be best if we did not let rage arise in the first place. I have encountered this on several occasions when women shied away from the term "rage in the belly." Men seem to be less uneasy about rage; so rage is also an issue of gender. Gendered issues implicitly address conceptions of masculinity and femininity, including the formation of roles and the performance of identities. Men perhaps allow themselves to become enraged because male rage makes an impression. Men and women surely feel rage equally, but perhaps gender roles allow women to express their rage less. Perhaps an enraged woman is more likely to be ridiculed. It is certainly worthwhile examining one's own resistance towards rage.

I am addressing rage here not as a moral or psychological problem, but in the context of social movements.[105] I want to call on two voices that have become very important for me: one is Audre Lorde, who described the painful necessity of rage most impressively. She was conscious that anger had become a transformative force in the Black women's movement:

> Oppressed peoples are always asked to stretch a little more, to bridge the gap between blindness and humanity. Black women are expected to use our anger only in the service of other people's salvation, other people's learning. But that time is over. My anger has meant pain to me but it has also meant survival, and before I give it up I'm going to be sure that there is something at least as powerful to replace it on the road to clarity.[106]

Audre Lorde wrote about the connection between pain and rage, about anger as a protest against injustice and hurt; at the same time she knew about rage's active nature: "Anger is loaded with information and energy."[107] Anger also acts for something that has still to be formulated, something that is not yet present. According to Lorde, rage is visionary.[108] Rage, anger: the quintessential feeling that the pain and hurt are wrong and unjust, and that we must take action against them.

Rage that arises as a reaction against oppression can also be a motor for countering domination.[109] For the Swiss author and lawyer, Iris von Roten, rage became a means to counter the self-opinionated complacency prevalent in Switzerland in the post-war years. In her study, *Frauen im Laufgitter: Offene Worte zur Stellung der Frau* [Women in Playpens: Speaking Openly on the Place of Women],[110] von Roten turned her rage into an engine for change; she subjected the male dominance of that time to critical analysis. (In 1958, Swiss women did not have the right to vote; they did not receive it until 1972. Lack of political emancipation also hindered women in their career choices.) Her literary work broke all the rules: many judged it to be insufficiently scholarly or decried it as lacking literary quality. Her language did not fit into any category. She was not intellectual enough or too much so, too journalistic or too dry. Von Roten's untiring attack on the status quo was nurtured by her feminist critique and rage. She searched for a language and a form that were broad enough, and ultimately her writing is visionary. Throughout her work, there is that rage against the self-opinionatedness of men; against the policy bourgeois women had of cozying up to men and not demanding anything for themselves; against the "Swiss mentality" that seemed tolerant and friendly, but was actually backwards-looking and mistrustful of women who wanted careers, who wanted to live independently; and against the laws spawned by men's domination and the mythology underpinning it.[111]

Since then, rage has also been analyzed methodologically, allowing us to discern the emotionality of texts. Sara Ahmed offers an analysis of the role of emotions in debates of international terrorism, asylum and migration, reconciliation and restoration. She also thinks about the role of emotions in feminist and queer thinking. She proposes the concept of a "politics of emotion," which enables collectives to form, stimulates the ability to remember, and characterizes the webs of relationship within nations, kinship groups, and religious communities.[112]

Insights such as these may encourage readers of the Bible not to overlook rage in its texts. Of course, not every rage is the same: the fury of the unsettled tyrant Herod (Matt 2:16) differs in many aspects from that of the hungry, which I hear as a force for change that will no longer put up with the injustice and the violence of hunger. For hunger is a violation of human beings, of their bodies, of the emerging generation, and of social networks, all of which hunger destroys. Their rage against it is vital: rage against the lack of bread, the loss of income, against the humiliation that perpetual hunger creates, and against the outrageousness of having to eat things that arouse disgust. Rage is a factor that puts an end to tolerance and calls social movements into being. The rage of the hungry also brings forth a theological perspective that is rooted in the Torah and was given concrete expression in the New Testament.

3.5 Text markers

The expression *text marker* implies that a text (a section, pericope, narrative, scene, story) is colored by specific words. Such coloration is provided by the text; i.e., authors or editors have put it there. While readers may mark up a text using a highlighter, the text itself provides marks like directives—road signs—to alert the reader and to prepare a way to understand it. But it is the reader who has to recognize and detect these marks so that they begin to make sense. In this sense the concept of text marker leads us into reception aesthetics, which examines the significance of the interaction between text and reader. As soon as particular words are repeated or appear in closer succession, a correlation emerges when reading that can indicate something beyond the text itself.[113]

Martin Buber and Franz Rosenzweig were schooled in rabbinical hermeneutics; their translation of the Hebrew Bible into German attempts to render the web of repetition visible. In his 1936 essay, "*Leitwort* Style in Pentateuch Narrative," Buber demonstrated how repetitions in the text of words he called *Leitworte*[114] reveal or clarify meaning for readers of Scripture. He refers to refrain-like *Leitworte* that create bridges or threads running through the narrative web of the text. However, "[i]nterpretation by *Leitwort* style can only be interpretation toward, demonstration can only be demonstration *toward*,—toward something that is to be perceived in its actuality, but not paraphrased in language or thought."[115]

We may regard text markers as *Leitworte* since they open up to readers a field that suggests hunger. That is to say, the shadow of hunger is not readily visible—it needs to be discovered. It does not become manifest through *Leitworte* in the sense of related words, but by tracking down particular marks in the text. The four text markers referred to above are not watertight proofs, but they do give directions. They function like signals that help slow down the flow of reading and make us look out for the signs of hunger. Sometimes, hunger is found in the immediate context. At other times, social-historical information about the food situation can open our eyes. We need to keep in mind economic conditions, political instabilities and tensions, droughts and other climatic extremes. Such observations together provide the ground on which we spread out the texts. In conjunction with the indicators mentioned earlier we attempt to find the shadow of hunger in the text, to open up a new access to individual, specific texts.

To sum up, these are the text markers once again:

1. talking about eating/food
2. silence about hunger
3. references to the Torah, which take over speech when words fail
4. rage in the belly, emotional restlessness, irritability

3.6 John the Baptist eats locusts

With this sharper eye, I now turn to a passage that refers to eating, the first of our text markers:

> Now John was clothed with camel's hair, with a leather belt around his waist, and he ate locusts and wild honey (Mark 1:6).
> Now John wore clothing of camel's hair with a leather belt around his waist, and his food was locusts and wild honey (Matt 3:4).

It is in no way customary to introduce a prophet with a description of his clothes or his diet. John's clothing identifies him from the outset with Elijah, for Elijah's clothing is said to include a leather belt around his waist (2 Kgs 1:8). But John's eating locusts is a unique feature of Matthew and Mark; Elijah did not eat locusts.

Many exegetes see John as living an ascetic lifestyle.[116] But we should enter a caveat here, because asceticism as such is not part of Judaism. Fasting on the Sabbath or before great feast-days is an aspect of ascetic practice, but we ought not to compare that with the Christian ascetics of later centuries. The atonement fast before Yom Kippur[117] lasts only two days. The Jewish practice of fasting does not aim to overcome the physical or to renounce the world. It is about social change and spiritual renewal, about trying for a new beginning in practicing the Torah, about practicing peace and justice in one's social interactions.

Elsewhere we hear that John was not eating or drinking (Matt 11:18) and that his disciples, like those of the Pharisees, were fasting (Mark 2:18). That too is interesting: When, for how long, and for what reason did the Pharisaic movement and the Johannine group fast? Is "fasting" the same as "not eating and drinking"? But here, at the beginning of the Gospels, is the verb "to eat" (Matt 3:4); John is introduced with his diet. The first communication about him is what he eats. We learn nothing about how long and how often he fasted, we hear nothing about how great or severe his hunger was; all we find is a remark about his diet.

Locusts were not normally on the menu in Palestine. But when there was a shortage of food, people had to adjust their diet and eat what they could find. William A. Dando refers to eating "famine foods,"[118] and Peter Garnsey enumerates what people had to eat in times of famine. He lists five categories of food that were not normally part of the population's diet but that were consumed during a food crisis.[119]

Hunger can severely disrupt diets, for example when people are forced to eat plants that do not nourish them (Job 30:1–4) or that are actively harmful (2 Kgs 4:38–40). Even a donkey's head made it onto the menu for hungry people:

> As the siege continued, famine in Samaria became so great that a donkey's head was sold for eighty shekels of silver, and one-fourth of a kab of dove's dung for five shekels of silver (2 Kgs 6:25).

The fact that John's strange diet is explicitly named right at the outset hints at a time of scarcity, when hunger had upset people's ordinary diet. Like other insects, locusts are a protein-rich foodstuff.

But we need more indicators of crisis than just the remarks about locusts. In the Old Testament the use of that term shows how dreaded swarms of locusts were, because they strip fields and destroy crops. The formative memory is in the exodus narrative, where swarms of locusts are described as a divine means of coercion (Exod 10:4). Beyond that, the term was used metaphorically to denote destruction and war.[120]

The New Testament also makes this connection between locusts and the devastation of war:

> 3 Then from the smoke came locusts on the earth, and they were given authority like the authority of scorpions of the earth. 4 They were told not to damage the grass of the earth or any green growth or any tree, but only those people who do not have the seal of God on their foreheads. 5 They were allowed to torture them for five months, but not to kill them, and their torture was like the torture of a scorpion when it stings someone. 6 And in those days people will seek death but will not find it; they will long to die, but death will flee from them. 7 In appearance the locusts were like horses equipped for battle. On their heads were what looked like crowns of gold; their faces were like human faces (Rev 9:37).

Here, locusts are associated with tortures that were to last for five months. They have the power to devastate the green fields. The locusts are pictured as grasshopper-like warhorses. This corresponds to other biblical images: in literary fashion, locusts are associated with destroyed plants, with war, and with GOD's wrath against those who deny the people freedom, like Pharaoh in Egypt.

Since John the Baptist is introduced in connection with locusts, so to speak,[121] we may situate him in a context of hunger, war, and the yearning for a new exodus.

3.7 What can we say about hunger in the time of John?

Two severe famines were documented in Palestine, in 25 BCE and 46 CE.[122] Both were associated with periods of drought,[123] but structural factors aggravated the situation. Years with extreme climatic conditions can be mitigated when good neighborly relations exist, so that catastrophic famine is averted. But that requires a region to have passable roads, reliable social networks, supply systems that have not been destroyed by social unrest, war, or additional factors of oppression (such as excessive taxes and rents that disregard failed harvests). We cannot say with certainty whether there were other food crises in John's time, around 30 CE.

Drought—when the autumn rains were weak, late or absent—presented communities with huge challenges, if it lasted more than two or three years. Seed reserves were used up, so that the following year's harvest was meager as well. The price of basic foodstuffs rose excessively as a consequence.[124] For poor populations, an enduring drought could result in a creeping famine accompanied by diseases, deficiencies of various kinds, high child mortality, and persistent weakening in women of childbearing age.[125]

Since terms such as "food scarcity" and "famine" are used vaguely even today and it is impossible to delimit them precisely, we cannot expect clear differentiation in ancient times either. The dividing line between scarcity and catastrophic famine is narrow. It does not take much for seasonal "pre-harvest hunger"[126] turn into a serious food crisis. In traditional cultures the time before the harvest is marked by scarcity, when substantial labor is required to prepare the ground and tend the crops, just as stocks from the previous harvest are dwindling. This is the time when less food is available and when winter has sapped people's energy. But if climatic and social conditions are as expected, a community can deal with those issues. It is the poor people who are hardest hit by rising prices in times of scarcity. They are more quickly forced to change their eating habits and to go begging. William A. Dando presents a diagram of the phases of famine,[127] which cannot be clearly separated one from another but merge into one another. He distinguishes between an overt, visible side of the hunger cycle and a corresponding covert, psychological side.

Peter Garnsey too, in his studies of famine in antiquity, emphasizes how difficult it is to define hunger precisely. He distinguishes between "famine" and "food shortage" and "endemic hunger."[128] This last is malnourishment, which leads to long-term damage and higher mortality, particularly in infants and children, and pregnant and nursing women. For him, "famine" is the catastrophic hunger that results in increased, measurable mortality. "Food shortage" refers to times when food is in short supply, which manifests itself in rising prices, social tensions, and the kind of hunger that in the worst case turns into famine. For our considerations it is important to take into account what malnourishment and shortage means, above all for the poor, and for mothers, who were affected even when the source texts do not mention hunger.

3.8 In search of water

In addition to John's explicitly mentioned meager fare, there are other references to his appearance during a drought. We should note the huge crowd that, according to Mark and Matthew, came together to meet him:

> And people from the whole Judean countryside and all the people of Jerusalem were going out to him, and were baptized by him in the river Jordan, confessing their sins (Mark 1:5).
>
> Then the people of Jerusalem and all Judea were going out to him, and all the region along the Jordan, 6 and they were baptized by him in the river Jordan, confessing their sins (Matt 3:5–6).

All Judea and the entire population of Jerusalem and the Jordan region left the places where they lived and went to the River Jordan.

The hermeneutic of hunger looks for reasons why the whole population gathered at the Jordan. In connection with John's unusual menu—locusts—we have to ask what moved all Judea, together with the city of Jerusalem and the people from around the Jordan, to go out to the banks of the river. Assuming that the prophet John was an attraction is not an adequate explanation, i.e., it is quite unlikely that so many people would drop everything just for his sake. Besides, this assumption does not take his diet into account.

What were the people looking for, out there by the Jordan? A verse in 1 Kings may help (18:5). During a great famine in Samaria, people looked for things to eat around springs of water where roots still found moisture, while everything had already withered elsewhere. The king, worried about his horses and mules, had his staff look for grass along springs of water and creeks, so that he would not have to kill his animals for lack of fodder.

Thus, we can now connect the prophet's peculiar food, which for centuries had been repeatedly associated in the biblical context with war and catastrophes, to the collective activities of the people. The people had to search for greenery for themselves and their animals, and that is why they went out to the Jordan and its tributaries.

The prophets often reflected theologically on irregular or absent rainfall. They understood it to be a sign of GOD having locked the heavens, in order to help the people turn back, to remind them of the obligations of the covenant. The prophet John, too, exhorted the people to confess their sins, to immerse themselves, and turn back to GOD. These exhortations may be seen in connection with drought and with the fear of a lack of rain. The writings of the prophets also contain rituals of reconciliation, attempts to assuage GOD and to pray for rain.[129]

The book of Joel, for example, describes a terrible drought and a plague of locusts; the priests are called upon perform rites of lamentation:

> 4 What the cutting locust left, the swarming locust has eaten.
> What the swarming locust left, the hopping locust has eaten,
> and what the hopping locust left, the destroying locust has eaten.
> 10 The fields are devastated, the ground mourns;
> for the grain is destroyed, the wine dries up, the oil fails.
> 12 The vine withers, the fig tree droops.
> Pomegranate, palm, and apple—all the trees of the field are dried up;
> surely, joy withers away among the people.
> 13 Put on sackcloth and lament, you priests; wail, you ministers of the altar.
> Come, pass the night in sackcloth, you ministers of my God!
> Grain offering and drink offering are withheld from the house of your God.
> 14 Sanctify a fast, call a solemn assembly.
> Gather the elders and all the inhabitants of the land
> to the house of the LORD your God, and cry out to the LORD (Joel 1:4, 10, 12–14).

The book of Joel was written in the fourth century BCE, and comes from a time when the land was ravaged by war and natural disasters. It is told from the perspective of GOD, who appears to have conspired against her people. But in their vulnerable situation the people raise their voice and remember the merciful divinity who had accompanied the people in the Sinai. The people now join together in a lament, to try to change GOD's mind:

> Who knows whether he will not turn and relent,
> and leave a blessing behind him (Joel 2:14).

The tender thread—the question: Who knows whether God will turn?—was all that the people had in hand: the memory of the God of Sinai and the possibility of turning back. And indeed, God does change her mind! God turns back because she is reminded of herself. God needs that memory—just as the people need it. God turns back and opens the heavens, pouring out her life-giving Spirit on everything that lives (Joel 3:1; cf. also Jdt 7:20–29).

There are also many stories in rabbinic literature that deal with this subject. We hear repeatedly of miracle-working rabbis who knew how to bring dry seasons to an end. They could call forth rains and avert drought with prayers (e.g., *m. Ta'an.* 3:8). The many such stories do not mean that there were equally many droughts, but that the people did not take the autumnal rains for granted. They were accustomed to praying for rain every year.[130]

In the Palestine region, the timing of the autumn rain was crucial. Deuteronomy 11:14–15 speaks of the early and the later rain. The early rain opens the wet season, the time to plough and to sow. If the early showers come too late, the sown seed cannot ripen by harvest-time. Later rains are the continuation of the earlier ones until April. If the wet season ends too early—before the onset of the later rains—the seeds will not reach maturity. Historical climate data from Jerusalem show that three or four years out of ten had irregular rain patterns that adversely affected the harvest.[131]

To summarize: John's consumption of locusts opens up an intertextual connection with Old Testament references to fields stripped bare, hunger, and the plagues in Egypt. For contemporary readers there was most likely something ominous about eating locusts. It certainly did not sound like a delicacy, but suggested hunger; when we well-off readers with enough to eat hear of locusts we might be tempted to think of crab with sweet-and-sour sauce, and wonder whether we might enjoy eating locusts and wild honey or find it disgusting. The Old Testament context clearly associates locusts with drought and war and what accompanies them: hunger.

In the context of the book of Joel and the later midrashic tales of miracle-working rabbis, John's food can also be seen as ritual fasting in the period when rain is expected to fall. Somehow God has to be moved to open the skies again! It seems plausible then that the prophet's foodstuff was a central component of his message. He was announcing a time of shortage, or perhaps a drought, or that a drought would last for longer. This is why the people would have to beseech God fervently, to move God to turn back, and to do the same themselves. Then, hopefully, heaven would not stay shut, the seed would grow, the storerooms would be filled, and hunger would be driven out.

3.9 You brood of vipers!

We have identified and elaborated the first two of the text markers—talking about eating, and silence about hunger. The prophet and his diet of locusts were introduced in a single breath. Characterizing John in terms of his eating locusts may hint at a massive change of diet, or at the fear that this might become reality for many people.

We cannot determine an explicit famine at the time of John's appearance. But it is quite likely that the poor suffered from chronic scarcity. Great crowds were prepared to go out to the Jordan, which is also evidence of widespread worries or fear. The prophet at the river addressed the people out gathering edible greens. He told them not just to take plants for themselves and their livestock, but to bring fruits themselves (Luke 3:8), that is, to practice solidarity, to turn back (Luke 3:10–14)—only that would avert GOD's wrath and open the heavens again. But what stands out most is that John berates the people out there.

> "You brood of vipers! Who warned you to flee from the wrath to come?"
> (Luke 3:7; also Matt 3:7).

Calling them this "brood of vipers" (NIV, NRSV)—other modern translations use phrases such as "you snakes" (GNB)[132]—is a severe rebuke. I suspect it contains text marker 4: rage, irritability, an outburst of anger—an emotionally irritated disposition that erupts out of hunger.

We can hear John's rage in his choice of words. He is incensed by the lip service paid, without leading to action. He reproaches the people for not really scrutinizing their behavior or being willing to change it. Yes, they have come out to him, but only to grab what is left of the vegetation. Or they are hoping for a rain miracle, so that they can get on with their lives as before. But he demands that they turn back to the Torah: he chastises those who have something and do not share it. Berating people also means holding them to account. He wants people to commit themselves. Whether the heaven will open is also up to them.

The prophet interprets the failure of rain to materialize as a consequence of people's behavior. Some have made GOD so angry that she has locked up the sky. Like other prophets before him, John gives a pedagogical interpretation: drought is one of GOD's means of exerting pressure, to open people's eyes and to guide them back into the paths of Torah, of the covenant with GOD. The prophet's criticism is directed primarily at the political leaders who mislead their people. They do not enforce the legislation governing the poor (Deut 24:17–22; 25:5–10), but circumvent it. They do not protect widows and orphans, but exploit them. They do not strengthen solidarity among the people, but undermine it. This is why the people must take a stand against their leaders' behavior. John reminds them of the Torah's praxis of justice; if they turn back and begin to live according to the Torah, GOD will turn and open the heavens.

John eats locusts and berates his people, he prophesies the wrath of God—the shut-off sky. If people want to have rain, if the sky is to open up again, and God is to become reconciled with them, then they must do something. John's rage should be recognized as a text marker that indicates the hidden, not yet visible hunger.

3.10 Trees, fruit, grain

Now that we are on the lookout for signals of hunger, we cannot fail to notice that in the Gospel of Luke, John constantly speaks about things to eat, about trees and their fruits, and of grain. We have designated talking about eating and silence about hunger as text markers 1 and 2. Here John is talking about eating while we do not hear a word about hunger; Luke (in contrast to Mark and Matthew) does not even mention the locusts. But what is very clear in Luke 3:11 is the call to share food with those who have nothing.

> 7 "You brood of vipers! Who warned you to flee from the wrath to come? 8 Bear fruits worthy of repentance. Do not begin to say to yourselves, 'We have Abraham as our ancestor'; for I tell you, God is able from these stones to raise up children to Abraham. 9 Even now the axe is lying at the root of the trees; every tree therefore that does not bear good fruit is cut down and thrown into the fire." 10 And the crowds asked him, "What then should we do?" 11 In reply he said to them, "Whoever has two coats must share with anyone who has none; and whoever has food must do likewise." 12 Even tax collectors came to be baptized, and they asked him, "Teacher, what should we do?" 13 He said to them, "Collect no more than the amount prescribed for you." 14 Soldiers also asked him, "And we, what should we do?" He said to them, "Do not extort money from anyone by threats or false accusation, and be satisfied with your wages" (Luke 3:7–14).

Bring forth good fruit, calls John. For the hungry, this is an intriguing speech: We, the hungry, who have nothing, we can bring forth good fruit? That would be wonderful, if our hands could make juicy melons and grapes grow—that would be worth talking about, with pleasure, for hours on end. Every good fruit passes before the mind's eye—figs, citrus fruits, passion fruit, carobs, pomegranates, dates. Juicy onions are a delicacy too and, of course, olives. Good fruits—the thought of them alone makes one's mouth water and the imagination take flight.

Plants and trees are life-giving. They grow an abundance of fruit and drop them to the ground for everyone without measure. The hungry need not go begging and fall to their knees before them. Fig trees grow in every crack in a wall and offer their fruit several times a year to the poor who cannot access the well-guarded vineyards.

John speaks of cutting down bad trees. In times of drought, trees that do not bear good fruit are cut down, which makes sense when water has to be rationed. A bad tree should not take water from a good one; trees can take up a great deal of water and still bear no fruit.

Of course, John's speech is also prophetic, that is, his words have a political and theological dimension as well. When he talks about cutting down unproductive trees, we are also hearing the biblical critique of kings; for the Bible often compares trees with kings. Good kings are a tree of life where there is space for life to flourish. Bad kings gobble up the water that other creatures need, offering them neither shade nor fruit.

There is a satirical song that illustrates the prophetic critique of the monarchy; it is attributed to Jotham on the occasion of Abimelech's election as king.

> "Listen to me, you lords of Shechem, so that God may listen to you.
>
> 8 The trees once went out to anoint a king over themselves.
>
> So they said to the olive tree, 'Reign over us.'
>
> 9 The olive tree answered them, 'Shall I stop producing my rich oil by which gods and mortals are honored, and go to sway over the trees?'
>
> 10 Then the trees said to the fig tree, 'You come and reign over us.'
>
> 11 But the fig tree answered them, 'Shall I stop producing my sweetness and my delicious fruit, and go to sway over the trees?'
>
> 12 Then the trees said to the vine, 'You come and reign over us.'
>
> 13 But the vine said to them, 'Shall I stop producing my wine that cheers gods and mortals, and go to sway over the trees?'
>
> 14 So all the trees said to the bramble, 'You come and reign over us.'
>
> 15 And the bramble said to the trees, 'If in good faith you are anointing me king over you, then come and take refuge in my shade; but if not, let fire come out of the bramble and devour the cedars of Lebanon'" (Judg 9:7–15).

According to Jotham, the function of a king-tree is to sway above the other trees, to outshine them but otherwise to be utterly absurd and pointless. This brings with it the loss of good fruit. Only one tree, the barren boxthorn (usually translated as "thorn bush" or "bramble"), agrees to play king. The good thing about a king-tree would be its life-giving shade, its leafy canopy under which humans and animals would seek refuge. But a bramble has no treetop that offers shade, only thorns that make it uncomfortable to be near. Brambles are highly flammable, and fire can devour even the fire-resistant cedars of Lebanon. The bramble's power is thus seen to be destructive.

In the book of Ezekiel, criticism is also directed at the king of Jerusalem. Because of his failure, God will leave him at the mercy of Babylon's foreign rule. But the Babylonian king will fulfil his task well. He will be a tree of life for many:

> 23 On the mountain height of Israel I will plant it in order that it may produce boughs and bear fruit, and become a noble cedar.

Under it every kind of bird will live; in the shade of its branches will nest winged creatures of every kind.

24 All the trees of the field shall know that I am the LORD.

I bring low the high tree, I make high the low tree;

I dry up the green tree and make the dry tree flourish.

I the LORD have spoken; I will accomplish it (Ezek 17:23–24).

John berates the people as a "brood of vipers," useless trees which, he threatens, will be cut down. He dares to criticize the royal house of Herod for its power-grabbing and its marital politics, as well as "all the evil things that Herod had done" (Luke 3:19). In response, Herod has the prophet jailed and executed (Luke 3:20; Mark 6:17–29). John perceives the Herodian court to be a useless tree that does not bear good fruit or offer shade. It does not care for the poor, but collects tolls and taxes for Rome and for the construction of ostentatious buildings.

John exhorts people to clothe the poor and to feed them (Luke 3:11).[133] He appeals for solidarity with the poorest, and compliance with the laws concerning the poor (Deut 24:6–22). Astonishingly, even the tax collectors ask for his counsel. They address him as "teacher," indicating that they are ready to learn from him. John tells them to stop squeezing out the last drop from people (Luke 3:13). Even soldiers stationed locally go out to John at the Jordan, asking what they should do, although they do not address him as teacher or prophet. The deprivation suffered appears to be so dreadful that not only the people, but also lowly members of the occupying forces are becoming concerned. Both of these groups, tax collectors and soldiers, were very unpopular with the local population, and they were feared because they used violence to take what they wanted. In John's speech, lived solidarity is paramount (Luke 3:11). It holds a community together and helps people survive times of adversity.

Having examined the appearance of John, I conclude: we look in vain for the word "hunger." What we do find in his speech is a lot about food—locusts and honey, good fruits, feeding others. But the prophet's rage is clear to see: "You brood of vipers!"

3.11 Elijah, the rainmaker

We now need to spot text marker 3: intertextual references, allusions to or explicitly quoted Torah passages that refer to texts with a background of hunger.

John's conspicuous clothing connects him from the outset with Elijah (2 Kgs 1:8).[134] And this obvious reference to Elijah denotes John as an important prophet. But that's not all: this garment alludes to a time of hunger, because Elijah was at the peak of his power at a time when famine reigned in Samaria. So the garment is a hidden indicator of the famine of that time and, because John wears it now, it characterizes the present, a drought that may well become a famine. Like Elijah, John is also a drought-time prophet.

Let us pursue this text marker in more detail: conspicuous clothing weaves the prophet Elijah into the text, and thereby into the circumstances under which he worked.

Elijah was regarded as a major rainmaker, who brought an end to drought and thus to famine (1 Kgs 18:41–46). God had sent him to a creek near the Jordan (1 Kgs 17:5), where ravens brought him bread and meat to eat. But soon the creek dried up as well, because there was no rain in the land (v. 7). Thereupon, Elijah sought shelter from a widow in Zarephath.

In the midst of a drought of many years, Elijah was able to make it rain. His rivals, the priests of Baal, tried to do the same, but without success. Elijah performed an unusual ritual: he took twelve stones, corresponding to the number of the tribes of Jacob (1 Kgs 18:31).[135] He used these stones to build an altar surrounded by a broad trench into which he poured water. He placed an offering on the altar, layered wood beneath it and began to pray. Suddenly fire fell from the sky—perhaps as a bolt of lightning—and consumed the burnt offering: God who is able to unlock the heavens was showing herself. After all, drought reigned because heaven was locked up. After this fiery sign, Elijah said to King Ahab, "Go up, eat and drink; for there is a sound of rushing rain" (18:41) and, lo and behold, the first rainclouds were approaching.

For us, such a ritual may be disconcerting. What is the point of building an altar with water all around it and a pile of wood? Perhaps if all else fails, we try whatever comes to mind until something works. But it all depends on how we understand the meaning of those stones: twelve stones correspond to the number of the tribes of Jacob. Elijah symbolically gathers the whole people, all the children of Jacob. Now that they are united, the ritual can succeed. For God, the stones that the prophet gathered together become Jacob's children. This shows how important it is that everyone came out to John, the entire population, including tax collectors and soldiers. The moment when people are united in solidarity, when they pour out their grief and pray together, they soften God's heart. Elijah was sure of that. And apparently so was John, as were huge swathes of the people, who flocked out to him.

John explicitly alludes to Elijah's rainmaking (1 Kgs 18:31) when he says:

> "Bear fruits worthy of repentance. Do not begin to say to yourselves, 'We have Abraham as our ancestor'; for I tell you, God is able from these stones to raise up children to Abraham" (Luke 3:8).

Recalling Elijah the rainmaker situates the appearance of John in a time of drought. He stands out there at the river, which may have shrunk to a rivulet, and waits for the fiery wrath of God. John is incensed by the lack of solidarity, by those who take for themselves and deprive others—like trees that gobble up water without bringing forth fruit. These trees will not survive the drought, but will be cut down. These greedy ones should not appeal to Abraham and think that they are part of the indispensable people of God—no, they can be cut down like a tree, at any time, as fruitless scroungers, and be replaced with lifeless stones. This critique is aimed at the royal house and all its collaborators. On the other hand, stones can by God's will also become Jacob's children.[136]

3.12 The heavens opened . . .

The prophet's passionate rage in the face of drought, under the threat of famine, and the irritability that comes when waiting and hoping are close to breaking, function as an image of the wrath of God about the prevailing injustice. When John immersed the unknown rabbi Jesus of Nazareth in the rivulet (Matt 3:13; Luke 3:21), the heavens finally opened and *pneuma* poured out, the Spirit's power came down.

> And lo, the heavens were opened unto him (Matt 3:16 KJV).

How do we picture heavens opening? I fear that many will think of a fresco in a Baroque church showing the interior of heaven with throngs of angels and God the Father; but who imagines an ordinary autumn shower? In our culture, we have a peculiar, distorting tradition, which tries in every conceivable way to lure us from connectedness with the earth, from life's reality and experiences.

The heavens open and the blessings of rain stream down. A voice from heaven thunders out (v. 17).[137] Thunderstorms announce their arrival: the autumn rains are coming! Perhaps it rained when Jesus was baptized—how wonderful that would have been for the crowds, if the sound of rain had been in the air . . .[138]

And the Spirit descended like a dove (Matt 3:16; Luke 3:22)—was it the first lightning? Did the long-awaited thunderstorm light up the sky and bathe everything in its light? The dove may confuse modern readers: the phrase "the Spirit in the form of a dove" makes us think, perhaps, of the urban pigeons outside St. Mark's in Venice, landing on the tourists.

The phrase "descending like a dove" describes how something arrived—not what it looked like, but what its coming was like, what its dynamics were and what effect it had: the Spirit found its target and its message arrived safely. The dove was regarded as a messenger; it was the herald and companion of the goddess of love.[139] So this phrase does not describe the form or shape of the Spirit, but the rapid, targeted arrival of a message: God's gift has come. If a message "strikes like lightning" this does not mean that those who receive it are scorched or even killed, but that the message has reached its target and has had an immediate effect, or has changed everything.

I picture the scene like this: after a long dry period—the autumn rain is delayed yet again—the people are afraid of looming famine. Substantial proportions of the population were poor and all too well acquainted with hunger; they longed for the green of the new seedlings, a sign of bread close at hand. They were prepared to pray, to immerse themselves, to turn back, to do what the prophet demanded (Matt 3:5; Mark 1:5; Luke 3:7), for it was apparent that God had shut up the heavens.

Many plunged into the trickle of the Jordan, bent over, and displayed their willingness to turn to God. Jesus, too, joined those who were willing to turn back, and was immersed. For days they were immersed one by one. Until finally, yes, finally, rumbling could be heard in the heavens, and the skies opened!

It would have been easy for Matthew to speak of rain. But he does not do so; he does not describe the climate or the weather conditions. He conveys his message of God's saving power in the language that his community understood very well: they had experience of drought, hunger, and the incompetence of the political leadership that robbed them of their land and their living. It was not just rain that was absent, but also safeguards against drought such as water reserves, systems of food storage, medical care. The rulers lacked the political will to invest in the land and its people. The early readers of the Gospels shared the fear of devastating droughts and knew the distress that results from exposure to drought, forsaken by all good spirits.

Ultimately, we have to leave the texts in suspense: Are Matthew and Luke talking about a drought that John the prophet brought to an end? Or do they clothe their message in a language that people tested by devastation and distress understood very well—hunger, privation, turning back, a new exodus—without there actually being a famine?

3.13 Forty days and forty nights

The heavens opened and distant, rolling thunder was heard. The muddled situation began to see movement. The power of the Spirit (*pneuma*) drove Jesus into the barren, uncivilized wilderness, the desert (Matt 4:1), where the devil was waiting for him.

> 1 Then Jesus was led up by the Spirit into the wilderness to be tempted by the devil. 2 He fasted forty days and forty nights, and afterwards he was famished.
> 3 The tempter came (Matt 4:1–3).

The heavens have opened amidst the rolling thunder (Matt 3:16–17), but the redemptive rain is still not falling. The atmosphere is strained to breaking point—and what happens? Jesus is driven into the desert. Why? It is the Spirit that leads him there. This is the omen for the bleak scene that follows—but it is a good sign, a protective power that Jesus desperately needs, for the scene is marked by Jesus' hunger: He was famished (v. 2).

Just as we should not imagine a white dove sailing down from the blue sky at the baptism of Jesus (Matt 3:16)—but the arrival of a message, the news that the divine gift was at hand—equally we should not picture a devil with horns and tail pursuing Jesus. This medieval idea can obscure our gaze.

By speaking of "the devil" the text refers to something mythical, something threatening. Whenever a text draws on the language of myth, as it does here, using terms such as *satanas* (v. 10) and *diabolos* (vv. 1, 5, 8),[140] it seeks to couch in language something that cannot be expressed using ordinary or everyday speech. The language of myth is able to articulate experiences of violence and powerlessness, using names, images, and narrative features that go beyond an individual's life experiences. It is fed from the collective memory of language. People gave a name to what menaced them, the evil that forced them into dependency, indebtedness, violent relationships, calling them devilish or demonic powers from which there was no escape. These powers ruled like a slave owner or a monarch who could destroy his subordinates. Today we prefer to talk about structural constraints or totalitarian structures instead of demons or devils, but we still understand the huge menace that this mythical wording expresses.

The text seeks to couch the experience of life-threatening violence in words—just as it had previously described a life-giving experience of the Spirit. It is so difficult to capture an experience of violence in words, for it transcends ordinary language, shattering it into fragments.[141] By using such words, the text makes it clear that Jesus was struggling with a power that many generations had already struggled with. This power is named *diabolos* (from the Greek: *diabolein*, to confound) because it messes up and destroys the social order. This mythical wording has given a collective and theological dimension to confrontation with this dark power.

Recourse to the language of myth is associated with Jesus' being famished (v. 2). Could this be a powerful experience of hunger forcing itself into language? It is obviously very difficult to put into words the experience of hunger as collective violence. Herta Müller referred to this:

> What can be said about chronic hunger.... How can you face the world if all you can say about yourself is that you're hungry. If you can't think of anything else.... No words are adequate for the suffering caused by hunger.[142]

Identifying the location characterizes the experience: the desert is a place of defenselessness, with no protecting city walls, and hardly any shade or sources of water. Jesus could not take refuge from that violence. He was left utterly at its mercy—like probably most of his contemporaries. Matthew portrays the face of hunger as a grotesque and devilish grimace. We have a glimpse here of an internal perspective on hunger that uses the language of myth to narrate the encounter with the devil.[143]

> Then Jesus was led up by the Spirit into the wilderness to be tempted by the devil. 2 He fasted forty days and forty nights, and afterwards he was famished.
> 3 The tempter came and said to him, "If you are the Son of God, command these stones to become loaves of bread" (Matt 4:1–3).

The combination of fasting and great hunger is extraordinary: "afterwards he was famished" (v. 2). This comment is unique. There is no practice of fasting in Judaism that prescribes a forty-day fast. Even later rabbinic Judaism refers only to days of fasting, but not to a sustained fast that encompasses day and night and lasts almost six weeks.

Jesus shared the hunger of his people; he suffered under the same harsh rulers. His experience of violence and hunger was similar to that of many other people. Thus, I read the forty days of hunger in connectedness with all the people who had gone out to John the Baptist. Like all the others, Jesus too had barely enough food to eat. The drought had taken its toll. It covered the region like a leaden cloud, like a shadow of death.

In specifying the number of the days and nights that Jesus fasted, Matthew does more than just characterize the duration and the radical nature of that hunger.[144] His reference to "forty days and forty nights" is borrowed from the Torah; he lets it speak where his own words would be too small and too weak (text marker 3).

> Moses entered the cloud, and went up on the mountain. Moses was on the mountain for forty days and forty nights (Exod 24:18).
>
> He was there with the Lord forty days and forty nights; he neither ate bread nor drank water. And he wrote on the tablets the words of the covenant, the Ten Commandments (Exod 34:28).

Both of these texts repeat the number forty. But only Exod 34:28 mentions that Moses fasted, that he "neither ate bread nor drank water." He took no food, and yet he was not famished. In the holy cloud where he encountered God, Moses did not—in contrast to Jesus—explicitly suffer from hunger.[145] The time Moses spent with God seems to be filled with intensity and energy. Moses immersed himself in the divine presence, he drank it in and was filled from God's nearness. The Torah, which emerges through his hands, is a portrait or a fruit of this nourishing encounter.

Matthew uses this reference to Exod 34:28 as the foundation on which to build his story. Moses did not hunger for forty days and forty nights, since his encounter with the divine nourished him. Jesus, however, did hunger greatly; he was utterly famished, so much so that he was visited by the devil, hunger's menacing shadow of death. While Moses in his rapture was able to write down the Torah, Jesus survived thanks to this Torah and to the memory of Moses' rapture. The Spirit did not abandon him, so that he was able to use the Torah as a protective shield against the devil. Jesus quoted the Torah three times. The image of the nourishing encounter between God and Moses, it gave him orientation, words, and power, until the angels came and cared for him (v. 11).

The Spirit and the Torah gave Jesus moral support, they became nourishment, so that he could outlast starvation until the devil left him. In this way, Matthew's Jesus fits seamlessly into the history of Israel. He is part of that people with whom God has made a covenant; a covenant that has proved to be life-saving and essential for survival in a time of crisis.

3.14 The hunger devil

The writer Herta Müller speaks of a "hunger angel." The hunger angel encompasses the totality of hunger as a humiliating, destructive violation that afflicts and infiltrates every inch of the hungry person. It sneaks into the brain, knows every nook and cranny of that person; it becomes an alter ego, a permanent partner who commands, comments on and knows everything better, to the point of driving someone crazy. And it grows beyond the person into their surroundings, creates mirages of things to eat, it twists the ears, eyes, and heart. It does whatever it wants and leaves nothing over for the hungry person. This is how Müller describes chronic hunger in the camp:

> Hunger is an object.
> The angel has climbed into my brain.
> The angel doesn't think. He thinks straight.
> He's never absent.
> He knows my boundaries and he knows his direction.
> He knows where I come from and he knows what he does to me.[146]

> The hunger angel had taken possession of me, my scalp was fluttering. My hair had just been clipped on account of lice.[147]

> The hunger angel was no longer inside our brains, but he was still perched on our necks. And he had a good memory, though he didn't need it, since our camp fashion was just another kind of hunger—eye hunger. The hunger angel said: Don't waste all your money, who knows what's yet to come. And I thought: Everything that's yet to come is already here. . . . The hunger angel warned: Pride comes before a fall. But I told him: We're alive. We only live once.[148]

The hunger angel is argumentative and needs to be countered with something. But it spreads into every part of one's head and beyond it into the stomach and the belly, it breathes down one's neck, grasping every fiber of the body. This angel encroaches as a matter of principle. And so it falsifies objects, hoodwinks people with imaginary smells of food and heart-warming colors, but is itself utterly cold and indifferent.

> Everything matched the magnitude of my hunger in length, width, height, and color. Between the sky overhead and the dust of the earth, every place smelled of a different food. The main street of the camp smelled like caramel, the entrance to the camp like freshly baked bread, crossing the street to the factory smelled like warm apricots, the wooden fence of the factory like candied nuts, the factory gate like scrambled eggs . . . It was magic and it was agony. Even the wind fed the hunger, spinning food we could literally see.[149]

This is how the hunger angel distorts reality; there is no escaping, even in one's dreams.

> I dive into sleep, and I dream.
>
> I'm riding home through the sky on a white pig. . . . But there's nobody there anymore, where am I supposed to go now.
>
> The hunger angel looks at me from the sky and says: Ride back.
>
> I say: But then I'll die.
>
> If you die, I'll make everything orange, and it won't hurt, he says.
>
> And I ride back, and he keeps his word. As I die, the sky over every watchtower turns orange, and it doesn't hurt.
>
> Then I wake up and use my pillowcase to wipe the corners of my mouth. That's the bedbugs' favorite spot at night.[150]

Whether one is awake or dreaming, the distortion of reality does have one saving aspect: smells, memories, colors awaken a part of life, awaken memory. As long as the hunger angel guards you, you are alive. However merciless and cold-hearted the angel, he is the only one who knows you and speaks to you, accompanies you and does not abandon you. Terrible as it is, his presence does offer a remote possibility of an encounter, a projection screen, a target to attack, and thus prevents speechlessness for the moment. I see the figure of that angel as both dreadful and protective.

I will attempt to elucidate the encounter of Jesus and the devil in the poetic-mythic density of Herta Müller's language:

1. The starting point and the foundation of the conversation in Matt 4:1f is bottomless hunger: Grown and developed in a time of drought, fed by persistent poverty, the hunger devil knows the emaciated rabbi from Nazareth and his background, limits, and weaknesses. He comes to Jesus, he knows where to find him. There is no escape.

2. Hunger creeps into the brain. The conversation in Matt 4:1f clearly depicts the force of the hunger that takes possession of Jesus. It spreads throughout his body, invades every thought, and cannot be chased away.

3. To ask whether Jesus encountered the devil as an external power or as something within himself is to ignore the might of hunger. Hunger sits in the control center and projects its distorted images onto the stones and the barren ground around Jesus. Dream and reality become intermingled, as do clear sight and psychic/physical distress. Categories like up and down, inside and outside, I and Not-I, bread and stone are muddled up (cf. *diabolos*, the confounder). Only poetic or mythical language is able to depict possession by the hunger devil with such clarity.

4. The dialogues between the hunger angel and the hungry self, just like the dialogues between the devil and Jesus, describe the struggle that must be withstood

every second, that is lost again and again and never won until bread drives hunger away. Like the hunger angel, the mythical figure of the hunger devil is an opponent in times of despair. The hunger devil comes to seduce Jesus, to tempt him to give up, to cave in and forget everything he considered holy and important. But in debating with the devil, Jesus succeeds in recapturing all that is holy and important to him.

3.15 With the Torah in his hand

The hunger devil keeps coming back, attacking Jesus again and again. Three attacks are described in detail as an example. The stones before his very eyes (v. 3)—don't they smell like lightly toasted bread? Throwing himself down and dying (v. 6)—finally resting in the arms of God: what yearning is spreading out its arms here? Submitting to hunger so that it leaves him in peace (v. 9), letting go completely: would that not be the greatest relief—death?

But if hunger is unrelenting, the Torah is even more tenacious. It renders the devil speechless. The power of the *Shema* ("Hear, O Israel"), the Jewish confession of faith, is great: the commitment to Yhwh proves to be nourishment, the survival rations. Matthew portrays the power of the Torah as life-saving.

> 3 The tempter came and said to him, "If you are the Son of God, command these stones to become loaves of bread." 4 But he answered, "It is written,
> 'One does not live by bread alone,
> but by every word that comes from the mouth of God.'"
> 5 Then the devil took him to the holy city and placed him on the pinnacle of the temple, 6 saying to him, "If you are the Son of God, throw yourself down; for it is written,
> 'He will command his angels concerning you,'
> and 'On their hands they will bear you up,
> so that you will not dash your foot against a stone.'"
> 7 Jesus said to him, "Again it is written, 'Do not put the Lord your God to the test.'"
> 8 Again, the devil took him to a very high mountain and showed him all the kingdoms of the world and their splendor; 9 and he said to him, "All these I will give you, if you will fall down and worship me." 10 Jesus said to him, "Away with you, Satan! for it is written,
> 'Worship the Lord your God,
> and serve only him.'"
> 11 Then the devil left him, and suddenly angels came and waited on him (Matt 4:3–11).

A close look at Jesus' first answer takes us into the book of Deuteronomy. The quotation (v. 4) reminds us of the long journey the people undertook through the desert in their exodus from Egypt. On that path, hunger was present.

> 2 Remember the long way that the LORD your God has led you these forty years in the wilderness, in order to humble you, testing you to know what was in your heart, whether or not you would keep his commandments. 3 He humbled you by letting you hunger, then by feeding you with manna, with which neither you nor your ancestors were acquainted, in order to make you understand that one does not live by bread alone, but by every word that comes from the mouth of the LORD (Deut 8:2–3).

The hunger devil in Matt 3:4 evokes a memory of the exodus, of the bread that was provided. Jesus remembers that, on their path to freedom, the people sometimes had too little bread. But this did not cause the exodus from the house of slavery to grind to a halt. Suddenly there was manna, raining from heaven. This episode on the road to freedom stands for other good things that the people had already tasted and experienced. The whole of creation had emerged from the mouth of Adonai (Gen 1:3)—the word of the Holy One causes the earth to bloom, rain to fall, and gives bread and justice (Isa 45:7–8, 23–25).

The second quotation (v. 7) takes us to Massah, a bottleneck on the road to freedom:

> Do not put the LORD your God to the test, as you tested him at Massah (Deut 6:16).

This is what happened at Massah:

> 1 From the wilderness of Sin the whole congregation of the Israelites journeyed by stages, as the LORD commanded. They camped at Rephidim, but there was no water for the people to drink. 2 The people quarreled with Moses, and said, "Give us water to drink." Moses said to them, "Why do you quarrel with me? Why do you test the LORD?" 3 But the people thirsted there for water; and the people complained against Moses and said, "Why did you bring us out of Egypt, to kill us and our children and livestock with thirst?" 4 So Moses cried out to the LORD, "What shall I do with this people? They are almost ready to stone me." 5 The LORD said to Moses, "Go on ahead of the people, and take some of the elders of Israel with you; take in your hand the staff with which you struck the Nile, and go. 6 I will be standing there in front of you on the rock at Horeb. Strike the rock, and water will come out of it, so that the people may drink." Moses did so, in the sight of the elders of Israel. 7 He called the place Massah and Meribah, because the Israelites quarreled and tested the LORD, saying, "Is the LORD among us or not?" (Exod 17:1–7).

At Massah, the thirsty people had put the Holy One to the test. Divine intervention was needed lest the exodus project fail. The hunger devil goaded Jesus on to quarrel with God, and demand that Adonai intervene and make water bubble forth out of the stones.

I imagine Jesus looking out over the land: drought, aridness, and hunger, as far as the eye could see. Immersion in the Jordan had not yet brought rain. Everyone in Jerusalem and the surrounding villages had followed the prophet John's call in the hope that God could be assuaged and that the rains would finally come. Even when the skies had opened, the fields remained brown, the animals lost their energy, and the people still had almost nothing to eat.

Changing stones into bread and making water bubble forth from the rocks—bread and water are the most essential foodstuffs. Even after the devil's third attack (v. 10), Jesus counters it with a passage from the Torah that tells of the rain and the grain that Adonai provides when his people work for him and only for him.

> 13 If you will only heed his every commandment that I am commanding you today—loving the Lord your God, and serving him with all your heart and with all your soul—14 then he will give the rain for your land in its season, the early rain and the later rain, and you will gather in your grain, your wine, and your oil; 15 and he will give grass in your fields for your livestock, and you will eat your fill. 16 Take care, or you will be seduced into turning away, serving other gods and worshipping them, 17 for then the anger of the Lord will be kindled against you and he will shut up the heavens, so that there will be no rain and the land will yield no fruit (Deut 11:13–17; but compare Exod 20:2–4).

Once again, Jesus recites the words of the *Shema*: "Worship the Lord your God, and serve only him" (Matt 4:10). Is that his answer to the opened heavens and the rolling thunder (Matt 3:16)? Jesus is fighting with the Torah in his hand. His weapon is the profession of faith of his people. Only the word from God's mouth, says Jesus, and consents to work with the power of the Spirit and the Torah against the shadow of death. The devil departs—having finally received his answer. Angels come and take care of Jesus (Matt 4:11).

The quotations from the Torah are more eloquent than we generally think. All three of Jesus' answers carry memories of hunger and thirst, of drought and the absence of rain. They put into words the context that we sketched out earlier. Countering hunger with the Torah may be the key to our examination of hunger. The Torah—not fine phrases or quotes to learn by heart, but the vibrant remembrance of hard times and how they were overcome, of the miraculous manna and of everything that had been called to life through the mouth of God, of the staff in the hand of the good leader, and of the commandment to everyone to work for Adonai with all their strength and all their mind—so that the heavens would open and the land bring forth fruit, and all its inhabitants be able to eat their fill and to rejoice.

3.16 First traveling companions

The story of Jesus' temptation is an insertion. It is narrated following John's baptism of Jesus in the Jordan. Paradoxically, after the heavens had opened, the Chosen One seems to go into hiding in the desert. Perhaps he has to process what he has seen. He has to grow into all that has already taken hold of him. That would be consistent but is a very esoteric or spiritual way of putting it. The text avoids this spiritualized sphere, working instead with explicit hunger ("and afterwards he was famished," Matt 4:2). Hunger does not vanish from the body, not even that of a great prophet. The desert is no safe hiding place but a place of defenselessness and exposure. Jesus is entirely at the mercy of hunger, like the entire population. It nearly breaks him. But the experience of the Spirit and the Torah give him strength to resist and to survive.

Jesus' battle with the hunger devil is linked without transition to the arrest of John in verse 12.

> 12 Now when Jesus heard that John had been arrested, he withdrew to Galilee.
> 13 He left Nazareth and made his home in Capernaum by the sea, in the territory of Zebulun and Naphtali (Matt 4:12–13).

Without any explanation, the Elijah-like prophet and rainmaker disappears from the picture. For people at that time, John's arrest must have been a bitter blow: all of them had gathered out there around him. He had become a spiritual leader and had denounced the greedy king as an unfruitful tree, whereupon Herod immediately had John arrested.

There is a direct line from Jesus' hunger (v. 2), to John (v. 12), the leader of the people, and to the people who rise up and join him (vv. 22–25). At some moment the hunger devil withdraws and angels come (v. 11), as the mythic language puts it. The angels bring news and announce a new departure. They bring tidings of forces that are ready to awaken and to join them: the first traveling companions.

We find these first companions here, the moment Jesus decides to continue the exodus project: he left Nazareth and went to the Sea of Galilee (Matt 4:13). Like many others who left their villages in the hills, he went looking for food around that large freshwater lake. There, Jesus met the companions he needed for the exodus project, people who were ready to work together as brothers and sisters so that GOD would let manna rain and rocks bubble forth water, at last.

3.17 The people in the land of the shadow of death

Jesus had been totally at the mercy of hunger's life-threatening violence. Without the Spirit's power and the Torah he would not have survived that time of starvation. But finally the devil departs and angels appear. Jesus leaves the desert, leaves Nazareth behind as well, and moves to the lakeside.

In my mind's eye, I see crowds of people streaming towards the lake, to its water. After the lonely desert experience there are now swarms of people:

> 14 so that what had been spoken through the prophet Isaiah might be fulfilled:
>
> 15 "Land of Zebulun, land of Naphtali, on the road by the sea, across the Jordan, Galilee of the Gentiles—
>
> 16 the people who sat in darkness have seen a great light,
>
> and for those who sat in the region and shadow of death, light has dawned"
> (Matt 4:14–16).

Psalm 107, a song of joy and relief, also contains the phrase "darkness and the shadow of death"—at least, in the King James translation. Those offering prayer give thanks to GOD for gathering together people who were lost, who were "hungry and thirsty, their soul fainted in them" (v. 5). The psalm relates how hungry people in the desert stray about desperately looking for food. In their despair they cried out to GOD, who set them free, led them out of the darkness, out of the shadow of death, and tore apart their fetters (v. 14).

> 1 O give thanks to the LORD, for he is good;
>
> for his steadfast love endures forever.
>
> 2 Let the redeemed of the LORD say so,
>
> those he redeemed from trouble
>
> 3 and gathered in from the lands,
>
> from the east and from the west,
>
> from the north and from the south.
>
> 4 Some wandered in desert wastes,
>
> finding no way to an inhabited town;
>
> 5 hungry and thirsty,
>
> their soul fainted within them.
>
> 6 Then they cried to the LORD in their trouble,
>
> and he delivered them from their distress;
>
> 7 he led them by a straight way,
>
> until they reached an inhabited town.
>
> 8 Let them thank the LORD for his steadfast love,
>
> for his wonderful works to humankind.
>
> 9 For he satisfies the thirsty,
>
> and the hungry he fills with good things.
>
> 10 Some sat in darkness and in gloom,
>
> prisoners in misery and in irons,
>
> 11 for they had rebelled against the words of God,
>
> and spurned the counsel of the Most High.

> 12 Their hearts were bowed down with hard labor;
> they fell down, with no one to help.
> 13 Then they cried to the Lord in their trouble,
> and he saved them from their distress;
> 14 he brought them out of darkness and gloom,
> and broke their bonds asunder (Ps 107:1–14 NRSV).

The psalm tells of experiencing the violence of hunger, described as the land of the shadow of death—or "darkness and gloom" as the NRSV puts it (v. 14).

Again I am amazed at how clearly the intertextual resonances lead us to hunger. Matthew does not mention hunger with a single word, but refers to the people who have suffered in darkness and those who lived in the shadow of death. These two phrases use the language of the Psalms to tell of the shadow of hunger that hung over Capernaum, the territory of the two tribes of Zebulun and Naphthali, the region of the Jordan, Galilee.

It is not just Psalm 107 that Matt 4:14 quotes, but also the prophet Isaiah. The land is marked by the presence of hunger and its people live in darkness and under the shadow of death (Isa 9:1). But Isaiah prophesies a good future to the territory of Zebulun and Naphthali:

> 8:21 They will pass through it hard-pressed and hungry; and it shall happen, when they are hungry, that they will be enraged and curse their king and their God, and look upward. 22 Then they will look to the earth, and see trouble and darkness, gloom of anguish; and they will be driven into darkness.
> 9:1 Nevertheless the gloom will not be upon her who is distressed,
> As when at first He lightly esteemed
> The land of Zebulun and the land of Naphtali,
> And afterward more heavily oppressed her,
> By the way of the sea, beyond the Jordan,
> In Galilee of the Gentiles.
> 2 The people who walked in darkness
> Have seen a great light;
> Those who dwelt in the land of the shadow of death,
> Upon them a light has shined (Isa 8:21—9:2 NKJV).

This passage from Isaiah reflects the prophet's empathy with the hungry, who are indignant, enraged, and at their wits' end. Looking for help they turn their faces upward, but neither their king nor their God seem to care about their hunger. Here Isaiah describes how rage in the belly changes everything, including the relationship to the king and to a God who cannot ease their suffering. The people turn away from both. Isaiah 9:2–6 seeks to offer another perspective:

> 2 The people that walked in darkness have seen a great light: they that dwell in the land of the shadow of death, upon them hath the light shined.
>
> 3 Thou hast multiplied the nation, and not increased the joy: they joy before thee according to the joy in harvest, and as men rejoice when they divide the spoil.
>
> 4 For thou hast broken the yoke of his burden, and the staff of his shoulder, the rod of his oppressor, as in the day of Midian.
>
> 5 For every battle of the warrior is with confused noise, and garments rolled in blood; but this shall be with burning and fuel of fire.
>
> 6 For unto us a child is born, unto us a son is given: and the government shall be upon his shoulder (Isa 9:2–6 KJV).

These bright verses are nonetheless a radical critique of the king. The prophet demonstrates that no relief is to be expected from the present ruler; that is why he speaks of his successor (Isa 9:6). A new generation will experience justice, the current royal house will disappear, and a new king will arise who will accept responsibility. This regime change is likened to the joy of harvest time and the exultation when spoils are divided. It is a vision of hope for the hungry.[151]

This passage makes explicit the rage in the belly that hungry people experience (Isa 8:21). The hungry become restless, they rise up in rebellion against their rulers, and curse their deity. They look upward but their eyes are downcast, somber, void of hope; the people are ready to turn violent. In Isaiah's days, the royal house reacted mercilessly, and it still does in the time of John the Baptist, consigning the people to deeper distress (v. 22). Herod, too, was wary of food riots; he therefore had John disappear, without a moment's hesitation. Fortress Machaerus had plenty of dungeons.

3.18 The beginning

The rest of the verses in Matt 4 sketch out the movement that began in Capernaum and spread from there. The first traveling companions other than the angels come into view; Jesus gathers people around him (Matt 4:17–22). Project Exodus—departure out of the land of the shadow of death, the land of hunger—has begun. Armed only with the word of the Torah, the small group goes into battle against the population's distress. They heal, drive out demons, and teach what the Torah can accomplish.

We looked out for the four text markers that draw our attention to the shadow of hunger. The word "hunger" does not appear in the Synoptic Gospels' accounts of John the Baptist. Hunger is evident only as a threat, as a fear-inducing drought, in the prophet's anger, in his diet of locusts and his clothing, which is reminiscent of Elijah, the hunger prophet. The texts are silent about John's hunger and that of the people. They are a prophetic lament and an indictment, and spell out the attempt of the prophet and the people to assuage God.

We find mention of hunger only later, when Jesus is famished (Matt 4:2; Luke 4:2), i.e., when he has clearly been hungry for a long time. Only now, in Jesus' encounter with the hunger devil, does the word "hunger" appear. The word itself is obviously dangerous; it takes much determination to write it down, to utter it aloud, but also to acknowledge it.

The many intertextual references to the Torah help bring out the shadings of hunger. By giving us its language and its trove of gathered experiences, the Torah helps again and again to describe present distress. In terms of method it is eminently worthwhile to look for the intertextual references and determine the context of a cited text.

From a prophet who eats locusts to Elijah the rainmaker, from the sealed and then opened sky to the yearning for bread and water, from the struggle with the hunger devil who holds the land in his clutches and the Spirit who drives the story onwards, and even strengthens Jesus during his encounter with the hunger devil and takes him to Capernaum, to the people in the land of the shadow of death: the beginning of the Gospels is marked by the hope for water and for life. The Spirit, *pneuma*, takes care of the people, allowing prophets like Elijah to rise up and the heavens to open, allowing Jesus to survive hunger and sending him where the people desperately need "light": healing, life, bread, a future.

The people had longed for that—ardently—and so they follow their prophet straight away:

> And great crowds followed him from Galilee, the Decapolis, Jerusalem, Judea, and from beyond the Jordan (Matt 4:25).

The people, the crowds, come from everywhere to John and then to Jesus—they are restless and ready to rise up. They do not need to be persuaded; they know that action is necessary now. The exodus can begin.

4.

The Blind Spot

HUNGER AND ANTI-JUDAIST PATTERNS OF THOUGHT

In this chapter I will discuss two pericopae from Mark's Gospel and one from Luke's. In the history of interpretation, these pericopae are described as "the cleansing of the temple" (Mark 11:15–19),[152] in which Jesus lambasted Israel's holiest of holies, as a "dispute about the Sabbath" between Jesus and the Pharisees (Mark 2:23–28),[153] and as Jesus' first public preaching in Nazareth (Luke 4:17–30),[154] which led to great discord between Jesus and his home town.

The headings alone show that the interpreters read these pericopae as moments of major criticism of Judaism, as a sign that Jesus is demarcating himself from his Jewish contemporaries and their rejection of his messiahship. I want to read these three pericopae as stories of hunger. I will search for the four text markers that allow us to sense the shadow of hunger, which extends into the text only by allusion. I would also like to investigate how these different assessments can come about— a pericope about differentiation, or a story of hunger. What sets the course for the different readings is, in my opinion, whether the material needs and experiences of the people concerned (here, the experience of hunger) are made visible. As soon as hunger is discerned, anti-Judaist models of interpretation become unnecessary. And even where hunger is hard to pin down (Luke 4:17–30), searching for it does enable us to free ourselves from the anti-Judaist tracks.

4.1 Trapped in patterns of thought

The well-known interpretations of the last decades, which arose after the Shoah, are tangible in commentaries on the Gospels, and are widespread. This is not specialist literature on individual passages in the text or on particular issues, but mostly readily accessible book series, into which much specialist literature has flowed, interpreted by the author or editor, and set in the context of how he reads the Gospels. While studying, and in pastoral ministry, many rely on these commentaries, because in each case they comment on a whole Gospel. But these works, although numerous, are not broadly based in theological terms. Whether Protestant or Roman Catholic, they generally neglect the social-historical foundation of their reading, and primarily pursue the historical-critical issue of the textual history (history of tradition or redaction criticism), rarely reflecting on their anti-synagogal perspective.

I would like to give the anti-Judaist[155] interpretations some space here, although not to embarrass the interpreters. They were active in a theological tradition that was for a long time a matter of course—just as the boundlessly androcentric way of thinking and speaking and self-reference to literature written almost exclusively by white men is still a matter of course in many places. It is important to me to demonstrate the unbroken line of anti-Judaist patterns, because these commentaries still stand in the libraries of numerous ministers and of educational institutions, and their influence prevails. I consider them to be historically interesting, but theologically problematic. They should be read with caution and with sufficient objectivity. This particularly applies to the interpretations by theologians who wrote *völkische Theologie* (National Socialist theology).[156] Their works too remain in many university faculties, without being identifiable as such for the younger generations.

Anti-Judaist patterns of thought include the assertion that the Christian religion is superior to all other religions. This attitude continues to hold sway over large parts of biblical interpretation even now.[157] It includes a construction of the past that presupposes a separation of Christianity from Judaism already at the time the New Testament was written. But these developments are increasingly being attributed to a later period.[158] After the Bar Kokhba revolt (ca. 135 CE) was crushed, the Jewish Christians of Jerusalem were expelled from the city, and lost their influence. But this step should not be equated with a separation of Jews and Christians. Today, it is reconstructed less as fracture or severing, and more as a gradual process, which took place in several stages and at several places over hundreds of years up to the fourth century (or even later), and which consists of approaches and intersections, divergences, and parallel developments.[159]

At the time the New Testament Scriptures originated, it can be assumed that no "separation" was yet in mind. Early Christianity can be understood only against a backdrop of contemporary Judaism and its developments in the Roman Empire. We should therefore also ask whether the vocabulary of "Gentile" and "Jewish Christians" often used in the interpretations describes anything meaningful at all for the period when the New Testament was written (ca. 40–100 CE), or is historically accurate, or whether it is much more driven by the ideological battles of later generations, which describe this time from a distorted angle.

We need to establish a different hermeneutical perspective from which the biblical texts can be read, a perspective no longer founded on unhistorical assumptions or on anti-Judaist patterns of thought. Simply criticizing these patterns of thought, without providing a different "pair of reading glasses," would be inadequate. This will become apparent if we allow different interpretations to be expressed, where some arguments are vehemently anti-Judaist while others attempt to appear moderate but suffer from being fundamentally unable to initiate any other interpretation. In this sense, the moderately anti-Judaist interpretations also remain trapped in the thought patterns of Christian superiority, in timeless statements that are applied without contextual reflection to all people, whatever their class, whatever their gender, whatever the century—whether hungry or sated. However, what I am assuming is that it is precisely this that makes a difference.

4.2 When hunger evaporates ...

As we have seen above, it is not always easy to discover hunger in the text. But sometimes it does immediately catch our eye:

> On the following day, when they came from Bethany, he was hungry (Mark 11:12).

Jesus was hungry (*epeinasen*). Mark reports this as an obvious fact. Since hunger otherwise tends to remain in shadow, naming it is significant for understanding the scenes that follow. Nevertheless, most of the interpreters of this passage known to me either overlook Jesus' hunger, or they interpret it as symbolic speech. Masking material hunger has far-reaching theological consequences, however, which I will demonstrate below; particularly when the interpretation remains trapped in anti-Judaist patterns of thought.

But first, here is the context of Mark 11:12–25:

> Jesus Curses the Fig Tree
>
> 12 On the following day, when they came from Bethany, he was hungry. 13 Seeing in the distance a fig tree in leaf, he went to see whether perhaps he would find anything on it. When he came to it, he found nothing but leaves, for it was not the season for figs. 14 He said to it, "May no one ever eat fruit from you again." And his disciples heard it.

Jesus Cleanses the Temple

15 Then they came to Jerusalem. And he entered the temple and began to drive out those who were selling and those who were buying in the temple, and he overturned the tables of the money changers and the seats of those who sold doves; 16 and he would not allow anyone to carry anything through the temple. 17 He was teaching and saying, "Is it not written,

'My house shall be called a house of prayer for all the nations'?

But you have made it a den of robbers."

18 And when the chief priests and the scribes heard it, they kept looking for a way to kill him; for they were afraid of him, because the whole crowd was spellbound by his teaching. 19 And when evening came, Jesus and his disciples went out of the city.

The Lesson from the Withered Fig Tree

20 In the morning as they passed by, they saw the fig tree withered away to its roots. 21 Then Peter remembered and said to him, "Rabbi, look! The fig tree that you cursed has withered." 22 Jesus answered them, "Have faith in God. 23 Truly I tell you, if you say to this mountain, 'Be taken up and thrown into the sea,' and if you do not doubt in your heart, but believe that what you say will come to pass, it will be done for you. 24 So I tell you, whatever you ask for in prayer, believe that you have received it, and it will be yours.

25 "Whenever you stand praying, forgive, if you have anything against anyone; so that your Father in heaven may also forgive you your trespasses."

When reviewing the exegetic literature on Mark 11:12–25—the story of Jesus' hunger, the "cleansing of the temple," and the cursing of the fig tree—it is striking that symbolic interpretations dominate, and that, as Luise Schottroff has ascertained,[160] they are overall very anti-Judaist: they relate the cursing of the fig tree to the Jewish people or their leaders. It is understood as God's final judgment on the people, the temple or the political ruling class, and even associated with the destruction of Jerusalem in 70 CE by the Romans. The cause for this divine judgment over Israel is given as the barrenness of the fig tree, i.e., the tree is understood as a metaphor for Israel. But this is by no means conclusive.

This symbolic reading causes hunger to evaporate leaving no trace in the commentaries. For example, John R. Donahue and Daniel J. Harrington state: "He was hungry: This is the only mention in Mark of Jesus being hungry."[161] Yet Jesus' hunger plays no further role in their reflections. Peter Dschulnigg mentions hunger in a kind of shorthand: "V. 12: time specification, change of location, hunger motif"[162]—and later as the motivation for seeking figs.[163] Wilfried Eckey does likewise, mentioning hunger one single time: "The statement that Jesus is hungry on his journey (12) gives a reason for what follows."[164]

While the more recent interpreters Harrington, Dschulnigg, and Eckey lose sight of hunger without comment, Joseph Ernst considers it "incongruous": "The extraordinary comment about hunger is so incongruous that we should contemplate a symbolic interpretation. If one keeps an eye on the metaphorical use of the image of the fig tree in the OT, an allusion to the problem of Israel could suggest itself. Jesus is 'hungry' for the devout approval of his people."[165]

Is the hunger of Jesus a hunger for acknowledgment? According to Joseph Ernst, the Messiah is searching for figs at the wrong time of year, and thus they stand for his compatriots who are refusing to follow him. Ernst views the search for something to eat as a discrepancy at the textual level: "The pericope contains some inconsistencies (Jesus [he alone!] is hungry, although he is coming from a hospitable house; Jesus is searching for figs at the wrong time; the tree withers, although it has only been threatened with barrenness), which urgently raises the question of the tradition and the literary form."[166]

But John R. Donahue and Daniel J. Harrington, too, ask why Jesus is searching for figs: "Jesus' behavior seems irrational, since as a native of Palestine he should not have expected to find ripe figs at Passover time."[167] Karl Kertelge therefore considers Jesus' search for fruit to be a deliberate absurdity in the narrative: "It was not the time of the fig harvest. Jesus' search for figs appears all the more paradoxical. This paradox is deliberate and ultimately leads to the drastic 'cursing' of the fig tree . . ."[168] Equally, Hans F. Bayer, who appears to take a great deal of care over details: "Over the coming days, Jesus stays overnight in Bethany, with his friends Lazarus, Mary, and Martha. From there, he travels 2.5 km up to Jerusalem every day. But why does Jesus curse a fig tree, from which he expects fruit prematurely, apparently without justifiable cause?"[169]

Hunger as the driving force behind the search for figs falls into the interpreters' blind spot: they rule it out, so to speak, they consider the mention of it to be a literary motive, without admitting its agonizing impact, and acknowledging it as the explanation for Jesus' apparently futile behavior. Instead of accepting poverty and hunger as a realistic explanation, textual discrepancies are assumed in the context of the tradition.

But it was entirely possible that hosts simply had nothing to share, as emerges in Luke 11:5–6, where a host rushes to his neighbor, because his own bread basket is empty:[170]

> 5 And he said to them, "Suppose one of you has a friend, and you go to him at midnight and say to him, 'Friend, lend me three loaves of bread; 6 for a friend of mine has arrived, and I have nothing to set before him'" (Luke 11:5–6).

This host considers it to be his duty to procure something to eat, so as not to let his guest go to bed hungry. More than ever, this should give us food for thought: Jesus has to leave, hungry, in the morning.[171] Jesus had often found lodging in Bethany—the hospitality of Martha and her siblings is well known. But evidently, this time, the hosts had to let Jesus depart hungry. This allows us to conclude a context of scarcity and need, to which the siblings in Bethany were evidently exposed as well. Mark, too, assumes this context: the people are out on the streets, they call "God, save us!" and draw attention to their distress, by waving foliage about and spreading their cloaks (Mark 11:8–11). "The entry into Jerusalem" is something I imagine as being less triumphal, but more like diving into an agitated and upset crowd of people, who are screaming out their need, and it doesn't require much for them to lose their temper (cf. Mark 11:18).

Luise Schottroff[172] sees the people in their need call for the Messiah, just as the blind beggar Bartimaeus in the previous story (Mark 10:48) does. They bring their sick; they are upset because of Jesus' teaching; they are the people who are like a flock of sheep without a shepherd (Mark 6:34). It is hunger that drives Jesus to investigate the fig tree for fruit (Mark 11:12). Schottroff considers Jesus making a mistake of timing (*kairos*) not to be a textual discrepancy, but something that shows the power of hunger.

From a long way away, Jesus sees a fig tree, and hurries hungrily over to it. Jesus' action appears irrational only if we blank out his hunger. He looks for figs; whether they are sweet or still hard is irrelevant. His disciples—in contrast to the commentators—are not repelled by his hope for a fig.[173] The reason for this may be that hunger was part of everyday reality for his companions.[174]

4.3 The poor fig tree

Fig trees grow everywhere, not just in carefully cultivated gardens, but also on the edges of paths and in cracks in walls. They do not need much, and bring forth their fruits almost all year round. But this fig tree in verse 13 does not bear fruit. The text gives the following reason: "It was not the season for figs."

Jesus cursed this fig tree: "May no one ever eat fruit from you again" (v. 14). This emotionally charged curse became the object of astonishingly arbitrary interpretations. Interpreters have encircled the fig tree with the question of what it could stand for. They have read it as a metaphor for the Jewish people, the religious leaders, the temple, the cult of sacrifice in the temple, the people of God, Judaism as a whole, or the Markan community.[175] But whatever it "symbolizes," in the end, the curse was associated with the rejection of Jesus the Messiah.[176]

Blanking out real hunger is the downside of the symbolic interpretation. It rests upon not viewing the fig tree as a fruit tree for hungry people, and therefore seeks a symbolic meaning that is independent of bodily needs, and where theological reflections do not include the political hopelessness of Palestine in those times. The unspoken prerequisite for symbolic interpretation is that we have to blank out the plight of the people, reflected in the host who was out of bread in Luke 11:5–6, the agitated crowds on the street (Mark 10:48; 11:10–11), and the obvious hunger of Jesus.

This blanking out of distress is underpinned by anti-Judaist conditions. Israel—not distinguishing whether this means the secular or spiritual leaders, or the popular masses, or the abstract theological concept of the people of God—is said to have rejected Christ Jesus and thus ceased to be G*od*'s chosen people.[177] Even twenty years after Joseph Ernst's (1981) commentary, we still find the same anti-Judaist shading, which amounts to the same judgment—more moderately in the words used, but with the same purpose. For Martin Ebner too, the fig tree serves as a "symbolic object."[178] He refers to a "metaphor based on" Hos 9:10 and Mic 7:1–4, where the figs are compared to pious and upright Israelites. However, Mark 11:14 is not about figs being cursed, but about a fig tree that has no (more) fruit. Ebner sees in this a Markan composition, which curses the tree that was supposed to bring forth the fruits (i.e., the upright Israelites). This tree, according to Ebner, can only be the temple. And this disregards the obvious explanation of Jesus' hunger.

Peter Dschulnigg, on the other hand, sees no fundamental rejection of the temple. He attempts to word things more cautiously: "The aforementioned curse of the barren fig tree (vv. 12–14) has been understood by many as a final condemnation of Israel by Jesus. However, this severely anti-Jewish interpretation fundamentally misunderstands Jesus' curse and the withering of the fig tree. . . . This negative and destructive violence of Jesus' word also casts an ominous shadow over his actions in the temple, which serves negatively to eliminate the abuses there, but positively to restore the comprehensive sanctity of the temple as a place of prayer for Jews and non-Jews."[179] His wrestling for an interpretation that is not anti-Judaist is palpable. But, just like Martin Ebner, he remains with a symbolic reading of the fig tree as the temple, and so no explanation arises that is free of anti-Judaism.

Neither Martin Ebner nor Peter Dschulnigg sees any difficulty in viewing a meager fig tree as a symbol for the magnificent temple complex of the Herodian royal house. But why should a fig tree at the wayside be read symbolically at all? Here the interpretation enters into illegalization, which is dangerous because it is arbitrary and ideological. Martin Ebner would like to avoid the thought pattern of Israel's rejection,[180] but as long as he reads the fig tree symbolically as the temple, he finds no way out. Conversely, there is some evidence for viewing the fig tree in Mark's story as a real tree rather than a metaphor: it is Jesus' hunger that drives him towards the tree he sees in the distance. He hurries over to it and finds only leaves, but no fruit. This is a disappointment for a hungry man. I see no indications in the text that mean reading this symbolically would be necessary or even appropriate. On the other hand, in the prophetic texts of the Hebrew Bible that are given as evidence, the figs or the tree are actually used figuratively. Being able to distinguish these should be one of the first tasks of exegesis.

But such a review, of what is being used metaphorically and what can be found at the wayside in reality, is not something to which the cited interpretations aspire. Rather, the interpreters' objective seems to be to condemn Israel. Judgment is made over

Israel—at least, this is how it appears to Karl Kertelge.[181] Walter Grundmann speaks of Israel's unworthiness, and of how the temple was abused and debased by the traders.[182] It is also difficult to see how the Gentiles can have been deprived of the temple in Jerusalem by the money changers and dove-sellers. Grundmann closes his reflections with the following sentence: "In any case, the word of Jesus is an indictment, speaking of the abuse and debasement of the temple and thus of Israel's unworthiness."[183] In any case? This surely applies only if the symbolic-arbitrary interpretation of the fig tree is read as a metaphor, and the cursing of it is understood not from the position of a desperately hungry person, but as a decree from the Pantocrator (the ruler of the world).

Wilfried Eckey denies Jerusalem the role as the center of God's people, based on Mark 11:17.[184] Joseph Ernst considers the temple to be meaningless from this point on.[185] Both Ernst and Eckey base their thesis that the temple is now being universalized, i.e., made accessible to Gentiles, on Isa 56:7. But the context of Isa 56:7 contradicts this argument: Isaiah is always reminding us that all who keep the Sabbath and do not profane it (v. 2), who hold fast to the covenant with Yhwh (v. 4), who minister to Yhwh (v. 6) and are Yhwh's servants (v. 6), will be gathered up by Yhwh and brought to his temple. Their sacrifices will be accepted. God gathers up the scattered people, for his *house shall be called a house of prayer for all peoples* (v. 7, cf. Mark 11:17). Isaiah is not trying to turn the temple into a place for Gentiles to worship in prayer rather than sacrificing, but to make welcome all who have been scattered among the nations or cast out—because they worship the name of God, and keep the Sabbath and God's covenant on Mount Sinai. The temple is kept open as a home for all Jews, not just for the Jews in Jerusalem, or the local population. A house of prayer for all—this is the vision of an open temple with the right to return or visit, a place of a new beginning.

4.4 The time of rage

If we survey the interpretations, we can sense a subliminal rage that is assumed to be emanating from Jesus. This rage is not made the explicit subject of discussion, and interpreters do not question what is behind it, to what or against what it could be directed. This is why I say it is "subliminal." Some examples: Jesus "punishes" the fig tree;[186] it is a "curse miracle";[187] Jesus' "protest" in the temple is repeatedly referred to as an "action";[188] Jesus "takes forcible action against people or property";[189] "against people" and "against objects";[190] he "attacks the lucrative trade in the temple";[191] the scribes and the high priests are challenged by Jesus' "indictment" and "attack."[192] The "definitive exodus from the temple in Jerusalem" is later superseded by Jesus' prophecy of the "complete destruction of the temple."[193] "Jesus' action" is not just an "emotional act" that we could explain away psychologically as "the wrath of God's son."[194]

Since the interpreters do not incorporate hunger into further developments, Jesus' rage is left in need of explanation. Instead of a "rage in the belly," fed by hunger and its associated powerlessness and violence, in these interpretations Jesus develops a rage towards the temple, i.e., towards Judaism itself. In the anti-Judaist patterns of thought, Jesus' rage has to be directed towards his people, the temple, and Israel. This thought pattern does not allow for another possibility.[195] In these interpretations, we find no attempt to see Jesus' rage as being directed towards the rich, or towards the traders or the institution of the temple bank.[196]

The symbolic interpretations make it very easy for unthinking Christian ideology to read into the text what we want to hear. We should therefore have recourse to a symbolic interpretation only if the text clearly demands it. Here though, Mark 11:15f is not about a metaphorical comparison with a tree, but about Jesus being hungry in the morning, because his hosts have had to let him leave hungry. He is not just plagued by appetite because he has missed breakfast. The text's explicit mention of his hunger encompasses the plight of his hosts, who have nothing to give him, and also forges links to the people who are seeking help on the streets (Mark 11:8–10).

Now I turn my attention to the rage of Jesus. He is hungry, and spies in the distance a fig tree that still has leaves on it. In the spring, the newly developed figs are still small and hard; but perhaps this tree carried none at all, not even little ones, so he is unable to assuage his hunger. This is, so to speak, the starting position. Jesus goes with a few people to the temple, where they find money changers and dove-sellers in the courtyard,[197] and they drive out the sellers and the buyers (v. 15).

Jesus' rage is palpable in the cursing of the fig tree as well as in the scuffle with the sellers and buyers in the temple courtyard, i.e., it is not directed exclusively against the money changers, but also against the fig tree. The next day the withered fig tree comes back into view (v. 20). Jesus does not take anything back, but adds an aggressively worded warning:[198]

> 22 Jesus answered them, "Have faith in God. 23 Truly I tell you, if you say to this mountain, 'Be taken up and thrown into the sea,' and if you do not doubt in your heart, but believe that what you say will come to pass, it will be done for you" (Mark 11:22–23).

Hunger means having diminished energy reserves. Lack of energy affects not only the body, but also the temper, and leads to irritability: "This behavioral shift has an emotional analog in apathy and sometimes irritability."[199] It is not my intention to relativize the actions and words of Jesus by psychologizing them—he only said this because he was hungry—but I would like to take Jesus' rage seriously in theological terms. This means that I read the rage of Jesus as "rage in the belly," something that arises from a basis of hunger. It is an indicator for the time of need, which oppresses the people and makes them restless. Jesus' rage shows that it is a time of scarcity, of need—and not "the season for figs" (v. 13).

> Seeing in the distance a fig tree in leaf, he went to see whether perhaps he would find anything on it. When he came to it, he found nothing but leaves, for it was not the season for figs (Mark 11:13).

Now it is no longer the season to wait for sweet figs, but the time to make impatience visible, to express the end of patience. Jesus announces the end of the period of waiting, of inactive hoping.[200] "No-sweet-figs-time" is the content of verse 13; this could be set as the heading of this pericope. As a contrast, let us remember the fig tree from Mark 13:28–33: the time of growing and ripening is visible in the fig tree that is becoming tender, as the twigs grow succulent.[201] Then it is the time for marveling, waiting, rejoicing. Summer is near, with its sweet fruits. This is a very different determination of time quality from that which comes to light in Mark 11:13f. Hunger reigns here. It is not the time for waiting. Summer appears to be far away—fruits that grow of their own accord are not in sight.

Now I will place this newly developed reading into a literary context. In the previous chapter, on the way to Jerusalem, Jesus encountered the blind beggar Bartimaeus (Mark 10:46–52), who called attention to himself and cried out loudly for help: "Jesus, Son of David, have mercy on me!" (v. 47). By the same token, the people on the street cried out: "Save us!"[202] (Mark 11:9f).

The cursing of the fig tree connects both of these cries for help. I also hear it as a cry for help from a hungry person who, together with the poor of Israel, is calling out in his distress. The fig tree without fruit is not in a position to relieve this distress. In this sense we can interpret the cursing as a prophetic-apocalyptic symbolic action, which makes visible the quality of the time: need is great, hunger and impatience are growing, relief is not in sight.

What reaction does this timing require? In his search for bread, for relief of need, for justice and life, Jesus goes into the temple. Where else? Not because he wants to battle against the central Jewish institution, but because he seeks Yhwh in the place where Yhwh is worshipped. But in the temple there is a confrontation between the hungry man and those who are occupied with buying and selling and continue to hope for good business. They do not share the rage of the hungry. They think themselves safe so long as business is booming, and in the impatient poor they see only the potential for unrest. But for Bartimaeus and for the people on the streets, the time of security, of carrying on as usual, is over: for them, apocalyptic impatience breaks out, the certainty that things cannot go on like this, that things will not go on like this.[203]

Bartimaeus is ordered to be quiet (Mark 10:48). Similarly, after the turmoil in the temple, the chief priests are looking for a way to silence Jesus (Mark 11:18). Putting distress into words and crying out for help goes unheard by many, including the high priests and scribes. When Jesus curses the barren fig tree, he denounces the time of need. Cursed be this time! Cursed be this hunger!

Then, the Markan Jesus makes it clear where blessings and success lie: God is on the side of the hungry; call upon him! Express your need! Cry out your injustice! Your God will give you strength to turn your distress around.

> 22 Jesus answered them, "Have faith in God. 23 Truly I tell you, if you say to this mountain, 'Be taken up and thrown into the sea,' and if you do not doubt in your heart, but believe that what you say will come to pass, it will be done for you. 24 So I tell you, whatever you ask for in prayer, believe that you have received it, and it will be yours" (Mark 11:22–24).

We have not yet left the context of hunger. "Rage in the belly" still reigns—prayer and supplication relate to this time of need. Even those who have not so much as a half-shekel are not shut out of God's house of prayer. These prayers have weight, because God in heaven is on the side of the hungry, and listens to those who plead, doggedly and impatiently. God does not silence those who are hungry and upset, but moves heaven and earth to make daily bread a reality for all. In Luke, Mary sings: "He has filled the hungry with good things, and sent the rich away empty" (Luke 1:53). Mark puts it like this:

> Whatever you ask for in prayer, believe that you have received it, and it will be yours (Mark 11:24).

Out of the trust in God's justice grows transformative power (v. 24), so that mountains can be moved, can vanish into thin air, or sink into the waters. The world can change. Pray for the world to change, for resources to be distributed fairly and equitably. Mountains of debt will melt like butter in the sun. Mountains of injustice will be cleared away, "made straight" (cf. Mark 1:3). Or, as Mary sang: "He has brought down the powerful from their thrones, and lifted up the lowly" (Luke 1:52).

Mark has not handed down an "Our Father" prayer, unlike Matthew and Luke. They link "prayer and supplication" clearly with our daily bread:

> 8 God, your father and mother, knows what you need even before you ask. 9 Pray then in this way: You, God, are our father and mother in heaven, hallowed be your name. 10 Your world of justice come. Your will be done, on earth as it is in heaven. 11 Give us this day the bread that we need. 12 Forgive us our debts, as we also forgive our debtors (Matt 6:8–12, author's translation; cf. Luke 11:2–4).

In God's just world everyone receives the bread they need. Matthew and Luke link the prayer for daily bread with the ability to forgive (Matt 6:12; Luke 11:4). In Mark 11:25–26, too, Jesus admonishes the impatient, even when they stand up and make strident demands, to remain prepared to forgive.

To summarize: A reading based on social history leaves anti-Judaist patterns behind and does not take the fig tree to be symbolic. It opens up an apocalyptic view of the world. The hungry enter the picture, they stand up, make demands; their rage is frightening. It is high time for change. Jesus tunes into the rage of the hungry, strengthens it, creates a memorial for it in the form of the withered fig tree; for rage should not be hushed. Now is not the season for (plucking) figs—but for the rage of those who have nothing, who have no bread to share and no money to change or to buy sacrifices for the temple.

Seeing the rage of Jesus takes some getting used to. It is appropriate rage. It can be a sign of distress and in this sense an extremely urgent request. But to get a glimpse of this rage, it is critical not to lose sight of hunger. Rage is evidence of the intensity of the hunger in the text, an indicator of determining the *kairos*, the time as the end of patience.

4.5 Sabbath in the fields (Mark 2:23–28)

Instead of reflecting on hunger as real distress and Jesus' rage as an apocalyptic characterization of the time—a season for anger, repentance, horror—the interpretations of Mark 11:12–25 are dominated by numerous anti-Judaist patterns. In the following story, too, where the disciples pluck heads of grain on the Sabbath (Mark 2:23–28), Jesus' interpretation of the Torah is often understood as making an anti-Judaist point against the Sabbath laws.

> 23 One Sabbath he was going through the grainfields; and as they made their way his disciples began to pluck heads of grain. 24 The Pharisees said to him, "Look, why are they doing what is not lawful on the Sabbath?" 25 And he said to them, "Have you never read what David did when he and his companions were hungry and in need of food? 26 He entered the house of God, when Abiathar was high priest, and ate the bread of the Presence, which it is not lawful for any but the priests to eat, and he gave some to his companions." 27 Then he said to them, "The Sabbath was made for humankind, and not humankind for the Sabbath; 28 so the Son of Man is Lord even of the Sabbath" (Mark 2:23–28).

This little episode describes a Sabbath scene. But here, Sabbath is not being celebrated at home, with candles, challah, and Kiddush cup. Here, people are roaming hungrily along the fields of grain, on the Sabbath. They start to pluck ears of grain and to eat the raw kernels. Some of the Pharisees see this happening and become thoughtful. We could actually say that their actions are forbidden on the Sabbath, couldn't we? The Pharisees pose this question without answering it. They then disappear from the text. We do not know whether they shared Jesus' answer, whether they agreed with it, or whether there was a further exchange of words.

Most interpreters have a firmly fixed and negative image of the Pharisees. In their opinion, the Pharisees are always in the wrong, they are always being provocative, setting traps and entangling Jesus in highly theological catch questions. This one question (Mark 2:24), intending to reflect theologically on what has been seen, is already described in the exegetic literature as a "dispute." To avoid such a charged atmosphere and a polarization, Dagmar Henze et al. suggest forgoing the term *Streitgespräch* (dispute) and instead calling it a *halakah debate*.[204] Most of the New Testament texts described as disputes should be understood in the Jewish tradition as clarifications, as substantive debates about different opinions, and reflections between equals on interpretations of the Torah. The purpose of these discussions is to develop a *halakah* for the present situation and its needs. Being right is not a priority; what is important is weighing up what is relevant here and now.

The interpreters notice, of course, that the story of David to which Jesus is referring cannot be found in the Bible in the way that Jesus tells it. 1 Sam 21:1–6 tells that story of David like this:

> 1 David came to Nob to the priest Ahimelech. Ahimelech came trembling to meet David, and said to him, "Why are you alone, and no one with you?" 2 David said to the priest Ahimelech, "The king has charged me with a matter, and said to me, 'No one must know anything of the matter about which I send you, and with which I have charged you.' I have made an appointment with the young men for such and such a place. 3 Now then, what have you at hand? Give me five loaves of bread, or whatever is here." 4 The priest answered David, "I have no ordinary bread at hand, only holy bread—provided that the young men have kept themselves from women." 5 David answered the priest, "Indeed women have been kept from us as always when I go on an expedition; the vessels of the young men are holy even when it is a common journey; how much more today will their vessels be holy?" 6 So the priest gave him the holy bread; for there was no bread there except the bread of the Presence, which is removed from before the LORD, to be replaced by hot bread on the day it is taken away (1 Sam 21:1–6).

None of the interpreters claims that the Markan Jesus is misquoting the text. But it remains inexplicable why Jesus refers to Abiathar rather than Ahimelech. Even independently of this mix-up, Mark obviously has Jesus quote very freely here. But rather: Jesus is reading the story of David contextually, and is relating it to the present situation.[205] This idiosyncratic hermeneutic of Jesus is remarkable.

But unfortunately some interpreters again use their observation of the difference to make an anti-Judaistic point: Fritzleo Lentzen-Deis emphasizes the greater authority of Jesus, which entitles him to use the Scriptures according to his needs, as well as to "break the Pharisees' Sabbath rules."[206] For Eckey this "greater authority of Jesus" fades into Christian freedom: "Here the freedom of the congregation of Jesus Christ regarding the Sabbath rules is reflected in the name of Jesus based on the Scriptures,"[207] while Karl Kertelge sees this difference as containing inaccuracies that have a theological basis: "The slight inaccuracies . . . allow us to perceive a certain latitude in quoting narrative texts. This is justified with this biblical example of 'Christian freedom' towards what the law commands."[208]

Jesus' form of quoting, his way of referring to the David story, is entered here into the dualism of law and gospel, of legalistic Jewish religion and Christian freedom from the law. Jesus, they say, is not just quoting freely, but is also breaking the Sabbath laws, which Lentzen-Deis here calls pharisaic, without being more precise. But the Sabbath law is not a pharisaic innovation; it is a core part of the Torah tradition. If Jesus really had distanced himself from the Sabbath law, this would have been a momentous step. But this is not the case here at all.[209]

I also have doubts about whether this model of law/freedom from the law should be applied to the story of hunger on the Sabbath. The model disregards the hunger of the disciples; equally, it disregards the Old Testament story of David and Jesus' own way of quoting it. The model has no context, it cannot be pinned down in the story of David or the episode of Sabbath in the fields.

4.6 The Jesuan hermeneutic of hunger

Jesus' disciples pluck ears of wheat, crush the raw grains in their hands, and eat them. We could read this action in very different ways. They could be plucking ears of grain out of contemplative boredom, simply because the wayside is so beautiful. But it is Jesus who brings hunger into play. Responding to the Pharisees' question, Jesus tells a story of David. He does not initiate a debate on "what is forbidden/what is permitted," but tells of David's hunger. This is why we cannot get around the issue of taking hunger seriously, theologically speaking. Jesus' hunger is so important that he reads it into the story of David:

> "... what David did when he and his companions were hungry and in need of food?" (Mark 2:25).

In 1 Sam 21:1–6 David goes out to the priest Ahimelech. He asks for whatever Ahimelech has at hand (v. 4). But the priest has nothing except the bread for placing on the altar. Impatiently, David demands it. But no words are used to mention David's plight or even his hunger. Then, David asks for a spear or a sword (1 Sam 21:8). He is arming himself with bread and a sword, to survive in the face of Saul's anger (1 Sam 20:33).

What is decisive is the perspective from which, the emphasis with which Jesus tells this little story. He could have highlighted David's boldness in demanding the showbread, he could have emphasized David's claim to power, in having the priest give him weighty symbols of power—bread consecrated to Yhwh and the sword of Goliath, whom he once vanquished (1 Sam 21:9). The story of David has no other reference to the Sabbath, and in this sense the story would be poorly suited as a basis for a discussion about the Sabbath. In David's own words, the bread he demands sanctifies his mission, and the sword promises further victories over opponents, who like Goliath will have no chance. But Jesus does not pick up on the symbols of power in the story of David. He underscores David's plight in having to flee from Saul. In Jesus' reading of 1 Sam 21, David is in distress; he specifies this distress as hunger and adds: David's people were suffering from hunger as well.

Jesus reads hunger into the story of David, into his flight, into his request to the priest—as though it were self-evident that someone who is fleeing will be hungry and dependent on the generosity of others. This self-evidence of seeing hunger where it is not explicitly mentioned corresponds to the hermeneutic of the hungry. They read the texts differently than well-nourished, satisfied people. They suspect the presence of hunger in gaps in the text, they know about its shadow, which hides in an impatient question or a bold demand. Hunger does not stop at the bread consecrated to Yhwh and, depending on the situation, puts the asker or the giver at risk. Thus, Ahimelech's family was later wiped out, because of the help they had given David (1 Sam 22:16–19).

Jesus puts David's distress into concrete terms. In referring to hunger, Jesus is of course including a larger group of people (1 Sam 23:24–26). Here, too, we can again perceive the hermeneutic of the hungry, who know that hunger is a collective phenomenon. Because if only one person were hungry, the others could help him or her out. Jesus is not just quoting freely by heart (and therefore imprecisely), or in Christian intellectual freedom, in order to circumvent carefully worded Jewish/pharisaic rules and regulations. Nor does Mark's Gospel accept discrepancies indiscriminately, in order to fit the story of David into the Sabbath episode.[210] Much more likely: right before our eyes is the Jesuan hermeneutic, which connects distress with hunger and recognizes hunger as a collective phenomenon.

David did not have people with him when he asked Ahimelech for help—Ahimelech clearly refers to his single-handedness (1 Sam 21:1). Nevertheless it becomes clear that David is going to share the bread with his people (v. 5). Later, the text explains that many people had gathered with David in their distress:

> 1 David left there and escaped to the cave of Adullam; when his brothers and all his father's house heard of it, they went down there to him. 2 Everyone who was in distress, and everyone who was in debt, and everyone who was discontented gathered to him; and he became captain over them. Those who were with him numbered about four hundred (1 Sam 22:1–2).

The distress of his people is mentioned clearly in 1 Sam 22:2; however, here the distress is mentioned not as hunger but as debt. The five loaves that David received from the hands of the priest and the sword were a kind of basic equipment, which would need to be multiplied over a short period.

4.7 Did you not read it like this?

Jesus refers in Mark 2:23–28 not only to 1 Sam 21:2–6, but also to the wider narrative context of distress, which takes in 1 Sam 21 and 22 as well.[211] The reading of these two chapters that Jesus undertakes, however, focuses on the provisions that David and his people needed in their distress.

This, precisely, is the issue: Jesus is demonstrating his reading of the Scriptures. He centers it on hunger and distress. This is why the Markan Jesus introduces his answer with a question about reading: "Have you never read what David did?" (v. 25). Jesus asks about the Pharisees' reading.[212] How do you read it? What do you put at the center? What is the starting point for your reading? What his answer says is: "For me, the distress and the hunger of all those who have gathered around David are at the center." And this answer encompasses not just David, but also the four hundred people who were with him in 1 Sam 22:2, just like the poor of Israel, from the time of David up to Jesus. They are at the center of the Jesuan hermeneutic of hunger.

So this story is not about Jesus allowing work to be done in the fields on the Sabbath, and justifying it in answer to the Pharisees' question by referring to David. He does not say: "I can do what I want, for I am greater than David. As the Messiah, I am above the Sabbath: if I want to break the Sabbath laws, then I will." Or: "Distress drives us to break the Sabbath laws; this is a situation of extreme distress, which demands extreme measures." Much more, this is about the question posed in the text: "How do you read the Scriptures? What is your starting point, your focus? From which perspective are you reading?"

The disciples fetch the bare minimum to eat. They are hungry every day, not just on workdays. On the Sabbath their activity is so obvious only because no one is working in the fields and most people are resting. The Pharisees are not asking whether Jesus can justify their actions. They claim that walking through the fields and plucking ears of grain is actually something that is forbidden on the Sabbath. In the actions of his hungry disciples Jesus may well see something that is forbidden, just as the consecrated loaves in the story of David were forbidden to unauthorized persons. But he does not focus on the topic of what is forbidden or permitted, but on the hunger, the distress, and the eating.

Jesus does not leave it at that either, with the priest handing over the showbread (1 Sam 21:7), but emphasizes even more David's and his people's act of eating:

> "[David] entered the house of God . . . and ate the bread of the Presence, which it is not lawful for any but the priests to eat, and he gave some to his companions" (Mark 2:26).

Three times there is a mention of eating in verse 26. This means Jesus is setting clear priorities: hunger and eating manifestly guide Jesus' reading perspective, i.e., 1 Sam 21:1f is read from the perspective of those who are interested in hunger and the stilling of this hunger. Jesus establishes this perspective clearly and centers the debate in Mark 2:25 around it.

The issue of what is guiding the reading—what is the guiding interest, the perspective of understanding—is also found in Mark 12:26 in Jesus' dispute with the rich Sadducees, about resurrection: "Have you not read in the book of Moses . . . ?" Jesus asks whether they are not reading the passage about the burning bush in Exod 3:2–6 to refer to resurrection. Whether they are reading this passage differently, whether perhaps they are locating the power of resurrection elsewhere than with Yhwh.[213] When we look up Exod 3:2–6, there is nothing literally about resurrection. Nevertheless, Jesus draws on this weighty passage of Scripture to demonstrate that Yhwh is the Living One. All who call upon him are therefore alive, i.e., related to Yhwh's aliveness. Resurrection as becoming-alive is, for the Markan Jesus, central to the name of God, Yhwh. This name guarantees aliveness, so to speak. God's name is given at the beginning of Exodus; those who call upon him begin their exodus out of the land of slavery. For the Markan Jesus, resurrection for liberation, resurrection into life, are thus crucially linked to the name Yhwh. The aliveness of God, the power of resurrection, become in Mark 12:26 the hermeneutic key for reading the Torah.

To compare, Luke's Gospel also broaches the issue of reading the Torah as being about the interpretive competence of those seeking answers. The Torah is not just read to be repeated, but to respond to a particular question. In it is sought—and correspondingly found. Every answer is thus the result of a search process, for which the seekers should be accountable. Kerstin Schiffner has mapped this out in detail.

> The question "how do you read the Scriptures?" which Jesus puts to a lawyer in Luke 10:26 is one of the fundamental questions that everyone who deals with Bible texts—whether professionally or privately—must address. It is not just about the "what," i.e., the content of the texts, and not just about the "who," i.e., the individual interpreter. Both questions are summarized but already superseded in the question of "how"—"How do you read?" This means: "How do you understand the things that are handed down to you? How do you deal with the memories that are formative for us? How do you write the history in which you yourself stand, the history of Israel with Yhwh, for your continuing life, so that it becomes a fulfilled one?"[214]

I consider Jesus' question in Mark 2:25 to be a signal that this story of hunger is not about observance of the Sabbath rules, and thus also not about whether plucking ears of grain is work or not. According to Deut 23:25, plucking ears of grain by hand is *Mundraub*, a form of pilfering that is permitted. *Mundraub* is not under discussion in connection with working or Sabbath laws. In this respect I am contradicting interpretations that, like Donahue and Harrington,[215] are unable to disengage from a dispute about laws. Here, Mark is sketching, strikingly, a hermeneutic of the hungry. He is not doing this as a defense of what the disciples have just done, but the reverse:

Jesus sees his disciples as part of that society which belongs to David, which is ground down by debt, which has a bitter life. But David began his journey with these people, and with them he erected a kingdom.

A Jesuan reading of the Scripture begins with these people who are hungry. They don't just belong to Israel; they define Israel. David and his companions are, throughout the centuries, the reference for the Markan Jesus as well. Bread belongs to them, the bread on the altar table and in the fields; it is the daily bread they need, from the hand of GOD in heaven.

Now we have read two different hunger stories from Mark's Gospel. In the first, we saw the hunger of Jesus, which erupted in an outburst about the fig tree and about money changers and traders in the temple courtyard. This characterized the present as a time for rage, which is clearly distinct from the time of waiting for sweet figs. In the second pericope, Mark 2:23–26, Jesus draws attention to the hunger of David and his companions. This reveals his hermeneutic key to reading the story of David, i.e., reading the Torah. At the center are the hungry of Israel. The Torah reading should be aligned with them—and not the other way around.

4.8 The four text markers

In our engagement with anti-Judaist and arbitrarily symbolic interpretations, we have seen how the shadow of hunger is overlooked. Although it is mentioned as such in the two Markan pericopae—once as Jesus' hunger (Mark 11:12), and once as David's (Mark 2:25)—the interpretations discussed do not really take hunger into account, let alone use it as a starting point for their reading.

In addition to explicit hunger there is also the shadow of hunger, i.e., indications of hunger without explicit mentions in the text. Perceiving this shadow of hunger is of course somewhat more difficult. In Chapter 3, above, taking Herta Müller's *Hunger Angel* as a starting point, I have already attempted to locate text markers that could help us not to overlook the shadow of hunger. I have worked with the following four text markers:

1. Talking about eating/food, which is very important to hungry people.

2. Silence regarding a hunger about which cannot be spoken, for which no words appear fitting.

3. The rage of the hungry, who are prepared to stand up and fight for their children. The irritability of the undernourished, who perceive themselves as being dominated by hunger. Rage expresses itself in the text, while hunger remains invisible.

4. And the intertextual references to other Scriptures, passages in the Torah that could be speaking of hunger. These Torah passages speak vicariously for the

hungry, they remind us of the experience of hunger and how it was overcome, they place the hunger of the present into the history of GOD and his people.

How can these text markers be found in the text passages we have examined?

1. *Talking about eating or food*: This can be found in both pericopae. The curse, "May no one ever eat fruit from you again" (Mark 11:14) contains the longing for sweet fruit as well. Eating figs—the listeners and readers know what this means: whether fresh, dried, or baked figs, they were part of the people's diet, they were important providers of sugar, as well as of pleasure. The curse gets to the painful heart of the barrenness, the lack of figs.

David not only fetches the holy bread, but also eats it (Mark 2:26): this is mentioned twice. And yet no one was actually allowed to eat it. Eating the bread is savored in a literary way. Hungry people will feel their mouths water when they imagine bread, eating bread, chewing it, savoring it.

2. *Silence about hunger*: Although hunger is mentioned surprisingly clearly, we get stuck at this particular word. There is no picture painted, there are no additional words or colors. We do not find out what it was like to be hungry even in the morning, or to wander about out of doors hungry on the Sabbath. We hear nothing about how long the hunger has lasted, how intense it is, what consequences it has. It is mentioned—but then the text is silent. The text continues, so to speak, with eating. That is much easier to talk about.

3. *The rage of the hungry*: This is very clear in Mark 11:12f. Jesus does not merely express his rage, he also makes the rage of the hungry into the defining feature of the time. His rage is not a coincidence, or a nervous indisposition on this particular day, but it instigates action, expresses itself in a food riot in the temple, and is reflected on theologically in the concluding verses (vv. 20–25).

In the second pericope, rage is barely visible. Perhaps we find a trace of it in the question, "Have you never read what David did?" (Mark 2:25). Putting this question to Pharisees demonstrates a certain irritation on the part of Jesus: the story of David is one of the most well-known parts of the Torah. Pharisees who did not know these passages would have been hard to find. In Mark 12:26 as well, when he poses this question, Jesus is exasperated (admittedly about the rich Sadducees).

4. *Intertextual references to hunger*: Hunger is the explicit topic of Mark 11:12f. The food riots also take place in this sense, with reference to Isa 56:7. But it is above all the comparative reading of Jesus' prayer (Matt 6:8–12 and Luke 11:2–4) that helps us, since both Matthew and Luke speak of daily bread, while Mark does not mention this prayer. In this passage he does speak of asking for something in prayer. He also mentions forgiveness, which is part of the prayer in Matthew and Luke. The prayer quoted in Matthew and Luke thus allows us to hear the prayer for daily bread in Mark 11:24–25.

In the second pericope, the intertextual reference is obvious. The hunger of Jesus' disciples becomes visible only through the reference to David's distress in 1 Sam 21:1–7, where Jesus lays out his hermeneutic.

4.9 Uproar in Nazareth (Luke 4:16–30)

And so, with sharper eyes, let us turn to a further pericope: Luke 4:16–30. This is also characterized by a history of anti-Judaist exegesis. I would like to try to liberate it from this and find a new way into it, guided by the above-mentioned text markers.

The Rejection of Jesus at Nazareth

16 When he came to Nazareth, where he had been brought up, he went to the synagogue on the Sabbath day, as was his custom. He stood up to read, 17 and the scroll of the prophet Isaiah was given to him. He unrolled the scroll and found the place where it was written:

18 "The Spirit of the Lord is upon me,

because he has anointed me

to bring good news to the poor.

He has sent me to proclaim release to the captives

and recovery of sight to the blind,

to let the oppressed go free,

19 to proclaim the year of the Lord's favor."

20 And he rolled up the scroll, gave it back to the attendant, and sat down. The eyes of all in the synagogue were fixed on him. 21 Then he began to say to them, "Today this Scripture has been fulfilled in your hearing." 22 All spoke well of him and were amazed at the gracious words that came from his mouth. They said, "Is not this Joseph's son?" 23 He said to them, "Doubtless you will quote to me this proverb, 'Doctor, cure yourself!' And you will say, 'Do here also in your hometown the things that we have heard you did at Capernaum.'" 24 And he said, "Truly I tell you, no prophet is accepted in the prophet's hometown. 25 But the truth is, there were many widows in Israel in the time of Elijah, when the heaven was shut up three years and six months, and there was a severe famine over all the land; 26 yet Elijah was sent to none of them except to a widow at Zarephath in Sidon. 27 There were also many lepers in Israel in the time of the prophet Elisha, and none of them was cleansed except Naaman the Syrian." 28 When they heard this, all in the synagogue were filled with rage. 29 They got up, drove him out of the town, and led him to the brow of the hill on which their town was built, so that they might hurl him off the cliff. 30 But he passed through the midst of them and went on his way (Luke 4:16–30).

The rage of the congregation in Nazareth is puzzling. What caused a warm welcome to turn so quickly into open rejection? The people drive Jesus from their midst—what they most want to do is throw him down the hill. They do not actually do so, however—Jesus passes through the midst of them unscathed.

The exegesis on this puzzling story is dominated by anti-Judaist patterns of thought, which aim to demarcate Jesus from the synagogue and to condemn Israel. The congregation's wave of anger is interpreted as an expression of their rejection of Jesus as the Messiah, and their leading Jesus out to the cliff as an attempted "lynch mob."[216]

Both Walter Schmithals and François Bovon identify the people of Nazareth with Israel. Nazareth "appears here as a representatively for all Israel," claims Bovon.[217] And for Schmithals, the people of Nazareth become "an example for all Jews."[218] The rage of those who have gathered in the synagogue is interpreted ideologically as a fundamental rejection of the Messiah.

I find it important to understand the rage of those in the synagogue (v. 28) in a way that does not perpetuate the anti-Judaist patterns. That Jesus did not just have friends, but also provoked resistance, is one thing. But seeing how a warm welcome at the start changes into naked anger is difficult to understand and also difficult to bear. The parallel passages in Mark 6:1–6 and Matt 13:54–58 are more reticent in this respect. They also contain the sentence about the prophet who has nothing to say in his hometown. But only Luke puts this sentence into a carefully developed context and reinforces the congregation's rejection. It is beguiling to fall into anti-Judaist patterns to explain the rage in the Lukan version, precisely because we cannot pigeonhole that rage.

So that we no longer read the rage from an anti-Judaist perspective, I suggest reading this pericope with the hermeneutic of the hungry, as we have sketched in the two pericopae from Mark presented above. Rage expresses itself, becomes loud, visible, while hunger remains hidden. Let us attempt to track down the four text markers:

1. Luke 4:16–30 does not talk about food. But we remember that immediately before Jesus' trip to Nazareth, he had been wrestling with the hunger devil in the desert (Luke 4:3–4). There, bread is mentioned several times: can anyone make bread from stones? And: One does not live by bread alone. But for this passage here, we have to note that there is no mention of food.

2. On the other hand, let us refer to the verse before the scene in Nazareth. Luke 4:2 states that Jesus was famished. It is the same Greek verb *epeinasen* (he was hungry) as in Mark 11:12. There is also the reference to the "severe famine" (Luke 4:25). Even the duration of this famine is described: 3 years and 6 months. But beyond that we find out nothing about the extent of the famine, the reasons for it, the victims, or the problems associated with it. Silence prevails on these matters.

3. Rage is clearly found towards the end of this pericope: in Luke 4:28–29 the crowd rises up, full of anger; the mood is tense. They want to drive Jesus from their midst.

4. On closer inspection, we find Torah references that have something to do with hunger, above all 1 Kgs 17:1: a story about Elijah and the widow of Zarephath, when the heavens were closed and a severe famine had come upon the land (Luke 4:25).

So we find three text markers in this story. Talking about eating/food (text marker 1) can, by contrast, be found only in its immediate proximity (Luke 4:3–4). Do we have reason enough to read this Nazareth scene as a story of hunger? How much do we prioritize the observation that text marker 1 does not appear in this scene? I will attempt to read the scene in the hermeneutic of hunger, although I am conscious that since text marker 1 is lacking, something is missing: talking about eating.

4.10 The great famine

Jesus' trip to Nazareth is one of a series of visits to synagogues that followed his sojourn in the wilderness. Jesus spent forty days in the wilderness/desert, where he ate nothing, until he was completely starving (*epeinasen*, Luke 4:2). This means that Jesus' teaching took its starting point in the inhospitable wilderness, where he had experienced hunger at first hand. This order of events, and the positioning of Jesus' teaching in the context of a fundamental experience of hunger, can be seen as a Lukan variant of Jesus' hermeneutic of hunger (cf. Mark 2:23–28).

> 16 He came to Nazareth, where he had been fed (Luke 4:16, author's translation).

For Luke, Nazareth is not just the place of Jesus' childhood, where he grew up or was brought up,[219] but a place of food (literally "nourished, fed" *tethrammenos*, v. 16). Following the description of Jesus' experience of hunger (v. 2), it appears right and proper to take up the basic meaning of this verb: Jesus went back to where he had been fed.

What expectations are associated with Nazareth for someone who has wrestled in the desert with the hunger devil? Does he return to the place where he was fed in childhood, to be fed again? Or were people in Nazareth suffering shortages—like Jesus in the desert—and did he go there to stand by them? Could it be that the uproar in Nazareth has something to do with hunger? That the angry people needed practical help in the form of bread, water, grain? That for their part they expected something from Jesus, e.g., an audacious deed, like David's when he fetched the showbread—or a spiritual deed, like a prayer that opened heaven?

Jesus goes into the synagogue in Nazareth. He receives the Torah scroll to read from. A little later, Jesus speaks about a great famine:

> 25 But the truth is, there were many widows in Israel in the time of Elijah, when the heaven was shut up three years and six months, and there was a severe famine over all the land; 26 yet Elijah was sent to none of them except to a widow at Zarephath in Sidon (Luke 4:25–26).

The "famine" in verse 25 refers to the famine that occurred in the time of Elijah. This is described in 1 Kgs 17:

> Now Elijah the Tishbite, of Tishbe in Gilead, said to Ahab, "As the Lord the God of Israel lives, before whom I stand, there shall be neither dew nor rain these years, except by my word." 2 The word of the Lord came to him, saying, 3 "Go from here and turn eastward, and hide yourself by the Wadi Cherith, which is east of the Jordan. 4 You shall drink from the wadi, and I have commanded the ravens to feed you there." 5 So he went and did according to the word of the Lord; he went and lived by the Wadi Cherith, which is east of the Jordan. 6 The ravens brought him bread and meat in the morning, and bread and meat in the evening; and he drank from the wadi. 7 But after a while the wadi dried up, because there was no rain in the land. 8 Then the word of the Lord came to him, saying, 9 "Go now to Zarephath, which belongs to Sidon, and live there; for I have commanded a widow there to feed you." 10 So he set out and went to Zarephath (1 Kgs 17:1–10).

In the days of Elijah there was a great drought. It becomes clear from the narrative context that the God of Israel had shut up the heaven because the kings—and Ahab above all—had offended her:

> Ahab son of Omri did evil in the sight of the Lord more than all who were before him (1 Kgs 16:30).

We see here how drought is understood as a consequence of the kings' failure to enforce the law. If drought is understood as being imposed by God, this does not mean being resigned to fate; quite the reverse. Thus, the drought does not appear inevitable, but as cause for criticizing the kings or oneself. God could be appeased, people could change their behavior, so that the drought would be ended.

Peter Garnsey points out that this concept was found in the ancient world, and not just among the Jews:

> The ancients did not face the dilemma of seventeenth-century European settlers in north America, for some of whom practical measures against natural disaster ... were seen as interference with the Divine Providence. ... Fate, immutable and predetermined, figures in Greek and Roman religious conceptions. However, in practice, the idea that the gods can be persuaded appears to have prevailed. Thus it is incorrect to assume that religious and non-religious responses were seen as different in kind, the one symbolic, the other practical, let alone that the two classes of response were in some way mutually incompatible. Christians and Jews, moreover, held a similar world-view.[220]

During the period of drought, Elijah retreated to a tributary of the Jordan, where he was miraculously fed by ravens. But one day, even this wadi dried up (1 Kgs 17:7). Elijah set off for Zarephath, on the coastal strip to the west—perhaps in the hope that the drought was less severe there. In Zarephath, he asked a widow for water (1 Kgs 17:10). The hospitality of this widow enabled Elijah to survive—and his help opened up a future for her. They helped one another in their need.[221]

The Old Testament does not, however, give the duration of this drought, which led to the "great famine," as three and a half years.[222] The Lukan Jesus extends the duration mentioned in 1 Kgs 18:1 by at least half a year. This gives it even more weight. I therefore consider this quantification of the time not to be a negligible detail, but a central moment in Luke's hermeneutic of hunger. It fits that Jesus calls this famine "severe": he is reminding his listeners explicitly that the famine raged severely in Samaria (1 Kgs 18:2). He also gives the reason for this distress: heaven was shut up (Luke 4:25).

4.11 The long fast

In the literary context as well, the shadow of a lasting, severe famine can be found. In Luke 4:2, we saw Jesus after forty days of fasting, famished in the wilderness. Stones grow instead of bread: the mention of bread that could be made out of stones appears as a reference to the drought-stricken land, which no longer brings forth wheat. Just stones everywhere, as far as the eye can see.

There are numerous indications in the Old Testament that supply problems and famines led to ad hoc days of prayer and fasting being proclaimed, in order to restore the people's relationship to heaven, to reconcile the congregation with GOD (1 Kgs 21:9, 12; 2 Chr 20:6–17; Isa 22:12–14; Joel 1:14; Jonah 3).[223]

A glance at the tractate *m. Ta'anit* may be very helpful here. In it, the days of fasting ordered by the authorities take pride of place. They include fasting to avert a disaster, in particular a drought. Eduard Baneth introduces this tractate with reference to the great significance of the winter rain: "In the Holy Land the winter period is the rainy season. . . . The rain that in normal years falls at particular, almost regularly recurring intervals, has an increased significance there. It is not supposed merely to stimulate the fields, but also to fill the cisterns with waters. If it fails to appear throughout the winter, or if the sparse clouds deliver too little of it, not only crop failure and famine, but also a lack of drinking water is the terrible consequence."[224]

The Mishnah (ca. 200 CE) tells of the events when, despite much prayer and fasting, the heaven could not be softened, and the people asked Honi to pray for rain:

> It happened that they said to Honi the Circle Drawer: "Pray for rain to fall." He replied: "Go and bring in the pesah ovens so that they do not dissolve." He prayed and no rain fell. What did he do? He drew a circle and stood within it and exclaimed before Him: "Master of the universe, Your children have turned their faces to me because I am like one who was born in Your house. I swear by Your great name that I will not move from here until You have mercy upon Your children." Rain then began to drip, and he exclaimed: "I did not request this but rain [which can fill] cisterns, ditches and caves. The rain then began

> to come down with great force, and he exclaimed: "I did not request this but pleasing rain of blessing and abundance." Rain then fell in the normal way until the Jews in Jerusalem had to go up Temple Mount because of the rain. They came and said to him: "In the same way that you prayed for [the rain] to fall pray [now] for the rain to stop." He replied: "Go and see if the stone of people claiming lost objects has washed away." Rabbi Shimon ben Shetah sent to him: "Were you not Honi I would have excommunicated you, but what can I do to you, for you are spoiled before God and he does your will like a son that is spoiled before his father and his father does his request. Concerning you it is written, "Let your father and your mother rejoice, and let she that bore you rejoice" (*m. Ta'an.* 3:8).[225]

I see here a few parallel narrative features to the story of Jesus' trip to Nazareth (Luke 4:16–30). Honi was urged to place his power of prayer at the disposal of the community. The people were hoping that he would be able to move the heavens to open. Honi felt morally obliged and in turn put pressure on GOD: "Your children have turned to me, because I am like a son of the house before you." We also find this expectation in our text, where the eyes of those who have assembled in the synagogue in Nazareth are turned anxiously towards Jesus (Luke 4:20).

Although what they desired did happen, and the sluices of heaven opened, in the end Honi reaped a reprimand: Shimon ben Shetah considered excommunicating him. Honi brought bad luck, and should from now on stay well clear of Jerusalem. This probably also hides rage about the circle drawer who caused the flood. Ultimately Honi was not excommunicated, because he was like a son of the house of GOD. In the Lukan pericope, too, we find the rage of the synagogue's congregation who want to drive Jesus out associated with some hesitation: they actually wanted to throw him off the cliff, but then they let him go, as the spirit of GOD was evidently upon him.

M. Ta'anit expresses impish criticism of the all-too-fervent prayers. Fasting brings nothing (the heavens remain shut) or too little (the rain only drips) or too much (an excess of rain falls). The tractate attempts to regulate prayers for rain, and Honi's excesses help people distance themselves from such excesses. Thus, the elder's speech at the beginning of this tractate concerns not only doing symbolic-ritual acts, but also turning from their evil ways:

> Brothers, it does not say of the people of Nineveh, "And God saw their sackcloth and their fasting," but, "And God saw their deeds, for they turned from their evil way" (Jonah 3:10). And in the Prophets it says, "And rend your heart and not your garments" (Joel 2:13) (*m. Ta'an.* 2:1).

We can understand the beginning of Jesus' speech in Nazareth in the same sense. Jesus is reading from the Isaiah scroll:

> 18 "The Spirit of the Lord is upon me,
>
> because he has anointed me

> to bring good news to the poor.
>
> He has sent me to proclaim release to the captives
>
> and recovery of sight to the blind,
>
> to let the oppressed go free,
>
> 19 to proclaim the year of the Lord's favor" (Luke 4:18–19).

Isa 61:1 is about the real practice of conversion, which is expressed in the proclamation of the "Jubilee."[226] The phrase "to proclaim release" refers in both Isa 61:1 and Luke 4:18 to the law on Jubilee (Lev 25:10). Every fiftieth year, according to Lev 25, all Israelites who had had to sell their property due to financial distress, or who had become debt slaves, would receive their land and their freedom back.[227]

And thus Jesus begins his sermon with a call to lived solidarity, based on the Torah—exactly as the elder in *m. Ta'anit* 2:1 had done.

To summarize the features that are similar to the story of Honi the Circle Drawer:

- Tractate *m. Ta'anit* begins by referring to the necessity of practicing solidarity and conversion rather than symbolic-ritual acts. The passage in Isaiah also points in this direction.
- In the Mishnah tractate, the community is expecting help from a competent man of prayer. All their eyes are fixed on him, as if he were the son of the house of GOD in heaven. In Nazareth as well, the eyes of all are expectantly fixed on Jesus (Luke 4:20).
- Honi allows the community to pressurize him into praying for heaven to open. Jesus reads from Isa 61 and calls to mind the leader who will save them, who will have the city rebuilt from its ruins. For the time being, he appears to take on the leadership role expected of him (Luke 4:17–21).
- Honi is held responsible for the result of his prayer. Since rain falls to excess, he incurs the wrath of the community. Jesus balks at being responsible for the emergency. He can do nothing without their cooperation. The congregation becomes angry with him (Luke 4:28).
- The rabbi wants to banish Honi from Jerusalem. But he lets Honi go, on the grounds that GOD listens to him. The people in Nazareth remove Jesus from their midst, in order to throw him off a cliff (Luke 4:29). But they let him go, so that he is able to "pass through the midst of them."

What does it mean that the Honi incident and the uproar in Nazareth have similar features? If we can identify narrative features and motivations in Luke 4:16–30 that are comparable to the events in *m. Ta'anit*, we can avoid anti-Judaist patterns of explanation. This means that we acknowledge a narrative continuity in both situations. Both start from the same Torah, take place within Jewish congregations, and refer to a rabbi or charismatic person who had a deep relationship with GOD. We see how the communities depend on this charismatic person or rabbi, how they approach him, how they really put him under pressure and then turn from him in anger. This puts the rage of the congregation in Nazareth in a quite different context than if we assess it from an anti-Judaist observation point.

On the other hand, this comparability does not mean that there was also a drought in Nazareth and the people wanted someone to pray for rain. In any case, we must note that there is no indication in Luke 4:16–30 of such a desire for rain. But let us pursue this path further, and then we will see that Jesus could indeed have prayed for the heaven to open.

> 21 Now when all the people were baptized, and when Jesus also had been baptized and was praying, the heaven was opened (Luke 3:21).

But here in Nazareth there was no sign of this. All the people (Luke 3:21) hoped for the heavens to open. The congregation in Nazareth was also part of these people. The people who had gathered in the synagogue hoped for an end to their distress. Their hope was founded on their experience of distress. We should not criticize their despair at the lack of rain, at the shut-up heaven, as a kind of "miracle addiction," as, e.g., Joseph Ernst does. He sees here a timeless commentary of Luke's about "an addiction to miracles, which is no longer satisfied with the proclamation of salvation."[228]

We have also found this hope in the Mishnah story of Honi. The hope is reflected in the many eyes that were fixed on him. We find these hope-filled eyes again in the synagogue in Nazareth (Luke 4:20). May the heavens open, right now! May GOD finally be propitiated. May rain come and end our distress.

Perceiving the shadow of hunger in the literary context and Jesus' accentuation of hunger in verse 25 changes our access to this difficult story. But if we skip over the severe famine, its duration and the reasons for it (the shut up heaven), the expectation of the people in Nazareth becomes incomprehensible, as does their urgent demand for prayer to ward off distress, and their disappointment when Jesus refuses to pray like this. All the exegetic literature I have seen on this overlooks the famine in Luke 4:25–26 and the hunger signaled in the literary context (vv. 2–3). All the greater is the puzzle of the sudden change of mood in the synagogue, all the more decisive the anti-Judaist reading of the outbreak of rage as a rejection of the Messiah.

4.12 A son of Joseph

The people in Nazareth were hoping that this native of the town would open heaven with the power of his prayer. The designation "Joseph's son" (Luke 4:22) expresses their expectations. Not just that Jesus was a son of the carpenter, who may have been poor—we don't know anything about this, unfortunately, as Joseph's trade is consigned to the realm of legend. But Joseph is a name with biblical tradition. When Luke brings his name into play here, and not Mary's, he is intending to tie into this Joseph tradition.

Joseph was the specially beloved son of Jacob, as also reflected by the beautiful Blessing of Jacob (Gen. 49:3–27), as well as the Blessing of Moses (Deut 33:2–27), which both reserve the greatest abundance of blessings for this particular son. The blessing beseeches the delights of heaven and earth to fall on Joseph (and his house)—water in abundance, fruits, herbs, all the green things of the earth, and the blessing of Adonai, who from the thorn bush heard the weeping of his enslaved people (Exod 3:2–7).

> 13 And of Joseph he said:
> Blessed by the LORD be his land,
> with the choice gifts of heaven above,
> and of the deep that lies beneath;
> 14 with the choice fruits of the sun,
> and the rich yield of the months;
> 15 with the finest produce of the ancient mountains,
> and the abundance of the everlasting hills;
> 16 with the choice gifts of the earth and its fullness,
> and the favor of the one who dwells on Sinai [or: in the bush].
> Let these come on the head of Joseph,
> on the brow of the prince among his brothers (Deut 33:13–16).

Joseph is not just one name among the sons of Jacob, but the outstanding name, which resonates with the tradition of the twelve tribes.[229] The title "Joseph's son" is thus not directed just at Jesus' father, Mary's husband, but at "the house of Joseph."[230] Here, Jesus is set in the tradition of Israel, addressed as a son of the house of Joseph. The abundance of blessings belongs to this house—an intense appeal in the face of possible drought and famine.

Joseph was sold by his brothers into Egypt, but when hunger weighed heavily on the land, the brothers had to go to Egypt themselves to buy grain (see Chapter 10).

> 56 And since the famine had spread over all the land, Joseph opened all the storehouses, and sold to the Egyptians, for the famine was severe in the land of Egypt. 57 Moreover, all the world came to Joseph in Egypt to buy grain, because the famine became severe throughout the world (Gen 41:56–57).

Egypt was the granary of antiquity—even though it did suffer repeated famines. If the Nile flooded the fertile regions at the right time, the land produced plenty of grain. Pharaoh had appointed Joseph as a supervisor of the land, and he began to make provisions against the absence of floods:

> 35 "Let them gather all the food of these good years that are coming, and lay up grain under the authority of Pharaoh for food in the cities, and let them

keep it. 36 That food shall be a reserve for the land against the seven years of famine that are to befall the land of Egypt, so that the land may not perish through the famine" (Gen 41:35–36).

So according to the story in Genesis, it is thanks to Joseph that, in the years of famine, when "the famine had spread over all the land" (Gen 41:56), the grain trade still functioned. And, although hunger was great in the land of Egypt, trade did not collapse, and the whole world came to buy grain from Joseph. The biblical tradition links the name of Joseph with his wisdom in providing for grain in hard times. The people's appeal to the son of Joseph in Luke 4:22 could be a further indication of years of famine, of the hard times that were also palpable in Nazareth.

But while Joseph found fame and honor abroad, his brothers had hated him. His dreams (Gen 37:5 and 37:9) landed him in trouble with his brothers. He dreamed that his parents and brothers would bow down before him. These dreams stirred up jealousy and rivalry. His brothers hated him for it (Gen 37:8) and thought him arrogant.[231] The sentence about the prophet who is not accepted in his hometown (Luke 4:24) would be understandable against this background. "His brothers" admire him, perhaps, but they cannot bear his dreams. Jesus comes to the city as a rabbi with spiritual gifts, and begins ambitiously by reading from Isa 61 (see below). They think him a well-educated, astute Torah teacher, and hope that he will open the heavens for Nazareth.

4.13 Physician, heal thyself!

As Jeshua ben Joseph, Jesus is situated in a great tradition, associated with grain stocks and the delights of heaven and earth, but also with high-flying dreams. If the people in Nazareth were suffering under the shut-up heaven, they had no more patience for this son of Joseph's dreams. They needed practical help, right now.

A wide gap yawns between the words of Isaiah in Luke 4:18 (good news for the poor, YHWH's Jubilee) and the reality of drought-stricken Nazareth. The city was his "mother," who had fed him; now it demands him to heal it ("Physician, heal thyself!" v. 23 KJV), but does not refer to his socio-political demands from Isa 61. The city's inhabitants wanted Jesus to heal the city by himself in a tour de force, without assistance or cooperation from them.

If we follow the expression "physician" into the Old Testament, it leads us to the story in Exodus, where YHWH is called a healer. Barely has the exodus community fled through the Sea of Reeds before the fleeing people suffer from lack of water. The people cry out to Moses. They are disappointed by him and his GOD. "What shall we drink?" they complain. Moses places them under obligation, and makes them responsible:

> He said, "If you will listen carefully to the voice of the LORD your God, and do what is right in his sight, and give heed to his commandments and keep all his

statutes, I will not bring upon you any of the diseases that I brought upon the Egyptians; for I am the Lord who heals you" (Exod 15:26).

If you follow his commandments, Adonai will give you water. The struggle for water perfuses the story in Exodus and leads repeatedly to conflict with Moses. The infamous grumbling of the people in Exod 15–17 has three times to do with thirst and hunger. The people cry, protest, fight for water and bread:

> 22 Then Moses ordered Israel to set out from the Red Sea, and they went into the wilderness of Shur. They went three days in the wilderness and found no water. 23 When they came to Marah, they could not drink the water of Marah because it was bitter. That is why it was called Marah. 24 And the people complained against Moses, saying, "What shall we drink?" (Exod 15:22–24).

> 2 The whole congregation of the Israelites complained against Moses and Aaron in the wilderness. 3 The Israelites said to them, "If only we had died by the hand of the Lord in the land of Egypt, when we sat by the fleshpots and ate our fill of bread; for you have brought us out into this wilderness to kill this whole assembly with hunger" (Exod 16:2–3).

> They camped at Rephidim, but there was no water for the people to drink. 2 The people quarreled with Moses, and said, "Give us water to drink" (Exod 17:1–2).

The assembly in Nazareth is upset about Jesus' reading and interpretation of the Torah, because they need more than mere words and visions. While Jesus was able to beat the devil into retreat with the spiritual force of the Torah (Luke 4:13) and assert that people do not live by bread alone, the Nazarenes take the other side: they need bread in the hand. Their disappointment in Jeshua ben Joseph is clear, their anger about his "dreams" and his not-helping. Luke's narrative refers back to the grumbling exodus community. Jeshua ben Joseph has a special blessing upon him; he could perhaps make something happen that would honor his name. The community in Nazareth had been hoping for the delights of heaven and earth, for full pantries. Their rage at the opening of neither a granary nor the heavens suggests the extent of their distress. As narrator, Luke does not shrink from this rage. In the uproar in Nazareth he recognizes the same distress as back then in Massah, Meriba, or Rephidim, when the exodus community had cried out for water. Jesus has to deal with resistance, just as Moses did.

An anti-Judaist reading will always come to the same conclusion: Israel rejected Jesus as the Messiah. But this pattern fails to recognize that conflicts with the prophets and leaders are inscribed into the story of Joseph and the story of the exodus. So just as the people fought with Moses without dissociating themselves from him, the people in Nazareth are also able to fight with Jesus without disengaging from the story of God. On the contrary: the Lukan exodus theology inscribes the altercation in Nazareth into Yhwh's liberation of the oppressed. Like Moses, Jesus is a great prophetic leader, who gets into conflicts and has to take a stand.

In addition to the exodus context, Luke stresses the context of distress. Thus, I see the rage of the assembled congregation as springing from their great need for rain, for reconciliation with heaven so that it will open. Just like this, the Israelites cried out for water, and people today still cry out for bread. Their protest has a clarifying function in the Lukan scene: they provoke Jesus into saying as clearly as possible what the result of his prophecy should actually be.

4.14 An explosive mix

Jesus read from the scroll of the prophet Isaiah. According to Luke what he read was a *Mischzitat*, i.e., verses from two different chapters of Isaiah, one after the other. The Greek text is quoted from the Septuagint. The question is, of course, whether this could be seen as a mix-up, i.e., a mistake, or whether this mix is a further authentic Jesuan reading of the Scripture, focusing on something that we need to find out.[232]

> 18 "The Spirit of the Lord is upon me,
>
> because he has anointed me
>
> to bring good news to the poor.
>
> He has sent me to proclaim release to the captives
>
> and recovery of sight to the blind,
>
> to let the oppressed go free,
>
> 19 to proclaim the year of the Lord's favor" (Luke 4:18–19).

The *Mischzitat* is carefully composed. It begins with Isa 61:1, then leaves part of a verse out ("to bind up the broken-hearted"), carries on with Isa 61:1 and then adds part of Isa 58:6 ("to let the oppressed go free")—and closes with Isa 61:1 again. The quote ends with the "year of the Lord's favor," before the end of the sentence in Isa 61:2, i.e., it leaves out the "day of vengeance." The composite quotation cannot have stood like this in a scroll of Isaiah, but suggests Luke's editorial hand.

Kerstin Schiffner sees in the *Mischzitat* references to keywords in Exodus, which she summarizes: "This is about liberation—liberation from earthly as well as 'supernatural' structures of oppression, to put it specifically: from the 'debt trap' as well as from the power of Satan."[233] Schiffner investigates above all the terminology for the "poor," the "oppressed," and the "captives," as well as for "release." Who are these poorest of the poor, the subject of Luke's composition?

Schiffner states that according to Exod 23:11 the poor are those who will be allowed to benefit from the fallow fields in every seventh year, as well as from the gleanings after the harvest. They are those to whom Yhwh will give special attention, so that the property owners will let them share in their property.[234] Release and debt cancellation are thus identical in a society that is familiar with debt slavery. "The people are captives—the dividing line should not be drawn sharply between e.g., economic indebtedness and debt slavery and enslavement under the power of Satan, which keeps people captive and small (cf. Luke 13:10–19)."[235] Solidarity with the poorest of the land therefore goes hand in hand with liberation from foreign rule. Liberation gives the "haves" responsibility; concretely, this means releasing the "have-nots" from debt. Then, Yhwh too will work for his people—if they do their part for liberation, in solidarity and responsibility.

Schiffner concludes that the composition of the two passages from Isaiah allows the cooperation of Yhwh with her people to be revealed. "While Isa 61 presents Yhwh as taking action . . . Isa 58 in return focuses on the people themselves and, going even further, gives them responsibility. . . . Liberation requires both sides, the powerful initiative of the God of Israel and equally the actions of her people."[236] Liberation comes not only from God, but also from out of the community. God gives the impulse, so to speak, the vision, the space, while it is creditors themselves who must cancel debts. Keeping the covenant—including the fallow year and the poor laws—must be realized by the community in solidarity. Then, God will not hold back her blessings, but will open the heavens and play her part so that liberation can sprout and take root.

Luke composes the scene so that it centers around the Torah. This is what the scene is about, its interpretation and how what it promises can today become true and real through communal action. The reading of Isa 61:1 (with the insertion of Isa 58:6) is a carefully weighed-up phrasing of the Jesuan programme—the cooperation between God and the people; but it is pitched too high, is too far-fetched for the Nazarenes in the time of their need. Those who have gathered in Nazareth demand immediate measures, concrete aid, such as a prayer for rain that will turn their distress around, a prayer for the heavens to open in Nazareth.

Wanting to throw Jesus out of their city and hurl him off a cliff (Luke 4:29)[237] is something we can read in the language of Exodus as well: come down from your high mountain (Sinai), where you can speak to God, face to face. Down here drought and distress reign; we are drowning in debt and land rents. A Jubilee Year is all well and good, but what help does it bring us, if nothing is growing in the fields? It's not up to us to give the land back to its former owners. We no longer own any land.—The people are moved by the Jesuan programme, but it pushes them too far.

Why doesn't Jesus give them what they need—what, no feeding of the hungry, no rain miracle? It is hard for Christians to admit that he *could not*. But let us see this in the context of Luke's Gospel. Jesus' teaching activity was still new at this point. He taught in the synagogues and this was appreciated (Luke 4:14–15). Only after the uproar in Nazareth did he teach with great authority (*exousia*) and not just with Spirit (*pneuma*)—an authority that he had perhaps gained precisely in these altercations in Nazareth. In Luke's story this teaching *activity*, which includes driving out demons

(v. 33) and healing the sick (vv. 39, 40–41), and finally bringing about Peter's plentiful catch of fish (Luke 5:4–11), begins only after the altercations in Nazareth.

If we read the cliff in Nazareth on a literary level, Jesus had started out too steeply for the village. This educated descendant of Joseph appeared to them to be a dreamer, whose dreams did not help them in their need. He did not prove himself a careful organizer, who was able to secure the grain trade even in years of famine. Behind the rage of the assembled people, we can sense their distress, their hope, and their disappointment. Yet Nazareth did not fall out of the scope of the story of GOD with his people, but put up a resistance that the young prophet had to withstand. Jesus went through the midst of them (Luke 4:30), so that he was fortified to continue on his path.

In summary, I consider it important to state that we must not turn this frictional energy in Nazareth into something that is anti-Judaist. Resistance and criticism accompanied Moses on his path to freedom. Jesus encountered such resistance too, as Luke narrates, and he grew with it. At the same time, by recognizing the underlying hunger, we can put the community's distress into concrete terms. They had reason to be anxious; debating on an empty stomach does not go well. Jesus did not yet have much with which to counter their hunger. He went through the midst of their rage, from now on he was acquainted with it—just like he had become acquainted with the satanic power in the hunger-zone at first hand.

Hunger is introduced as a factor in Luke 4: a prophet like Jesus could not avoid it. He had to get to know it, share it, endure it. The associated expectations and fears of small communities reached him and formed him. Nazareth remains the starting point for Jesus' teaching activity in Luke: what he learned here prepared the ground, so to speak, for everything from then on.

5.

The Geography of Hunger

A FAMINE OVER ALL THE WORLD (ACTS 10-12)

So far, the hermeneutic of hunger has taught us to look under stones, to lift them up and turn them round: people do not like to write about hunger, or to talk about it. What is going on there, in the shadows, in the unspoken, is not only astonishing but paramount in acquiring a historically appropriate access to the texts.

The dark has to do with both the textual sources, and also with ourselves, i.e., we have blind spots, clouded lenses, where the perception of hunger is concerned. It always means work, turning our gaze away from the shining lights to the inconspicuous, or to incidents mentioned only briefly, incidents that are not in the limelight of the narrative, but at its margins.

> *Denn die einen sind im Dunkeln*
> *Und die andern sind im Licht.*
> *Und man siehet die im Lichte*
> *Die im Dunkeln sieht man nicht.*
> Bertolt Brecht, *Die Dreigroschenoper*[238]

I would like to show a further variant of the hermeneutic of hunger, when hunger finds its way into the spotlight. In Acts 11:28 hunger is, exceptionally, not left in the dark: a severe famine will come over the whole world. This concerns the great famine, which encompassed a wide area, which was predictable and was heralded:

The Geography of Hunger

> One of them named Agabus stood up and predicted by the Spirit that there would be a severe famine [*limos*] over all the world; and this took place during the reign of Claudius (Acts 11:28).

If we take Acts 11:28 as the focus that suddenly lights up out of the darkness, we can carefully feel our way backwards and forwards in the literary context of chapters 12 and 11 and 10, in order to recognize the figures and events in the shadow of hunger, which were already making ripples in the run-up to 11:28. How do these chapters tell the story of famine? Is it just signaled—as a prophecy—or can it already be painfully sensed at particular places? Where and how does hunger turn into famine? Who first calls it a famine? How do the affected people or communities act?

Ultimately, we must also ask about the theological consequences that the impending famine brings with it. What does the fear of famine do to the people? Where is GOD, when famine comes? Where do the hungry situate GOD, GOD's Spirit and assistance? What theological ideas are mobilized? The clear announcement of famine in Acts 11:28 makes us prick up our ears to the whole literary context, and the question goes with us: So what does GOD do, when famine comes?

5.1 Agabus in Antioch

There is a passage in Acts where there is nothing to quibble about, nothing concealed to draw out; nobody—whether well-fed and indifferent to hunger or not—could fail to spot this passage:

> 27 At that time prophets came down from Jerusalem to Antioch. 28 One of them named Agabus stood up and predicted by the Spirit that there would be a severe famine [*limos*] over all the world; and this took place during the reign of Claudius. 29 The disciples determined that according to their ability, each would send relief to the believers living in Judea (Acts 11:27–29).

In verse 28 we find the Greek expression *limos*, which means "shortage, scarcity" and is synonymous with our "famine." A great shortage of food is mentioned here. Speaking prophetically (*prophemi*, v. 27) means "speaking before," less in the sense of "predicting" but more like "saying loudly and clearly in front of someone, making public, announcing."

We can imagine the situation like this: a few women and men came to Antioch in Syria from far-off Jerusalem. They are described as prophets, i.e., women and men who spoke before the congregation and stated certain things publicly. One of them is mentioned by name: Agabus (Hebrew for "locust").[239] His name is remembered along with his message; it appears to be inextricably linked to him:

> Agabus stood up and predicted by the Spirit that there would be a severe famine [*limos*] over all the world; and this took place during the reign of Claudius (Acts 11:28).

Claudius was emperor of Rome from 41 to 54 CE. We know from different sources that a severe famine rocked the eastern part of the Mediterranean region in the late 40s.[240] Parts of Greece as well as Syria, Palestine, and Egypt suffered shortages. This wide geographical area is described in Acts 11:28 as "all the world." For the population of this eastern region it was indeed the whole world: it was impossible to send out caravans or ships to bring back seeds and grain from neighboring countries. The distances were too great to remedy the famine in this region within a reasonable period of time.[241]

The note at the end of Acts 11 thus reminds us of this comprehensive famine in the eastern Mediterranean. So what do we do with it? Why does this reminder survive in Acts at all? Certainly the reaction of the disciples in Antioch is important: they pooled all they could spare, and had this collection sent to Judea (vv. 29–30). This makes visible a solidarity that reaches out far beyond the province's borders. Judea lay several hundred kilometers south of Antioch.

The people from Jerusalem, who had endured this long journey during a period of scarcity, had accepted hardships. Their journey took a long time and was dangerous. Agabus was one of the travelers. His descriptive name has come down to us, as well as his courage in standing up: "He stood up"—this expression means more than just getting up, raising himself—especially in connection with God's Spirit.[242] Agabus stood up against the paralyzing fear, the leaden shadow that had been cast over the communities. He started something, he broke the silence that reigned in the city's neighborhoods and the synagogues. He recognized the shadow of hunger and named it publicly, gave word to what many feared or did not want to be true: "A worldwide famine is coming."

Mentioning the Spirit in connection with Agabus' speech qualifies his speech as effective. God's Spirit (*pneuma*, v. 28) stirred up the listeners, who allowed the message to sink in, reach its target. The people were shaken, moved, stricken by his speech. A speech full of the Spirit can awaken compassion, so that the listeners realize what is at issue. They felt connected to the brothers and sisters in far Judea, and decided to do whatever was in their power. The Spirit's effect is discernible in this reaction. The Spirit transforms the listeners into people who are affected, makes isolated congregations into a community in solidarity beyond all boundaries.

Word of the great famine was heard in Antioch. During the Roman Empire, Antioch was the capital city of the province of Syria (now Antakya in Turkey), estimated to have had about 450,000 inhabitants. This made it one of the largest cities in the Roman Empire, after Rome and Alexandria. The River Orontes, which flowed through its heart, connected the city with the Mediterranean, and the caravan routes to Persia,

Syria, and India made the city an economic center in the ancient world. Spices, silk, fine woods, and luxury goods were carried from India and China to the Mediterranean. Syria itself supplied oil, wine, cedar wood, purple dye, and furniture. The key cities along the caravan routes and the Mediterranean also included Tyre and Sidon (see below).

Agabus and the people from Judea had not traveled to wealthy Antioch by chance. They were hoping for support from the community on whom they relied. Here, the famine was evidently still unknown. Here, people were still able to gather together goods that they did not themselves need immediately, and send them to Judea.

5.2 Unrest in Tyre, Sidon, and Jerusalem

During this period, when scarcity spread and the congregation in Antioch gathered support, other places in the eastern regions experienced unrest under King Herod. Following on from our verse about Agabus:

> 1 About that time [*kairos*] King Herod laid violent hands upon some who belonged to the church. 2 He had James, the brother of John, killed with the sword. 3 After he saw that it pleased the Jews, he proceeded to arrest Peter also (Acts 12:1–3).

Although a new chapter is starting, the narrative context is not left behind. Verse 1 follows on directly with the phrase "about that time." Now we hear of unrest in Jerusalem, some distance from Antioch. Both Jerusalem in Judea and Antioch in Syria had been incorporated into the Roman Empire. Judea was ruled by a Roman client king, at that time the Herodian royal house. King Herod Agrippa I always had huge debts; he was the grandson of Herod the Great and a friend of Emperor Claudius, which ensured his political survival. He died in 44 CE (Acts 12:23).

Why does this king intrude into our view? Why does Acts tell of these arrests? The link to Antioch and Agabus is "about that time." According to Peter Garnsey, *kairos* is also one of the expressions that might indicate scarcity and food crisis—along with *limos*, *sitodeia*, *spanis*, *aporia*, *aphoria*, *endeia*.[243] If we follow Garnsey, Acts 12:1 means "about that time" not only in the sense of "contemporaneously," but during this scarcity, at the same time as the crisis was spreading.

Thus, Acts describes what was happening at another place during this crisis. The Jewish congregation in Antioch started a collection for their brothers and sisters in Judea, who were having a hard time not just because of the food shortage but also because of the added social and political tensions.

"About that time," Herod felt compelled to take steps to master the situation. He had a few people from the community surrounding Peter arrested and executed; he wanted to execute Peter as well, without giving reasons (Acts 12:19). It was probably to set an example of his power.

It is well-known that, in times of hardship, social tensions arise that explode into violence. Among the Jews of Tyre and Sidon, the formerly Phoenician port cities, there was a desperate battle for survival as well:

> Now Herod was angry with the people of Tyre and Sidon. So they came to him in a body; and after winning over Blastus, the king's chamberlain, they asked for a reconciliation, because their country depended on the king's country for food (Acts 12:20).

It cannot be fathomed for certain what exactly happened in the port cities of Tyre and Sidon at that time. Perhaps there were bloody uprisings at the port, attacks on Jewish houses, or parts of the city set on fire.

The historian Josephus narrates that, shortly before the war broke out around 66 CE, the insurgents in Jerusalem set fire to the palaces of the high priests and the royal family, and did not rest until the archives in which the debt records were kept had burned down.[244] This destroyed the impoverished people's obligations towards their creditors. Only now could the "poorer sort" take part in the revolt, because they no longer had anything to fear.

If we follow the wording of Acts 12:20, the Jewish community agreed that it was better to join forces with a royal official than to oppose Herod and his power structure. Thus, they tried to win over Blastus, the king's chamberlain, and "asked for a reconciliation, because their country depended on the king's country for food" (Acts 12:20).[245] So yet again, hunger is a hidden topic.

After the worldwide famine is heralded in 11:28, we see how tensions boiled over and order threatened to slip out of the hands of the powerful. They took inappropriate measures and tried to master the situation through intimidation.

5.3 The famine began in Joppa

In 11:28 the news of a catastrophe reached the flourishing city of Antioch. Following this, we hear of arrests, executions and riots in Jerusalem (Judea) and the Phoenician port cities to the north.

But where did the famine actually start? Who first experienced it? Famine arguably already reigned in Judea, at the time the delegation with Agabus set off for Antioch. The beginning of Acts 11, set in Jerusalem, is already preoccupied with food (vv. 3, 7–9). Here we hear Peter, surrounded by the congregation, telling of his journey to Joppa and Caesarea. The brothers and sisters want to know exactly what happened in Caesarea (v. 3).

In Acts 11 Peter repeats, in his own words, what the readers have already been able to read in Acts 10: Peter was staying in Joppa and was then invited to Caesarea by Cornelius' people. Clearly and concisely: While Peter was in the tanner's house by the sea around noon, he was hungry (10:10). His hosts were aware of this. They made efforts to prepare something to eat. But it appears to have taken some time—for Peter climbed up onto the roof to pray.

We could read this—Peter's hunger at noon—as a quite ordinary appetite. But if we keep our eye on what develops in the subsequent chapters, up to Agabus' speech about the worldwide famine (11:28), we should not prematurely assume it means just "appetite." In connection with Peter's prayer, which, so to speak, accompanies his hosts' preparation or procurement of food, the hunger mentioned here appears to be more all-encompassing. Peter prayed in Joppa, contributing what he could to his hosts being able to get hold of something edible.

Joppa lay on the Mediterranean, approximately 65 km from Jerusalem. Next to Joppa lay Lydda, where Peter was at the time (9:32–35). From here, he was called to neighboring Joppa because it was reported that Tabitha had died (9:37). Tabitha is the only woman in the New Testament who is expressly referred to as *mathetria*—disciple. She must have been a woman of great importance in the eyes of the congregation; it is written that she "was devoted to good works and acts of charity" (9:36).[246]

This woman, who was important to the congregation in little Joppa, became ill, or to be more precise: weak, feeble, faint. Then she died. The community called for Peter to come at once. Peter hurried to Joppa and they showed him who Tabitha had been and what she had done for the widows. The widows then showed him items of clothing they had made together with Tabitha or in her house,[247] and lamented her death greatly (9:39–41).

The word "hunger" is not mentioned here. But there was profound sadness in Joppa, even despair. Where did this despair come from? The brothers and sisters certainly did not call for Peter for every death. Tabitha was an extraordinarily important pillar of the community. The only indication of scarcity we can see is in the verb "to become weak" (v. 37). Tabitha became so weak that she died. Was she a prominent victim of the famine? Did the congregation fear for its survival once Tabitha, the benefactor, was gone? Did the community send for Peter not just because of Tabitha, but because of the hunger that affected everyone?

I suspect that the narrative context of scarcity (*limos* in 11:28 and *kairos* in 12:1, up to the offer of peace in 12:20) began here in Joppa. Peter was summoned, because there was no end to the distress in Joppa, and even this important benefactor of the community, who had provided work for many widows in her house, had fallen victim to it.

The first to be affected by the famine were the little places in the middle of nowhere, far away from the major trade routes and transshipment ports, far away from rich families who were perhaps still offering grain for sale. And in this little place it is first the women, and precisely the widows, who appear in this connection. Their joint efforts made them able to resist poverty and scarcity for a time. But now, when even their benefactor had given up the ghost, they knew only one thing: We must get help from outside—it can't go on like this.[248]

Tabitha is a key figure in this story of hunger. Her death (9:37) started the ball rolling, and they sent for Peter (9:38); he was then invited to Caesarea (10:5); other prophets traveled from Jerusalem (11:27) to Antioch, while those in Jerusalem waited for news and aid (11:29). However, only in wealthy Antioch was the famine publicly announced and described as a great catastrophe (11:28). But Peter had already become acquainted with this in Joppa (10:10), in the house of a tanner, where he had been summoned because of Tabitha.

It is remarkable that Acts situates the start of the famine so precisely. The famine begins in little, insignificant Joppa, among widows—women outside the patriarchal family structure. By the time it is noticed in Antioch, many poor people have presumably been carried off like Tabitha. But Acts also shows ways and strategies to counter hunger: the widows in Tabitha's house were working together until they could no longer do so, and then they sent for external assistance. They called attention to their distress—Peter rushed to help, and his prayer (10:9) set heaven and hell in motion.

5.4 Parenthesis: Drawing boundaries

Before we look over Peter's shoulder, we must mention the exegetic history of Acts 10—11:18. It is the case that the interpreters do not perceive hunger or take it seriously, but focus on the demarcation between Jewish and Gentile Christians.

This demarcation is underpinned by the question of the community in Jerusalem ("the circumcised believers"), of whether Peter had eaten with "men who still had their foreskins" (11:3). This sets the key points that concern the interpreters: they assume that Peter jettisoned the Jewish dietary laws when he ate with the Roman centurion—and they hold this vision in Joppa to be a key experience for the anarchic mission to the Gentiles. To maintain this thesis, it is enough that, in his vision, Peter sees all manner of animals that he is supposed to eat, and speaks of "unclean" and "abominable" (see below). "The issue is the acceptance of the first Gentiles into the community hitherto composed only of Jewish Christians."[249] Interpreters refer to it as Cornelius' conversion, a paradigmatic conversion of a Gentile.

The focus on the Jewish-Gentile relationship threads its way through numerous interpretations and allows us to discern a fascination for discourses on demarcation.[250] Jews and Gentiles, or pharisaic Jews (in Jerusalem) and Gentiles are always discussed as two discrete groups standing opposite one another in this story; their relationship needs further clarification.

The concept of demarcation understands sharing meals only in the light of the Jewish dietary laws prohibiting table fellowship.[251] Rudolf Pesch on this: "The focus of the ... Cornelius story lay apparently not on the issue of admitting Gentiles to baptism without prior circumcision ... but on the issue ... of the table fellowship between Jewish and Gentile Christians."[252] Pesch understands Peter's vision of the sheet from heaven as a rejection of the Jewish dietary laws. Division into permitted and forbidden foods is, according to Pesch, thus cancelled by GOD in person. For Christians this differentiation would no longer play a role; that is what Peter is learning here. Thus, in this interpretation Peter appears as a Jew who is slowly giving up his resistance to contact with the unclean heathens.

This ignores the fact that the text of Acts 10–11 leaves open what was actually eaten in the house of Cornelius. Was it vegetables and bread? Or meat and fish? Did the little delegation from Joppa receive a kosher meal? Did they pray together, wash their hands, make a peace offering to the Emperor? The text does not say a single word about this.

The demarcation discourses that concern the interpretation of our passage have had a long-lasting effect.[253] They are used to construct identity, sketch boundaries, and defend them; these discussions bring about the traditions of demarcation. But I doubt whether they are helpful in understanding a specific text such as Acts 10—11:18, at least because it contains terms that during the first century CE were open in many respects.[254]

The text does not allow us to determine precisely whether Cornelius was a "Gentile"—as the exegesis commonly assumes—or not. He is described as a devout man who constantly prayed to God (Acts 10:2), and who had generously given alms to the Jewish people. So in no case was he a clueless heathen. But this is the only thing that is clear. He could even have been Jewish. Or he could have been kindly disposed towards the synagogue; a sympathizer. But whether he viewed himself, or the congregation viewed him, as Jewish, as someone who belonged or was just an ally, the text does not say.

Shaye J. D. Cohen[255] shows what different levels of distance from or closeness to the Jewish community we can find in ancient texts. In any case, it is nowhere near clear whether someone was "really Jewish" or "just a sympathizer"—for there was no unambiguous membership, no systematic recording or definition of such a thing. If new worshippers counted themselves as part of the synagogue, that was sufficient, and the synagogue had to accept them. Beyond that, there was much that had to remain open. If Jews moved to a new place, but kept their distance from the synagogue there, were they Jewish or not? Who would know? Who would want to know anyway? And what for?

The Mishnah (ca. 200 CE) was first to define the conversion ritual. However, it remains open how many Jewish congregations at this point followed the Mishnah, or even knew it. Paula Fredriksen[256] demands a fundamentally new reconsideration of our vocabulary. The definitions and presuppositions[257] that determine our reconstruction of antiquity were passed down by those who were the victors of history, and do not reflect the situation in which the texts were written and to which they were reacting.[258]

Let us note: In the period when Acts of the Apostles was written, the criteria for belonging to the synagogue had not yet actually been defined. We cannot say with any certainty that Cornelius was not a Jew. He prayed to the Jewish God—constantly—and practiced his faith by giving alms to the synagogue. But let us not get bogged down in "belonging" or "not belonging," because the text can also leave this open. Let us try to sideline the demarcation discussions, and to discern the foreshadowing of hunger.

5.5 A terrifying vision in Joppa

Peter is staying in Joppa, at the house of Simon the tanner, when hunger strikes him. Acts of the Apostles presents Peter's hunger as the starting point for a vision. The vision and hunger appear to go together. Hunger opens Peter's eyes; heaven opens up before him and he sees something coming towards him:

> 10 He became hungry and wanted something to eat; and while it was being prepared, he fell into a trance. 11 He saw the heaven opened and something like a large sheet coming down, being lowered to the ground by its four corners. 12 In it were all kinds of four-footed creatures and reptiles and birds of the air. 13 Then he heard a voice saying, "Get up, Peter; kill and eat." 14 But Peter said, "By no means, Lord; for I have never eaten anything that is abominable or unclean before God." 15 The voice said to him again, a second time, "What God has declared clean, you must not call abominable" (Acts 10:10–15, adapted from NRSV).

Peter sees a kind of sheet coming down. On it he sees all kinds of animals. A voice calls him to stand up, to slaughter the animals and eat them. Peter is appalled, and refuses. The voice insists, and brings GOD into play, i.e., puts forward a theological argument, to change Peter's mind. Why does Peter react with such horror? He is so exceptionally hungry and would really like to eat! But Peter is disgusted. He calls what he has seen "abominable or unclean before God." He will not eat such disgusting things.

Instead of switching to the ideological level—GOD commands Peter to forget the Jewish dietary laws—we should consider that hunger forces people to eat things which are not in their diet, and which they normally find disgusting. For example, in his investigations of famine and food shortage in antiquity, Peter Garnsey[259] distinguishes five categories of food that were eaten in times of need, although they were avoided in good times, or were even taboo:

1. Livestock not in ordinary circumstances destined for slaughter
2. "Inferior" cereals (damaged by pests or weather)
3. Animal food (such as vetch or acorns)
4. Natural products such as roots, twigs, leaves, bark, leather
5. Human flesh

THE GEOGRAPHY OF HUNGER

The Roman historian Flavius Josephus, reporting about the Roman siege of Jerusalem, says: "The price of corn was fantastically high, and now that the City was walled round and they could not even gather herbs, some were in such dire straits that they raked the sewers and old dunghills and swallowed the refuse they found there, so that what once they could not bear to look at now became their food."[260]

Peter had spent his life eating only food which was clean. Now he is outraged at being asked to eat unkosher things. This unreasonable demand is made because of the food shortage, which has grown into a famine (Acts 11:28). He will have to change his diet—perhaps even eat rotten grain, or fall back on animals that he would otherwise never, ever eat.

Peter is not alone in his outrage. Ezekiel, too, was aghast and distraught when he saw in a vision that, because of a great famine in the besieged city, he should bake barley-cakes on human feces:

> 12 You shall eat it as a barley-cake, baking it in their sight on human dung. 13 The LORD said, "Thus shall the people of Israel eat their bread, unclean, among the nations to which I will drive them." 14 Then I said, "Ah Lord GOD! I have never defiled myself; from my youth up until now I have never eaten what died of itself or was torn by animals, nor has carrion flesh come into my mouth" (Ezek 4:12–14).

Comparison with Ezek 4:14 shows clearly the humiliation of hunger,[261] which appalls Peter and Ezekiel. Ezekiel has to eat substandard bread, even baked on human feces, for during the siege of the city normal food and even normal fuel had run out. Ezekiel is horrified at the idea that he will in future have to live on carrion and eat rotting meat.

This situation is not just life-threatening but also humiliating. In Ezek 36:30 we find the connection between hunger and insult again:

> 29 I will save you from all your uncleannesses [*ek pason ton akatharsion hymon*], and I will summon the grain and make it abundant and lay no famine upon you.
> 30 I will make the fruit of the tree and the produce of the field abundant, so that you may never again suffer the disgrace of famine among the nations.
> 33 On the day that I cleanse you from all your iniquities [*kathario*], I will cause the towns to be inhabited, and the waste places shall be rebuilt (Ezek 36:29, 30, 33).

The hungry are insulted by the well-fed (v. 30). However, after the catastrophe, GOD does provide reconciliation in the form of an abundance of food, so that all the nations see that the humiliation of Jerusalem has come to an end. With the abundance, the insult will stop, everyone will once again be able to eat properly, decently, according to their own customs. In the case of Jewish people, this means being able to eat in accordance with the Torah's dietary laws.

In Ezek 36:29–33 the verb "to declare clean" (cf. Acts 10:15) is also used in connection with moral impurity. This differentiation of moral and Levitical/ritual impurity is compelling for Jewish literature. In connection with the siege of Jerusalem, the prophet Ezekiel is not concerned with ritual impurity, but with the leaders' crimes, guilt, and political mismanagement, which had played the city into the hands of her enemies. This guilt is "paid off" through the suffering of the people; afterwards there will be a new beginning for everyone.

The interpreters' assumption that Acts 10:15 suspends the dietary laws rests on the concept of "Gentile Christianity free of the law,"[262] which this vision legitimizes. But the concept is historically premature for the first century CE. In addition, the verb "to declare clean" does not indicate the context of the Levitical dietary laws. It never occurs in Lev 11 in connection with food. But the assumption that contact with heathens is defiling is also problematic. Ben Witherington admits that there was no formal Jewish law declaring the heathens to be unclean and prohibiting contact with them.[263] Jonathan Klawans also makes it clear that the claim that sinners were impure, and Jews associating with them would be violating the norms of purity, is just an error based on the lack of differentiation between moral and ritual impurity.[264]

So we must not set Peter's vision into the context of problematizing the dietary laws, just because the verb "to declare clean," or the negative expressions "unclean" and "abominable" occur, as though GOD would personally declare the dietary laws to be nonsense. It is not GOD who forces Peter to give up his morals, but the worldwide famine.

In this sense, Acts 10:15 is not aiming to dissolve the categories "permitted" and "not permitted," but is building on them. It makes the impending famine so malleable and so dangerous that these profoundly self-evident categories have to be crossed out in order to remain alive at all. This crossing-out does something to the dignity of those affected; it damages their self-understanding as people.

Peter's vision in Joppa thus does two things: it mercilessly shows Peter that a great famine is coming. He and his people will have to eat things that disgust them. This is why Peter reacts with horror and outrage, and rejects what is being announced. "No, Lord GOD, never!" But yes, really, and this is the initially hidden aspect of this vision: God is on the side of the hungry. When the Jewish congregations suffer from hunger, when they are humiliated, this should not be understood as distance from GOD. GOD will even declare the terrible food to be pure, so that they can survive. Or to put it another way: even disgusting food comes from GOD's hand and aids survival. Ultimately, we should not overlook the statement that this sheet with the strange food comes down from heaven. Even this food is a gift from heaven. It is heaven that will open over the hungry. GOD will be merciful; hunger does not have the last word.

On this, I would like to refer to a striking passage from the Mishnah. Mercy towards the hungry takes precedence over adhering to the Torah's dietary laws. Thus, in *m. Yoma*, using the example of fasting on Yom Kippur (the Day of Atonement): "If one is seized by a ravenous hunger, they feed him even unclean things until his eyes light up" (*m. Yoma* 8:6).[265] So even unkosher things can be eaten by the hungry. This is not about surmounting the dietary laws, but about surviving.

We should no longer view Peter's vision with discussion against a backdrop of demarcation, but in the light of mercy towards the hungry.

When the vision is narrated, readers of Acts already know that Cornelius has sent out his people to fetch the hungry group from Joppa (Acts 10:5). So God has already acted to benefit the congregation in Joppa—even though Peter is not yet able to see this.

5.6 Deadly sieges

With an eye towards Ezekiel, who sees the siege of Jerusalem in his visions, we have touched on the most extreme form of hunger that could strike a population. We must therefore engage with this starving of the people. Otherwise we read the phrase the "siege of Jerusalem" too quickly and do not take account of what it actually means.

Our story about Joppa and Caesarea, Antioch and Jerusalem, is not about a siege. But: Acts was written towards the end of the first century. Although it tells of the 40s and 50s, it speaks to people who lived after the siege of Jerusalem and its destruction. Following a four-year war, Jerusalem was completely destroyed by Roman legions in 70 CE. These legions came in ships to Caesarea, a great Roman Mediterranean port. From this base they set about besieging Jerusalem. After four years the starved and depleted population was massacred or sold into slavery.

Acts was written down a single generation after this drama. Everything in it that is written about Jerusalem is thus in the past—the temple, the city, the flourishing life, the congregation surrounding Peter and Tabitha. But the memory of the siege and its famine must still have been alive—all the more so, because at around this time they still hoped the temple would be rebuilt.[266] We should therefore take a closer look at the background to this memory.

Besieging a city was a widespread instrument of conquest in antiquity.[267] Hunger was used as a weapon. A city could be under siege for months or years. Their gates were controlled by the enemy forces, ramparts were dug around the city, and water sources occupied (cf. Jdt 7:7).

In the book of Judith, the little hill town of Bethulia is besieged. It is part of the war strategy to cut off the population from their sources of water:

> 12 Let your servants take possession of the spring of water that flows from the foot of the mountain, 13 for this is where all the people of Bethulia get their water. So thirst will destroy them, and they will surrender their town. . . .
> 14 They and their wives and children will waste away with famine, and before

A siege meant war against the whole population: children, women, elderly people—and the enemy army did not have to suffer. Ezekiel repeatedly mentions the triad of the sword, famine, and pestilence:[268]

> The sword is without, and the pestilence and the famine within: he that is in the field shall die with the sword; and he that is in the city, famine and pestilence shall devour him (Ezek 7:15).

Jerusalem had already been besieged by the Babylonians during 589–586 BCE[269] and was finally forced to surrender by being starved out (Jer 32:24; 52:6; Ezek 5:16-17). Jeremiah was threatened with death by starvation, because there was no bread left in the city (Jer 38:9). The following description of the storming of Jerusalem by the Babylonians also relates how the men fit for military service abandoned their city to its fate and saved their own skins.

> 3 And on the ninth day of the fourth month the famine prevailed in the city, and there was no bread for the people of the land.
> 4 And the city was broken up, and all the men of war fled by night by the way of the gate between two walls (2 Kgs 25:3–4; see also Jer 52:6–7).

Samaria was besieged by Aram in the ninth century BCE, so that a severe famine developed. The siege led to a donkey's head costing 80 shekels of silver and a quarter of a kab of dove's dung 5 shekels (2 Kgs 6:25). The prices show the immeasurable need in the city. It becomes even more distressing in the story of mothers who eat their own children (2 Kgs 6:28–29).

> 19 Pour out your heart like water
> before the presence of the Lord!
> Lift your hands to him
> for the lives of your children,
> who faint for hunger at the head of every street.
> 20 Look, O Lord, and consider!
> To whom have you done this?
> Should women eat their offspring,
> the children they have borne?
> Should priest and prophet be killed
> in the sanctuary of the Lord? (Lam 2:19–20).

> 3 Even the jackals offer the breast
> and nurse their young,

> but my people has become cruel,
> like the ostriches in the wilderness.
> 4 The tongue of the infant sticks
> to the roof of its mouth for thirst;
> the children beg for food,
> but no one gives them anything.
> 5 Those who feasted on delicacies
> perish in the streets;
> those who were brought up in purple
> cling to ash heaps (Lam 4:3–5).

> Surely, parents shall eat their children in your midst, and children shall eat their parents (Ezek 5:10).[270]

Josephus' report about the Roman siege of the small city of Gischala in the First Jewish-Roman War 66–70 CE makes similar things visible. The leader John of Gischala seized his chance in the night-time to flee the besieged city with his soldiers.[271] He gathered his men, together with their families, and fled towards Jerusalem.[272] Hardly had he left the besieged city when he left the slower refugees behind, so that they could not hamper his own flight.[273] Those left behind began to call out, begging not to be given away. Women and children cried out for their husbands and fathers, but John exhorted his people to make haste and get away before the Romans could catch them.[274] The crowd got lost in the darkness; the weaker ones were crowded out of the way by those who were stronger. The next morning, Titus sent soldiers after the people who were fleeing and slew six thousand women and children, taking a further three thousand captive.[275]

The cries of their own wives and children did not manage to move the fleeing soldiers to take their families with them. Schottroff reads Mark 13:17 against the backdrop of Josephus: "Every man runs as fast as he can. According to military logic, the first victims during flight are one's own women and children. Not named explicitly are the aged, but they too are among the casualties; elsewhere they are named with women and children. Mark 13:17[276] makes plain the logic of military thinking in which women and children, not to mention pregnant and nursing women, are only a hindrance during flight. Wars are not conducted for their protection or for their freedom. They are fought for the freedom of the freeborn men. During the flight from Gischala, women protest in vain to the men who follow the orders of John."[277]

I also understand Josephus in this certainly quite critical sense, when he reports the breakdown of solidarity within the besieged city.[278] He describes how hope flared up among the beleaguered people in Jerusalem, after they had won a small victory. But "God was blinding their eyes" so that they did not see "the famine that was creeping towards them," for up till then they had fed "on the public miseries and [drunk] the

City's life-blood."²⁷⁹ Now poverty had them in its grasp and had wiped out many of them. But the rebels still thought that destroying the people would be useful; they wished no one who had made peace with Rome to survive.²⁸⁰ For three days they denied the Romans access to the city; but when Titus' attacks became stronger, they fled the city.

Josephus also describes the increasing hunger in Jerusalem under siege, and how the rebels fought more and more amongst themselves: "as the famine grew worse, the frenzy of the partisans increased with it. For as corn was nowhere to be seen, men broke into the houses and ransacked them. If they found any, they maltreated the occupants for saying there was none; if they did not, they suspected them of having hidden it more carefully and tortured them."²⁸¹ If they had found some wheat or barley, they shut themselves up immediately and ate it, some without even grinding it, and others baked it—"Nowhere was a table laid—they snatched the food from the fire while still uncooked and ate like wolves."²⁸² The more powerful someone was, the more he had to eat. "Thus it was that wives robbed their husbands, children their fathers, and—most horrible of all—mothers their babies, snatching the food out of their very mouths; and when their dearest ones were dying in their arms, they did not hesitate to deprive them of the morsels that might have kept them alive. . . . Children pulled the very morsels that their fathers were eating out of their very mouths, and . . . so did the mothers do as to their infants"—even from the dying they took "the very last drops that might preserve their lives."²⁸³ When the partisans saw a locked door, they broke it open, ripped the bread out of the hands of people who were eating, even squeezing their throats. "They beat old men who held onto their crusts, and tore the hair of women who hid what was in their hands."²⁸⁴ "Torments horrible even to hear about they inflicted on people to make them admit possession of one loaf." And this was all done not out of absolute necessity, but "rather they were keeping their passions exercised and laying in stores for use in the coming days . . . to keep their madness in exercise and to make provisions for themselves for the following day."²⁸⁵ These men even went so far as to rob people who, in mortal danger, had crept outside at night to gather wild plants and herbs.²⁸⁶

We should read this report by Josephus from a critical distance: Josephus is writing from the side of the besiegers, the Roman army. As a Jew this cannot have been easy for him. He therefore describes the rebels as cruel and accuses them of perpetrating violence and barbarism against the civilian population within the city walls—while the Roman besiegers appear much more civilized, almost liberators, who ultimately rescued the city from its sad fate. This whitewashing flies in the face of historical reality: barbarism was unfortunately not always to be found on one side alone. Nevertheless, I consider the individual scenes that he paints to be not unrealistic illustrations of how hunger can rage in a siege.

If starving people was a strategy of war, the famine that followed a defeat was a consequence of war. "Hunger is not just the terrible experience in a siege situation, but also the experience of any post-war period. Since the fields are devastated, the harvest destroyed, the fruit trees felled, there is nothing more to eat."[287] And thus the triad of the sword, famine, and pestilence persists well beyond war's end. The consequences of famine and persistent scarcity are weakness, bowel diseases, cholera, hunger edema—injuries heal slowly, infection leads to gangrene, and lack of hygiene to epidemics.

This dismal backdrop makes Ezekiel's terror (Ezek 4:14) at his vision more understandable. Ezekiel was scared to death. He had to announce a message that could not be blacker. Peter was similarly terrified (Acts 10:14)—in literary terms his reaction clearly refers to Ezekiel—although his vision in Joppa was not of a siege, but of a famine that had gripped a wide area. He presumably knew about the unrest in Tyre and Sidon and the unpredictable harshness of Herod. Food shortages, linked to riots, risked leading to war. Uprisings in large cities provoked the occupying forces.

5.7 "Siege-Documents" from Nippur

I would like to highlight another aspect of sieges, and go into it in more detail. The brief, terrifying descriptions of the sieges broach the subject of relationship of the parents to their children, and particularly of mothers to their infants, on several occasions. Children who tear the bread out of their elderly parents' hands, mothers who eat their children—hunger doesn't just humiliate people, it dissolves civilization, transforms society into a collection of barbaric individuals, for whom nothing is sacred any longer. A parent's love—above all a mother's love—stands here for dependability in a society, for protection and the sequence of generations, which famine conditions dissolve.

But I would also like to remember the hungry voices in Neh 5:1–5 (see Chapter 2, above). In the fifth century BCE, parents lamented that poverty and hunger were forcing them to sell their children into debt slavery:

> 2 For there were those who said, "With our sons and our daughters, we are many; we must get grain, so that we may eat and stay alive." 3 There were also those who said, "We are having to pledge our fields, our vineyards, and our houses in order to get grain during the famine." 4 And there were those who said, "We are having to borrow money on our fields and vineyards to pay the king's tax. 5 . . . we are forcing our sons and daughters to be slaves, and some of our daughters have been ravished; we are powerless, and our fields and vineyards now belong to others" (Neh 5:2–5).

Poverty and hunger destroy the community, evidenced by the dysfunctional primary relationships. But while some are even forced to sell their children, there are also people who become rich in these times, who profit from need and poverty, and who acquire children at giveaway prices.

In this connection, I find Adolph Leo Oppenheim's work on siege-documents from Nippur[288] very thought-provoking. Nippur was one of the very ancient cities in Mesopotamia, on the Euphrates. The documents come from a family archive, which was excavated in the back courtyard of a house. They are twenty-eight clay tablets, twenty-five of which are contracts (plus three letters). The name of the archive's main character is Ninurta-uballit. These contracts were concluded in the period between 656 and 617 BCE.

Nine of these contracts concern the sale of persons. Only once is it a boy being sold; the rest of the sales are of girls. The sellers are their parents, usually their mothers. Oppenheim states that "the fact that women appear as sellers in these texts could be due to the war situation. The husbands had perhaps been killed or were in the service."[289] The emergency situation, for mothers who were alone and had to fall back on their own resources, was certainly great and evidently forced them to sell their children. We should also ask ourselves whether it was easier to sell daughters than sons.

The special thing about these sale documents is that the children were sold *in order that they might live*. Oppenheim translates from the Babylonian: "Take my small child (daughter) and keep (her) alive (*bullutu*)! She shall be your small child ([slave]-girl). Give me x shekels of silver so that I may (have something to) eat (*akālu*)!"[290]

This sale contract was intended to keep both the sellers and the sold children alive. The prices given in the documents (sometimes they are left out) are extremely low: 6, 11, 12, 15, 22 shekels. During this time of need, one shekel would buy approximately one measure of barley, which was an extraordinarily high price (for barley). Selling a human being for a few measures of barley is evidence of an equally extraordinary emergency.

Two documents (NT 300 and NT 301) state: "During (the time when) the gate of Nippur was closed (and when) the equivalent (of what could be bought for one shekel of silver was) one sûtu of barley."[291]

This clearly makes links to the siege of Nippur, when the city gate was locked. During this time the price of barley exploded. Barley was always worth less than wheat, which presumably became utterly unaffordable during this period.

Another document states: "PN, my husband, went to his fate. There is famine in the country ... and I have (therefore) marked my two small sons ... with the (brand in the form of the) star (of Ishtar) and dedicated them to the Lady-of-Uruk; do keep (them) alive, they shall be temple-slaves ... of the Lady-of-Uruk!"[292]

The sale of these small children was always concluded with a mention of the famine. This justified the sale. According to Oppenheim, it is a sign that, in a society in which parents do not normally sell their children, a transaction of this kind required an excuse. The price was also often left out of the contract (!), which presumably indicates the shame of selling one's children for a measure of barley. The mention of the emergency (instead of the price) defines the criteria for the sale: permitted under exceptional circumstances, normally immoral.

These sales did not lead to debt slavery. In this sense, the mothers were selling "voluntarily," i.e., certainly under the pressure of need, but not under pressure from a creditor. The sale is intended to lead to life—the child was sold so that it might live, so that it might continue to stay alive. Ninurta-uballit bought children in order to raise them. Later they could, for example, be married off and bring in a lucrative bride price, which would pay off his investment. Or the relatives could buy the child back, something that a few of the documents set down expressly. But the contracts make it clear that there were great differences in the besieged city: Ninurta-uballit obviously had enough grain to feed his own family and additional people. He was even able to capitalize on the hunger of others.

Cities were often besieged, but only rarely captured. The usual situation was rather the one we can observe in Nippur: in this period, Nippur was harshly besieged for six months by the Babylonian army under Nabopolassar—but was not taken. The army was suddenly withdrawn due to other events. However, it remains shocking that such a short siege could lead to such great famine and despair.

5.8 Caesarea, the imperial city

After these depressing digressions, we return to Peter in Joppa. He was hungry, saw a terrifying vision, and before he had time to understand it, a Roman centurion's men were on the doorstep. They brought an invitation, and accompanied Peter and some of the brothers and sisters to Caesarea. After a day's walk they arrived in the port city (Acts 10:23). In Caesarea, Acts 10:1 tells us, there lived a Roman centurion (commander of a century, i.e., a captain), who was on good terms with the Jewish community (10:2).

In Caesarea there were a great deal of military. The Roman garrisons were sited here. Caesarea Maritima (Caesarea-by-the-Sea; there were several cities named after Caesar) was an imperial city, which Herod had developed (between 22 and 9 BCE) and dedicated to Caesar Augustus. Herod made the formerly Phoenician town into a magnificent Roman metropolis, reinforced the port facilities, and established Roman amenities such as a theatre, a hippodrome, and much more, so that in a short time the population had grown to 100,000 people.[293] The Roman administration of Judea resided here as well.[294]

Caesarea had a long, peaceful heyday. But around 50 CE, tensions between Jews and non-Jews grew, between the pro-Roman and anti-Roman population.[295] About 60 CE there were large-scale pogroms and riots in the city; from here the wave of actual violence, which led to open war against Rome, kicked off. In Caesarea there were mass crucifixions, and the Jewish quarters were plundered.[296]

Flavius Josephus tells of a dispute about a piece of land near the synagogue, which belonged to a Greek (i.e., a non-Jew). The Jewish congregation wanted to buy this land, to extend access to the synagogue. However, the Greek did not want to sell his land to the congregation, but started to erect buildings on it.[297] Overzealous members of the community attacked the construction workers, which led to further acts of violence. A pogrom swiftly erupted: over a few hours the people of Caesarea massacred 20,000 Jews, so that Caesarea was emptied of its Jewish inhabitants. Even those who ran away were pursued, and they were taken in chains to the galleys.[298]

The Jewish-Roman war accelerated the development of Caesarea. From 67 CE there were 60,000 soldiers stationed in the city, who needed to be fed and entertained. In July 69 CE, while at Caesarea, the commander, Vespasian, was proclaimed Emperor, which involved enormous celebrations. The soldiers received a gift and the city a new, privileged status: *Colonia Prima Flavia Augusta Caesarea*.

As the war reached its peak, hundreds of Jews died in the arenas and theatres of Caesarea, in combats with gladiators and wild animals.[299] Titus celebrated his brother's birthday in Caesarea by having Jewish prisoners executed. The destruction of Jerusalem in 70 CE ushered in Caesarea's golden era.

When Peter comes to Jerusalem, he is subjected to intensive questioning (Acts 11:3). The brothers and sisters want to know exactly what had happened in Caesarea. Had Peter eaten and drunk with the Romans? Had he done things together with them, while they were sending prophets to Antioch to organize support? Had he been able to agree to something with the heathen soldiers, something that would be useful to Jerusalem? Peter thereupon gives a detailed narration of his vision in Joppa. His horror at the impending famine is even more obvious here than in the first story. Peter makes it clear that he has not for one second forgotten his sisters and brothers in Jerusalem. He went to Caesarea full of care and hunger, but in the house of Cornelius he experienced surprising things (cf. Acts 11:17).

It is interesting that in Peter's visit to Jerusalem we find out nothing about the raging famine. Was there a famine in Jerusalem at all? If we did not know that the congregation in Jerusalem had sent out prophets, and that Herod had cracked down in Tyre and Sidon as well, we would be able to assume that everything in Jerusalem was in order: the text says nothing about the situation. But we now know that silence need not be read as reassurance. The anxious enquiries from the brothers and sisters about what had happened in Caesarea makes it clear that they were on edge.

This silence about the situation in Jerusalem has another effect as well: Jerusalem is not presented as a city to be pitied, as a victim, but as a place where people are still thinking and questioning. People here are thinking, questioning, talking, narrating, and rejoicing. We hear not a single word about the famine which, according to Josephus, had claimed thousands of lives in 67–70 CE. In the eyes of those who handed down this episode, Jerusalem appears as a place where Peter was able to formulate and reflect on his experience. The narrators remember Jerusalem before the siege, before the terrible breakdown of solidarity that the siege brought about. Jerusalem is not remembered as being hungry and suffering need. Jerusalem is the spiritual home of the community, the center of reflection and remembering, tightly woven into a net of solidarity and empathy. This memory may be accurate—or it can be read as utopic.

To summarize: The geography of the famine that took shape in Acts 9:33—12:17 encompassed a wide area, from little Joppa to the south of Caesarea, via Tyre and Sidon, up to rich Antioch, and down again to Jerusalem (see also Chapter 6). This sketches for us not just an area of famine, but also reports on communities that organized their survival during this period: paths are struck, support is fetched. People do not wait passively for the famine. The widows in Joppa send to Lydda for Peter, the congregation in Jerusalem sends prophets to far-off, wealthy Antioch. The people in Tyre and Sidon negotiate with Blastus, the king's chamberlain, to avert the worst. GOD sends her messengers to Cornelius in Caesarea. Cornelius has Peter and the brothers and sisters fetched from Joppa.

Thus, these chapters tell of hunger and of the counterforces that are mobilized. The heavens open—GOD sends down a tablecloth full of living creatures, for he is a GOD of the hungry and knows about their distress. The spirit of GOD acts in the communities, and takes care of connections and solidarity and rescue measures.

These chapters are not about overcoming the Jewish dietary laws, or about transforming Judaism in the direction of Christianity. The discussions about demarcation should no longer be brought to bear on this text; they obstruct our access to the reality of both then and now. Survival is, after all, a question of solidarity. These chapters of Acts show that GOD is there where people act in solidarity, where they transcend boundaries and go long distances so that they might live. This is not the time for debates about demarcation and purity.

The communities surrounding Peter and his brothers and sisters prove that they can survive in difficult times, because they are connected to the communities in Judea and elsewhere. This interconnectedness is based on the biblical belief in the one GOD, whose Spirit mobilizes, arouses mercy, and makes cohesion possible across wide distances.

6.

Good Deeds in Times of Hunger

(ACTS 10—11:28)[300]

Acts 10–12 covers a wide narrative scope. Geographically, it encompasses several hundred square kilometers, from little Joppa in the south of Caesarea, via Tyre and Sidon, up to prosperous Antioch, and down again to Jerusalem. Its contents are also substantial, which is why we must revisit a few scenes and verses of this narrative context.

Above all, I would like this further round of analysis to include the Jewish tradition of the righteous. This, too, determines how food is treated: the righteous donate food from their surplus and share their bread with the hungry. We shall see that a reading also has to include the Roman-Hellenistic ideal of benefactors, of *liberalitas*, the politically accepted form of generosity. How do the two systems of righteous Jews and of Roman benefactors relate to one another? What did the Roman authorities do, and those who called themselves patrons, in times of hunger? For biblical faith it is of utmost importance to ask: what do the well-fed do for the hungry? Where can the hungry find support? What can they rely on?

6.1 Links

In the preceding chapter we looked at a vision that the hungry Peter had, and which horrified him (Acts 10:14). We compared his revulsion with that of Ezekiel, who envisioned the siege of Jerusalem and associated with it a catastrophic famine approaching the city (Ezek 4:14). Later, Agabus uttered the word "famine" (*limos*, Acts 11:28). His prophecy resulted in an act of solidarity in rich Antioch.

Hunger brackets Acts 10–12, though it is barely addressed. Yet the hermeneutic of hunger reflects this silence about hunger, particularly the silence of those who know hunger, because famine can only ever be talked about negatively, even if, or precisely because it is lurking in the background. My liberation-theology perspective, which is sensitized towards hunger, focuses on the fatal sickness of Tabitha in Joppa, the unrest in Tyre and Sidon, Herod's brutal crackdown, and the diplomatic steps taken by the Jewish community towards the king's chamberlain Blastus, as visible consequences of the famine.

The hermeneutic of hunger reads Peter's vision in Joppa against the backdrop of famine, which is explicitly named in 10:10. Peter receives an answer to his prayer. In his ecstasy he sees something that has to do with his hunger and the hunger of his people. I put the reading of this vision socio-historically in the category of a time of famine, which 11:28 describes as extending throughout the world. Hunger is the golden thread running through Acts 10–12, and thus also the thread that we must not lose sight of when decoding this vision of Peter's.

In the Christian interpretation, on the other hand, Peter's vision and his subsequent stay with the Roman centurion are read in an anti-Judaistic hermeneutic, against a negative backdrop: the Jews had not acknowledged Christ. Instead, they stubbornly observed their law and refused liberation from it by not accepting the gospel. Peter, so this interpretation continues, had been instructed by GOD in his vision to cast off Jewish dietary laws (*kashrut*). He was thus able to accept the centurion's invitation to go to Caesarea and to eat with him there. Peter ate with Gentiles because GOD had ordered it, which offended the community of believers in Jerusalem (Acts 11:2) and created conflict. In this interpretation, GOD did away with the Jewish dietary laws, and abolished the difference between Jews and Gentiles.[301]

That it could actually be about such concrete things as hunger and food appears impossible in the ideologically charged hermeneutic of demarcation. But food lies at the core of communities: at the table it is decided who may or can eat with whom, and who is excluded. At the table hierarchies are confirmed or undermined, standards affirmed or called into question. At the table there are fights, experiments, and celebrations. The community constitutes itself through shared meals—or is undermined if the food is not shared fairly or at least handed out in a reasonable way. In the Christian exegesis tainted with anti-Judaism, the story is essentially about overcoming Judaism, and about distancing oneself from it, or about mission in the sense of proselytizing individuals or communities.

It is time we got rid of the old trench warfare between religions (Peter overcomes his Jewish background; Cornelius becomes the first Gentile Christian), which makes us blind to interreligious connections that were and still are vital. It is not the observation of imposed laws that helped or help us—and neither is it the freedom to do whatever one likes—but a lively engagement with things that are essential to us, matters of life and death, things that affect us fundamentally. Having to change one's diet—e.g., suddenly having to eat insects or rats—doesn't just provoke disgust, but challenges our identity: we feel humiliated, abased. We aren't barbarians! We don't eat such things! Disgust says a lot about what we consider valid and what we fundamentally reject. This applies also to the emerging, important discussion about vegetarian or vegan food culture. Industrial food production is accused of barbarism; "inhumane" livestock farming and "meat production" calls forth abhorrence. How can Christian people still enjoy eggs from battery hens? What processes of demarcation prevent our acknowledging the living conditions of animals?

These discussions about what we put on the table help establish our culture, since they name our values and have the ability to change or reinforce our behavior. They also clarify how we understand ourselves within traditions we have adopted. Whether we insist on having the right to eat everything, however it is produced, or whether we align ourselves with another tradition that upholds moderation and particular ethical values, whether solidarity with countries of the southern hemisphere becomes visible on our table, or whether we do not even want to reflect on our eating behavior—these discussions circle around our identity as people, Christians, humanists, and affect our actions towards other living creatures and other people.

Discussions about safeguarding humanity—as sketched by the Torah—are reflected in Peter's vision and his revulsion (Acts 10:10f). This is about one's own identity within the adopted tradition. These traditions quite centrally include the Torah: in Peter's oppressive circumstances, the Torah is gauged against the hunger and injustice he is experiencing. What does it have to say about the frightening situation in which he finds himself? Where do the communities find GOD in the face of hunger?

6.2 Cornelius—Jew or Gentile or what?

There is much to read in the Bible commentaries about Peter as a Jew (or Jewish Christian) going into a Gentile household and eating there. This places the focus on Gentile Christianity free of the law, i.e., no longer observing the Jewish commandments (see Chapter 5, above). Cornelius is viewed as a Gentile who has converted to Christianity without being circumcised, while Peter has had to jettison the dietary laws so that he is able to eat in the house of Cornelius the Gentile.[302]

This interpretation takes seriously the question of the community in Jerusalem, who heard of the visit to Caesarea (11:1) and now want to know from Peter what precisely happened: "Why did you go to uncircumcised men and eat with them?" (11:3). This question makes it possible for us to presume that Peter and those who had accompanied him from Joppa received something to eat, as Acts 10 does not describe this controversial shared meal itself.

And yet this interpretation does entail some problems: it focuses on the separation of (Christian) Jews and (Christian) Gentiles and it dates this extremely early historically. It also leaves out the political and social context of hunger. Acts does not specify whether Cornelius was a "Gentile" or not. Cornelius lived in the emperor's city Caesarea, and was in the Roman service—both of these would explain the question posed by the Jerusalem congregation. Because living "among the nations" demands that Jewish people conform socially, in a way that is visible precisely at the dinner table.

The question the community in Jerusalem raised becomes all the more understandable if we consider that, at the time Acts was drafted, Jerusalem had been destroyed by the very Roman cohorts stationed in the port and garrison city of Caesarea. We can certainly assume that the brothers and sisters in Jerusalem felt some aversion towards the residents of Caesarea, who had massacred the city's Jewish community in a bloody pogrom (before the outbreak of the Jewish-Roman war). They may also have been hostile towards a city that profited in many ways from the downfall of Jerusalem, and advanced and blossomed during and after the war (see Chapter 5, above). That Peter went to this hated city, and even enjoyed table fellowship with people who may have taken part in pogroms and war, would of course have been difficult for the brothers and sisters to stomach.

I find it problematic when exegetes interpret the distrust and the distance of the community in Jerusalem (Acts 1:3) towards the inhabitants of the coastal area and of Caesarea as due to "Jewish superiority, privilege and exclusivism,"[303] and thus blank out the context of war and pogrom. The brutal pogrom against the Jewish population of Caesarea took place in 66 CE—i.e., only twenty years after the famine in the 40s, which is referenced here in Acts 10–12. But for the first readers of Acts, which is mostly dated around 80–100 CE, the pogrom was a fact like the Jewish-Roman war, and influenced their perspective in reading it. We should not therefore overlook either—the pogrom or the war—when reading this chapter.

> 1 In Caesarea there was a man named Cornelius, a centurion of the Italian Cohort, as it was called. 2 He was a devout man who feared God with all his household; he gave alms generously to the people and prayed constantly to God. 3 One afternoon at about three o'clock he had a vision in which he clearly saw an angel of God coming in and saying to him, "Cornelius." 4 He stared at him in terror and said, "What is it, Lord?" He answered, "Your prayers and your alms have ascended as a memorial before God. 5 Now send men to Joppa for a certain Simon who is called Peter; 6 he is lodging with Simon, a tanner, whose house is by the seaside" (Acts 10:1–6).

Cornelius is attached to the Jewish community in Caesarea. He is pious and prays to the God of Israel—not just occasionally, but "constantly," i.e., in all things his prayers are directed towards the God of Israel. He gives alms generously (v. 2), and these alms are known unto GOD (v. 4). He is therefore connected to the community, not just secretly or inwardly, but also outwardly, practically, helping the community (cf. Luke 7:5). Shaye J. D. Cohen lists three elements showing that someone belongs to the Jewish community: observance (i.e., practicing the Jewish laws), exclusively worshipping the Jewish God, and being integrated into the Jewish community. Cornelius fulfils these three elements. The text says nothing about how Cornelius views himself, or whether the community considered him a Jew, whether the brothers and sisters in Jerusalem viewed him as a proselyte (i.e., someone who has converted) or as a Jew in the Diaspora ("among the nations").[304]

The "unambiguous" criteria for being Jewish had not yet been defined when Acts was written.[305] Acts of the Apostles introduces Cornelius through his connection to Israel—whether he "really" was a Jew (through birth to a Jewish mother, or through conversion with circumcision, immersion, and acceptance by the local community, as rabbinic Judaism later ordered) or a sympathizer who occasionally went to the synagogue, observed the Sabbath and worshipped the God of Israel, is not stated. Cornelius prayed to the God of Israel, he gave alms to the synagogue community, and in verse 2 he is described as righteous and God-fearing.[306] The text thus encourages us to think of Cornelius in close relationship with the Jewish community, despite being a Roman centurion in the imperial city Caesarea.[307]

6.3 A centurion who has visions

Cornelius had a profession and a corresponding social position. He was stationed in Caesarea, a city with a distinctive history. He prayed to the God of Israel and had visions. I would like to investigate this step by step.

> 3 One afternoon at about three o'clock he had a vision in which he clearly saw an angel of God coming in and saying to him, "Cornelius." 4 He stared at him in terror and said, "What is it, Lord?" He answered, "Your prayers and your alms have ascended as a memorial before God" (Acts 10:3–4).

Cornelius saw how an *angelos* (the Greek word merely means "messenger")[308] from God came to him, and he heard the message. The dialogue between the two is described precisely. Where exactly this afternoon encounter took place,[309] we do not find out. Cornelius was also given a mission: to send for Peter from Joppa (Acts 10:5–6). Just these few verses were probably enough to shake the contemporary readers' concept of a centurion. Cornelius is depicted as a centurion who prays and has visions. The commander of a century, he receives an order himself and carries it out unquestioningly.

Following hungry Peter's vision (Acts 10:10–16), the two storylines of Cornelius in Caesarea and Peter in Joppa come together. Cornelius' soldiers stand in front of the tanner's house, where Peter is a guest.

> 17 Now while Peter was greatly puzzled about what to make of the vision that he had seen, suddenly the men sent by Cornelius appeared. They were asking for Simon's house and were standing by the gate. 18 They called out to

ask whether Simon, who was called Peter, was staying there. 19 While Peter was still thinking about the vision, the Spirit said to him, "Look, three men are searching for you. 20 Now get up, go down, and go with them without hesitation; for I have sent them." 21 So Peter went down to the men and said, "I am the one you are looking for; what is the reason for your coming?" 22 They answered, "Cornelius, a centurion, an upright and God-fearing man, who is well spoken of by the whole Jewish nation, was directed by a holy angel to send for you to come to his house and to hear what you have to say." 23 So Peter invited them in and gave them lodging (Acts 10:17–23).

The fact that Roman soldiers from Caesarea are standing at the door is explained carefully to Peter by the Spirit. Having soldiers at the door can be frightening. Either they are searching for food—by force if necessary—or they have been ordered to pick someone up. The Spirit tells Peter that this latter is the case, but he should not worry about it. So Peter is not being detained or arrested, but invited. For Peter this was something that needed explanation. For safety's sake, he asks the soldiers about it (v. 21).

This intermezzo shows us how unusual a friendly invitation from a centurion must have been for Peter—and for contemporary readers. This makes it clear once again that the cultural distance between Joppa and Caesarea, between the tanner's simple house and the Roman centurion, must have been great.

6.4 Generosity versus *liberalitas*

What did the rulers—whether Caesar, his vassals (e.g., the royal family of a province), or the Roman administrative authorities of a city—do when a famine started to emerge in a region or a city? Using this question, I would like to probe the social history and political background of our story.

The Roman emperor promoted himself as a great benefactor. But his charity was the expression of political calculation, and less of philanthropy. "Bread and circuses" was a governing principle of the Roman imperial era. The rulers had themselves celebrated as benefactors; their munificence (*liberalitas*) integrated them into the system: festivals, gifts, and grain distribution marked them as potent pillars of society. *Euergetism* (from the Greek: "doing good deeds") meant that rich citizens marked their claim to leadership of a particular community by distributing part of their wealth—funding games, donating grain, erecting public buildings such as baths, theatres, and aqueducts.[310] Such donations were not least the expression of aristocratic rivalry.

Angela Standhartinger speaks of meal distribution at festivals that was a sign of *liberalitas*, and grain distribution that emperors and other benefactors regularly carried out.[311] Grain distribution was intended for the citizens' basic supply, and also helped candidates for office to win the hearts and minds of the people.[312] However, "the citizens" were not those in need, but members of privileged families entitled to receive particular quantities of grain. The poor, the slaves, and travelers presumably also occasionally received something when grain was distributed, but actually they were not in the benefactors' sights, as the Roman system of meal distribution reproduced the hierarchical society rather than correcting it.[313]

Cities with direct access to the sea (such as Antioch and Caesarea Maritima) could look after themselves more easily than landlocked cities (such as Jerusalem). They were able to buy shiploads of grain, while the cities inland had to organize insecure and expensive transport. The greater the food shortage, the longer and more expensive the transport routes became. Peter Garnsey points out that a further factor should be included: if the authorities acted quickly, they could import grain at a low price. The longer they watched to see how the shortage developed, the more expensive the import. But it is evident that this waiting was often a calculation, since rising prices meant greater profits could be made. Garnsey concludes that the rich therefore often brought their grain stocks to the market late, so that they could demand horrendous prices.[314]

How did the emperors react to famines? Very little is recorded about this. It appears to be an exception that in 19 CE, the emperor Tiberius reacted to a rise in the price of wheat by fixing a maximum price and compensating traders for their losses. In 6 CE, Augustus had expelled the gladiators, slaves brought in for sale and foreigners; he packed senators and their entourages off to their estates, rationed grain in the city, and cut back on expensive celebrations.[315] But Garnsey notes that such measures are unique in the historical record of Rome. In 32 CE, reports of popular protest at the price of wheat reached Tiberius: he chided the Senate for not disciplining the populace. But beyond this, Tiberius did nothing to alleviate the food shortage.

Euergetism as a state-forming principle did not mean support for the general public in time of need. It was indeed part of the ruling ideology in antiquity to refer to the wise provision of goods, which the rulers obtained from the provinces. But this provision took place one-sidedly with regard to the conquerors and their endless rapacity,[316] not with regard to the people of the provinces.[317]

The ruling class, whose self-perception was very remote from the masses, felt continually threatened by the population at large. This explains the systematic violence with which the popular masses were treated. The nobility constructed relationships of dependency—patronage—to consolidate loyalty from the lower classes towards the higher ones, "for safety." A patron could rally tenants, freedmen, associations, and communities of all kinds around him, and benefit them in various ways in order to ensure their loyalty. For example, a wealthy *popularis* (descendant of the non-gentry) was able to tie his hungry clientele to him by freely distributing grain. They would, so to speak, eat out of his hand.

Whether a *popularis* like Julius Caesar provided benefits out of genuine sympathy for the needy or out of an ambition to mobilize the political power of a crowd in the streets was a matter of vivid debate and partisan accusation in his own day.[318] His willingness to provide the masses with food and cancel their debts may however have contributed to his murder (in 44 BCE); although it achieved broad support from the people, it was also a power factor, and a cause of rivalry.

6.5 Two benefactors: Spurius Maelius and Marcus Sulpicius Felix

The city of Rome in the time of Augustus had a population of about a million to feed—a number that no European city reached again until the nineteenth century. It was the provinces that fed Rome and the Roman Army of approximately 300,000 or 400,000 men.

Any surplus that the farmers produced in good crop years were squeezed out of the provinces and consumed by the capital city, by the court, the administration, and the military. Stocks, seed reserves, secure supply routes, protection against speculation with seed—these were unheard of in the provinces. It was not the State's duty to provide for the population in bad times.

Sometimes there were rich people who opened up their granaries and sold their grain, instead of hoarding it as usual and selling it only later at the highest prices. More rarely, there were *euergetes*, benefactors who let the people buy cheaply, or helped them out. The Roman administration considered these good deeds benefiting the masses to be politically motivated, and feared they would stir up the people against their rightful rulers.

The Roman historian Livy[319] gives an account of Spurius Maelius, a Roman equestrian who distributed grain free to the hungry masses.[320] The people cheered him, but the authorities were unhappy to see this capriciousness. Maelius was murdered on the orders of the dictator Q. Cincinnatus, and his house destroyed.[321] Spurius Maelius had overstepped his role as a private patron at the point when he "served" not just his own clientele but also those of other patrons—even though they were doing nothing to combat hunger. His actions were criticized as populism and aiming at tyranny, and his fate was read widely as a cautionary tale.

The cities in the provinces had to fend for themselves in times of famine, and depended on rich citizens as potential benefactors. For these citizens it was a political tightrope walk to support their city, without crossing someone more powerful. Support was generally reserved for those with citizenship of that particular city; they had the backup from the leading families, so that they were able to provide charity, within certain limits, whenever they wanted.

An inscription on a column from Sala (now Chellah, Morocco, ca. 144 CE) is one remarkable exception, as the benefactor it names is a Roman prefect, i.e., not a scion of the city. Marcus Sulpicius Felix was part of the Roman occupational force and yet he still helped the population in need, by taking supplies from the troops and giving them to the city. A translation of the inscription, which is on a stone column, reads:

Rage in the Belly

> For Marcus Sulpicius Felix, son of Marcus, from Rome, of the tribe of Quirinus, our liberator and patron, Prefect of the first cohort of Germans, military tribune of the sixteenth Legion [named] Flavia Firma Fidelis, military tribune of the third Ulpian cohort of Petraeus (comprising 1000 men), who was elected and retained in order to collect duties in part of the province of Armenia, as well as Cappadocia, equestrian prefect of the second wing of the Roman citizens from Syria, because of his genuine commitment to the city of Sala, his friends have dedicated [this statue] and attached the decree of the decurions.[322]

This inscription introduces Marcus Sulpicius Felix according to his military career: he was Prefect of the first cohort of Germans and a cavalry officer of the second wing of Rome's Syrian citizens. Nevertheless, he was active in Sala, in North Africa, as liberator and patron. Lines 15 and 16 of the inscription then mention his charitable acts:

> . . . or that he encompassed the city at its rather vulnerable points with a very great wall, but at very little cost, or that, during prohibitive difficulties in the grain supply, he left most of the abundance of his provisions to our advantage yet without detriment to his soldiers.[323]

Among other things, the prefect fortified the city by building the city wall. He also helped the city "during prohibitive difficulties in the grain supply." These two phrases indicate how valuable his commitment to the city was. Without the wall, it was defenseless against looting. Without a secure grain supply the city's population was vulnerable to speculators and to hunger. His intervention probably prevented riots in Sala.[324] The words of this inscription are chosen carefully. It states expressly that the prefect never neglected his troops—presumably for his own protection from his superiors.

6.6 Cornelius, centurion of the Italian cohort

We can compare the inscription on the column in Chellah with the description of the centurion Cornelius in Acts. Like Marcus Sulpicius Felix, Cornelius is described according to his military career, and to what he had done.

> 1 In Caesarea there was a man named Cornelius, a centurion of the Italian Cohort, as it was called. 2 He was a devout man who feared God with all his household; he gave alms generously to the people and prayed constantly to God (Acts 10:1–2).

He was commander of a century of soldiers from the Italian cohort. The mention of his good deeds also reminds us of the liberator and patron Marcus Sulpicius Felix, who acted in the interests of the city's population. Cornelius acted in the interests of the Jewish population in Caesarea, which had grown quite large before the war.[325]

I believe we can even recognize a third correspondence between the details in Acts and the ancient inscription: the careful choice of words, so as not to create a pitfall for the cherished prefect, can also be found in Acts 10:7–8, when Cornelius selected his best men and briefed them cautiously:

> 7 When the angel who spoke to him had left, he called two of his slaves and a devout soldier from the ranks of those who served him, 8 and after telling them everything, he sent them to Joppa (Acts 10:7–8).

Cornelius did not just send any three soldiers, but selected his messengers with care. His intentions must not be misinterpreted as political meddling, and he therefore explained "everything" to them precisely. The expression "a devout soldier" is itself noteworthy and indicates that Cornelius was instructing a soldier who had an equally unspoiled relationship to the Jewish community, or who may even have been Jewish.

The Prefect of Sala had access to the troops' food supplies. It is reasonable to assume that, as a centurion, Cornelius would also have had access to food supplies for his century in the port city of Caesarea. It was thus invaluable for the synagogue community to have a centurion as their benefactor during a food crisis.

But why did Cornelius send for Peter? The envoys kept this under cover and said only that Cornelius wanted to hear what Peter had to say (Acts 10:22).[326] Of course Peter would go with them, even if they gave no reason: an invitation from a centurion in Caesarea is not something to turn down unpunished.[327]

When Peter came to Caesarea, Cornelius was waiting for him, together with his relations and close friends. The centurion approached him, "fell at his feet and worshipped him" (vv. 24–25). The text emphasizes that the Roman officer, whose place in the social hierarchy was way above the fisherman from Galilee, paid respect to him in his own house. Cornelius justified this by saying that a man[328] had assured him that his prayers and good deeds would come before GOD. He should send for Peter—which he did at once (vv. 31–33).

6.7 A just man in Caesarea

Cornelius did not behave in a way that conformed to his position in the Roman hierarchy. His hospitality was based on listening to GOD (10:2), not on the Roman ideal of *liberalitas*.

> 34 Then Peter began to speak to them: "I truly understand that God shows no partiality, 35 but in every nation anyone who fears him and does what is right is acceptable to him" (Acts 10:34–35).

Cornelius fears GOD and makes efforts to do what is right. The reception that he and his household prepared must surely have surprised Peter. Here, we hear for the fourth time about the alms and the righteous deeds of Cornelius (vv. 2, 4, 31, 35). Thus, Acts of the Apostles presents Cornelius in line with the Jewish ideal of the righteous. A just man (v. 22 KJV) gives the needy what they need—bread for the hungry, a blanket for the naked, etc.[329] According to the Torah, these people are entitled to receive the basic necessities of life. The ideal of a righteous person thus goes beyond family solidarity and also includes support for strangers and prisoners.

Cornelius' good deeds for the needy made room for them in his vision of a good life; he did not limit these good deeds to his own social class. His family and his closest friends knew about this, since he had rallied them around him while waiting for Peter. Cornelius is thus showing that he has not had to act in secret, but in consensus with his household. So his household was prepared to share in his good works, or at least, they did not reject his ideal of justice and solidarity.

Doing good works correlates with the divine image in the Jewish tradition: it is a mark or a reflection of GOD's mercy.[330] While acts of charity from a Roman citizen generally reflect the *liberalitas* of the system, or the "munificence" of the wealthy towards people like themselves,[331] the actions of the just are directed towards the needy and the wretched, towards widows and orphans, strangers, and the naked (who really did have hardly anything with which to cover themselves).

The Bible abounds with images for doing good, for giving alms, and for exercising justice. Tabitha, the disciple Peter awakened in Joppa, was also characterized by her good deeds:

> 36 She was devoted to good works and acts of charity (Acts 9:36).

For this, Tabitha was given the honorary title "disciple," and Cornelius the honorary title "righteous man."[332] Both are part of the same tradition of showing neighborliness, which also includes, for example, Tobit and Job:

> I, Tobit, walked in the ways of truth and righteousness all the days of my life. I performed many acts of charity for my kindred and my people who had gone with me in exile to Nineveh in the land of the Assyrians (Tob 1:3).

> 16 Give some of your food to the hungry, and some of your clothing to the naked. Give all your surplus as alms, and do not let your eye begrudge your giving of alms. 17 Place your bread on the grave of the righteous, but give none to sinners . . . 19 At all times bless the Lord God, and ask him that your ways may be made straight and that all your paths and plans may prosper (Tob 4:16–17, 19).[333]

> 12 Because I delivered the poor who cried,
> and the orphan who had no helper.
> 13 The blessing of the wretched came upon me,
> and I caused the widow's heart to sing for joy . . .

> 16 I was a father to the needy,
>
> and I championed the cause of the stranger (Job 29:12–13, 16).

And Job cursed himself in case he had not acted righteously, saying:

> "If I have withheld anything that the poor desired,
>
> or have caused the eyes of the widow to fail,
>
> 17 or have eaten my morsel alone,
>
> and the orphan has not eaten from it" (Job 31:16–17).

For these benefactors—Job, Tobit, Tabitha, and Cornelius—piety and practice belong together; they live by the Torah, they practice the Jewish tradition of giving alms to the poor, which in that era had no parallels in the surrounding world.

6.8 Thanks from Peter's mouth

The social reversal that Cornelius introduced, by bending the knee to his social inferior, Peter, brings fruits: Peter does not appear as a needy beneficiary of alms, but as a wise teacher who is generous with his knowledge. In his welcome to Peter, Cornelius has acted righteously according to the Torah—for which he would not expect gratitude.

In the house of Cornelius, Peter opened his mouth (*anoixas to stoma*, v. 34). This phrase appears in the King James Version but was lost from later English translations—a telling phrase, especially for someone who was still very hungry. It therefore seems a pity to translate it simply as "he spoke." Readers who know about Peter's hunger in Joppa (Acts 10:10) would expect that he opened his mouth finally to eat. But the text makes no allusion to hunger or food. Peter opens his mouth—and words flow out of it. Peter allows them to flow, to gush forth as if generated by the Spirit, as they did with the prophet Ezekiel, who opened his mouth to speak the truth, which was full of pain and suffering:

> 2:8 But you, mortal, hear what I say to you; do not be rebellious like that rebellious house; open your mouth and eat what I give you. 9 I looked, and a hand was stretched out to me, and a written scroll was in it. 10 He spread it before me; it had writing on the front and on the back, and written on it were words of lamentation and mourning and woe.
>
> 3:1 He said to me, O mortal, eat what is offered to you; eat this scroll, and go, speak to the house of Israel. 2 So I opened my mouth, and he gave me the scroll to eat. 3 He said to me, Mortal, eat this scroll that I give you and fill your stomach with it. Then I ate it; and in my mouth it was as sweet as honey (Ezek 2:8—3:3).

Peter's speech is related to Ezekiel's opening his mouth. Just like Ezekiel, Peter suffers from hunger, and understands that a much greater and more severe famine will come upon everyone. Ezekiel had to prophesy this precisely. At this point, Peter understands his vision of the animals (Acts 10:11–16).

What Peter said had great consequences in the house of Cornelius. It brought something about. It wasn't just words, but words with power to reach the listeners and move them to become active. So Peter opened his mouth and spoke:

> 36 The word which God sent unto the children of Israel, preaching peace by Jesus Christ: (he is Lord of all:)
>
> 37 That word, I say, ye know, which was published throughout all Judea, and began from Galilee, after the baptism which John preached;
>
> 38 How God anointed Jesus of Nazareth with the Holy Ghost and with power: who went about doing good, and healing all that were oppressed of the devil; for God was with him (Acts 10:36–38 KJV).

Peter begins his speech with: "The word which God sent"—We can find this expression in Ps 107:20 as well:

> 18 they loathed any kind of food,
>
> and they drew near to the gates of death.
>
> 19 Then they cried to the LORD in their trouble,
>
> and he saved them from their distress;
>
> 20 he sent out his word and healed them,
>
> and delivered them from destruction (Ps 107:18–20).

Psalm 107 is a song of thanksgiving from people who have experienced hunger and repression.[334] The people suffered "trouble" (v. 2), they "wandered in desert wastes" (v. 4), were "hungry and thirsty" (v. 5), "they loathed any kind of food" (v. 18). With this, Psalm 107 opens up the same context that we have seen for Ezekiel (Ezek 4:14) and Peter (Acts 10:14): a famine that forces people to change their diet and eat disgusting things. This clarifies the particular level of food crisis.[335] Peter's speech of thanks notably echoes this song of thanksgiving from hungry people.

"Sending out the word" in both Acts 10:36 and Ps 107:20 means sensing the healing presence of GOD in a time of great need. This presence can manifest itself in bread, in grain, in life-giving rain, in support and help of all kinds, giving the needy relief or even satiety, healing, or vitality (Ps 107:9, 20). The psalm describes the situation as being marked by hunger and violence, so that the oppressed cry out to GOD (compare Ezek 2:8—3:3). The psalm reminds us of the faithfulness of GOD, who keeps his word. He heals their suffering and lets them arise out of their deathly agony. He proves to be a God who takes the side of the hungry, appreciates their need, and helps them.

We have seen above that Peter was hungry in Joppa, and that he was disgusted by the food his vision foretold, allowing him to gauge the extent of the famine (Acts 10:10–15). But now Peter has recognized that GOD has sent her word, and sees her steadfast faithfulness in Cornelius having brought him and his companions to his house from Joppa. Here, in this house, Peter experiences healing and new life, fullness and peace. The experience of hunger is not named expressly, but still provides the basic tenor of the story.

As well as the reference to Ps 107, which introduces the context of hunger and violence, and a wording reminiscent of Ezekiel's, in which he "opened his mouth" and received the power of the Spirit so as to complain (Ezek 2:8; 3:2), we also find a further expression, which we have already discussed in connection with hunger: the devil (*diabolos*, v. 38).[336] The term "devil" captures the degrading violence and dehumanizing power of hunger. Experiences of hunger and violence are devilish, because they draw people into their deadly sphere, into the shadow of death, making them suffer, debasing them.

Acts only touches lightly on hunger at this point, without letting it have its say. But we find intertextual references with the wording from Ps 107:20 and Ezek 3:2. Hunger, suffering and violence are referenced in a concealed way using the mythical name *diabolos*. Peter opens his mouth like Ezekiel, yet out of his mouth we hear not complaints but the thanks of a hungry man.

6.9 Jesus the benefactor

Peter reminds them of what happened in Judea:

> 37 That message spread throughout Judea, beginning in Galilee after the baptism that John announced: 38 how God anointed Jesus of Nazareth with the Holy Spirit and with power; how he went about doing good [*euergeton*] and healing all who were oppressed by the devil, for God was with him (Acts 10:37–38).

What is Peter referring to here? We should not jump too quickly to understanding this in terms of traditional theological language as "GOD's salvation through Christ." It is primarily about the movement associated with John the Baptist. John called the people out to the Jordan—when the autumn rains had, yet again, failed to materialize, the streams had dried up, and even the Jordan had become a trickle. As we saw in Chapter 3, John called angrily upon them to come to their senses and turn back: "You brood of vipers! Who warned you to flee from the wrath to come?" (Luke 3:7). The hope for reconciliation gathered the population out there with John, who urged them to confess their sins, to turn back again and be immersed in the Jordan so that GOD would bring about a new beginning and allow rain to fall.[337] It appears to me that linking Peter's to John the Baptist's movement, and the years of hardship when the *diabolos* had laid his iron hand upon the population, forms an important bridge to the present situation.

Let us look once again at how things had begun with John, which Peter is referring to here. An ominous shadow had been cast over the people. This is why, in the land of the shadow of death, John called for this baptism/immersion, so that their relationship to GOD would regain its balance, and the people would once again be able to eat their fill. The absence of rainfall had brought about a drought, a food shortage, that hit the poor the hardest. But the rain stayed away, because GOD did not allow it to rain—or at least, this is how the prophecy is interpreted: justice had to be restored in the relationships between people, had to be a part of the political system in the first place, otherwise the heavens would remain closed and the devil wreak havoc.

John called upon the people to do their part for reconciliation, so that GOD would open the heavens again. Many allowed him to immerse (baptize) them—even Jesus took a step towards GOD, ready to start again. Thereupon, GOD anointed him with the holy power of the Spirit. Now the healing presence of GOD started to become perceptible, visible, tangible. Jesus went about doing good—for GOD was with him.

Thus we have both sides in view: the violence and the terrible need, which Peter summarizes as "the devil," which lies like a leaden shadow upon the land—and John, who pits himself against this shadow, and Jesus, who does much good—*euergeton* (Acts 10:38). Peter describes Jesus here as a benefactor. The author of both of Luke's works (the books of Luke and Acts) is alone in the New Testament in using this expression. At a time when the emperor and kings, princes and commanders called themselves *euergetes*, the New Testament Scriptures are evidently very reticent in using this expression.[338]

The author of Luke's two works mentions benefactors and good deeds in two further passages.

> 24 A dispute also arose among them as to which one of them was to be regarded as the greatest. 25 But he said to them, "The kings of the Gentiles lord it over them; and those in authority over them are called benefactors [*euergetai*]" (Luke 22:24–25).

> 9 "If we are questioned today because of a good deed [*euergesia*] done to someone who was sick and are asked how this man has been healed, 10 let it be known to all of you, and to all the people of Israel" (Acts 4:9–10).

In Luke 22:25, Luke criticizes the upper-class benefactors who refer to themselves as such, but who exercise violence. (The English translation ("authority") weakens the original Greek meaning and thus also Luke's criticism.) In Acts 4:9, it is again Peter who uses the word *euergesia*: the good deed consisted in healing a man. This good deed led to Peter's being accused, i.e., it aroused the authorities' distrust. This distrust of a self-proclaimed "benefactor" was widespread in the Roman State, as we saw in the story of Spurius Maelius (see above), who was murdered for being a populist.

So the author of Luke and Acts is criticizing the politically compliant use of the term, i.e., those wealthy "benefactors" who exercised violence under that guise, as well as the distrust of the elite who keep drawing attention to their good deeds and defending them. It is all the more noticeable, then, that Jesus is called *euergeton*. His good deeds are given by God, they hark back to Yhwh, who gives healing power and holy Spirit, peace and reconciliation. But those who know the Roman system of *euergetism* know that it is precisely these good deeds that led to Jesus being killed ("hanged on a tree," v. 39). So the characterization of Jesus as a "person who does good deeds" also includes the critical observation that a benefactor who takes care of poor people cannot remain unpunished in Roman society.

With the mention of "the devil," the power struggle becomes even more obvious: under this political system, hunger and violence spread in Palestine; the devil subjugated many people. Jesus stepped up against God's deadly adversary, the *diabolos*, with spiritual and transformational power (*dynamis*), and allowed justice to prevail. He was got rid of; yet God had him rise again on the third day.

> 37 That message spread throughout Judea, beginning in Galilee after the baptism that John announced: 38 how God anointed Jesus of Nazareth with the Holy Spirit and with power; how he went about doing good and healing all who were oppressed by the devil, for God was with him. 39 We are witnesses to all that he did both in Judea and in Jerusalem. They put him to death by hanging him on a tree; 40 but God raised him on the third day and allowed him to appear, 41 not to all the people but to us who were chosen by God as witnesses, and who ate and drank with him after he rose from the dead (Acts 10:37–41).

For Hosea, the consequence of turning back to the living God is revival on the second day and restoration on the third day: the defeated people will rise up and live (Hos 6:1–2).[339] Acts attaches importance to this third day (as does Luke 24:46) and thus also to the importance of reading Hos 6:2 alongside it. The rising of the people, of the defeated and wounded Israel are thus center stage: on the third day, the people will rise up and live—here, Hosea's promise, his vision streams out of the mouth of the hungry Peter.

To summarize: Peter reminds us of the starting point, the experience of privation under the devil's yoke, of how John the Baptist's movement at the Jordan began to reconcile with God and open the closed heavens. Jesus became a key figure: he was anointed with power so that he could do good among the people. But his *euergetism* as a benefactor of the poor of Israel was prohibited by the Roman system, and led to his death.

Peter ends his speech with the happy, amazed statement that it is still possible to experience this benefactor, to eat and drink with him like those "who ate and drank with him after he rose from the dead" (Acts 10:41). Here in Caesarea it is possible to see the Risen One, where people eat and drink with one another, where generosity abounds towards the hungry and needy, as it did in the house of Cornelius the righteous.

6.10 Charity from God's hand

Let us now re-examine Peter's vision in Joppa: it occupies an important place in this story, intensifying Peter's hope and despair. Intensification often takes place in images and metaphors; everyday language gives way to one interwoven with an invisible thread. With the necessary calm, we can feel our way through these threads and images once again.

> 11 And saw heaven opened, and a certain vessel descending upon him, as it had been a great sheet knit at the four corners, and let down to the earth:
>
> 12 Wherein were all manner of four-footed beasts of the earth, . . . and creeping things, and fowls of the air (Acts 10:11–12 KJV).[340]

I am astonished that the fisherman from the Sea of Galilee does not see any fish! Peter was living in Joppa, a little harbor town on the Mediterranean—the tanner's house was "by the seaside," as 10:6 tells us. Would fish not be the obvious thing to satisfy Peter's hunger? Unfortunately, we do not know what exactly was going on with fishing in Joppa at that time. Fishing rights lay with the Roman emperor, even in this part of the eastern Mediterranean.[341] The fishermen had to lease their right to fish: from the local community, the city, the temple, or the State. They often had to lease the nets or the boats as well, since they lacked the capital to buy them.[342] The idea that Simon the tanner could simply go and get a couple of fish out of the sea is therefore not appropriate. Fresh sea fish was expensive and ordinary people, including the tanner, were generally unable to afford it. But salt fish? Pickled, preserved fish? It may be assumed that during a general food shortage—i.e., a lack of grain—the prices for other goods rose as well, and ultimately there was a shortage of everything.

In any case, we cannot let this absence of fish in the vision pass without comment. It is, after all, a fisherman's vision. If he does not mention fish, there must be a reason for it. Let us note: Peter does not see fish in his vision, but he does see *tetrapoda* (four-footed creatures; livestock), *herpeta* (creeping things; reptiles), *peteina* (fowl of the air; birds). In the second mention of his vision, in Jerusalem, Peter supplements it with a fourth kind of animal: *theria* ("beasts of prey; wild beasts," Acts 11:5–6).

These four kinds of animal that Peter lists do not belong in the itemization of the dietary laws in Lev 11, although this is repeatedly claimed.[343] Lev 11 always mentions these animal types (as well as animals that live in water) in particular detail, since it lays down precisely when they are edible and when not. But they do not appear vaguely and generally, as they do here. On the other hand, we find the same vague listing of the four animal types in the book of Genesis. This opens up a different and unexpected view of these animals than the one in the dietary laws. The four animal types draw a picture of the good creation, in which all find food:

> 24 And God said, "Let the earth bring forth living creatures of every kind: cattle and creeping things and wild animals of the earth of every kind." And it

> was so. 25 God made the wild animals of the earth of every kind, and the cattle of every kind, and everything that creeps upon the ground of every kind. And God saw that it was good.
>
> 30 And to every beast of the earth, and to every bird of the air, and to everything that creeps on the earth, everything that has the breath of life [*nephesh*], I have given every green plant for food." And it was so (Gen 1:24–25, 30).

These animal types are created as living creatures on the fifth day. In verse 24 it is the earth that has brought them forth, in verse 25 it is GOD who has made them. The two processes of creation stand in parallel. GOD is pleased with this diversity of life, and in verse 30 GOD expressly mentions the green plants, which had already sprouted on the third day (!). Everything that has breath is to receive this vegetation as food. GOD gives the breath of life (Hebrew: *nephesh*) and the earth lets green plants grow—so that no one has to suffer hunger.

Thus, in mentioning these four types of animal, Peter's vision reminds us of the good creation. The God of Israel has created these living and breathing creatures. And in divine care, the earth brings forth food for all living creatures upon her. The fish are fed by the sea, not by the earth. They have no breath, *nephesh*. Herein lies the reason, I suspect, why they do not appear in the vision: they are different from the four types of breathing animal and different from humans. In this sense the earth is the great benefactor of all, and everything that has breath, all life—as well as the food it needs—comes from GOD's hand.

> 10 He became hungry and wanted something to eat; and while it was being prepared, he fell into a trance. 11 He saw the heaven opened and something like a large sheet coming down, being lowered to the ground by its four corners. 12 In it were all kinds of four-footed creatures and reptiles and birds of the air. 13 Then he heard a voice saying, "Get up, Peter; kill and eat." 14 But Peter said, "By no means, Lord; for I have never eaten anything that is abominable or unclean before God." 15 The voice said to him again, a second time, "What God has declared clean, you must not call abominable" (Acts 10:10–15, adapted from NRSV).

The vision—both visual and auditory—is ambiguous for Peter. While still plagued by hunger, he sees the heavens open, and something like a vessel or a sheet come down, on which are the three types of animal (or four, if we include Acts 11:5–6). But what he hears repulses him: he is supposed to slaughter these animals and eat them (v. 13). Most reptiles and birds, as well as many wild animals and domestic ones, do not belong to the diet of Peter and his people.

What happens on the auditory level (cf. Chapter 5) tells of the coming famine, which will force the community to eat abominable things. This perturbs Peter, and he vehemently refuses the horrifying demand. It is precisely this refusal that makes it clear to the readers that Peter has understood the announcement of a famine; his reaction is described similarly to that of the prophet Ezekiel, who responded with biting indignation to the announced famine.

And yet Peter still felt that he had not properly understood what he had seen in the vision (as distinct from what he had heard). Although he was painfully aware of the message about impending famine, he was still chewing over the images of this gift from heaven, this abundantly filled vessel (Acts 10:17, 19). Where were these heavenly vessels to be found during the famine?

Only in the hospitable house of Cornelius did Peter begin to understand (v. 34): the vision showed the *providentia* of GOD, the Creator's care and provision for his creations. GOD had sent his Word long ago—to Cornelius, to Jesus, who was anointed with the *dynamis*, the transformational energy of GOD, and to John, whose call on people to accept immersion initiated the movement to turn back to GOD. Long ago, the Creator had prepared *nephesh* (the breath of life, *pneuma*) and food (Gen 1:24f). GOD is a caring GOD, a beneficial GOD, as the Torah says. Even before Peter went up on the roof and started to pray, GOD had sent her word to Cornelius and brought about the rescue of the community in Joppa.

Peter was as yet unable to see this positive link. Only in Caesarea, encountering the hospitality of Cornelius, did he begin to understand what he had seen (10:34): the generosity of GOD. He saw the four kinds of animal of GOD's good creation.

The animals on a sheet-like vessel, which come to Peter from heaven, are from GOD's hand, and are in GOD's hand. They may be clean or unclean in terms of the dietary laws, they may taste good or bad to the palate or the stomach. They may be delicacies or they may be totally inedible: they share the same breath and food. These details may not be biologically correct, since the animals' food chain varies a great deal; but in the biblical view they all rely on that which the earth brings forth. The breathing creatures (humans and animals, but not fish) share *nephesh*—the breath of life.

In the house of Cornelius, this insight gushes out of Peter's mouth. He shares it generously with everyone—whereupon the Holy Spirit, *pneuma* (v. 44), falls upon all those present. This proves Peter's interpretation; it really is true. All living creatures share the *nephesh* of GOD—the listeners realize this truth at once. The house of Cornelius fills with the life-giving Holy Spirit (*pneuma*). Those who had come with Peter from Joppa can now hear those who are gathered in Cornelius' house (v. 46). This is where bonds are forged in the power of communication; *pneuma* as a uniting breath is the basis of community. The four animal types may vary greatly, but *nephesh*, having breath, links them and marks them as creatures made by GOD's hand. Out of these throats now streams praise for GOD in the soldiers' language—if we read Acts 2:11 as well, we hear the colorful Italian cohort along with them:

> 9 "Parthians, Medes, Elamites, and residents of Mesopotamia, Judea and Cappadocia, Pontus and Asia, 10 Phrygia and Pamphylia, Egypt and the parts of Libya belonging to Cyrene, and visitors from Rome, both Jews and proselytes,

11 Cretans and Arabs—*in our own languages we hear them speaking about God's deeds of power*" (Acts 2:9-11; author's emphasis).

Peter and his people are now invited to stay in the house of Cornelius (v. 48). It was presumably not just greens that they shared, but also salt fish preserves, which accompanied the Roman army wherever they went—even into the hungry east of the Empire—and together they survived the famine.

6.11 Turning back to life

Hungry people are filled, strangers become friends, and yet more: enemies become friends in the house of Cornelius—at least for a moment, creation seems to be as good as it could be in the world.

Here, Cornelius' vision takes on concrete shape. He had prayed constantly to GOD (Acts 10:2): even if we do not know what he was asking for or what troubled him, his prayers were the starting point for this encounter. I doubt that he was praying for baptism in Jesus' name—or whether he simply wanted to become a Christian, without having to be circumcised (as the interpretations generally emphasize). It strikes me as much more convincing that Cornelius was troubled by the impending famine throughout the region. He was praying for rain, for deliverance out of the shadow of hunger. Or he was asking for guidance, for how he could be useful to GOD in this time of distress.

His prayer, and the messenger who directed him towards Joppa, belong together. Cornelius proved himself a benefactor for the poor in Joppa, a politically sensitive issue, as these poor people most certainly did not belong to his clientele. Benefactors lived dangerously at that time—think of Spurius Maelius or Jesus of Nazareth, or even Tobit, persecuted for their charity to the poor.[344]

The *pneuma* connected the assembled people to one another, and made it clear to them that they were not just creatures of the same GOD, but also brothers and sisters, who shared *nephesh* and food. A shared vision of the world as it should be, could be, interlinks these women and men. Peter was able to formulate a common focus. He opened his mouth—and suddenly the atmosphere in this house changed, suddenly there was bread for everyone, and there was a *dynamis* in which the people arose and ate and drank—a vision of the healing of the people, as can also be seen in Hosea (Hos 6:2; see also Chapter 9).

I consider this vision to be profoundly biblical. It would be wrong to define it as Christian, in contrast to that which is Jewish. It cannot be divided between the two religious communities. It belongs to both—even though it has to do with Jesus, since Jesus stands in the Jewish tradition of the righteous, and in the tradition of GOD the benefactor. This biblical tradition contrasts sharply with the Roman model of *liberalitas*.

Later on in Jerusalem (11:4f), Peter tells of the wonderful transformation that he and his small band from Joppa had experienced in Caesarea. He is unable to explain it except like this: The soldiers were transformed by *pneuma*—the Holy Spirit—for they shared their food, they shared *nephesh*, and praised GOD. Members of the Roman army became life-savers. Is this not a sign of GOD's faithful presence in times of hunger? Is it not a sign of Christ's resurrection? His presence was palpable in this house; the shared meal took place just as it always had while Jesus was alive.

The sisters and brothers in Jerusalem put what they had understood in a nutshell: even the Roman soldiers in the house of Cornelius can turn back towards life (11:18), they turned away from death and killing and took the side of the needy, they became life-savers. The soldiers embodied what it means to be baptized in the name of Jesus.

6.12 Conclusions

Acts 10–12 sketches vital maps for community survival: the Jews in Antioch organize "relief" for sister communities living in Judea (11:19). Herod's chamberlain is won over (12:20) and enables food to be supplied to the community. The story of Cornelius shows a further option: in Roman Caesarea, among the Gentiles, there are benefactors in the Torah's tradition of the righteous, who are prepared to support the synagogue community (10:1–2).

The communities beset by hunger had a lively interest in finding out how they could survive and how their GOD could help them to do so. Acts 10–12 reminds us that GOD sides with the hungry, opening up possibilities of support on different levels. Peter's conviction that GOD sent her word is fundamental to this. Her word had opened his mouth, so that he is able to put misery into words. At the same time GODS word moved Cornelius to open up his house and his food stores.

If a boundary is being undermined here, it is not that between Jews and Gentiles, but that between the hungry and the well-fed, or between the so-called "ordinary people" (the Jewish craftsmen, fishermen, tanners, weavers—like Tabitha) and the Italian cohort. This was an important boundary especially during the time of Acts, following the Jewish-Roman war: the people in Jerusalem had experienced the violence of the cohort, the starvation during the occupation, and the looting. For them there was a lethal boundary between Roman soldiers and the population of Jerusalem. The hospitality of Cornelius the centurion circumvented this boundary.

Without the question put to Peter by the community in Jerusalem we would not find out anything about a shared meal (Acts 11:3). The text says nothing about whether the centurion's house was kosher or vegetarian, or whether they ate "in the manner of Gentiles." We find out just as little about what the Risen One ate (10:41). Instead, the focus is on doing justice in the name of the God of Israel (10:2), on sharing food with the needy, overcoming the distance between the Roman soldiers and the community in the tanner's house in Joppa, hospitality in times of famine.

The use of the word *symphagein* (eating together) in both Acts 11:3 and 10:41 is significant. It links the meal in the house of Cornelius with the meals in Emmaus (Luke 24:30) and Jerusalem (Luke 24:43). Eating and drinking together "after he rose from the dead" (Acts 10:41) transforms the people eating into a community; put biblically: into one body, a collective body (see also Chapters 8 and 9). Not everyone experienced the murdered Christ after his death, but only those who had eaten and drunk with him. The verb *symphagein* transforms those eating together into a "we," who can see anew and differently from before, who share a common vision of how the world could be.

Eating together seems to create a deep bond against the power of death, of hunger, of the devil (Acts 10:38–41), allowing the people in Jerusalem to sum up: Even "people among the nations" such as these soldiers in Caesarea can turn back and come alive ("the repentance that leads to life," Acts 11:18). Even soldiers can rise up from under the shadow of death, can stand in solidarity with the poor and needy, and turn to the justice of the God of Israel.

This reading of Acts 10–12 contains a kind of Christology that may be called Petrine. It can be sketched based on Peter's vision, his experience of hunger, his speech in the house of Cornelius, and its radical difference from the politically motivated Roman *liberalitas*, which did not include the poor but only the families of citizens, the pillars of society. On the other side are men and women like Tabitha and Cornelius, benefactors in the tradition of the Torah, who sought to give the needy the essentials of life. Jesus, too, was one of the few benefactors towards the poor, and he died the death of a benefactor in the times of the Roman emperors—for the emperor and his court alone laid claim to the right to play benefactor. The tradition of the righteous and John the Baptist's *Umkehrbewegung*—a movement of turning back—belong to this Petrine Christology, as do the subversive moments of the executed benefactor (Acts 10:37–42).

Acts 10–12 tells of survival strategies in times of hunger. The way the narrative unfolds offers help to readers about what to do when faced with hunger. It is crucial that the hungry retain their dignity. Peter, representing the hungry, comes not as a petitioner or an intruder, but as an invited and honored guest. Peter's speech is, in return, a gift from Jerusalem to the world. In the house of Cornelius, cultural exchange is taking place, in mutual respect and in gratitude.

7.

Laughing at Table

DANIEL, BEL, AND THE DRAGON

The earliest detective in world literature must be Daniel. The prophet's courage is legendary, as is his wit, which he uses to save lives and bring down kings. His warning *"Mene, Tekel"* ("weighed in the balance and found wanting"; Dan 5:25) was repeated whenever it was important to recognize the signs of the times and stand up to power. We encounter Daniel's detective side primarily in the later, Greek additions to the book of Daniel, which originated in the period between 100 BCE and 100 CE.

Because they came down to us only in Greek (in the Septuagint version and Theodotion's translation), they were no longer included in the Hebrew Bible. Thus, these Daniel episodes (Susanna, Bel and the Dragon) are apocryphal supplements to the Bible's book of Daniel.[345] Although the episode about Susanna, who was harassed by two elders while bathing, has been widely taken up by the visual arts, the stories about the deity Bel and the dragon have remained largely unknown, despite being both funny and down to earth.

In these stories, Daniel is confronted with the task of proving to the king that Bel is not a proper god, although it devours a huge amount every day. Daniel succeeds, as we shall see. The priestly families have tricked the king and have to pay for this with their lives. But hardly has the situation been clarified, when Daniel has to face the next challenge: he is expected to worship the city's dragon. Again Daniel refuses, saying he will worship only a truly living God. Daniel has to prove that this dragon is not alive. He manages this—but now the city's anger is turned towards him, because he has destroyed their idol and their dragon; he is thrown into the lions' den and is saved only with help from Habakkuk.

Both of these apocryphal stories are about eating. A god that eats a lot instills awe—as does a hungry dragon! A creature that demands a lot, devours a lot, is powerful and must therefore be alive. Daniel questions this premise. He is convinced that living power is something different from what the Persian king is setting before him. But while the power of the god and its dragon is easily unmasked, the hungry lions in the den pose a serious threat.

I want to tell these stories one after the other, situating them in their historical context and with a commentary that enables us to reflect on further shadings of the language about eating and its theological force.

7.1 Framework conditions

Before we look more closely at the "Bel and the Dragon" episodes, let us take a look at the political conditions of the time in which they were written. In the biblical stories of Daniel it is already the case that the hero's actions take place in the fairy-tale space of a past era that diverges from the period when the text was written. The book of Daniel has been dated back to the time of Babylonian rule, or the Persian court, the pomp and splendor of which were legendary.[346] By the time the story was written down, the old Babylonian and Persian empires had long since become smaller and less significant. Their luster existed only in legend. The contemporary political situation could be bypassed using this narrative trick, which lightened the story and created clear space for the listeners. They did not have to analyze the confusing present or position themselves within it, but were able to concentrate on the essential issues against a shimmering backdrop. Nebuchadnezzar and Cyrus were kings in days gone by. Criticism of the royal court and the priesthood in the stories did not concern current kings and priests, so it was distanced from reality and therefore unthreatening.

The book of Daniel originated in a time of unrest, when Palestine was the pawn of the great powers Greece, Syria, and Egypt (ca. 170–160 BCE).[347] It was written partly in Hebrew and partly in Aramaic. This bilingual state is a mark of the times, in which Hebrew was losing significance and Aramaic was becoming the new lingua franca. Only a few generations later further stories of resistance emerged, which gave the people encouragement and laughter as well. These three episodes were written in Greek between 100 BCE and 100 CE, a time that was shaken by wars and revolts.

In a period of political vacuum—while the great powers Greece and Egypt were occupied with battles elsewhere—the Hasmoneans united the nationalist-conservative forces behind them and succeeded in liberating Judea from foreign rule.[348] For almost a hundred years (166–63 BCE), the Judean state managed to defy the great powers' stranglehold. But nationalist-conservative autonomy finally led to political isolation, which was then exploited by another, young superpower: around 63 BCE Pompey and his army marched into Judea, without having to reckon with retaliation from the great powers. Judea became incorporated into the Roman Empire as an eastern province.

Rome appointed vassals, kings with favors from Rome who collected high tributes from the cities and regions. A large proportion of these tributes flowed directly to Rome, the rest into the king's coffers.

The people went empty-handed; not even the prestigious buildings of Herod the Great could conceal that fact. Herod's household plundered the regions so severely that revolts and social unrest multiplied. Ultimately even Rome dropped the Herodians, as their rule had proved increasingly unpredictable and costly. So the Emperor dispatched governors, Roman prefects, to the province of Palestine (from 44 CE). But even the Roman administrators were not really able to keep the impoverished masses in check, through either games or mass executions.[349] The peasant farmers had lost their lands and were drowning in debt, so that bands of robbers and politically motivated guerrillas attracted an increasing number of followers.

The spiral of violence went on and on, until rioters set fire to the municipal archives of the port city of Caesarea:[350] this incinerated the debt records of the impoverished population, who could then join forces with the rioters without their debts making them vulnerable to blackmail. Around 66 CE Roman warships landed at the port of Caesarea, ready to pacify Judea, a process that took them four years, at the end of which Jerusalem had been razed to the ground and all military resistance broken.

At some point during these painful decades, the apocryphal Daniel stories were written. They show that internal resistance, including cultural resistance, was unbroken. Rome had turned a whole people into its enemy. For generations to come the Jews were perceived as being critical of Rome, or even enemies of Rome. Their skepticism towards great powers, and towards the Roman superpower in particular, was the freedom they could hold onto. Daniel is a brainchild of this skepticism towards great powers, a hero of the Jewish resistance, who defeats the most powerful foes without force of arms. But how, precisely, does he defeat them?

7.2 Daniel and the god Bel

> 1 When King Astyages was laid to rest with his ancestors, Cyrus the Persian succeeded to his kingdom. 2 Daniel was a companion of the king, and was the most honored of all his friends. 3 Now the Babylonians had an idol called Bel, and every day they provided for it twelve bushels of choice flour and forty sheep and six measures of wine. 4 The king revered it and went every day to worship it. But Daniel worshipped his own God. So the king said to him, "Why do you not worship Bel?" 5 He answered, "Because I do not revere idols made with hands, but the living God, who created heaven and earth and has dominion over all living creatures." 6 The king said to him, "Do you not think that Bel is a living god? Do you not see how much he eats and drinks every day?" 7 And Daniel laughed, and said, "Do not be deceived, O king, for this thing is only clay inside and bronze outside, and it never ate or drank anything."

8 Then the king was angry and called the priests of Bel and said to them, "If you do not tell me who is eating these provisions, you shall die. 9 But if you prove that Bel is eating them, Daniel shall die, because he has spoken blasphemy against Bel." Daniel said to the king, "Let it be done as you have said."

10 Now there were seventy priests of Bel, besides their wives and children. So the king went with Daniel into the temple of Bel. 11 The priests of Bel said, "See, we are now going outside; you yourself, O king, set out the food and prepare the wine, and shut the door and seal it with your signet. 12 When you return in the morning, if you do not find that Bel has eaten it all, we will die; otherwise Daniel will, who is telling lies about us." 13 They were unconcerned, for beneath the table they had made a hidden entrance, through which they used to go in regularly and consume the provisions. 14 After they had gone out, the king set out the food for Bel. Then Daniel ordered his servants to bring ashes, and they scattered them throughout the whole temple in the presence of the king alone. Then they went out, shut the door and sealed it with the king's signet, and departed.

15 During the night the priests came as usual, with their wives and children, and they ate and drank everything. 16 Early in the morning the king rose and came, and Daniel with him. 17 The king said, "Are the seals unbroken, Daniel?" He answered, "They are unbroken, O king." 18 As soon as the doors were opened, the king looked at the table, and shouted in a loud voice, "You are great, O Bel, and in you there is no deceit at all!" 19 But Daniel laughed and restrained the king from going in. "Look at the floor," he said, "and notice whose footprints these are." 20 The king said, "I see the footprints of men and women and children." 21 Then the king was enraged, and he arrested the priests and their wives and children. They showed him the secret doors through which they used to enter to consume what was on the table. 22 Therefore the king put them to death, and gave Bel over to Daniel, who destroyed it and its temple (Bel 1–22).

7.3 Stories of resistance

The Greek additions to the book of Daniel were written under the pressure of the growing Roman power in the Middle East. Here, Daniel is the confidant of the Persian king (Bel 2). The First Temple, destroyed by the Babylonians, was rebuilt under Persian rule (ca. 415 BCE). The Persian government had an interest in strengthening Judea to safeguard its own position, and therefore permitted temple worship in Jerusalem again. This contributed significantly to the cultural survival of the beleaguered population. In comparison with Assyrian and Babylonian rule, the Persian kings were mild. But they did intervene actively in society when it suited their own preferences.[351]

This meant the mild rule also had its downside. But where exactly does this downside begin? What critical distance has to be maintained, and where can one just go along with the king, with the Persians? Where exactly did people have to be careful, so as not to end up adopting the king's household god, taking on his view of the resources, and believing his universe to be the only true one? The king was the guarantor for peace and food safety. His was the hand that fed them all, wasn't it? But what about the hands who prepared food, cultivated it, distributed it, owned it? How far can one go along with things, and when is it going too far?

The Daniel story characterizes the king as friendly and approachable, but he does not leave Daniel in peace. He even demands that Daniel accompany him into the temple of Bel and worship the image. The king worshipped Bel[352] in the form of a magnificent idol, in an equally magnificent temple, and a large body of priests maintained his cult. Daniel goes along—but he does not want to worship Bel. The conflicts begin.

This most recent Daniel episode is a caricature. Everything is black and white, overdrawn. Sensitive souls may criticize, but it does have an advantage: you get to the heart of the matter very quickly.[353] This late Daniel story draws the prophet as an early detective: he unmasks the gang of fraudsters using a method of creating footprints. But are the facts really as simple as they appear? Even though the case is solved rapidly, the episode throws up questions that we should not drop too hastily.

7.4 Of secret doors and footprints

The Daniel and Bel episode is a tale of a prank. In the first century BCE, the world order in the Middle East began to falter. The Romans extended their empire, and the small state of Judea had little with which to counter them. After the Roman armies marched into Judea (ca. 63 BCE), the Judean elite began collaborating closely with Rome, enabling them to preserve their wealth for the time being. The farmers, on the other hand, had to supply bread and olives to the enormous armies, and the cities had to deliver tributes to the victors. The top and the bottom layers of society drifted apart very quickly.

In this period, a new Daniel story suddenly appeared. In it, Daniel is the king's confidant—as in the Old Testament book of Daniel. The king is somewhat silly; another familiar element. But this time the story is about Bel, this king's god, the effigy of which stands in a temple and is ostentatiously worshipped.

Since Christianity was declared the state religion under Emperor Theodosius in the fourth century, the Christian GOD has had a monopoly. A god from a bygone universe of deities quickly becomes ridiculous to modern readers, as soon as it lays claim to power. We know, after all, that there are no such gods, that the monotheistic religions fundamentally worship the same GOD, and we therefore feel superior to the polytheistic systems. We can join with Daniel in laughing about the tin gods and the king, who appear so stupid to us enlightened readers.

But tucked behind these symbolic or literary figures are core issues that still bother us today. The question: "Who is the greatest and most powerful in the land?" is uncomfortably topical in our Western democratic society. Multinational corporations and banking systems claim the biggest slice of the pie for themselves, and laughter can catch in the throat when faced with their arrogance towards the welfare state and most of the population. With stories about power and profit, about old-boy networks and their loopholes, we are right in the middle of what's going on now.

As this little story has it, the idol Bel receives twelve bushels of choice flour, forty sheep, and six measures of wine every day. Forty sheep for an effigy! Bel is the lord over the land; the name Bel means "lord" or "master." He guarantees prosperity in the country. All profits, all harvests are thanks to him. This religion is so simple: the lord guarantees prosperity and security, and thus the community's survival. He therefore has the right to be fed with the goods he causes to be produced. But a flock of sheep per day is truly a lot. From whom have they been taken? Which farmers or tenants have been deprived of them?

> So the king said to him, "Why do you not worship Bel?" 5 He answered, "Because I do not revere idols made with hands, but the living God, who created heaven and earth and has dominion over all living creatures." 6 The king said to him, "Do you not think that Bel is a living god? Do you not see how much he eats and drinks every day?" 7 And Daniel laughed, and said, "Do not be deceived, O king, for this thing is only clay inside and bronze outside, and it never ate or drank anything" (Bel 5–7).

That Bel consumes such huge quantities every day is, for the king, a sign of his power. A great power system demands its tribute—the greater the power, the greater the tribute. So Bel's healthy appetite is not just a detail of the narrative, but a mirror of what power is understood to be. A huge amount goes into the god—and in turn he can do a huge amount![354] And his priests, too, hang on his strength and power; the whole temple personnel and their families also eat their fill. Alongside them, the craftsmen and temple servants, the artists and tradesmen also receive work and bread. They are drip-fed, so to speak, by this system of power.

We can compare Bel to modern power systems. These days we would say that "Bel" is a brand, a label that could apply to various systems producing money ("blessings") and consuming billions overnight again. They have to be fed with enormous amounts every day: sometimes they appear productive, but sometimes more like a black hole into which whole countries can plunge. Currencies depend on such systems of power and money; they can be larger than the gross domestic product of a country, and if they crash the country cannot cope. This link between products, dominance of the country, enormous sums being destroyed, and almost infinite demands for special rights may seem familiar to readers who are attentive to current affairs in our days of banking and financial crisis.

For Daniel this connection between the idol representing the beneficial order and its demand to be venerated becomes an issue of power. For the readers it is also important to recognize what defines the difference between GOD and an idol, between a power that brings blessings, and a hollow image. How can we actually make this difference visible, and communicate it?

The king is unsettled and annoyed by Daniel's answer. Daniel has mentioned his suspicion that the king is being deceived. Now the king wants to the priests to tell him who is eating the daily rations, if not the god Bel personally. He wants them to prove that it is Bel—and if they cannot, the king will no longer need them. This also means that the priesthood has to justify its raison d'être, by demonstrating that Bel is alive and powerful. If they cannot do so, they become superfluous.

> 10 Now there were seventy priests of Bel, besides their wives and children. So the king went with Daniel into the temple of Bel. 11 The priests of Bel said, "See, we are now going outside; you yourself, O king, set out the food and prepare the wine, and shut the door and seal it with your signet. 12 When you return in the morning, if you do not find that Bel has eaten it all, we will die; otherwise Daniel will, who is telling lies about us." 13 They were unconcerned, for beneath the table they had made a hidden entrance, through which they used to go in regularly and consume the provisions (Bel 10–13).

The seventy priests of Bel do not allow themselves to be intimidated. They ask the king to procure the daily ration as usual, and to shut and seal the temple door. The next morning he will see for himself that Bel has eaten and drunk everything. These priests don't come up with anything else, but carry on business as usual. Are they so certain that their system works and need not be corrected? Or do they lack the imagination to behave differently?

They rely on their secret door. Under the table, directly where the rich offerings lie, there is a hidden entrance, through which they can enter the sealed temple unnoticed. At night, when all the monitoring systems are sleeping, they collect the wine casks and sheep and sacks of flour, to fill their bellies. And the wonderful side effect is that everyone else thinks the god Bel has eaten it all.

Daniel is courageous and dares to say what he sees, even though this does not please the king at all. He is able to interpret his dreams (Dan 1:17; 2:27–45) and read signs on the wall (Dan 5:17–28). But here the case is quite different: how is Daniel to reveal the power elite's loophole?

Now the prophet's detective streak appears: he has fine ash spread in the temple, creating an invisible carpet of ash on the floor:

> 15 During the night the priests came as usual, with their wives and children, and they ate and drank everything. 16 Early in the morning the king rose and came, and Daniel with him. 17 The king said, "Are the seals unbroken, Daniel?" He answered, "They are unbroken, O king." 18 As soon as the doors were opened, the king looked at the table, and shouted in a loud voice, "You are great, O Bel, and in you there is no deceit at all!" 19 But Daniel laughed

and restrained the king from going in. "Look at the floor," he said, "and notice whose footprints these are." 20 The king said, "I see the footprints of men and women and children" (Bel 15–20).

Knowledge of ancient Eastern temples as the residence of a deity—complete with throne and throne room, staterooms, living rooms, and bedrooms for the god—is assumed. The ancient Eastern deities had a divine court, in addition to their own divine extended families: viziers, ministers, advisors, messengers, and doorkeepers were allowed to serve the god. This court thus embodied the general *conditio humana*: they were created for the sole purpose of ensuring that the god was fed and maintained.

> As in palace compounds, living rooms and staterooms were also grouped in houses of worship, together with service rooms around spacious courts where kitchens and bakeries, breweries, and slaughterhouses would be located. Numerous temple officials, workers, craftsmen, functionaries, and priests together carried out the task of providing food for their master and his companions. For example, in the household of Marduk of Babylon, fine meals and foodstuffs of all kinds were produced from raw materials, provided by the gardens and estates, which supplied the livestock and temple waters and other produce. Twice a day . . . the priests and temple servants . . . served Marduk and his companions a lavish feast, during extensive rituals, associated with songs and prayers. In the king's court they exercised the privilege of looking after the king-god.[355]

Daniel's engagement with the ancient Eastern deities is thus also a struggle about human destiny. The balance of giving and taking—the deity gives blessings, fruits of the land; the people return some of this produce to the deity's court—is the basis of culture and civilization. Political regimes have always used this balance to their advantage: they allied themselves with deities, had themselves adopted or legitimized by them, aligned their rule with the divine cosmic order. The present political regime may be violent or economically disastrous, but it is appointed by the gods and the subjects must therefore serve it. This interpretation of order lacks any space to think about the effects of a regime, to criticize it, to demand changes. Biblical religion, too, is not immune to having interpretations turned into ideology that support the system. But it is precisely such Daniel stories that attempt to open up free spaces and to undermine the using of religion and images of God in a way that is dissociated from concrete realities.

At night, the priests and their families came in through a secret door and did what they had always done. They did not feel compelled to rethink their behavior, which left clear traces. We are not talking here of fingerprints, but of footprints. The fine coating of ashes that Daniel had spread made these footprints very obvious—if one were looking at the floor. The king looks at the table, which is empty, and at the image whose power he admires. He believes in the power of the lord, the lords above.

Daniel laughs at his naivety and even has to hold the king back so that he does not wipe out the evidence. *"Look at the floor,"* he said, *"and notice whose footprints these are."* Bel does not have so many feet; someone else must have been walking there!

The people told this story of his prank and laughed. And they were in need of laughter. The Roman army had left massive footprints wherever it was stationed. Daniel encouraged the people not to be intimidated. He called a spade a spade; he used his wits to uncover the hidden machinations.

And yet Daniel was unable to stem the tide of political developments in the Palestine of his day. Even his GOD, who did not want to be fed daily, but who is the creator of heaven and earth, did not hold back the Romans. They expanded ever further and took what they wanted. Judea was incorporated as a province, devoured by their boundless greed for power and wealth. The Roman officials governed the country in accordance with their rules and demanded more tributes every year. But here, in this little story, resistance is possible. The people laugh about the naïve king and his belief that an effigy was able to eat. The people know they may be unable to change anything, but they do not have to believe what is set in front of them.

I think also of our waste of resources, of the ecological footprint of our society and economy, as well as of the traces that we leave in our daily actions. The religious question becomes ever more clearly a question of power: What is the God we believe in? Are we relying on having loopholes? Do we prefer to look away from the consequences of our belief? What we believe in, what we support, build up, and keep alive—all this has far-reaching consequences.

The tradition of Daniel insists that resistance is necessary and does good. Distance from the imperial god is important, laughing about the king does us good; but ultimately what is important are the traces we leave behind. An awareness that all our actions—or inaction—will leave traces is part of trusting GOD in our daily lives. This religious awareness acknowledges the footprints we leave in the world around us, and on our planet.

7.5 Daniel kills the dragon

> 23 Now in that place there was a great dragon, which the Babylonians revered. 24 The king said to Daniel, "You cannot deny that this is a living god; so worship him." 25 Daniel said, "I worship the Lord my God, for he is the living God. 26 But give me permission, O king, and I will kill the dragon without sword or club." The king said, "I give you permission." 27 Then Daniel took pitch, fat, and hair, and boiled them together and made cakes, which he fed to the dragon. The dragon ate them, and burst open. Then Daniel said, "See what you have been worshipping!" 28 When the Babylonians heard about it, they were very indignant and conspired against the king, saying, "The king has become a Jew; he has destroyed Bel, and killed the dragon, and slaughtered the

priests." 29 Going to the king, they said, "Hand Daniel over to us, or else we will kill you and your household." 30 The king saw that they were pressing him hard, and under compulsion he handed Daniel over to them.

31 They threw Daniel into the lions' den, and he was there for six days. 32 There were seven lions in the den, and every day they had been given two human bodies and two sheep; but now they were given nothing, so that they would devour Daniel. 33 Now the prophet Habakkuk was in Judea; he had made a stew and had broken bread into a bowl, and was going into the field to take it to the reapers. 34 But the angel of the Lord said to Habakkuk, "Take the food that you have to Babylon, to Daniel, in the lions' den." 35 Habakkuk said, "Sir, I have never seen Babylon, and I know nothing about the den." 36 Then the angel of the Lord took him by the crown of his head and carried him by his hair; with the speed of the wind he set him down in Babylon, right over the den. 37 Then Habakkuk shouted, "Daniel, Daniel! Take the food that God has sent you." 38 Daniel said, "You have remembered me, O God, and have not forsaken those who love you." 39 So Daniel got up and ate. And the angel of God immediately returned Habakkuk to his own place. 40 On the seventh day the king came to mourn for Daniel. When he came to the den he looked in, and there sat Daniel! 41 The king shouted with a loud voice, "You are great, O Lord, the God of Daniel, and there is no other besides you!" 42 Then he pulled Daniel out, and threw into the den those who had attempted his destruction, and they were instantly eaten before his eyes (Bel 23–42).

This is another story of resistance, because the people simply needed more resistance, more courage, and more laughter as well. The political climate in the first century BCE was unstable. Rome spread her power as far as the Middle East, and consumed little countries without batting an eyelid. In the daily lives of ordinary people this meant growing poverty and social unrest: the Romans brought systems of leasing and customs duties, which weighed heavily on the small farmers.

People still told stories of a dragon[356] so powerful that it devoured enormous quantities of food. Its throat had to be constantly stuffed, or it would spew streams of fire or water, depending on the story.[357] This naturally also reminded people of the heraldic animal of Babylon,[358] which caused fear and terror wherever it appeared.

If anyone could put a stop to the dragon, it was probably Daniel, this most cunning of all prophets. But the question was *how* he would do it. He was not like St. George the knight who, tucked into a suit of armor and armed to the teeth, was able to slay a dragon. Daniel was cunning and shrewd. But would he escape with his life, if he battled with the dragon?

23 Now in that place there was a great dragon, which the Babylonians revered. 24 The king said to Daniel, "You cannot deny that this is a living god; so worship him." 25 Daniel said, "I worship the Lord my God, for he is the living God. 26 But give me permission, O king, and I will kill the dragon without

sword or club." The king said, "I give you permission." 27 Then Daniel took pitch, fat and hair, and boiled them together and made cakes, which he fed to the dragon. The dragon ate them, and burst open. Then Daniel said, "See what you have been worshipping!" (Bel 23–27).

There are systems of power that pump themselves up, that swell and distend and do not know their own limits. Their power is based on their appetite; they have to be fed to keep them in check. The king reveres the powerful dragon, since it commands fear and terror. Daniel laughs at this, because the dragon is dumber than a doorknob, and doesn't even notice what it eats. The dragon eats whatever it can get its teeth into—sheep, humans, olive groves, whole regions—but it does not notice if something is indigestible. The cakes made of pitch, fat, and hair cause it to burst open. The people probably had to laugh at this new prank of Daniel's—he made a good job of that!

This is the first message of the little story: Don't be afraid of dragons; they can't do anything except consume. Dragons aren't really able to cope with life, they stare unblinkingly and open their throats, that's all. Their appetite will be their downfall.

But what happens then? When a large system explodes because it does not know its limits? The story does not end here. The dragon bursts like a soap bubble—but now its followers come and demand that Daniel must pay. The king hands Daniel over to the enraged dragon-devotees, and they throw Daniel into the lions' den.

> 31 They threw Daniel into the lions' den, and he was there for six days.
> 32 There were seven lions in the den, and every day they had been given two human bodies and two sheep; but now they were given nothing, so that they would devour Daniel (Bel 31–32).

The Ishtar Gate on the Processional Way in ancient Babylon depicts magnificent lions, the goddess Ishtar's sacred animal, representing her unapproachable, dangerous side. It is thus no coincidence that Daniel is thrown into the lions' den: the lions are part of the same power system as the dragon and Bel. Daniel's victory over them attracts the anger of Ishtar, i.e., the power that stands behind Bel and the dragon. Ishtar's lions make it clear that there could be no debate with Ishtar. Her power was unshakeable. The lions meant that any contradiction, any resistance was nipped in the bud. The lions' den is the place where accounts are settled—like the Roman arena, in which thousands of animals were hounded and, together with humans (as late as the sixth century CE), were slaughtered.[359]

Now no trick will help; Daniel is stuck. He cannot break free, either through his wisdom, or with a prank. The lions' den will not simply burst in mid-air. The narrators of this story were surely confronted with anxious faces: what do you mean, who can help now? What will work, when nothing else does? Who will stand by us in times of great need? God, ADONAI, yes, GOD should help, he should always do that—but what would GOD's help look like, if someone is sitting in a lions' den surrounded by seven hungry lions?

7.6 Habakkuk's cookshop

This is perhaps the most exciting moment of the story: Who can help now? The superficial powers have been defeated, Bel has turned out to be a colossus of clay, his heraldic animal a stupid glutton. But despite all this, the power system is nowhere near being shaken. Behind every layer of power that is exposed, another one appears. The listeners realize that, even behind the lions' den, further dangers may lurk. And in any case, Daniel has been in the lions' den once before (Dan 6:17–24).

How can Daniel be saved? The listeners have perhaps interjected their experiences, mobilized their stories of rescue or their ideas of how to liberate Daniel now: God could send angels to make the lions peaceable. The youngest children have perhaps called out that, above all, God now has to make sure Daniel does not starve in the lions' den for, like the lions, he is not being given anything to eat. Indeed, such an observation could well have come from a little girl or boy. It focuses attention away from the imposing lions and towards the frail prophet, sensitively connecting their own experiences of hunger with Daniel's situation. The point now is this: What do we think, how are we to get out of the lions' den—or out of the debt trap, the climate catastrophe, the spiral of violence? The story now takes an unexpected turn:

> 33 Now the prophet Habakkuk was in Judea; he had made a stew and had broken bread into a bowl, and was going into the field to take it to the reapers. 34 But the angel of the Lord said to Habakkuk, "Take the food that you have to Babylon, to Daniel, in the lions' den." 35 Habakkuk said, "Sir, I have never seen Babylon, and I know nothing about the den." 36 Then the angel of the Lord took him by the crown of his head and carried him by his hair; with the speed of the wind he set him down in Babylon, right over the den. 37 Then Habakkuk shouted, "Daniel, Daniel! Take the food that God has sent you." 38 Daniel said, "You have remembered me, O God, and have not forsaken those who love you." 39 So Daniel got up and ate. And the angel of God immediately returned Habakkuk to his own place (Bel 33–39).

The story refers back to the well-known, venerable prophet Habakkuk. The text that bears his name is part of the Hebrew Bible. It was written ca. 600 BCE, when Babylon was still a great power. It is therefore an eminently suitable narrative reference. Injustice and violence were the order of the day, and Habakkuk's Scripture begins with the words:

> 2 O Lord, how long shall I cry for help,
> and you will not listen?
> Or cry to you "Violence!"
> and you will not save?
> 3 Why do you make me see wrongdoing
> and look at trouble?

> Destruction and violence are before me;
> strife and contention arise (Hab 1:2–3).

Habakkuk is a compassionate and indignant prophet, who observes—he does not stare fixedly, without batting an eyelid (like a dragon), but trembling and quivering (Hab 3:16). He perceives the violence, the imminent war and associated with it: impending hunger.

> 17 Though the fig tree does not blossom,
> and no fruit is on the vines;
> though the produce of the olive fails,
> and the fields yield no food;
> though the flock is cut off from the fold,
> and there is no herd in the stalls (Hab 3:17).

Where have the flocks gone? Habakkuk laments the fields and stalls plundered to feed foreign armies, and this is reminiscent of Bel's daily portion, complete with his insatiable dragon. Like Daniel he has no faith in the embodiments of foreign claims to power. They are only made of wood, of stone—there is no life-creating force within them; quite the opposite. They teach lies when they claim to bring life, blessings, peace (Hab 2:18–19). He sees through them as embodiments of the victors, the military superpowers of that time.

Habakkuk's criticism of idols is along the same lines as Daniel's. The magnificent effigies are only wood or stone—and yet Daniel is now in the lions' den, where the goddess Ishtar's power base threatens to devour him. Idols are nothings, but behind them stand powers that consume lives, that devour whole tracts of land and appropriate whatever they want. Accordingly, these deities want people to feed them. Anyone who questions this will have to feed the lions of Ishtar with his or her own body.

How can this system be interrupted? Habakkuk cooks. He prepares food, not for his deity but for hardworking people. Habakkuk has compassion for them, and knows that they need food. Criticism of the magnificent effigies of gods that gobble up whole harvests is rooted in the vision of men and women as creatures of GOD, who are not responsible for feeding deities. They labor and should be able to enjoy the fruits of their labor. They should be caring for one another rather than for magnificent gods.

Daniel would get no further, were it not for people like Habakkuk. The story shows Daniel as a vulnerable man who, even if he is clever and brave with his words, remains dependent on others. He needs food and support, or he will perish. He finds this support in his tradition—embodied in the venerable Habakkuk, who sails to him from another time, another story—but it is the same historical tradition. In this tradition, it is not dragons and dangerous lions that set the tone, but the voices of prophets who recognize the people's plight.

Incidentally, Habakkuk's Scripture ends with his quick, light steps:

> 19 GOD, the Lord, is my strength;
>
> he makes my feet like the feet of a deer,
>
> and makes me tread upon the heights (Hab 3:19).

So Habakkuk is extremely agile. Perhaps he is the quickest of all the prophets. He almost flies, drawn by GOD, to where there is hardship, where he is needed. It is astonishing that Habakkuk in the apocryphal Daniel episode is running a cookshop. Habakkuk cooks a stew and breaks bread into it—a stew he is cooking for the hardworking agricultural laborers. Habakkuk has no idea of the lions' den; he does not care to know even where it is. But he is seized by his mop of hair and flown into the lions' den, "with the speed of the wind," along with his stew.

With Habakkuk, a wind of change enters the story. Rescue comes from outside, from an unexpected quarter. Or would it be better to say: help comes from home, from the ancient prophets, the old prophetic tradition, which nourished the people in times of crisis? Is this about remembering the concept of being human in mutual care and dependency? Daniel can no longer be a lone warrior; he needs saving powers, helping hands, food, and solidarity.

Habakkuk brings the story to a satisfying end—but he also changes the listeners' perspective. Grand words were uttered at the king's court, about power, about devouring and being devoured. But out in the fields, where Habakkuk is, people are concerned with the work of harvesting, and a stew with chunks of bread, about humanity and living.

This marks the GOD of Daniel. His power rests in mobilizing people to do something about hunger; they do not think themselves too important to bring the laborers something to eat, and they are not too frightened to visit someone in the lions' den. Daniel depends on such women and men.

7.7 Interruptions

The two Daniel episodes follow one another seamlessly. Hardly has Bel been demolished when the gluttonous dragon is there; and no sooner has the dragon ruptured from overeating, when Daniel is thrown into the lions' den. The same happened to him in the book of Daniel: one intrigue followed another, one threat gave way to the next. Despite all Daniel's interventions and those of his GOD, the kings did not really appear capable of learning. Hardly was one despot dead when his successor had himself installed. Every triumph proved to be temporary, for there is always one more lions' den. This den is the last-named place in the story, thus making it clear: even if Daniel has escaped it this time (Bel 42)—the place itself, the pit of the powerful, remains.

The poet Hilde Domin therefore does not speak of overcoming the lions' den. She turns a little voice into a great one, a voice that dares to call things by their real name. To uncover the devouring force, with nothing but our breath—this means being alive, having the power to hold fast to one another, and to wrest life from the lions at least for a while.

> Salva nos
>
> This is our freedom
> naming the real names
> fearlessly
> with a little voice
>
> calling to one another
> with a little voice
> naming the all-consuming by name
> with nothing but our breath
>
> *salva nos ex ore leonis*
> holding open the maw
> in which to live
> is not our choice.[360]

The Daniel episodes do not tell of final victories either, but of the existence of ordinary people, who are threatened by lions over and over again. But in this situation—which Domin describes as living in the maw of the lion—resistance is all the more important.

Even though the individual episodes—especially this last one with its rough humor, mythical dragon, and flying Habakkuk—do not appear to be interested in reality, in what is possible and what not, the stories nourish our eschatological imagination. They give us insights into the world, into how it could be better, more just, more lively. They give rise to hope that things could be different—and they outline a direction for us.

Andrea Bieler and Luise Schottroff adopt the term "eschatological imagination" in their book *The Eucharist: Bodies, Bread, and Resurrection*.[361] However, they do not follow the line of eschatology that developed from the seventeenth century as the study of the Last Things, the *eschata*. That eschatology is based on the idea that time proceeds in a linear fashion and that GOD (along with the holy goods such as liberation, resurrection, new life) will come, after much time has elapsed. Schottroff and Bieler turn away from this elapsing, linear idea of time and develop an understanding of eschatology as the radical criticism of an idea of time as a continual process.

The conventional differentiation of present and future eschatology remains rooted in linear thinking, just as much as the thesis of the delay of the Parousia.[362] Eschatological imagination, on the other hand, is transformative and permeable for liberation. According to Schottroff and Bieler, eschatological imagination can be found in the speech of those who are in the middle of battles for survival, of marginalized people who long for the end of oppression. Womanist theology, developed by Black feminists, directs its gaze less to liberation and more to survival. It concerns the power to enable children to survive—without losing their dignity or their backbone. Both Joan M. Martin and Emily Townes[363] refer to apocalyptic images that were also sources for the old spirituals, "He's Going to Wake Up the Dead," or "When the Saints Go Marching In": the eschatological imagination allows the present to become permeable to GOD's proximity. The expectation of a just world lets us lift up our heads and our voices now, lets the dead stand up and sing.

The two Daniel episodes can also be read eschatologically, given that they allow the listeners to laugh and take a deep breath; because the stories of power and violence can be interrupted, not once and for all, but *again and again*. It becomes obvious that meals are a central factor. Food can be a means to give life, or to take it. There are simple, life-sustaining meals to interrupt labor and structure the day. And there are raids to provide nocturnal feasts. There is food that stuffs without nourishing. And there is an excess of food, a limit that should not be surpassed—nor be undercut, otherwise hunger will rage. The feeding of lions marks another line that must not be crossed. Feeding them with the corpses of humans reveals the powers to be godless, without scruples. These stories thus develop a differentiated language of eating. Eating conditions people, to complicity, to maintaining the system—or it can provide interruptions and breathing spaces.

Mealtimes are always culturally determined.[364] They are not just about nutrition and food, but about preparing it and producing it, about the relationships between the people eating, about power relationships. Thus in eating, one incorporates a personal identity—it embodies to whom one belongs, to which group. The enactment of eating is therefore always the expression of personal and cultural identity. Mealtimes structure the day in the simple farmer's life as well as at the king's court. Not just domestic family meals, but also public, ceremonial feasts create points of orientation in the cycle of the year.[365] So the rulers' birthdays, their weddings and funerals were points of reference in the year, structuring the time of their reign. These feasts gave cohesion to a village community or to a family.

Eating thus guarantees the continued existence of a biological body, but also that of a power structure, of an institution: the existing order needs ideological underpinning. If this fails or changes, the system starts to falter.

There are two opposing eating behaviors in the two Daniel episodes. One is found in the ritual meals of the deities and their courts, who are there to guarantee the continuity of their reign. Bel and the dragon are fed repeatedly, as are the lions. As soon as these meals cease, things become muddled.

What Habakkuk does, however, is on a different level. Habakkuk cooks a simple stew for the hungry laborers. His little cookshop is barely able to satisfy all of them. The task is too great; it should actually fall to the owners of the fields and the vineyards who have people work for them. But these employers are obviously neglecting their responsibilities; they provide too little bread, or the wages are too small to start off with, so Habakkuk intervenes. His cooking is just a small contribution to survival; it does not guarantee that the laborers in the field have food on the Sabbath as well, and that they get through the winter. His cooking interrupts everyday hunger—nothing more.

We can also understand the prophet who cooks and brings food as the embodiment of the Torah, the word that gives life. The Torah nourishes people, strengthens them, gives them life—so it is quite fitting to show a prophet cooking. If he passes on the Torah, if he interprets it in such a way that it interprets life and fills it with meaning, if by criticizing and warning people he calls them back to the righteous path of GOD, then he enables life. A good prophet is someone who delivers food, someone who cooks in a cookshop, who is present where there is impending hunger and injustice, need and isolation.

The Daniel episodes do not string together into a narrative of progress, but tell of interruptions. These bring hope and laughter into the story of the court, which Daniel disrupts, turns upside down, inspires with real life. Again and again, the listeners can come alive with Daniel, who perforates the system, upsets it—but is still unable to put an end to it. In these episodes, religion is the art of interruption, of creating breathing spaces, of sparking glimmers of hope—it opens windows into GOD's future.[366]

8.

Thirst for More

(1 COR)

8.1 Everything that has breath

It is time for us to talk about thirst. The urgent need for water, for any kind of liquid, is something we can assuage easily here in Western Europe. Water is still abundant in this region, and houses everywhere have had running water for a long time. Drinking water is available for anyone who is thirsty, whether from public drinking fountains or taps; many restaurants and bars provide it free of charge. And so the same applies as to hunger: we now barely know thirst, unless what we mean is small and easily quenched—when we get up in the morning, or if it's hot during the day.

Is there a difference between hunger and thirst? Is it true that thirst is more closely associated with longing than hunger is? The unquenchable thirst for freedom, adventure, love, recognition . . . but things are not so clear. We cannot settle the hunger for bread on the material side and thirst for recognition on the spiritual side. This does not work, because these two sides do not exist as such, but are always mixed, interwoven, interlaced. The impulse to play "hunger" and "thirst" off against one another in a qualitative sense is an intellectual game for the well-fed, a game that gets us nowhere in exegetical terms.

And yet: can thirst also arouse rage in the belly, or only an undefined longing? Can we also arouse hunger, or only appetite? We can certainly arouse a thirst for more, for something that is not yet manifest, something that thirst in a sense can only anticipates. It is the case that the verb "to thirst" has undergone a great process of spiritualization in Western cultural history. To our ears, it sounds like "thirsting" for freedom or love—and not so much like material thirst. If we spiritualize "thirst" as undefined longing for immaterial goods, we are not prepared for the biblical view of needs: thirst for clear, healthy water is part of the hunger for daily bread.

Water was a precious resource in the regions of Palestine, Israel, and Syria, where there were no great rivers or forests to store water. Timely autumn rain and abundant spring rain (Job 29:23) were immensely important for agriculture. The thirsty earth and the dry soil are mentioned often (Ps 63:1; Isa 35:1; 41:18; 48:21; 53:2); the desert as a place of thirst and death never seems far away (Exod 17:3; 2 Sam 17:29; Wis 11:4).

Thirst, drought, dried up, thirsty, parched, arid, withered—without water there is no life. In biblical language this means: water and the breath of life are closely connected.

Water flows down a person's throat and literally enlivens them with new vitality. This experience of revitalization is wonderful and leads the Israelites to reflect on GOD, the giver of water and of breath. GOD gives breath, while everything that breathes remains dependent on water. Thirsty throats thus pant for water:

> As a deer longs for flowing streams,
> so my soul longs for you, O God (Ps 42:1).

In the ancient Orient, the throat was the part of the human body where a man expressed himself completely, a woman made herself heard, with his voice, her needs, fears, reactions, demands. The throat connects humans with what they need, with food as well as air. The throat was regarded as the seat of life. "Throat" (Hebrew: *nephesh*)[367] is an all-encompassing, holistic term. In ancient Eastern thinking, bodies are either living (animated by the breath of life) or dead; a soul that exists in isolation from the body is unthinkable in the ancient Eastern understanding, as it is for the Jewish and thus also the early Christian one. The breath of life, which flows to and fro in the breathing throat, expires with death, and returns into the comprehensive breath of GOD.[368]

The longing for water, for fulfilment, for an answer in a time of need, is captured in this verse:

> I stretch out my hands to you;
> my soul thirsts for you like a parched land.
> 7 Answer me quickly, O LORD;
> my spirit fails (Ps 143:6–7).

The throat is the channel for communication and for needs, including breath.

> Let everything that breathes praise the LORD!
> Praise the LORD! (Ps 150:6).

Exchange takes place in the throat; this is where food, water and air are taken in. The green plants of the earth are intended to become food:

> And to every beast of the earth, and to every bird of the air, and to everything that creeps on the earth, everything that has the breath of life, I have given every green plant for food (Gen 1:30).

These breathing creatures include humans (Gen 2:7). After the Flood, the relationship between humans and other creatures changed (Gen 9:2–4). But what does not change is thirst, which continues to connect all creatures that breathe.

Everything that has the breath of life drinks water: birds, reptiles, cattle, wild beasts, and humans. There are many different basic foodstuffs for humans, and some animals eat things that others never could. Living creatures are highly differentiated in terms of their solid food, and live in their ecological niches. But water, like air, is the stuff that connects all of them.

8.2 Hunger and thirst

Hunger and thirst appear to be an inseparable duo for the poor. Paul shared with many poor people an endangered existence, which repeatedly led to hunger and thirst. He often speaks of this pair, which he wouldn't even wish on his enemies, and from which not even hard work can protect:

> If your enemies are hungry, feed them; if they are thirsty, give them something to drink; for by doing this you will heap burning coals on their heads (Rom 12:20).
>
> To the present hour we are hungry and thirsty, we are poorly clothed and beaten and homeless, 12 and we grow weary from the work of our own hands. When reviled, we bless; when persecuted, we endure (1 Cor 4:11–12).
>
> In toil and hardship, through many a sleepless night, hungry and thirsty, often without food, cold and naked (2 Cor 11:27).

The poor in Corinth lived in cheap tenements on dirty streets and attempted to make ends meet on the breadline. Corinth was a city with two ports, a trading center for goods, including slaves. The city was not yet one hundred years old when Paul visited. Many freed slaves and new settlers lived in the city, sent there by Julius Caesar.

The living standards in Corinth were comparable overall with those in other cities of the Roman Empire. There was a gulf between the small group of the ruling elite and the rest of the population. The elite group is estimated to have been about 3 percent of the total population; they owned the fertile lands and enjoyed urban luxury. Merchants, specialized craftspeople, and a few military veterans made up about 7 percent who did not do too badly. The remaining 90 percent lived on the breadline, or below it.[369] As Luise Schottroff points out:

> The living conditions for the majority of the population in the cities of the Roman Empire were unsanitary and harsh. Poor people's dwellings in tenements

did not have a kitchen or sewage disposal; many were windowless. The stinking filth on the streets and the violence in everyday life made living dangerous. Children grew up under such conditions between the adults. Only half of the newborns reached their tenth year of life. The First Letter to the Corinthians assumes these living conditions.[370]

In the synagogues of the ordinary people, Paul read and interpreted the Torah, talked to people, motivated them to stand together and change their situation together.

> Consider your own call, brothers and sisters: not many of you were wise by human standards, not many were powerful, not many were of noble birth. 27 But God chose what is foolish in the world to shame the wise; God chose what is weak in the world to shame the strong; 28 God chose what is low and despised in the world, things that are not, to reduce to nothing things that are (1 Cor 1:26–28).

In these lines at the beginning of Paul's Letter, it becomes clear that he is speaking to the poor. At the same time, a revolutionary movement is emerging: "the wise" will be shamed and those who represent something in the world will have their power taken from them. Those who know hunger and thirst will rise up, will stand up, because GOD wants them to live. This is the gospel of the poor, which also rings through Mary's Magnificat in Luke's Gospel:

> 52 He has brought down the powerful from their thrones,
> and lifted up the lowly;
> 53 he has filled the hungry with good things,
> and sent the rich away empty (Luke 1:52–53).

Hunger and thirst are a real, permanent threat for the poor and lowly. There is therefore no reason for either Paul or Luke's Mary to be referring to "symbolic" or "spiritual" hunger. Rather, this is about the hungry throat, which can sing of GOD only when it has the breath of life. As soon as this breath departs, the throat becomes silent. So poor people are in a situation where singing and praising GOD passes them by. But now, says Paul, GOD has called the poor.

8.3 Thirst for more

According to Paul, it is time for these people to rise up out of their precarious situation and demand life. But how can an uprising of the poor succeed? The wealthy citizens of Corinth will have no scruples about counterattacking. How are the poor supposed to liberate themselves from their defenselessness and lack of perspective? How should it be possible for them to receive a better life?

It is high time for resurrection in Corinth—not just for the resurrection of dead bodies, but for the living, hardworking bodies of women and men, as well as for the bodies of children, so that they can grow and blossom. Paul tries to speak of a resurrection that can be sensed not just in the hereafter, but in life, not just in the depths of one's heart, but in the midst of the community.

> But someone will ask, "How are the dead raised? With what kind of body do they come?" (1 Cor 15:35).

The question that Paul takes up here sounds modern. How are the dead supposed to come again? Will they still have a body for that? Or will they come in a transparent body, a body of light; or disembodied, only as a voice, or as a memory . . . ?

The question about the body of the dead who will return is, however, not just a metaphysical one that ties us in speculative knots. It is much rather a question of power. What power do the dead have when they rise? Does their rising bring something about? Does it change anything in the living conditions of the poor? If not, they may as well stay put and—of all people, for once at least!—rest from their daily struggle against hunger and injustice.

A poem by Dorothee Sölle from the 1980s reflects poetically this search for an effective force: what the rising of the dead brings about for those who perceive it. It moves the world, because it is able to strengthen the living.

> At a peace gathering
>
> We are only ten thousand I said
> there are many more of us here
> the dead of both wars
> are with us
>
> A journalist came and asked
> how could I know that
> haven't you seen them
> I ask the clueless guy
> haven't you heard your grandmother
> groaning when they started it up again
> do you live all alone
> without any dead who drop in
> for a drink with you
> do you really think
> you are only yourself?[371]

Sölle connects a commitment to peace with mysticism. For her, those who have died are not locked away behind a glass wall, irrelevant to present and future generations. Here, the dead are those murdered by the last two wars, victims of aggressive policies, victims of nationalism and anti-Semitism. These dead do not drop in physically, of course, not as bodies of flesh and blood, not as semi-transparent ghosts. The encounters that Sölle sketches here are of a different kind.

The dead are the reason for demonstrations against armaments and organized violence. They play an ethical role; they drive the living onto the streets, they demand response and commitment from the living. They have not disappeared from our lives, our memories, our history, merely because they are dead. Sölle perceives them as a support: they help us to stand up for peace, to hear the quiet voices and to remain vulnerable.

The dead are not at all far away. They drop in here and there, they make the living become restless and question the course of events. They whisper in sleepless nights and remind us of the injustice that took place, and that is currently taking place. But through the presence of these dead, Sölle concludes something surprising: "Do you really think you are only yourself?" This calls a boundary into question. We are more than is visible. You are not just yourself, you are also determined by what others hope for. You are a more extended existence than just a single body, you are part of a "We," part of something shared, something that extends the borderlines of an individual. Fundamentally, the individual body transforms here into a joint "We-are-more-bodies."

This "We are more" has a quantitative and a qualitative side. The murdered dead support our commitment to peace and therefore make it so urgent as well. The dead do not leave the demonstrators alone, but back them up. Beyond the direct ethical impact, there is also an implied spiritual dimension: the dead share with the living the longing that makes them restless, that doesn't let them sleep. So that, Sölle postulates, the thirst for life does not die. On the contrary, this thirst connects the dead and the living, brings them together.

Why do the dead "drop in for a drink with you"? Why not to sit with us, to cry, to share silence? There is comfort associated with drinking an evening glass of wine, and the suggestion of familiar social interactions; this expression implies matter-of-factness. "Having a drink" does not mean tea or coffee, but something alcoholic, the kind of drink that makes boundaries permeable. In addition, "having a drink" normally takes place in the evenings, at night, not in broad daylight. This means the dead show up when we come to rest, when we let go, allow memories to rise, gaze into the night. It is no longer the hunger for bread that connects the living to the dead, but an unquenchable thirst.

The thirst for life contains a religious momentum, similar to the yearning for everything that is still to come. It is similar to the drive to hurl oneself into the arms of life.[372] This drive is close to the deep, disquieting knowledge that we are not just what we are able to live in any one moment. We can grow, can change ourselves and the world; and this transformation also poses the question of power.

A shift of the resurrection into the hereafter is generally speaking apolitical, because doing so leaves the social and political circumstances unchanged. Dorothee

Sölle's discussion of resurrection, as well as Paul's, includes the political dimension, the desire to change the circumstances. This dimension demands a "We," to overcome an isolation that is individualistically limited to a single body, while being alive is only conceivable in exchange with other beings, with the world. Seen biblically, resurrection is bound up with immersion in a network of relationships, making individuals into a "We-are-more-bodies."

Today, on the other hand, individualistic expectations—that I will experience my own personal resurrection (and mostly, after my physical death)—are widespread. At the same time people reject these expectations for being implausible. A network of relationships doesn't often come into view at all in connection with resurrection. Individual resurrection appears absurd—a fairy tale for people who are grieving, for those who cannot accept transience—and has absolutely no significance for the world. But this means we are relinquishing the talk of resurrection, of a "We-are-more-bodies," too cheaply. Resurrection has less to do with "believing in . . ." than with experiencing a refreshing gush of solidarity, which all have a right to experience, but most lack the opportunity. Demanding this opportunity and not forgetting it is a thread of continuity running through the Bible.

How can we speak today of resurrection—of rising again[373]—in such a way that people want to rise up? That they do not try to content themselves with the frontiers around them, with what they can actually have. The Bible speaks tirelessly of another world being possible—and how we can yearn for it, how we can work towards making this world, beyond violence and hunger, grow before our very eyes. This also includes the conviction that rising up/rising into a "more-body" is possible. The consequences that arising have for society and for the body are what I now want to investigate.

8.4 With what kind of body will they come?

Paul takes up the audience's question in 1 Cor: with what kind of body will the dead come? Relatives of deceased persons know what state the body of their dead is in. Whether they are long decomposed or cannot be found, whether they have been mutilated or disfigured through violence. It would be alarming if emaciated corpses who had long been dead suddenly stood at our front door.

> 35 But someone will ask, "How are the dead raised? With what kind of body do they come?" 36 Fool! What you sow does not come to life unless it dies. 37 And as for what you sow, you do not sow the body that is to be, but a bare seed, perhaps of wheat or of some other grain (1 Cor 15:35–37).

With what kind of body will they come? This question easily generates absurdities. Paul chooses his words carefully, with recourse to the Jewish wisdom tradition.[374] How are we to talk about the miracle of transformation if we hold a single bare seed in our hands? We need the vision of golden yellow wheat to be able to be amazed at all—this seed turns into wheat, and many seeds into an undulating wheatfield! But it remains difficult to find fitting words for this transformation.

In 1 Corinthians, Paul wrestles again and again with speaking about the transformation of the body in such a way that something of this miracle can be perceived. He uses mythological images and poetry to clothe experiences in language, experiences that go beyond the conventional linguistic resources that are characterized by discourse.[375] Referring to the miracle of the seed's greening life-energy, which it carries within it, and for which we barely have the words, Paul directs the reader's interest away from theorizing or speculating about the future of the (deceased) body, and back to something obvious. Steering the gaze back like this to the realm of nature is in line with the Jewish wisdom tradition. The people are involved with seeds every day, in the fields, milling them, cooking, and eating. And yet they have no idea what really lies within these seeds.

> 16 We can hardly guess at what is on earth,
> and what is at hand we find with labor;
> but who has traced out what is in the heavens?
> 17 Who has learned your counsel,
> unless you have given wisdom
> and sent your holy spirit from on high? (Wis 9:16–17).

And yet it is obvious . . . like a single seed, infinite numbers of which are toasted or milled for food. What is it in these dry little seeds that actually nourishes us? Perhaps the energy we get from eating them also has something to do with the transformative power that lies within the seed. For out of an unassuming seed, a green plant can appear, out of many seeds a fruitful field, out of this field in turn, flour, bread—and out of this bread, children, women and men gain energy to live.

People are able to observe the visible, tangible, edible creation as a place where GOD's fingers are at work, where her wisdom has designed everything. Creation is thus a place of GOD's revelation, of her wisdom, which can be recognized in everything. And yet we cannot explain how something grows, how something changes its form.

In the Gospels, too, we find this line of sight towards the obvious, towards specific things created by GOD's hand, which transform themselves through growth or maturation:

> Look at the fig tree and all the trees; 30 as soon as they sprout leaves you can see for yourselves and know that summer is already near. 31 So also, when you see these things taking place (Luke 21:29–31).
>
> And why do you worry about clothing? Consider the lilies of the field, how they grow (Matt 6:28).

Look at a single seed! If you do not understand how something new can come out of this, how then do you intend to understand the transformation of the body? For human bodies are just as much part of GOD's creation as the plants. Bodies can change, just as plants can. This "transformation gene" lies within all life that comes from GOD's hand. And another thing is clear: Paul does not demarcate between spheres of life and death, between the world of GOD and her (ephemeral, painful, frail) creation.[376] The miracle of transformation lies in the midst of life, lies dormant with the seed in our hand. But we barely have the wisdom, the words, to speak of it.

Paul is conscious of how difficult it is to speak about resurrection so that it appears credible, desirable, real. We can see his reference to the obvious along the same lines as in Mark 4:14, where sowing the seed is compared to the lessons of the Torah: "The sower sows the word." For some, it falls on fertile soil; in other places birds on the wing scoop it up, or thorns choke it. Whether the seeds turn into something, whether the word produces something, is not in the sowers' control. How can we speak about flourishing, so that it becomes true?

8.5 We all

Paul is not only speaking of the dead who will be changed, but also of the living who will be embraced by transformation.

> We will all be changed (1 Cor 15:51).

This addresses the collective dimension of transformation. "We all" will be transformed by GOD's greening power.[377] Paul does not just mean the congregation he is addressing in Corinth ("you in Corinth will be transformed"), but is including himself and those who accompany him. At the end of the Letter the gaze opens out onto all communities in the province of Asia (1 Cor 16:19–20). "We all"—this is a comprehensive term that does not seek any demarcation between groups.

Paul untiringly uses various images to impress this comprehensive, collective dimension on his audience, and to broaden their view:

> 26 If one member suffers, all suffer together with it; if one member is honored, all rejoice together with it. 27 Now you are the body of Christ and individually members of it (1 Cor 12:26–27).

There is a long history of body metaphors, which have often been used to legitimize hierarchies in the community.[378] Paul, however, is not interested in justifying hierarchical structures;[379] he opens our gaze out towards creation, towards the miracle of transformation, which will leave nothing untouched. And the marveling gaze sees no hierarchies: Paul mentions humans, animals, heavenly bodies, in the same breath so to speak, since everything can sing of GOD's glory (1 Cor 15:39–41). And so the body metaphors in Paul do not belong in an idea of order that legitimizes hierarchies, but in a mystic horizon of connectedness with everything that is alive.

The little congregation in Corinth can perceive itself as part of a great body: it belongs, it is plugged into a history, a future, a project—it is "more." It has a share in the vision of a messianic community, the traces of which could be seen at that time in the eastern Mediterranean region in particular. The Corinthian congregation, an individual, poor community, is a part of a network in which they all stand up for each other. If one community is in distress, this affects the whole network (see Chapter 5, above), which is strengthened through the brilliance of each individual community, shining out into the network around it.

In the same broad view, Paul draws attention to the key role played by solidarity among the communities. This solidarity is expressed in the collection for the poor of Jerusalem, which Paul helps to organize (1 Cor 16:1–4). The theological significance of the collection lies in making the network of relationships visible.[380] The community in Corinth thus makes materially visible that they are part of the people of God, and that they do not forget Jerusalem. This material side belongs to the body as well: the Corinthian congregation is an integral part of the Messiah project.

Now their gaze has opened onto the whole of creation and onto the miracle of transformation, a latent greening or shining which lies in everything. GOD's finger creates a diversity of life *in this world*—not just in a later or transcendental world. At the same time, Corinth has become visible as part of a relationship network. "We will all be changed." An individualistic transformation of everyone for himself or herself alone is not in view here.

With what kind of body do they come? This question, according to Paul, leads nowhere. In the first place, everyday language is unsuitable for speaking about the transformational ability that lies within everything living. Poetic language or the wisdom tradition of the Bible may help us to find words, metaphors. It is as though GOD's creation had left a glimmer in everything, a fingerprint, the point at which wonderment begins. And then Paul speaks of "we all." Not just "they," the dead, but "we all." With this, Paul binds the dead and the living together, and does not allow them to be divided from one another by death.

Finally, he inserts the question about the resurrection of the body into the vision of Israel familiar with collective bodies of hope. In her interpretation of 1 Corinthians, Luise Schottroff makes it clear how important this motif of the collective body is for Paul.[381] The "body of Christ," she says, is not used as a metaphor here, but reflects the idea that the people of God stand before GOD as a collective. The idea of a collective person, who stands before GOD, is part of the whole biblical tradition. *Adam* can mean all humanity; the *Son of Man* (Dan 7:9–28) encompasses the new humanity, the righteous people; the unyielding resistance of the *Suffering Servant* (Isa 53) brings about the liberation of the people. The idea of an individual figure (*Israel, David, Zion*) becomes the collective idea of a people or a community. The servant of God can be a particular person, but also the people of God. Identification and belonging are brought about through such collective figures.

The small communities in Corinth and elsewhere are connected to one another through shared visions, shared experiences, and shared problems, and they share in one another. They know about each other, for example, through the lively correspondence of Paul, and the traveling of the brothers and sisters, who covered astonishing distances. The people, who under the *Pax Romana* had to work so hard and under such harsh conditions that they barely had the opportunity to raise their heads and get a wider perspective (1 Cor 16:15),[382] are incorporated by Paul into a comprehensive body-network, in which they are able to find space, a purpose, and friends.

We are many, we are more—we can have these experiences in life. We can all be touched and spoken to, we can all transform. Our skin is thinner, our responsibility greater, our history richer than a single person would think. We are not alone with the project of the Messiah, in which an infinite number of hands and feet are working. Paul allows us to grow slowly into the collective body of the Messiah, who gives us space and power to stretch out and feel that we are connected.

8.6 The Spirit—a drink?

So how does it happen, this growing into a collective hope-body? Concluding his description of the individual different tasks of the parts of the body, Paul speaks of drinking:

> For in the one Spirit we were all baptized into one body—Jews or Greeks, slaves or free—and we were all made to drink of one Spirit (1 Cor 12:13).[383]

"Drinking of the Spirit" is metaphorical language. How should human beings drink the Spirit, or be watered with the Spirit? The Spirit is not a beverage. Nowadays we would take "drinking spirits" to refer to an alcoholic beverage. In Paul's time, "a drink" would have been beer or wine.[384]

There is a textual variant of verse 13b that reflects our question and attempts to answer it in its own way. A tiny change in the handwritten text has turned *pneuma* into another word *poma*: spirit has become a drink.[385]

In this late variant of the text (from the fourteenth century), Paul speaks of drinking a beverage—not the Spirit. This turns Paul's metaphorical language into a confirmation of medieval ecclesiological practice, making Paul's statements about the unity of the congregational body in baptism (v. 13a) appear to associate "drink" with the chalice of the church, the Eucharist.

This tiny change in the text appears late and should therefore not be exegetically preferred. It does, however, permit a view into the ecclesiological reading of verse 13, which was commonplace under the influence of the medieval church's eucharistic practice. The unity of the hierarchically structured church was made visible ritually with the sacraments of baptism and the Eucharist: members of the congregation are incorporated through the chalice of the Eucharist (through drinking) into the one body of the church, so that they all possess, recognize, live *one* spirit.[386] They all receive the same chalice to drink, and this binds them into one collective body with one spirit. The downside of this textual variant is that it homogenizes believers and eliminates any contradiction.

Paul's expression "we were all made to drink of one Spirit" refers, in terms of cultural anthropology, to the uniting force of drinking together.[387] Sociological research has shown that sustenance in the form of eating and drinking can be understood as a kind of currency, which connects people with each other, and which can be used to trade services, obligations, belonging, and indeed more.[388]

Drinking is considered to be bonding, and yet less formal than eating,[389] as it allows greater flexibility. Alcoholic beverages, in particular, create a high degree of identification within the drinking group, blurring the boundaries between individuals. According to the anthropologist Mary Douglas, drinks "give the actual structure of social life." There are beverages that are the key to the transition from free time to work time (such as coffee), while others ease the transition from work time to recreation (alcoholic drinks).[390]

If we read verse 13b from these perspectives of cultural anthropology, drinking together creates a bond. It is the power of the Spirit that brings forth this connection, a fruit of the Spirit, a gift for the community. The transformation from individual parts of the body into a collective body, the emergence of an awareness of the body and a feeling of belonging together, takes place through drinking, or being made to drink—the Greek form is passive—together.

The medieval textual variant has distorted the drinking together in this respect, by losing sight of the Spirit while focusing on the eucharistic chalice. Additionally, in the medieval Eucharist, only the clergy drank from the transubstantiated chalice, and not the laity. Strictly speaking, this eliminates the shared group drinking, which is horizontal in hierarchical terms, in favor of a representative, vertical drinking.

8.7 Watering

In spite of the late textual variant and its convenient suggestion, Paul surely did not have the medieval Christian practice of Holy Communion in view. In 1 Cor 12:4–13, he sketches how different members with different gifts form a body. The body is conceived of as a collective one, in which all find their space and their task, and every part of it is needed. As cultural anthropology has pointed out, drinking together strengthens bonding. The language of drinking thus reinforces this connection between the members.

"To drink" in connection with "Spirit" (v. 13) refers, within the Bible, not to the Eucharist, but to the act of creation. In Gen 1:2 too, the spirit of God sweeps over the face of the waters, suggesting the potential proximity of life. Anything can arise at this proximity, stretching out an energy field in which sparks can jump.

When God created life in its diversity, a spring rose from the earth and watered everything:

> 5 when no plant of the field was yet in the earth and no herb of the field had yet sprung up—for the Lord God had not caused it to rain upon the earth, and there was no one to till the ground; 6 but a stream would rise from the earth, and water the whole face of the ground—7 then the Lord God formed man from the dust of the ground, and breathed into his nostrils the breath of life; and the man became a living being (Gen 2:5–7).

A spring moistens the field and allows green things to sprout. Without water, life is unimaginable. The Bible's sharp eye sees that the soil must be moist so that God can work it. Adam is created out of this watered earth—and the vitalizing power of God's Spirit. Here again, water and spirit are interlinked.

The verb *potizein* in verse 13b means "to give somebody to drink," to water. Paul uses the passive form, "being watered." *Potizein*, as used in the New Testament, generally indicates life-giving water.[391] Every living being needs water to live, and thus *potizein* has an ethical dimension in biblical writings:

> Whoever gives even a cup of cold water to one of these little ones (Matt 10:42; Mark 9:41).
>
> I was hungry and you gave me food, I was thirsty and you gave me something to drink, I was a stranger and you welcomed me (Matt 25:35).
>
> If your enemies are hungry, feed them; if they are thirsty, give them something to drink (Rom 12:20).
>
> Does not each of you on the Sabbath untie his ox or his donkey from the manger, and lead it away to give it water? (Luke 13:15).

Paul uses *potizein* in 1 Cor 3:6 as "watering" when he speaks of the development process of the young community in Corinth:

> I planted, Apollos watered, but God gave the growth (1 Cor 3:6).

Here again we have the moistening of the earth as a background, which is necessary so that growing and breathing life can emerge (cf. Gen 2:5–7).

In terms of social history, we must also consider the context of a large Roman city. In the cities everything had to be purchased, except water. The Greek orator and philosopher Dio Chrysostom lived at around the time of Paul (ca. 40–110 CE) and knew the conditions in the cities:

> For the poor of this type suitable work may perhaps be hard to find in the cities, and will need to be supplemented by outside resources when they have to pay house-rent and buy everything they get, not merely clothes, household belongings, and food, but even the wood to supply the daily need for fire, and even any odd sticks, leaves, or other most trifling thing they need at any time,

and when they are compelled to pay money for everything but water, since everything is kept under lock and key, and nothing is exposed to the public except, of course, the many expensive things for sale.[392]

Like water, GOD's Spirit is also accessible to all and costs nothing. GOD lets water and justice rain from Heaven, free to everyone who wishes to drink them (Isa 55:1). The rabbinic tradition also acknowledged this link: "Just as water is free for all, so, too, is Torah free for all" (*Sifre Devarim* 48.7).[393] And the words of the Torah, like water, create life, awaken the greening power in everything, which begins to stretch and stir.

8.8 Watering the bones . . .

Paul wrote the Letter to the community in Corinth around 54 CE. When he speaks of "giving something to drink, watering," he cannot therefore, in any circumstances, have been thinking of the priestly Eucharist. He did not know any medieval churches, but he did know the synagogues[394] of his time, in which he taught and studied. A mural in the synagogue in Dura-Europos depicts a biblical scene that could be important in understanding Paul's field of vision.

The murals in the synagogue in the Syrian desert city of Dura-Europos show that there were not only geometrical patterns (mostly mosaics) to marvel at, but also biblical scenes.[395] The mural on the north wall is interesting in our context: it shows a prophetic vision of Ezekiel in the valley of the dry bones, with a few body parts scattered around. Several hands reach down from heaven, and pull the people up, stand them up. Small winged beings join the body parts together into whole persons, who finally stand together in a group. This depicts the prophet's vision in Ezek 37:1–14:

> 1 The hand of the LORD came upon me, and he brought me out by the spirit of the LORD and set me down in the middle of a valley; it was full of bones. 2 He led me all around them; there were very many lying in the valley, and they were very dry. 3 He said to me, "Mortal, can these bones live?" I answered, "O Lord GOD, you know." . . . 5 Thus says the Lord GOD to these bones: I will cause breath to enter you, and you shall live (Ezek 37:1–3, 5).

The message of this mural is recalcitrant: the people of Israel will not end on the graveyard of history.[396] GOD does not let his people go, but continues his relationship with them. Thus, death and violence do not have the last word. The Eternal One fills the prophet with spirit, so that he teaches the Torah to the dry bones. Over several attempts, the bones then start to come together, flesh grows upon them, sinews form, skin stretches over them (vv. 7–8). The prophet has to breathe spirit from the four winds into the shattered bodies, so that they begin to live (vv. 9–10):

> 10 I prophesied as he commanded me, and the breath came into them, and they lived, and stood on their feet, a vast multitude.

> 11 Then he said to me, "Mortal, these bones are the whole house of Israel. They say, 'Our bones are dried up, and our hope is lost; we are cut off completely'" (Ezek 37:11).

In verse 11, the bones complain, because they feel cut off. They can already speak again, but they cannot live as isolated body parts. The prophet therefore has to help them, and make it clear that they are one people, that GOD is with them and will be with them (vv. 12–14).

Before the eyes of the synagogue's congregation, the separate, severed body parts come together, bone by bone. The community sees how many hands animate the lamenting bones, so that the house of Israel, with many members, arises. The house of Israel becomes recognizable as consisting of groups of people, i.e., the house is a collective body, assembled by these many hands. It is no coincidence that this image is found in a synagogue, a space in which people read the Torah, learn, and pray. Ezekiel's vision of the opened graves and the return to the land of Israel sketched a place of hope in which they could re-invent themselves (vv. 13–14).

The synagogue at Dura-Europos sets this dream of returning home center stage, decorating the Diaspora community's assembly room with it. This painting is a defiant message: the house of Israel lives on today, despite destruction by the Assyrians, Babylonians, and Romans.

To summarize: instead of interpreting the drinking in 1 Cor 12:13b ecclesiologically, i.e., by referring to the sacrament of the chalice, I have read it with reference to the following four aspects:

1. Being watered by the Spirit creates bonds between people. This is in line with the sociological interpretation of drinking together, which dissolves boundaries between individuals, joining those who drink together into a drinking community, bonding them as a group.

2. Theologically, the memory of creation from Gen 2:5–7 resounds with the (passive) "being watered": the soil of the fields (*adamah*) was watered so that GOD can form a body out of earth, the body of Adam. Water is vital for all beings, as is GOD's Spirit. This vitality of GOD's Spirit can be experienced by drinking water or even just by being offered water to drink.

3. In the cities of the ancient world, water was free to all. Water and the Torah are free, without costs in the true sense of the word. The Spirit is there for everyone; like water, it flows from the words of the Torah and animates the parts of the body and creates a common hope-body out of them.

4. The mural in the synagogue at Dura-Europos illustrates this: The dismembered bodies are miraculously joined together by heavenly hands, so that the dead get up on their feet and come together again and again as the people of Israel (Ezek 37).

8.9 Conclusion: Hope-bodies

In Dorothee Sölle's reading, the dead do not come to share a meal. They no longer suffer from hunger. The living do not have to share their meager bread with their dead either. But according to Sölle, they "drop in for a drink" with us. It appears as though thirst links everything, through all time, beyond the frontiers of death.

With what kind of body do they come? Not with a hungry body, or a body of any kind. This is actually about our transformation, about the extension of our bodies into a hope-body. We will all be changed, not just the dead. Resurrection encompasses both the living and the dead. This uniting thought is based on the creative force of GOD, which acts in everything. The Greek text of 1 Cor 12:13b expresses this action as "being watered" with the Spirit (which the English versions render as "being made to drink" of the Spirit). Drinking together, according to Paul, binds the individual members into a greater, comprehensive hope-body, which—touched by GOD's greening, or the power of the Spirit—together, begins to move.

> Again II
>
> Make me
> into water again
>
> I want to stream
> in the stream
>
> to flow out
> into the sea
>
> Rose Ausländer[397]

The stream of life, which unites us with the dead, with those left behind, as well as with everything that is alive, is also a body of hope, in which we can immerse ourselves. In Ausländer's poem it consists of water, which dissolves, heals, unites—a body of water into which we can plunge and submerge, which waters us and carries us, and which flows towards the sea. Into the sea! This direction is clear, no more arduous gradient, no effort, no strain, but flowing into the distance, into the freedom of the sea—in a "more-body" that encompasses everything.

8.10 Outlook

The poor of Corinth lived on the streets, and lodged in gloomy back rooms, but together they were the temple of GOD. For the power of the Spirit was alive in the midst of the synagogue's congregation, when the Torah was read and listened to, and when solidarity was practiced in daily life. When, together with Paul, they resisted poverty, when they helped each other out and shared bread, then together they built a shared house, a space of protection and hope.

> For we are God's servants, working together; you are God's field, God's building (1 Cor 3:9).
>
> Do you not know that you are God's temple and that God's Spirit dwells in you? (1 Cor 3:16).
>
> Now you are the body of Christ, and each one of you is a part of it (1 Cor 12:27 NIV).

The field, the building, the temple, or the "house of Israel" and the body illustrate shared identity and the common bond of the many. They are called upon together to live as a collective body before GOD.

"You are the body of Christ"—this gives the many, who seek their livelihood in the throng of people, membership of a collective. Paul wraps the poor in the metaphor of the body of the Messiah, like a warm coat under which the Corinthians can slip. The Messiah is a hope-body, which can be traced back far into the history of Israel; it is much older than Jesus of Nazareth. The Psalms, too, refer to a king whom GOD will appoint for his people—and this was in the post-royal era following the destruction of Jerusalem around 586 BCE. The kingdom had fallen, but not the figure of a just king, who would work for the welfare of the poor.[398] The figure of the Messiah in Paul does not refer to a wise king, but to an enemy of Roman imperial rule who was tortured and crucified because he was part of a liberation movement in Palestine. Making reference to this figure, understanding him as a hope-body for the poor, is part of Paul's perspective.

Paul localizes GOD's Spirit on the side of the Crucified, i.e., not on the side of those who were victorious or successful, but together with the bodies who were sold or cast out, those who were regarded as worthless in the Roman arenas, in animal baiting, gladiator fights, or mass crucifixions.[399] The same power, says Paul, that animated the dead in Ezekiel's vision of the battlefield, also summoned the crucified Messiah from the grave—and now leads the defeated out of their gloomy tenements. You are not garbage, says Paul, GOD lives among you. For one another you are not strangers, but a united body before GOD—reach out to one another, have confidence. Life awaits you!

The image of the body's neediness acquires new weight in the age of climate change and its noticeable consequences. It is not the earth that is a vale of tears, not the human body that is problematic because of its sexuality and its weakness. It is the mentality of maximization, the lust for profit, that empties and warms the oceans. Political power will have to be renegotiated between the countries of the global North and the South, the generations who will have to live with this ransacked Earth and those who only care about their short-term profit.

It would be cynical for resurrection to count only for the afterlife. Risen beings as incorporeal angels, who flit about on paintings or in legends or films, are like volatile hopes that play no real role in human life. Resurrection has political, social, and tangible consequences for our bodies, which are meant to be places of life, which want to laugh and to eat, to love, and to work.

And yet hope of resurrection cannot be equated with an ethical appeal to speak out for others. It unites creation theology and Christology, the dimensions of poetry and power. For when we are "more," we will transcend boundaries that we took for granted. If *one* thirst unites the dead and the living, this thirst is stronger than death. This changes our language, which is not accustomed to speaking about this type of thirst. The hope that all—including the dead—will rise to live scrambles all the boundaries. This hope seeks permeable spaces, criss-crosses the spheres of life and death, the here and the hereafter, the at first and the afterwards, the local and the temporal.

To and fro wanders the love between the living and the dead, to and fro flutters the longing; death is not far away, but neither is life. Poetry and mysticism have to take the lead here, because a permeable language is starting to sing and dance, and to keep silence. In any case, it just won't do to leave resurrection to the dead and to defer thirst for life to the afterlife. The living should also have reasons to shout for joy and to be jubilant. No way is there nothing to laugh about down here.

9.

"A Ghost Does Not Have Flesh and Bones"

WHAT DO WE HAVE TO COUNTER HUNGER? (LUKE 24:39)

9.1 What is Luke 24 about?

In the last chapter of Luke's Gospel, the Resurrected eats before the very eyes of the people who have gathered (Luke 24:43). This is the only time in Luke's Gospel that eating is shown so plainly. Readers cannot have the least doubt: somebody asked for food—and somebody ate fish. But this immediately begs the questions: Who is this somebody? Who is resurrected? What exactly is resurrection? What is this eating about?

This scene must shake any idea of resurrection being purely spiritual, because it focuses on the body and its needs—appetite or hunger—as well. In the midst of Jesus' gathered friends, a real body appears, made of flesh and blood, with skin and bones, hands and feet. This body is hungry again: it is alive.

> 36 While they were talking about this, he himself stood among them and said to them, "Peace be with you." 37 They were startled and terrified, and thought that they were seeing a ghost. 38 He said to them, "Why are you frightened, and why do doubts arise in your hearts? 39 Look at my hands and my feet; see that it is I myself. Touch me and see; for a ghost does not have flesh and bones as you see that I have." 40 And when he had said this, he showed them hands and feet. 41 While in their joy they were disbelieving and still wondering, he said to them, "Have you anything here to eat?" 42 They gave him a piece of broiled fish [and honey], 43 and he took it and ate in their presence (Luke 24:36–43, adapted from NRSV).

The connection of resurrection and eating raises the relentless question of the Resurrected's body. It is once again the question we discussed in relation to Paul (see Chapter 8, above):

> "With what kind of body do they come?" (1 Cor 15:35).

While Paul uses poetic-mythological language to describe the miracle of transformation, sketching a comprehensive organic network, Luke's Gospel treats this issue narratively. Its final chapter tells of the time of despair following Jesus' death, which transforms step by step before the readers' eyes and leads to the fish-eating scene in Jerusalem.

Even though Luke's Gospel recounts the story very carefully and clearly, understanding Luke's vision of resurrection is a challenge for readers. It is easy to carry one's ideas of resurrection into Luke 24, and readers can overlook what Luke is sketching out carefully, right in front of them. In the process of reading, memories of other gospels, sermons, or prayers mingle with the Lukan text and form the reader's individual understanding. This process makes it difficult to perceive what precisely the text is saying.

Luke[400] places what occurred in Jesus' time and shortly afterwards into the context of the political history (Luke 1:1–4), which reached a crisis for the Jews under Roman rule. This is a challenge for many readers of the Bible today: it means that the text is about a liberation movement, not about a very individual relationship between oneself and GOD, but about a societal, collective, social, political dimension. The Jewish people in the east—one of the many peoples incorporated into the Roman Empire—longed for freedom, autonomy, and a correspondingly better life. Roman rule in the eastern province of Palestine was hard, and made no provision against hunger, drought, or social injustice.

The Jews—in all their diversity and with all their rifts—worshipped GOD in the temple in Jerusalem; the Torah gave them orientation in daily life, and the Torah's many stories and narrative tradition formed their sense of history. Into the history of his people with their GOD, Luke now embeds the events surrounding Jesus' execution in Jerusalem, the hopes pinned on the Messiah, and also the experiences of the new life that was palpable despite the shattering of the Jesus movement. And he is a master, from whom we can learn a great deal.

The concluding chapter of the Gospel, Luke 24, leads the reader to a shared meal with the Resurrected. So there is a final meal for Jesus in the company of his disciples (Luke 22:14f)—and a meal after his death, again in the company of the disciples. While the last meal before Jesus' death is remembered in the church's eucharistic practice, the meal with the Resurrected remains without echo in the church. I consider this to be an omission that has robbed the Christian communities, and the church, of much energy.

For a hermeneutic of hunger it is certainly impressive that the shared meals do not end with Jesus' death. Jesus' last supper is not the last meal eaten by the circle of disciples. We can add further meals in Luke's Gospel: the little supper in Emmaus, the meal in Jerusalem. Astonishingly, it is the Resurrected who is hungry, who asks for something to eat (Luke 24:41). Hunger, the shadow of which we can discern in the Gospels, does not die. As soon as the disciples gather together, hunger is in their midst: Do you have anything to hand to ward off hunger? The question should still be asked of any Christian gathering, church or congregation, in rich or poor communities: What do we have to counter hunger?

I want to investigate the process of transformation, as narrated by Luke 24. The turning point is formed by eating fish with the Resurrected. This is why the hermeneutic of hunger is also legitimate in relation to the resurrection, i.e., if "arise and eat" are intertwined, the question of what the resurrection signified for hungry people must also be located within the hermeneutic of hunger. I will thus consider the combination of arising and eating as a key question. What kind of body arises in Luke 24? Is it really an individual physical body? What kind of body is hungry? How is it made, if it has "flesh and bones" (v. 39)? And: what is it hungry *for*? In the next section, I sketch the following steps:

1. The narrative thread of Luke's Gospel starts with the search for Jesus' body after his execution and the visit to the grave. If we feel our way along this thread, we will realize that the body of Jesus is no longer to be found, but a new body will nevertheless assemble itself before our very eyes. We will investigate this closely.

2. At the end we recognize the risen body—with eyes and heart, hands and feet, flesh and bones—as a hope-body, as we have also seen in Paul (see Chapter 8, above). This messianic body of hope—consisting of the assembled disciples, the narrative community of Luke—is hungry!

3. This community, however, does have something with which to counter hunger—Luke's narrative tells us they produce "broiled fish and honey." We also need to pay attention to this story: sweet honey, in particular, has generated a theological tradition rich enough to make readers' mouths water.

4. Luke's Gospel links this food with the Torah, the words that can give life. They are edible words—words that melt in the mouth and enliven the body. "These are my words," (Luke 24:44) rejoices the Resurrected, and Luke's Gospel closes with great joy (v. 52) and the song of praise (v. 53) from the narrative community, who have something with which to counter hunger.

9.2 Disturbed conditions

Eating is at the heart of this process of transformation from grief to joy, from death to life:

> "Have you anything here to eat?" 42 They gave him a piece of broiled fish, 43 and he took it and ate in their presence (Luke 24:41–43).

This meal takes place after Jesus' death. But we have never been able to read so clearly that Jesus ate while he was alive. Although Jesus was welcomed into houses (Luke 4:38; 7:36; 10:38; 11:37; 14:1; 19:5; 22:14), Luke's Gospel never mentions what he ate, or even whether he ate at all. The text is obstinately silent on this. This silence about Jesus' eating speaks volumes. It has something to do with a knowledge of hunger; in the whole of Luke's Gospel, we never read about cooking or preparing food or meals, or about shopping at the market. No fisherfolk bring their catch. We see no one harvesting, or watering their vegetables.

If we hear of a fig tree growing in a vineyard, it is only to find out it was barren (Luke 13:6). If we hear of children asking their parents for an egg or a piece of fish because they are hungry, it is recounted as a question that shows conditions were disturbed:

> 11 Is there anyone among you who, if your child asks for a fish, will give a snake instead of a fish? 12 Or if the child asks for an egg, will give a scorpion? (Luke 11:11–12).

Even just the suggestion that a father could offer a snake to eat, or a mother a scorpion, is disconcerting. The barren fig tree and the hungry child's plea are indications of a food shortage. Such narratives do not add a colorful note; they do not make the mouth water. Since we barely hear anything else about fruit trees or children, these mentions are all the more important—but they give the text a rather gloomy shading. We can also add the prayer for daily bread to this mood. In this context of scarcity they become an object lesson of a practice of trust, of knowing that GOD is on the side of the hungry. This is why we have to plead persistently, to become shameless:

> 5 And he said to them, "Suppose one of you has a friend, and you go to him at midnight and say to him, 'Friend, lend me three loaves of bread; 6 for a friend of mine has arrived, and I have nothing to set before him.' 7 And he answers from within, 'Do not bother me; the door has already been locked, and my children are with me in bed; I cannot get up and give you anything.' 8 I tell you, even though he will not get up and give him anything because he is his friend, at least because of his persistence he will get up and give him whatever he needs" (Luke 11:5–8).

To obtain bread, the host has to bother his neighbor, who does not want to get up at midnight and share his bread. If his sleep is disturbed, he will in the end get up and hand over the bread, so that he can get back to sleep. The host, in whose home the traveler has sought shelter, has nothing in the house to offer. This shows how precarious the household's situation was. The prayer for daily bread should be seen in the context of this household.

Before our very eyes, we see conditions that are disrupted by hunger. If, from his birth up to his execution, Jesus never chews bread in comfort or drinks water in the sight of the readers, never bites into a fig or a spring onion, these are conscious narrative omissions that outline the shadow of hunger. Almost unnoticed, a longing threads through Luke's Gospel: to be satisfied for once. And here, at the end, this longing is brought to the table.

But why only here? After his death? How can a person who is executed, who rises again, eat? What is this about? It is about the body that rises. What are its characteristics? There are discussions about this; we have to talk about it. The body that rises is so real that it can also eat, says Luke. Do we share his opinion? Or do we think that a person who has been executed, who choked to death hanging on a cross and lay in a tomb for three days, cannot possibly rise up and eat fish? That would be believing in fairy tales! Is that what Luke wants to make us believe? We can understand this idea as wishful thinking by shocked mourners. But is that what Luke is telling us? Should our trust in GOD be based on this great resurrection miracle?

I would like to let Luke take me by the hand and lead me through this world of ideas—resurrection, transformation, fractures, upsets, and fantasies. Then I can start to see that the resurrected body is solid, real, and then again immaterial, transparent, of a different nature. It oscillates in the narrative theology of Luke 24. On the one hand, he asks for food, takes it and eats before the eyes of witnesses. He walks with them to Emmaus, breaks bread with them. On the other hand, he suddenly vanishes from their sight (v. 31). How is this possible? How is this meant? And at the end, after the meal of fish, how should we imagine his disappearance into heaven (v. 51)? What is Luke actually telling us? Isn't he expecting too much of us? This oscillating narrative theology puts our idea of resurrection to the test.

9.3 Desperately seeking Jesus

Women came to the tomb, following the day of Sabbath rest, with prepared aromatic oils (Luke 24:1). They found the stone rolled away from the tomb, but they did not find the body of Jesus (vv. 2–3). The oils in the grieving women's hands were intended for the body that had been tortured and killed. But the body of Jesus (*soma Iesou*) was not to be found in the tomb.

> And they found the stone rolled away from the tomb, 3 but when they entered, they did not find the body of the Lord Jesus.[401] 4 While they were perplexed about this, behold, two men suddenly stood near them in dazzling clothing; 5 and as the women were terrified and bowed their faces to the ground, the men said to them, "Why do you seek the living one among the dead? 6 He is not here, but he has risen. Remember how he spoke to you while he was still in Galilee" (Luke 24:2–6 NASB).

Two men in dazzling clothes entered the tomb and stood beside the perplexed women. They spoke of "the living one," *ton zoonta*. The living one is not here, they said, he has risen. But they did not mention the name "Jesus." Is "the living one" someone other than "Jesus"? The living one spoke to the women while he was still in Galilee, said the two men. This makes it clear, for one thing, that these women had been disciples right from the start; they had belonged to the Jesus movement from its beginnings in Galilee. For another thing, it provokes the readers: the way he spoke to you—that can surely be none other than Jesus! Why do they not mention his name, but speak of "the living one"?

Here the narrative begins to shimmer. Only this is clear: the body of Jesus is not to be found in the tomb. You don't find a living person among the dead—but what does this mean in terms of Jesus' body? Has he come to life again and wandered off? Or does this body have some different form of life, so that he cannot be found in material terms? Finally, we must investigate the question of whether "the living one" actually does mean Jesus or rather a form of GOD, the "living one" as referred to in Revelation, for example:

> 17 When I saw him, I fell at his feet as though dead. But he placed his right hand on me, saying, "Do not be afraid; I am the first and the last, 18 and the living one. I was dead, and see, I am alive forever and ever" (Rev 1:17–18).

The seer in Revelation describes a visual and auditory vision. Seeing and hearing this figure frightened the prophet deeply so that he fell down as though dead. First he heard a voice (Rev 1:11), and then he described what he had seen:

> 12 Then I turned to see whose voice it was that spoke to me, and on turning I saw seven golden lampstands, 13 and in the midst of the lampstands I saw one like the Son of Man, clothed with a long robe and with a golden sash across his chest. 14 His head and his hair were white as white wool, white as snow; his eyes were like a flame of fire, 15 his feet were like burnished bronze, refined as in a furnace, and his voice was like the sound of many waters. 16 In his right hand he held seven stars, and from his mouth came a sharp, two-edged sword, and his face was like the sun shining with full force (Rev 1:12–16).

What John's Revelation formulates here in detail, Luke refers to only in passing: the dazzling clothes of the two men suggest a vision, as does the fright of the women in the tomb. They were terrified and bowed down deeply (Luke 24:5). They did not fall down as though dead like the prophet in Revelation, but "bowed their faces to the ground," as the text has it.

The shining figure in Revelation says he is the living one. He shows himself and can be heard. In Luke, the two men tell the women they should not seek the living one among the dead, and remind them of words that he taught them. This lays two tracks that will lead to the living one: turn away from the grave, and remember the life-giving words of the Torah.

In the first verses of this chapter, Luke showcases the body of Jesus. It was going to be covered in aromatic oils and honored, as proof of the love and faithfulness of his disciples. They climb down to the caves, into a tomb, they even lie flat on the ground. In this position they experience something about the living one, who is not to be found in the burial cave. The women remember his words (v. 8). Now the remembering immediately unfurls its power: they get up, turn around, abandon the tomb. They have understood that the living one is not to be found among the dead. They turn to their sisters and brothers, telling them everything ("the eleven and all the rest," v. 9). Now, in proclaiming their news, they emerge in the text by name and are no longer just referred to as unspecific "women": Mary Magdalene, Joanna, Mary the mother of James, and the other women who belonged to the Jesus movement (v. 10).

It is striking that the wording in verse 3, *soma Iesou kyriou*, "the body of Jesus, the Lord," does not reappear right up to the end of the Gospel. The women disciples did not find his body in the tomb, but it does not appear elsewhere either. Let us put it like this: On a textual level, the body of Jesus remains untraceable.

After Jesus died on the cross (Luke 23:45) and Joseph, a member of the council, a good and righteous man from Arimathea, had taken the body down, wrapped it in linen cloths and laid it in a rock-hewn tomb (v. 53), this body remains hidden. The women do not find it and the two men in dazzling clothes confirm this not-finding: It is not here. This makes the search really take off. In memory, in his words—that is the direction indicated (vv. 6–8).

9.4 The name of Jesus

But let us follow Luke's narrative thread, which leads the readers first to Emmaus. Two members of the Jesus movement were walking to the village of Emmaus. On the way they began to talk about everything that had happened.

> 15 While they were talking and discussing, Jesus himself came near and went with them, 16 but their eyes were kept from recognizing him (Luke 24:15–16).

Two people are walking along, a third joins them, so the three of them walk on together. But Luke does not put it like this. He implies that "Jesus himself" came near and accompanied them. Can the executed man, whose body cannot be found, now suddenly be here? Verse 16 makes it clear at once that something was strange: "their eyes were kept from recognizing him." The two verses have a lot to offer.

In the search for the body of Jesus we are already encountering Luke's oscillating narrative technique at work. Jesus appears—from where, actually? Out of nothing?—and comes nearer and nearer, walks along with them, speaks to them—and yet his friends, amazingly, do not recognize him.

Would we have recognized him? Readers have an advantage in that the narrator explains that it is Jesus who approached them, something that is not clear to the walkers. We tend to assume that we would have recognized Jesus, if we had been there. But unfortunately we weren't there at the time and today . . . we no longer see Jesus. We make do with believing that the Resurrected finally ascended into heaven and was removed from our eyes. But hold on: How did we get to thinking we would have recognized Jesus on the road to Emmaus? We haven't seen him at all—in contrast to his disciples and friends. How should we be able to recognize him, if we have never seen him in the first place? How should we be able to recognize him without an explicit "hint to the reader," if he approached us on the path that we walk today?

But the simple reading—here comes the Crucified, freshly risen from the tomb—is disallowed by Luke himself. If things had been that simple, his friends and disciples would also have recognized him. A tortured man who has just been reanimated should be recognized as such, at least. Yet in verse 16, Luke hangs up a great big caution sign. Verse 16 shows that things were not as they appear: the eyes of the two disciples were unable to recognize him at all.

The verb "to approach, to come near" (Greek: *engizein*) breaks through any direct, simple way of reading. Jesus comes near—but he doesn't come near enough for them to recognize him. There is a blur in this coming-near, as in the scene as a whole. It must remain open whether Jesus comes near to them "only" in memory, as they begin to talk intensely with one another, contemplating passionately, trembling with emotion. As they say later: "Were not our hearts burning within us?" (v. 32). Does not the coming-near consist precisely of talking about everything with one another and pouring their hearts out to each other? They feel alive again, and overcome the paralysis of death. We could go even further and say: "talking about everything" also includes interpreting the Torah, arguing about its promises, digging deeper, and expressing doubts about the end of the liberation movement. It will continue to exist, you'll see, for GOD wants the liberation of his people. Then "Jesus" would have come nearer in their memory, as their Torah-teacher, as they, like him, interpreted the Torah in light of current events.

The approach of Jesus is thus not made clear narratively, but remains fuzzy. The body of Jesus, this poor, ill-treated corpse that has lain in the grave for three days, was not seen on the road to Emmaus. Correspondingly, we do not find the expression "body of Jesus" here. On the other hand, memory and the passionate discussions of the Torah on the road unfurled their power—so greatly that Jesus somehow came nearer. How exactly did that happen? The two disciples relate the Torah to present events. The "things that have taken place there in these days" (v. 18) are to do with GOD, with his word, with liberation—they articulate the hope that has been dashed (v. 21), with the hope of Israel as a backdrop.

As soon as the disciples were able to relate the Torah to the present, the word of GOD came alive. The same will also be the case later in Luke 24:44: remembering "his words" helps to process the catastrophe. The term "his words" also shimmers. Are these the words that Jesus spoke? Or are they the words of GOD, words from the Torah, which YHWH gave? If "talking about all these things" (v. 14) means talking about the events in Jerusalem against a background of the Torah, then we have overcome this either-or. For they are words of the Torah, interpreted in the present, whether by the walkers to Emmaus or by Jesus as Torah-teacher: the words of GOD placed into this situation.

This would then equally apply to what the women report:

> 8 Then they remembered his words, 9 and returning from the tomb, they told all this to the eleven and to all the rest (Luke 24:8–9).

The women are not just recounting what they have experienced, but also remembering the words of the Torah, i.e., the hope of Israel, the Spirit's power in the prophets, the suffering of GOD's servant, etc. They remember the power of the Torah and proclaim this to the brothers and sisters, i.e., they place the Torah's words into their present situation, thus interpreting the situation and recalling the Torah.

The final chapter of Luke's Gospel began with the search for Jesus, for his body. Jesus appeared on the road to Emmaus—he came nearer, but as a body? Or as a teacher, with whom one can talk even if he is not physically present? Whose close listening and passionate commitment to the text, to the Torah, to the poor, can accompany us, even if he himself is not there? The two disciples did not see him. Their eyes were prevented, blocked, clouded; in their grief they did not see what happened.

After "Jesus" came near the two disciples on the road, we encounter his name only one more time. Asked what exactly had happened in Jerusalem, they answer:

> He asked them, "What things?" They replied, "The things about Jesus of Nazareth, who was a prophet mighty in deed and word before God and all the people" (Luke 24:19).

The two talk about him. They situate him in the past: Jesus was a prophet. Thus, "Jesus" has found his place in the memory of those who are on the road together and ponder with one another. Jesus of Nazareth is dead. Everything has expired with his death, and the hopes of the Torah make no sense in the present; they have become meaningless, empty. The appeal that the two hear does not concern their talk about Jesus in the past, but their interpretation of the things that happened in Jerusalem. In the current events—the brutal crucifixion—they find nothing left of the hopes that had appeared in Jesus' lifetime. The appeal (vv. 25–27) means this: You must read things differently.

9.5 Jesus in the translations

The name of Jesus does not appear again in Luke's text. Most translations do use it, however. The translators insert it very deliberately, and thus the translations do not follow Luke's text precisely. They do not take seriously what the women and the walkers to Emmaus had to learn: that because Jesus has died, this is about a lively remembering of the interpreted words of the Torah. The women sought the body of

Jesus—they did not find it, but they did find the power of remembering "his words." The walkers were outraged at the absurdity of what had happened, and the words of the Torah stuck in their throat. On the road to Emmaus, they had to learn to look at current events with the eyes of Torah readers.

By inserting the name "Jesus," the translations of the Bible prevent readers from seeing clearly. They also introduce a particular idea of resurrection into Luke's Gospel, which is foreign to it. We must therefore elaborate on these insertions.

Many English translations of the Bible—and German versions too—repeatedly introduce bold subheadings into the text, which are not to be found in the original Greek text. It is always questionable whether these subheadings are really necessary. In any case, they steer the reader's understanding. They can of course be perceived as an aid to reading, yet these subheadings are misleading where the theological understanding of the original Greek text experiences considerable change. This is the case, for example, in Luke 24:36:

> Jesus appears to his disciples
>
> 36 While they were talking about this, Jesus himself stood among them and said to them, "Peace be with you." (NRSV)

The NRSV's subheading states that it was Jesus who appeared to his disciples. But this is not the case in the Greek text, which would be better reflected by the following corrections:

> 36 While they were talking about this, ~~Jesus~~ he himself stood among them and said to them, "Peace be with you." 37 They were startled and terrified, and thought that they were seeing a ghost. 38 He said to them, "Why are you frightened, and why do doubts arise in your hearts? 39 Look at my hands and my feet; see that it is I myself. Touch me and see; for a ghost does not have flesh and bones as you see that I have." 40 And when he had said this, he showed them ~~his~~ hands and ~~his~~ feet. 41 While in their joy they were disbelieving and still wondering, he said to them, "Have you anything here to eat?" 42 They gave him a piece of broiled fish, 43 and he took it and ate in their presence (Luke 24:36–43, adapted from NRSV).

If we consult the Greek text, we can see that the name "Jesus" does not appear in Luke 24:36. The NRSV translation inserts the name, as well as the subheading "Jesus appears to his disciples." This sets the course for readers of the Bible. Resurrection means: Jesus comes out of the grave in person, terrifies his friends, shows them his limbs, wants something to eat, and eats before their very eyes to demonstrate that he has risen. But this understanding of resurrection comes about only because the name "Jesus" was added to Luke's text.

Luke leaves it open who this "he himself" is, who is standing among them and speaking. Many English translations cannot bear this openness, and fill it with the name "Jesus," adding the subheading "Jesus appears to his disciples" in bold to ensure that readers will imagine it all correctly. The risen Jesus shows himself to his disciples, before he is finally carried up into heaven (v. 51).

The NIV takes a similar course, inserting the name "Jesus" in verse 28, so that there can be no doubt about who was walking with the two Emmaus disciples:

> 28 As they approached the village to which they were going, Jesus continued on as if he were going farther. 29 But they urged him strongly, "Stay with us, for it is nearly evening; the day is almost over." So he went in to stay with them (Luke 24:28–29 NIV).

The Good News Bible inserts "Jesus" at several other places as well:

> 15 As they talked and discussed, Jesus himself drew near and walked along with them; 16 they saw him, but somehow did not recognize him. 17 Jesus said to them, "What are you talking about to each other, as you walk along?"
>
> ...
>
> 25 Then Jesus said to them, "How foolish you are, how slow you are to believe everything the prophets said! 26 Was it not necessary for the Messiah to suffer these things and then to enter his glory?" 27 And Jesus explained to them what was said about himself in all the Scriptures, beginning with the books of Moses and the writings of all the prophets (Luke 24:15–17, 25–27 GNB).

We can no longer refer to this as a blurring of the narrative. It is writ large that it was Jesus who joined them, walked with them, talked with them—only strange that the disciples did not recognize him.

In verse 36, where the disciples are gathered in Jerusalem, the Good News Bible does not have "he himself" appear, nor even "Jesus himself" as in the NRSV, but "the Lord himself." This is a serious breach. Up to now, the Resurrected has been "Jesus," from now on it is "the Lord." This questionable translation decision is, however, not made transparent.

> While the two were telling them this, suddenly the Lord himself stood among them (Luke 24:36 GNB).

9.6 Whose hands and feet?

Luke 24:40 suffers another insertion, not just in the Good News Bible, but also in the NRSV and the NIV:

> And when he had said this, he showed them his hands and his feet. (NRSV)
>
> He said this and showed them his hands and his feet. (GNB)
>
> When he had said this, he showed them his hands and feet. (NIV)

All of these translations change verse 40 of Luke's text. Instead of "he showed them *the* hands and feet," the English translations all introduce the possessive pronoun "his" hands (and "his") feet. This delicately guides the readers in what they should be imagining.

The Lukan text uses the possessive pronoun "my" on one occasion, in verse 39, in the direct speech of the Resurrected. But the second time he showed "the" hands and feet, not "his hands." The presentation thus shimmers once again before our eyes. We have just put together a picture: the Resurrected standing in their midst—he holds up his hands and points down to his feet, although this second gesture does seem a bit strange. Does he lift up his long robe a little, to show his feet? Or does he lift up one foot after the other? This doesn't quite work—but we imagine the act to be done in a way that is fitting and somehow makes sense, in context. But why should the risen Jesus point to his feet, to make it clear who he is? I would point to my face, not to my hands and feet!

The Resurrected speaks of "my" hands in verse 39, but whose hands is he pointing to in verse 40? Luke leaves it open whose hands and feet we are looking at. In the search for the body of Jesus, this is not insignificant. Is it important to see Jesus' hands and feet in order to believe it is he? What would his limbs make clear?

Jesus' body was crucified. Luke makes this link between the name "Jesus" and the execution relentlessly explicit. The Greek text of Luke 23 mentions the name Jesus nine times: Luke 23:8, 20, 25, 26, 28, 34, 42, 46, 52. It is Jesus of Nazareth who was executed. Crucifixion was a humiliating and cruel type of execution. It destroyed Jesus' body and exposed it to public shame. The population of the Roman Empire was familiar with this method of torture, and was reminded of it repeatedly. Violent criminals, slaves, and political agitators were crucified. There were several mass crucifixions following uprisings in first-century Judea, not even sparing women and children.[402] Death by suffocation came only after several hours; as time went by, suspended by their arms, the bodies would no longer be able to breathe. The bodies would be tied or nailed on, and suffocation was often prolonged by giving them a small seat to perch on. The painful death was finally brought about by breaking the legs, as mentioned in John 19:31–33.

After this public torture, Luke no longer shows Jesus' body. Since his entombment (Luke 23:52), he has withdrawn from all prying eyes, through the darkness of the tomb and through the linen cloths in which he was wrapped. The group of women do not find him, and according to Luke, no one else finds him either. It is important to see this respect for the executed body; although (consciously or unconsciously) reading John's Gospel alongside does cause some confusion, as in contrast to Luke, it does bring the tortured body into view quite starkly.

9.7 Excursus to John

John's Gospel also describes an encounter with the Resurrected, although it is very different from Luke's narrative. In our context, it is important that in John 20–21 the name "Jesus" really is in the Greek text, repeatedly. Against this backdrop, the omission of the name in Luke 24 should stand out. In addition, the word *kyrios*, Lord, can also be found in John's scene—quite differently from the meal scene in Luke 24.

> 19 When it was evening on that day, the first day of the week, and the doors of the house where the disciples had met were locked for fear of the Jews, Jesus came and stood among them and said, "Peace be with you." 20 After he said this, he showed them his hands and his side. Then the disciples rejoiced when they saw the Lord [*kyrios*] (John 20:19–20).

Thomas was, however, not present when Jesus came, and did not believe what the disciples told him afterwards. He insisted he would not believe unless he could see and touch the body of Jesus:

> "Unless I see the mark of the nails in his hands, and put my finger in the mark of the nails and my hand in his side, I will not believe" (John 20:25).

Thanks to Doubting Thomas, we find out precisely why the Jesus of John shows his hands and his side. There is a second meal scene among the disciples:

> 26 A week later his disciples were again in the house, and Thomas was with them. Although the doors were shut, Jesus came and stood among them and said, "Peace be with you." 27 Then he said to Thomas, "Put your finger here and see my hands. Reach out your hand and put it in my side. Do not doubt but believe" (John 20:26–27).

Here, the body of Jesus as a tortured man comes into sight. While in Luke 24 we hear and see nothing of stigmata, John mentions his side, which must bear a gaping wound into which Thomas could reach. But the feet remain unmentioned, although John does stress that Jesus is able to go through closed doors. This feature of the narrative cannot be found in Luke's Gospel either.

If we read the two Gospels together, without seeing their independent features or differentiating the associated christological statements they make, we are writing a new gospel of our own, which is not to be found in the New Testament. Luke's and John's narrations are each coherent in themselves and consistent with their respective Gospels. Luke leaves much open, he works, so to speak, with gaps that make us think. He confuses us with his shimmering narrative technique, which does not eliminate the blur but plays with it instead. If he is now clearly not using the name "Jesus," then this means something. If he cloaks the tortured corpse in linen and lays it in the tomb so that no one will find it again, then this is an important feature of Luke's Christology. While in John's language the body of Jesus has risen again, Luke steers us to a new body, one which is assembled between the lines, but before our very eyes. This Lukan language contains autonomous christological potential, which I will now pursue.

9.8 What kind of body rises?

Let us turn back to Luke 24. The question of the body still preoccupies us. What kind of body rises again? We have learned with the women in the tomb that the body of the living one (v. 5) is not to be found among the dead. "The living one" must be sought in memory and in the words of the Torah (v. 8), or so the female disciples proclaim, as do the disciples on the road to Emmaus. "Jesus" finds a place in memory (v. 19), which lives and propels us; a place in a past that stays connected to the present and thus has impact on the understanding of what happens in the present. While breaking bread in Emmaus, the two disciples recognize "him." But who is this, precisely? Who was on the road with them? Luke remains discreet again and leaves out the name and the body of Jesus.

> 28 As they came near the village to which they were going, he walked ahead as if he were going on. 29 But they urged him strongly, saying, "Stay with us, because it is almost evening and the day is now nearly over." So he went in to stay with them. 30 When he was at the table with them, he took bread, blessed and broke it, and gave it to them. 31 Then their eyes were opened, and they recognized him; and he vanished from their sight. 32 They said to each other, "Were not our hearts burning within us while he was talking to us on the road, while he was opening the Scriptures to us?" 33 That same hour they got up and returned to Jerusalem (Luke 24:28–33).

Once again: the omissions of "Jesus" are significant on a narrative level. Some Bible translations force an unambiguous Christology on readers, before they have had the chance to examine their own ideas. The translations insert the name, to ensure that Jesus rises again, and no one else. This changes the role of the disciples. They appear to be slow on the uptake, blind, incapable—while the readers have it easy and know that this is Jesus. And so it escapes most Bible readers that their advantage is fabricated by translations of the Bible and not by Luke.

Luke (unlike John) does not insert any supernatural encounter. A dead body that passes through walls, but is still alive, is something we seek here in vain. Nevertheless Luke constructs a mystery, which began with the search for the body/corpse of Jesus.[403] Let us note: The two disciples are walking despondently to Emmaus. Hardly have they begun to talk with one another and to ponder, than "Jesus came near to them." But what does this mean, exactly? Who exactly came near to them? Is a person with them on the road, whom they do not recognize, an unknown Torah-teacher? Or is "Jesus" alive and close by in their conversation? We as readers are questioned directly by the text as to what we see before us. This question applies to the scene in

"A Ghost Does Not Have Flesh and Bones"

Emmaus as well: Is Jesus sitting at the table? Jesus, just as he was before his death? Or the crucified, broken body of Jesus, marked by torture? Or another person, who somehow reminds them of Jesus? Or a ghost, who looks like Jesus, but who evaporates on closer examination?

We must distinguish between the idea of resurrection that floats around in our minds—sometimes drawn on unreflected set pieces from our childhood, or influences from religious art—and the one which Luke sketches with careful strokes of the pen. Luke patiently makes several attempts to describe what is important to him, and to lead us to the questions that we must put to ourselves. After the tomb scene there is the scene on the road, then the breaking of bread in Emmaus, followed by a brief scene of exchange between the companions who had all experienced something (Luke 24:33–35).

In the midst of their lively exchange a further vision or apparition arises, which unsettles the joint narrators:

> 36 While they were talking about this, he himself stood among them and said to them, "Peace be with you." 37 They were startled and terrified, and thought that they were seeing a ghost. 38 He said to them, "Why are you frightened, and why do doubts arise in your hearts? 39 Look at my hands and my feet; see that it is I myself. Touch me and see; for a ghost does not have flesh and bones as you see that I have." 40 And when he had said this, he showed them hands and feet. 41 While in their joy they were disbelieving and still wondering, he said to them, "Have you anything here to eat?" 42 They gave him a piece of broiled fish, 43 and he took it and ate in their presence (Luke 24:36–43, adapted from NRSV).

Any readers who have so far held fast to the possibility of "Jesus" appearing as a ghost receive Luke's clear denial of this: "A ghost does not have flesh and bones as you see that I have" (v. 39). This definitively rules out this particular way of reading the text. The risen body is no transparent entity; there is still no trace of anything supernatural.[404]

Luke 24:36–43 states nowhere that "Jesus" in any way has appeared as a risen being.[405] His name is not given here either. But we must ask ourselves who "I myself" can be (v. 39). This leads us to the next question, of who is actually rising here. In verse 33, it is the two disciples who hurried from Emmaus back to Jerusalem—it is they who rise up. Then, we remember, "rising up" and "rising again" is the same verb in Greek. Here, Luke is using *anistemi*.[406]

> And they rose up the same hour, and returned to Jerusalem (Luke 24:33).

The two walkers discovered on the road that their hearts were beating again, or even burning. In their shared conversation they rediscovered their passion for interpreting the Torah, and they understood what they had previously failed to grasp. Their hearts have become warm again and now, in verse 33, they rise up. We could also translate this as "they rose again." They are deeply moved by what they have experienced, and hurry to their brothers and sisters in Jerusalem. They had not been physically dead, but very downcast. Their hope was damaged, if not destroyed.

That they suddenly get up and hurry to Jerusalem expresses their new vitality. Now they want to see their companions again, and seek them out. They begin to share what they have experienced, seen or heard, what they have encountered in the meantime. And in doing so, it comes out that the others have also experienced something. Their experiences of resurrection form a narrative community. So far, this is the only "body" that we can recognize. The two who were going to Emmaus get up. Their hearts burn again, and are revived. They become members of the narrative community that is forming in Jerusalem:

> 33 That same hour they got up and returned to Jerusalem; and they found the eleven and their companions gathered together. 34 They were saying, "The Lord has risen indeed, and he has appeared to Simon!" 35 Then they told what had happened on the road, and how he had been made known to them in the breaking of the bread. And they rose up the same hour, and returned to Jerusalem, and found the eleven gathered together, and them that were with them, 36 While they were talking about this, he himself stood among them (Luke 24:33–36).

In the reinvigorated narrative community of disciples, who come together in Jerusalem for the first time since the crucifixion, something becomes perceptible. While they are talking to one another, recounting their impressions, something takes place in their midst. In the text, *autos* (Greek: "self, himself") suddenly stands there (v. 36).[407] Is it the lively storytelling, the exchange of experiences, that causes *autos* to take shape? *Autos* is present in the midst of them, similarly to Matthew's phrasing:

> "For where two or three are gathered together in my name, there am I in the midst of them" (Matt 18:20).

What appears here has nothing to do with the *stigmata*, and neither is it a vision suffused with celestial light. Luke allows nothing to flash, not even the tip of a robe, nor an angel, nor a beam of light. Nevertheless, the assembled sisters and brothers are afraid, shaken by a tangible presence.

"It is I, *autos*" shows them his hands and feet in Luke 24:39. In verse 40, he shows *the* hands and *the* feet. On one occasion they are "my hands" and the other they are "the hands." Here, precisely, Luke is oscillating greatly. To whom do these hands belong? Are they the hands of Jesus? No, he does not reappear, his name is missing, his body remains removed from our view.

Which hands and feet are they? Which hands and feet were assembled? Here in Jerusalem the hands and feet of the disciples met, the women who took aromatic oils to the tomb, Mary Magdalene, Joanna, Mary the mother of James—their hands; the feet of the walkers who hurried back from Emmaus to Jerusalem and who had risen up; and those of Simon Peter (v. 34) and a few others (v. 33). So many hands and feet were gathered here together! So much potential, so many actions, and so many long journeys could be taken together! Do we see these hands—or do we deliberately overlook them and prefer to keep looking for supernatural hands?

The *autos*, the "it is I myself" suggests the limbs of the people assembled there. "His hands and feet" consist of the living, flesh-and-blood hands and feet of those who have gathered. They are the risen limbs of the Messiah, who can serve (practice of the hands) and follow (practice of the feet).

Paul puts it in very similar terms in 1 Corinthians, and we can link to his vision here (see Chapter 8, above):

> Now you are the body of Christ (1 Cor 12:27).

"It is I, *autos*" is the impulse for the formation of the collective hope-body of the Messiah. Those who have gathered begin to understand themselves as being parts of a collective body. Through the sharing of memories and experiences, in seeking the relevance of the words of the Torah, their community becomes more than the sum of its parts. Another quality becomes perceptible, something welds them together, binds them together—it is *autos*, this shimmering "third party," open towards the God of Israel, who is alive and present in her/his words, open towards the Crucified, who interpreted these words, lived them, embodied them, and open to everyone who is present. *Autos* condenses into a hope-body, which arises before our very eyes, which overcomes mourning, and eats.

9.9 Eyes and heart, hands and feet, flesh and bones

While the body of Jesus in Luke 24 cannot be found, on a textual level a new body assembles: with new eyes (v. 31), a burning heart (v. 32), hands and feet (vv. 39–40), and made of flesh and bones (v. 39). These body parts must be understood against the backdrop of Old Testament anthropology.

In Hebrew, there is no expression for "body." Hans Walter Wolff has pointed out that the Hebrew names for organs and body parts stand, like pronouns, for a whole human being.[408] The body part and its actions are thus viewed together. The parts are thus synecdoche for the whole person. It should however be noted that the Hebrew use of language sometimes differs considerably from modern body imagery.[409]

I want now to investigate the body parts that are mentioned in Luke 24, against the background of Old Testament anthropology:

1. It starts with *the eyes*: These are the first indication of a transformation. In Luke 24:31 they start to open, to see in a different way, and consequently to perceive. Even in verse 16, their sight is associated with perceiving or not perceiving. The

Old Testament attaches more importance to seeing and to eyes than to hearing. The word for "eye" appears 866 times, but "ear" only 187 times.[410] Seeing and understanding generally belong together.[411] In the New Testament, those who believe and those who see are identical; in this sense the many healings of blind people always have more than one meaning. Luke 24 recounts how the same eyes are at first unable to perceive (v. 16), because they were downcast (literally "surrounded by darkness," v. 17), then while breaking bread, their eyes open and the two walkers understand.

2. The second organ to be mentioned is *the heart*: "Were not our hearts burning within us?" (v. 32). The two walkers remember that their hearts warmed to the words of the Torah and its interpretation. Talking on the road warmed their hearts. However, in the Bible the heart is not the seat of the emotions, but the seat of reason and understanding, of considering and making decisions.[412] They thus grasped the words of the Torah with their hearts. The human heart also preserves memory, remembrance (Judg 16:15; Luke 2:51). This all comes into effect in Luke 24:32. Eyes and heart have to do with recognizing and trusting, remembering and understanding. In verse 38 the heart of the narrative community once more comes into view: the cognitive process threatens to falter, and thus the gaze is redirected to hands and feet.

3. In Luke 24:39-40 hands and feet come into view. With over 1,600 mentions, "hand" (Hebrew: *yad*) is one of the most common words in the Hebrew Bible.[413] Human action is concentrated in the hands. In the New Testament, the term "to serve" indicates action—handling things, giving a hand—and thus the importance of the work of hands. Serving and following (*diakonein* and *akoluthein*) can in the Synoptic Gospels virtually be described as technical terms for discipleship.[414]

4. *Feet* are mentioned explicitly in Luke 24:39-40 together with hands. They are of course implicitly already in play, for the two men who are walking to Emmaus— as when they get up (v. 33) and hurry to Jerusalem. Feet or legs are mentioned about 250 times in the Old Testament.[415] The foot embodies the human world, its connection to the earth, its stability, and its flexibility. Hands and feet express how people live, whether what they do and strive for endures and makes sense, and much more. In verses 39-40, these two body parts come prominently into view, drawing attention to the discipleship, to the practice of the hands and the feet,[416] the serving and following, and thus encompassing so much more than the parts of the body themselves.

5. Only when *flesh covers the bones* can spirit, movement, life flow into the body. Flesh and bones are the basic provision for life at all, and are the distinctive characteristics of humans, who recognize themselves in flesh and bones.[417] A body belongs to a family, to a people, to a community, through its flesh and bones.

Here in Luke 24:39 "flesh and bones" is an important double term, expressing vitality, cohesion, and belonging.

So, the new body is described using three double terms: *eye and heart, hand and foot, flesh and bone.* This brings into view a body that sees and understands, that is able to serve and follow. It is energetically alive and cohesive—something we will take up again below. These body parts and thus this body do not at any moment signify a re-animated "Jesus." Here, resurrection means: A new body composes itself, a collective hope-body arises out of the wreckage of the trauma surrounding the execution. The companions, disciples, brothers and sisters in Jerusalem are integrated into this body, they take part in this body, they are part of it—together, they form the hope-body.

In Luke 24:33–36, this body is made up of the narrative community.[418] The individual preceding scenes each provided a part of the whole: The hands brought the aromatic oils, the feet undertook the walk to Emmaus, the eyes watched the breaking of bread, and the heart burned while discussing the Torah; flesh and bones arrive at the moment of gathering, of the building of a new family or community, so that *autos* becomes present among them (v. 36). The hope-body is assembled in these verses. They sit down together, their stories join together. The hands and the feet of those gathered there have flesh and bones; they are able to move mountains. They are not impotent, but strong and resilient. Together they are a family—whose kinship we might now perhaps express as "they are one flesh and blood." In those times blood was not understood to transmit familial traits. But you could see similarity between brothers and sisters, kin and ancestors: they share one flesh and bones.

At this point I would like to remind us again that we should not mix Luke's Christology with John's. John 20:25 has the disciple Thomas find the holes of the nails in the body of Jesus. His hands and his side (John 20:20—not his feet!) are marked by the crucifixion. But in Luke there is nothing about wounds.[419] The hands and the feet assembled here are in no way injured or weakened, but simply alive, and have already shown in the narrative of Luke 24 that they are capable of action.

9.10 Have you anything here to eat?

We have seen in Luke 24 how a new body assembles itself. Now this resurrected body would like to eat:

> 41 "Have you anything here to eat?" 42 They gave him a piece of broiled fish,
> 43 and he took it and ate in their presence (Luke 24:41–43).

Fish was an important foodstuff in Palestine.[420] There was very probably a salt fish industry at the Sea of Galilee, which is also evidenced by the name *Tarichea* for Magdala (Aramaic: *Migdal*). *Taricheos* is preserved fish. The salted fish were wrapped in fig leaves and layered into sealed clay pots. These were traded from the

Black Sea to Spain.[421] Fresh fish was generally expensive; cured or dried fish was for the poor people.

Here in Luke 24:41, it should be noted that the disciples were apparently sitting together without anything to eat, as the fish was brought only upon request. Since the text gives no indication that a meal had preceded this scene either, we should ask ourselves whether those assembled in Jerusalem were fasting together. Only once the body had composed itself anew, once life had begun to pulsate, did an appetite develop, i.e., did he ask for food.[422]

How should this question be understood? I do not think it incidental that the question of whether there is something to eat comes up. It would be quite different if the Resurrected had said: "I am hungry." Or commanded: "Bring me something to eat!" The risen body appears questioning, curious, interested. "Have you anything to eat here?" could also be a question about how they are: Are you well, have you already eaten? The question refers to those who are present—the subject of the sentence is "you"—and to what they are sharing with one another. Do they have something that connects them? What do they have to fortify themselves?

The assembled people show that they do not lack food. They know where they can get hold of a fish that is already prepared. It is the first time in the whole of Luke's Gospel that the disciples have and give food. From their hands, the Resurrected takes the good things that they have. It is the first time that this giving-taking situation is described: the disciples draw on a wealth of resources. They do have something with which they can counter hunger.

9.11 Honey

I would like to discuss this in more detail. What do the women and men who form into a hope-body here have to counter hunger? A piece of broiled fish. I find it fascinating that some old texts add to Luke 24:42:

> They gave him a piece of a broiled fish and of an honeycomb. (KJV)

This additional phrase, for which source evidence is relatively strong,[423] is revealing. The fish is sweetened with honey—this is not just a culinary enrichment, but links the eating scene to a rich biblical tradition.

Honey is an opulent gift of nature in a time that had not yet experienced sugar from cane or beets. Fructose grew everywhere, and could be enjoyed in figs, dates, melons. But honey was a gift from the bees, who collected nectar with uncanny diligence. Honey was a fruit from heaven, a gift that had to be found. But manna from heaven, which the Jewish people found in the wilderness, also had to be collected. In the morning it lay as honeydew on the bushes; but it rotted if kept overnight.[424] Heavenly food was thus also connected with the lesson not to hoard, not to become greedy, but to take only what was needed for the day, what was necessary to live.

It is not good to eat much honey: so for men to search their own glory is not glory (Prov 25:27 KJV).

The Song of Solomon talks of eating honey in the middle of a banquet of love:

I come to my garden, my sister, my bride;
I gather my myrrh with my spice,
I eat my honeycomb with my honey,
I drink my wine with my milk.
Eat, friends, drink, and be drunk with love (Song 5:1).

In the ancient world, a reading of the Song of Solomon developed in both Judaism and Christianity that related love allegorically to the love between God and humans. Athalya Brenner explains this in terms of the historical background: "worrisome times of military upheaval, conquest of the land by the Romans, destruction of the Second Temple in Jerusalem, the failure of anti-Roman uprisings, and the loss of all organizational structures for the Jewish community. In sum, those were times of crisis that also led to the development of Christianity in the first and second centuries. When it seemed as if God had left the people of the covenant completely in the lurch, the allegorical reading of the Song brought new affirmation of God's steadfast love and mercy toward Israel."[425]

The insertion of the honeycomb into Luke 24:42 connects seamlessly with this interpretation: The Messiah's followers felt they had been abandoned (vv. 20–21). If we read verse 42 while remembering the banquets from the Song of Solomon, then we see the love of God towards Israel confirmed in this eating scene: God will never forsake her beloved people. The relationship between God and Israel is steadfast, like that of the lovers in the Song of Solomon. The fish dipped in honey makes a snack into a banquet of love and faithfulness. The book of Wisdom, which was written in the first century BCE in Alexandria, Egypt, is along the same lines. The wise women and men wrestle with their faith in God, since actual living conditions are so hard it appears useless to hold fast to a God.[426] While they are this insecure position, they are reminded of Yhwh's heavenly food, the manna that secured life for the people in the desert—and the associated lesson of moderation, of not taking more than they needed.

The book of Wisdom extols wisdom as being sweet, for it comes from God's hand, down from heaven, like honey and manna, and corresponds to the sweetness of the Torah, which was brought down from Sinai. Its words have healing power, and it even brings people up from the underworld.

> 12 For neither herb nor poultice cured them, but it was your word, O Lord, that heals all people. 13 For you have power over life and death; you lead mortals down to the gates of Hades and back again. 14 A person in wickedness kills another, but cannot bring back the departed spirit, or set free the imprisoned soul. . . . 20 Instead of these things you gave your people food of angels,

and without their toil you supplied them from heaven with bread ready to eat, providing every pleasure and suited to every taste. 21 For your sustenance manifested your sweetness toward your children; and the bread, ministering to the desire of the one who took it, was changed to suit everyone's liking ... 26 so that your children, whom you loved, O Lord, might learn that it is not the production of crops that feeds humankind but that your word sustains those who trust in you (Wis 16:12–14, 20–21, 26).

People can kill others—but not liberate them. Humans cannot bring about the return of the departed spirit. But GOD prepares what is needed to sustain life, as bread from heaven: manna, the food of angels. This is also along the same lines as in Luke 24: the execution, which lies leadenly upon the friends of Jesus and destroys their hope of liberation, is contrasted with the snack of sweet fish. This meal is a result of faithful engagement with YHWH's word, which revives people, and is like angel food, the bread of heaven, full of sweetness.

In Greek antiquity, ambrosia and nectar were the food of the gods, quite in line with this understanding. *Ambrosios* means "immortal."[427] Nectar is withheld from mortals, for it is only for the immortals, the gods, because it makes those who drink it immortal. But conversely, the biblical wisdom tradition tirelessly praises the word of GOD, the Torah, as being sweet and life-giving for all, young and old, wise or naive.

In the apocryphal book Joseph and Aseneth,[428] we find honeycomb as angel food that has transformative power.[429] Chapter 16 of Joseph and Aseneth describes in detail how an angel comes to Aseneth and asks for a honeycomb:

> 4. And Aseneth went into her inner room and found a honeycomb lying on the table; and the comb was as white as snow and full of honey, and its smell was like the breath of life. 5. And Aseneth took the comb and brought it to him; and the man said to her, "Why did you say, 'There is no honeycomb in my house?' And lo, you have brought me this." 6. And Aseneth said, "My lord, I had no honeycomb in my house, but it happened just as you said: did it perchance come out of your mouth, for it smells like myrrh?" 7. And the man stretched his hand out and placed it on her head and said, "You are blessed, Aseneth, for the indescribable things of God have been revealed to you; and blessed too are those who give their allegiance to the Lord God in penitence, for they shall eat of this comb. 8. The bees of the Paradise of Delight have made this honey, and the angels of God eat of it, and no one who eats of it shall ever die." 9. And the man stretched his right hand out and broke off a piece of the comb and ate it; and he put a piece of it unto Aseneth's mouth.
>
> ...
>
> 15 Then the angel stretched forth his hand and took of the honeycomb and break it; and he ate a little, and gave the rest to the mouth of Asenath, saying—16 "This day hast thou eaten of the Bread of Life, and are anointed with the Holy Chrism. 17 Beauty is given thee for ashes; for virtue shall never go

from thee, neither shall thy youth wither, nor thy fairness fail; but thou shalt be as the strong city builded as a refuge for the children of our Lord, Who is King for ever more." 18 Then the angel touched the honeycomb, and it became unbroken as before.[430]

In relishing the honeycomb, Aseneth is transformed (v. 16). Honey causes her beauty to flourish and makes of her a well-fortified city, a shelter for many. The textual variation of Luke 24:39 may be reminiscent of verse 16 of the Joseph and Aseneth story in particular. The honey helps the delicate young body to grow, flesh and bones will blossom through eating the heavenly food, here: the honeycomb. Something new comes about through this eating, something that has never been present before begins to appear, a real space of hope, asylum, a collective hope-body.

Aseneth is encouraged to eat of the honeycomb, just like Ezekiel, who has to eat a scroll that tastes of honey (Ezek 3:3):[431]

> "Mortal, eat this scroll that I give you and fill your stomach with it." Then I ate it; and in my mouth it was as sweet as honey (Ezek 3:3).

Ezekiel describes how sweet the word of GOD can be, and how good it is. It gives him the gift of smooth, flowing speech, which he needed urgently as prophet.

But the message that the eloquent prophet of Revelation has to convey can be bitter:

> So I took the little scroll from the hand of the angel and ate it; it was sweet as honey in my mouth, but when I had eaten it, my stomach was made bitter (Rev 10:10).

Flowing honey in the context of antiquity refers to miraculous, heavenly food. It comes from heaven, from the air—it is not manufactured by the sweat of one's brow, but found, bestowed upon those who seek. In the wisdom literature, wisdom is a divine gift and—in addition to the idea of it as a tree that brings forth fruit (Sir 24:12–22)—is associated with the sweetness of honey, which gladdens the heart, and smoothens the tongue, so that one can speak fluently in beautiful words that give strength to others.

> 13 My child, eat honey, for it is good, and the drippings of the honeycomb are sweet to your taste. 14 Know that wisdom is such to your soul; if you find it, you will find a future, and your hope will not be cut off (Prov 24:13–14).

Honey transforms the mouth, transforms speech, makes eyes light up, and brings charm to an encounter. Honey revives people and has them grow wings to carry them into the future, into the open horizon. The links between teaching, the word of GOD, and wisdom with honey are very clear in the biblical tradition, and it is therefore no wonder that honeycomb has found its way into the text of Luke 24:42.

9.12 We will live on the third day

Luke 24 describes a resurrection process in minute detail. We have observed how a new body is assembled, with heart and eyes, hands and feet, flesh and bones. This body exists only in the collective—together, the individuals are alive, they are carried by a hope, they remember together and are on the road together. The body of Jesus does not appear again—but the words he taught remain alive.

> "These are my words" (Luke 24:44).

For Luke, reading the Scriptures, engaging with the word of Yhwh in Moses and the Prophetic Scriptures is absolutely necessary in order to process the crucifixion of Jesus. Only this way can the disastrous event be understood as the death of a righteous man, and what this death means for the poor of Israel. The whole of chapter 24 wrestles with not letting the brutal violence that broke the body of Jesus stand as a victory of the powerful.

I would like to recapitulate this briefly here, so that we can focus on the struggle for the meaning of the Scriptures in the post-execution period. In Luke 24:4, everything begins with the disciples' perplexity. Their teacher has been executed. Their friend and teacher, who was a righteous man and a prophet, has been murdered. The Roman occupational force has prevailed, not the will of God. They have seen how he was laid in the vault (Luke 23:55). But now the stone has been rolled away from the tomb (Luke 24:2), the corpse cannot be found. How should they understand this? Is there a context into which to set their experience, or have the Romans triumphed, and there is nothing more to say? How should they behave, in light of their overlords' triumph? Is there something they can do, to express their love and loyalty?

The mystical experience in the tomb casts them back to "his words" (v. 8):

> "[T]he Son of Man must be handed over to sinners, and be crucified, and on the third day rise again" (Luke 24:7).

The women would surely have remembered that Jesus had predicted his death (Luke 9:45 and 18:31–33). But that would just be a repetitive remembering. As well as the proclamation of suffering, the women also remembered the hope for resurrection on the third day. Jesus was convinced that someone who stood up for justice would appear to the powerful as a threat, and they would therefore kill him. But he was also convinced that, out of this death, further courage and great determination would grow: his death would not paralyze the hope for liberation and the people's courage, but strengthen it. Jesus took this defiance from the Torah. When he announced his death (in Luke 18:33), he linked it with the hope of "rising on the third day": The death of the righteous man will not be meaningless but will give power to many, on the third day. Jesus did not invent this hope for resurrection on the third day, but found it in the Scriptures:

> 1 "Come, let us return to the LORD; for it is he who has torn, and he will heal us; he has struck down, and he will bind us up. 2 After two days he will revive us; *on the third day* he will raise us up, that we may live before him" (Hos 6:1–2, author's emphasis).

This ancient saying by the prophet Hosea[432] reminds us of GOD's faithfulness, which will never cease—not even in times of violence, pain, and death. Turning away from the rulers, not letting oneself be beaten down by the Romans, but continuing on the road with GOD—this memory flares up in Luke, as early as the tomb scene.

When Mary Magdalene, Joanna, and the other Mary remembered "his" words and proclaimed them to their companions, they too were speaking of rising again on the third day. "On the third day we will live" (cf. Hos 6:2)—they are not merely reporting what they have seen in the tomb, but are proclaiming the Torah. For with the memory of the proclamation of suffering and of resurrection on the third day, the disciples are creating an initial link to what has happened to them, and to the word of GOD. On the third day after the catastrophe—this is how the Torah refers to it—GOD's power can be felt again. GOD does not give up. Above all, GOD does not give her people up. They remember these words, which reflect the catastrophe they have experienced, and give the words new breath. Hos 6:2 leads them into the Now of the present, on the third day after the catastrophe they have just experienced.

Hos 6:2 is about a collective rising of the people—"we live"—and not a miraculous resurrection by an individual. With their reference to the invigorating power of YHWH, the women are drawing attention not to the resurrection of one man, but to the reviving power inherent to the Torah, which raises up the collective. Those who read the Torah together, share it, live it, can expect divine reviving power on the third day.

"The words" seemed to the apostles to be empty rhetoric, and they did not believe the women (Luke 24:11).[433] The apostles were not yet capable of understanding the events in the light of Hos 6:1–2. They had heard the words of the Torah, and surely also knew them, but these words appeared "empty." This, in my opinion, is the low point of the Lukan community. With the murder of Jesus, the Torah has lost its life-giving power. "The words"—GOD's words—have no effect on the apostles. But the first disciples, who followed Jesus from the time in Galilee, who searched for him and were the first to remember the Torah, have laid tracks. In verse 15, we saw two of them pondering these words and talking about them. The walkers who encountered him on the road asked about "these words" (v. 17). This started a discussion about words of the Torah, which led to the confession:

> "But we had hoped that he was the one to redeem Israel" (Luke 24:21).

Yet this hope, which the Torah had awoken in them, has been shattered. The two disciples are therefore deeply despondent. The stranger on the road almost despairs of the disciples' blindness:

> "Oh, how foolish you are, and how slow of heart to believe all that the prophets have declared!" (Luke 24:25).

Here we hear a voice full of trust in the Torah, which is still as valid as ever, and provides an orientation, even in the present unjust situation, with the breaking of a righteous man through Roman brute force (v. 26).

> Then beginning with Moses and all the prophets, he interpreted to them the things about himself in all the Scriptures (Luke 24:27).

Later, the two disciples remembered this conversation, with burgeoning enthusiasm:

> "Were not our hearts burning within us while he was talking to us on the road, while he was opening the Scriptures to us?" (Luke 24:32).

Now they were able to connect the words of the Torah with what they had witnessed in Jerusalem (v. 35). Their companions also began to join the conversation; mystical experiences and discussions of the Torah mingled, reports of experience, and a quest for meaning interwove into a tapestry of meaning.

> While they were talking about this, he himself stood among them (Luke 24:36).

Finally, we might think as readers, finally he is here! But *how precisely* is *who* there? As a ghost, as an apparition, as an ethereal body who will evaporate after a few days? How do we envisage resurrection now—spiritually, cerebrally, supernaturally? Has Jesus appeared, like a flashback interjected into a film, a dream that everyone is dreaming—and then disappeared after all? And shortly afterwards, leaving the disciples behind, on their own? Or have we understood that it is the narrative community that rises again as a new body? That it is they who are transformed into a messianic body, which continues to live on through the centuries, so that the words are realized anew, again and again?

Luke's Gospel rejects a purely spiritual understanding of resurrection:

> "Look at my hands and my feet; see that it is I myself. Touch me and see; for a ghost does not have flesh and bones as you see that I have" (Luke 24:39).

Verse 39 is directed explicitly against a spiritualized hope. This is not just about "talking about it," about mental exchange, about believing in stories. Those who only remember words without allowing their transformative power to come alive in the present are, to all intents and purposes, remembering empty husks—like Peter, who found only linen cloths in the tomb (v. 12). But also, the interesting conversation that warms the heart (v. 32) would have got stuck halfway, if the disciples had not arisen and hurried to their brothers and sisters. And even when recounting the events and pondering them in Jerusalem (v. 36), it is not enough that everyone is talking to one another. The action of procuring food and eating it before everyone's eyes is needed.

The new body of companions proves that it has become capable of acting: now, when they are able to provide food, the meaning of the Scriptures has arrived in the present. Now they have something with which to counter hunger!

9.13 These are my words!

Now we too have been on a long journey. When breaking bread together in Emmaus, the two disciples' eyes were opened (v. 31), but they still had nothing in their hands. They hurried to their companions, recounted, listened, reported—and then the hope-body began to grow together. It got up and was hungry at once:

> "Have you anything here to eat?" (Luke 24:41).

Now, when they do not just have eyes that can see and a heart that can warm, but also hands and feet, flesh and bones—now they can fetch something to eat. They bring a piece of broiled fish to the table—and some honeycomb, as a later textual tradition has it. Now the new hope-body can refresh itself. And we read:

> 43 and he took it and ate in their presence. 44 Then he said to them, "These are my words that I spoke to you while I was still with you—that everything written about me in the Law of Moses, the Prophets, and the Psalms must be fulfilled." 45 Then he opened their minds to understand the Scriptures, 46 and he said to them, "Thus it is written, that the Messiah is to suffer and to rise from the dead on the third day" (Luke 24:43–46).

Now, when they have fish and honey to counter hunger, their minds open and they can understand what is written. The Torah no longer appears to be empty rhetoric (v. 15), their eyes are no longer blinded, they are no longer foolish and slow to understand (v. 25). Now they have access to the living words, which taste like fish and honey, and which give them a remedy—even against hunger and death.

Finally, we must now look more closely at the phrase, "These are my words." These four words stand between the process of eating and the opening of the mind. We can thus relate them backwards to eating—or make reference to what follows. If we relate them back to the meal, they mean: My words taste like fish and honey; they are good, they are easy to digest, they make the mouth water and gladden everyone's hearts. With them, with my words, you can come alive together, you will be equipped to counter even hunger and violence. If we relate the sentence ("These are my words") to the following verse, then it means: I told you that Christ would suffer in this way and would rise again on the third day. What you are experiencing here together is right, is exactly what I meant. Now a hope-body has arisen, in which GOD's power is alive and active. That is the meaning of the Scriptures, which you now embody.

I think both ways of reading are possible, and permitted. But I would like to point out something further. In Luke 22:19, Luke used a very similar phrasing, which we know from the Words of Institution in the Eucharist. The last time Jesus shared bread with his companions in Jerusalem, when breaking bread, he asked them to continue to share bread in memory of him. And he placed the bread and his body into a context:

> This is my body—*touto estin to soma mou* (Luke 22:19).
> These are my words—*houtoi hoi logoi mou* (Luke 24:44).

Now, in Luke 24:44, "my words" appear in place of "my body" (Luke 22:19). The dead body (*soma*) is sought, but does not reappear. The women are directed towards "his words," they remember them, and pass on their interpretation—but these words appear empty, incomprehensible, and time is needed until they are clothed "in flesh and bones" and can be shared as broiled fish and honey in the resurrected community. The body is so to speak replaced, refilled, re-sketched, by the words that give life.

This leads to a eucharistic theology in the hermeneutic of hunger (see also Chapter 10).

Christ is present among those who have gathered together; they become his hands and feet. The words of the Torah are remembered in such a lively way that they taste like broiled, spiced fish and sweet honey, and make the mouth water. This moment is a celebration. For at this moment, the Roman occupiers have no power over the narrative community. The companions overcome grief, fear, and a crisis of purpose. They have a heart, hands, feet, flesh and bones—and they can remember, make connections, and feed one another.

Now they share a legacy that does not become dusty or rotten, but is in a form that they (and we) can fall back on at any time. Broiled fish and honey can be preserved. They conjure these up—now they are able to do so. The Resurrected eats and is satisfied. The phrase "These are my words" can also express his satisfaction with his students. He has taught them and now they can feed one another, pass on the message. Now there are witnesses who can pass on the Torah as the bread of life—as food for the hungry.

Luke's resurrection theology oscillates. It puts our ideas to the test and takes us into the period following the crucifixion, long before any dogmatization of the nature of Christ (*vere homo—vere deus*), or paintings of the resurrection in churches. Luke's story constantly awakens new questions. Would *we* have recognized him? Would *we* have trusted the Torah, despite the violence we had experienced? Could *we* make the connection between what had happened and the Torah's words? Could *we* conjure up living words like broiled fish? And do *we* never forget that countering hunger is our primary and urgent task? Do *we* belong to a collective hope-body that rejects violence and works, with its hands and feet, for peace?

There are still many questions we could add. Did the disciples really produce fish, or is that just a metaphorical way of speaking about the Torah's effects? Were they transformed, newly assembled into a messianic body, which throughout the centuries has continued to live and work with other people? Or did Jesus really rise again? If so, how? Materially, in a spiritualized way, just for a single moment? Are "my words" the words of Yhwh or the words of Jesus? Is it important to remember the words that Jesus spoke—or is it important to relate the words of Yhwh, which Jesus and the prophets and the Scriptures taught, to the present, to events of our own time?

The community discovers the life-giving words of the Torah anew, tests them out on the defeat suffered, spices them with splinters of experience, and marvels at the power of the Torah to withstand everything that challenges it (v. 41). The Torah is introduced here in its tripartite form: the Law of Moses, the Prophets, and the Psalms (v. 44). These rich testimonies pose critical questions for the present, as well as providing historical references, theological orientation, and spiritual fortification. Everything that the disciples have experienced with Jesus of Nazareth, including his crucifixion, can find its place in the story of Yhwh with his people, and reflects the faithfulness of Yhwh to the poor of Israel. The crucifixion does not make the Torah absurd, an "idle tale"—as the disciples think in Luke 24:11. The Torah, the word of Yhwh, turns in verse 44 back into food, which can fortify, move, heal people, give them impetus, bowl them over, and raise them up. Chewing over the Torah strengthens the bones, makes the flesh bloom, and transforms individuals, allowing a new hope-body to grow together where the words are related to the present, and are lived. The body of the Messiah—made of heart and eyes, hands and feet, flesh and bones—takes shape, where people embody the words of the Torah. This is the Eucharist meal with the Resurrected, surrounded by the resurrected.

In the mouth, the words of God taste like fish sweetened with honey. They can be recognized by this taste (v. 44): "These are my words." The words of Moses, the Prophets, and the Psalms provide nourishment, they taste sweet and spicy, and they raise people up. So the words of the Torah can be eaten, devoured, even slurped. This metaphor of eating for receiving and processing a lesson is not foreign to our culture. However, connecting the verbs of eating theologically with the Torah, or with the words of Yhwh, has been neglected. This neglect went hand in hand with a disdain for the body. Sucking and chewing are verbs with sensual references, they refer to bodily abilities and needs, not just the spiritual, mental level. Devouring, drinking, and eating lead to incorporating, embodying, and thus to transforming the body: the bodies who absorb, who appropriate the word begin to blossom (like Aseneth), begin to rise up (like the people in Hos 6:2), and to reconstitute themselves (like the disciples in Luke 24).

10.

Eating a Transformation

THE LAST SUPPER IN THE HERMENEUTIC OF HUNGER

In this chapter I want to take a look at Jesus' last meal before his death, concentrating on the story in Mark's Gospel (Mark 14:22–26). Let us therefore leave aside the other texts that have also greatly influenced eucharistic theology (Matt 26:26–28; Luke 22:19–20; 1 Cor 11:23–26). It would be a task in itself to read these carefully in the hermeneutic of hunger as well. I would like to take Mark's Gospel to investigate whether or how our reading of the last meal of Jesus—and thus also the Christian Last Supper—changes if we work with the hermeneutic of hunger. We are not beginning with the Words of Institution and the various denominations' traditional interpretations of the Eucharist, the differences that distilled out during the sixteenth century and led to great trench warfare;[434] we are starting with hunger.

It is indisputable that shared meals in ancient Israel and antiquity in general constituted ritual.[435] Communal meals were part of all kinds of gathering, including worship (Exod 24:11; 1 Sam 1:9; Neh 8:10, 12).[436] It is thus not unreasonable for the Christian communities to have a meal that is a central part of worship. But why was it precisely this last shared meal before Jesus was executed that constituted a ritual for the Christian churches? Why not the meal with the Resurrected, as we have seen above (Luke 24:29–31, 36–43; John 21:10–14)? In his speech in the house of Cornelius, Peter referred to the meal with the Resurrected (Acts 10:41; see Chapters 5 and 6, above). Why is it not the feeding of four thousand (Matt 15:32–39; Mark 8:1–9), or five thousand people (Matt 14:13–21; Mark 6:34–44; Luke 9:10–17; John 6:1–13) that is the focus for Christian communities?

A table always has a limited numbers of places; it includes some and excludes others. A table fellowship therefore always has to reflect on who is admitted to the table, and who is not. We therefore start by considering who was sitting at the table when Jesus ate with others for the last time before his death. We are used to presenting Jesus at table in a circle of twelve disciples. The twelve belong to this tradition that has characterized the Last Supper, just as much as the betrayal by Judas. How different would be the message of a tradition that remembered Jesus, not at a table with twelve men, in an enclosed room, but outside in the open air, amid crowds of people?

We must begin by going into the number twelve. As a metaphorical number of hope, "the Twelve" is part of the tradition of Israel; it opens up a future and a life for the community surrounding Jesus as well. In relation to Mark's Gospel, we should then ask where, when, and how the twelve have been introduced. The "commissioning of the twelve" (Mark 3:14) is a momentous translation decision that will have to be discussed, as the Greek text of Mark presents us with a major exegetical challenge. The way the twelve are introduced in Mark's Gospel, they are an open group of "disciples," i.e., with new students joining the group all the time. Not far from the "commissioning of the twelve," the text mentions not being able to eat (Mark 3:20), and the many people who were seeking something. The disciples' learning and the people's hunger appear to be connected.

The Feeding of the Five Thousand (Mark 6:34f) is introduced in connection with the teachings of Jesus, i.e., the multiplication of the loaves is based on this teaching. What did it involve? What did Jesus teach here in Mark 6:34f? Of course the answer must be: he was teaching the Torah. And Jesus' disciples in this story were students of the Torah. They were learning to relate the Torah to their real lives. This story is about hungry people receiving something to eat. The Torah students were learning to relate particular aspects of the Torah—though not all the parts of the Torah, all the Laws and sayings of the prophets, and stories, and Psalms—to their present hunger. They were learning how to counter hunger. We will take this quintessential teaching with us for a new reading of the shared Last Supper in Mark 14:22f.

10.1 Bread in the hand at long last

When Jesus blesses bread in Mark 14:22, the readers of Mark's Gospel can breathe a sigh of relief. Ever since he left Bethany hungry (Mark 11:12, see Chapter 4, above), Jesus has eaten nothing. At least, there is no eating to perceive in the text, and so the readers who know about the hunger of Jesus and his people have to endure, with him, until Mark 14:22. Here, at last, Jesus can recline at table, surrounded by his friends, and eat.

> 17 When it was evening, he came with the twelve. 18 And when they had taken their places and were eating, Jesus said, "Truly I tell you, one of you will

betray me, one who is eating with me." 19 They began to be distressed and to say to him one after another, "Surely, not I?" 20 He said to them, "It is one of the twelve, one who is dipping bread into the bowl with me. 21 For the Son of Man goes as it is written of him, but woe to that one by whom the Son of Man is betrayed! It would have been better for that one not to have been born." 22 While they were eating, he took a loaf of bread, and after blessing it he broke it, gave it to them, and said, "Take; this is my body." 23 Then he took a cup, and after giving thanks he gave it to them, and all of them drank from it. 24 He said to them, "This is my blood of the covenant, which is poured out for many. 25 Truly I tell you, I will never again drink of the fruit of the vine until that day when I drink it new in the kingdom of God." 26 When they had sung the hymn, they went out to the Mount of Olives (Mark 14:17–26).

Hunger pervades Mark's Gospel, running through it like a golden thread, beginning with the locusts of the prophet John (Mark 1:6; see Chapter 3, above) and leading, via John's disciples and the Pharisees who were fasting (Mark 2:18), to the story of hunger in Mark 2:23–38, where Jesus presents his hermeneutic of hunger (see Chapter 4, above). So right from the start we can sense the shadow of hunger that lay over Galilee. When Jesus calls the daughter of Jairus back to life, he immediately adds that they should give her something to eat (Mark 5:43). In Mark 6:34, there follows the story of the feeding of the multitude, which is reported twice—in Mark 8:1f as well. There, the story begins: "There was again a great crowd without anything to eat" (Mark 8:1). Following the feeding, the disciples again have too little food with them (Mark 8:14). Finally, Jesus sets off hungry in the morning from Bethany (Mark 11:12). And later on, Jesus' vivid speech in the temple refers openly to the coming adversity:

> "For nation will rise against nation, and kingdom against kingdom; there will be earthquakes in various places; there will be famines" (Mark 13:8).

After this, we see Jesus exhausted in the house of Simon the leper (Mark 14:3). In the Greek text, there is no reference to eating; the leper's house sounds much more like a poorhouse, a hostel for the homeless and ill.[437]

The only time the shadow of hunger retreats for a moment is in the two great feeding miracles. Otherwise, it weighs heavily on the land. Perceiving the long-running hunger changes our reading of the Last Supper fundamentally: the Passover meal in Mark 14:12f ends the hunger—or at least interrupts it. Jesus gives thanks for the bread they have yearned for, and blesses it (vv. 22–23). The text thus places the bread and the cup in the hands of a hungry man. That alone is a fundamental message.

In the history of Western exegesis, this message has been overlaid with the announcement of Jesus' betrayal. The Words of Institution begin: "In the night when he was betrayed" (1 Cor 11:23) and thus color the Last Supper with the shadow not of hunger but of betrayal. Only someone who remembers Mark 11:12, the hunger and the despair of Jesus, which led him to curse the fig tree, and to the food riot in the temple courtyard, can hear the silence about chronic hunger. This shadow of hunger does not wipe away the betrayal, but gives it another color: it took place in the context of hunger. One hungry man betrays another.

Mark sets the Last Supper in this context. Quite differently from the painter Leonardo da Vinci, whose famous painting *L'ultima cena* shows Jesus with empty hands.[438] Da Vinci sets this scene in an elegant villa of his own time, and in the landscape of Tuscany, which can be seen through a window. The men present come from Italy's fifteenth-century upper class. None looks malnourished. On the table, as well as plenty of tableware, bread and a few small fruits, careful observers can also spot meat, or at least bones. The contextualization of the Last Supper into the Western European world of the wealthy puts betrayal at the center. Judas can be recognized at the table with a bag of money in his hand. At this table, everything is about money, there are the haves and the have-nots. But there are no hungry people. The thought of hunger does not occur at all.

I mention this painting because even today it continues to influence our ideas of the Last Supper. It presents a meal among men, who are all well-heeled, light-skinned, and Western European. There are no women, children, or invalids; there are no dark-skinned, Oriental, or poor people. The question of who is admitted to this table and who is excluded is key. In antiquity, too, shared meals were among the key institutions that formed communities. Group identity was symbolically coded and characterized through meals.[439] Table fellowships are always about inclusion and exclusivity, about belonging, about social position, and about relationships cemented at the table.

> When it was evening, he came with the twelve (Mark 14:17).

Who, in Mark 14:12ff, is eating at the table at the last shared meal during Jesus' lifetime? Who are these twelve?

10.2 The twelve at Jesus' table

The iconography of Jesus' last meal, which is steeped in tradition, has time and again presented the exclusive masculinity of the disciples. From Leonardo via Tintoretto, from Byzantine mosaics to modern church windows, the Last Supper appears as the ceremonial sealing of a male circle. The few new representations of women at the Last Supper have had the power to provoke, but have not achieved any resounding change in perceptions.[440]

The iconography of the Last Supper and the church's practice of the Eucharist—particularly in the Roman Catholic and Orthodox traditions—form a perspective of exclusion. One sex is—tacitly but consistently—excluded. Only one skin color is accepted. Disabled people, children, and the ragged are not present at this fundamentally important meal. This depiction of the twelve white, well-fed apostles at a festive meal actually looks like a successful steering committee, one we recognize from numerous institutions today.

But this perspective of exclusion contradicts the presentation in the Gospels. Does this iconography and this eucharistic practice preach the gospel at all? What messages does this table send out? Do the poor proclaim the gospel at this table (cf. Luke 7:22), or do the rich preach their own gospel to one another? Linking this table of men to the announcement of betrayal creates a peculiar drama. One of the twelve will shortly be excluded—this announcement hangs over the table fellowship like the Sword of Damocles. Combining the perspective of exclusion with betrayal is pregnant with consequences. It legitimizes the status quo, putting the exclusive table fellowship into the right from the outset, and those who are excluded into the wrong.

Women followed Jesus from Galilee to the cross, and kept faith with him beyond his death. The explicit mention of the women at the crucifixion (Mark 15:40), as well as in the empty tomb (Mark 16:1f), make it unlikely that women were barred from Jesus' last supper. But while this meal developed into one of the sacraments and formed a basis for the Eucharist, the women's witness, although impressive, did not affect the development of church rituals. We could ask provocative questions: Are the people sitting at the table more important than those who stood under the cross, or who received the message of resurrection? Where were the twelve during the crucifixion and afterwards? Why should it be theologically unimportant that the twelve were missing at the crucifixion?

Most representations of the Last Supper show Jesus and "the twelve" (Greek: *dodeka*). We must therefore ask whom the New Testament texts designate as these twelve. Are they particular individuals, twelve in number? Who is allowed to sit at the Lord's table? Didn't Jesus sit with a larger circle of disciples than the twelve? And did these disciples also include women?[441]

A series of exegetic observations open up a fascinating field.[442] At the last shared meal while Jesus was alive, the Synoptic Gospels mention different groups at the table—*dodeka*, *apostoloi*, and *mathetai*:

> Mark 14:17: When it was evening, he came with the twelve (*dodeka*).

But in Mark 14:12, 14, 16, 32 Mark speaks of the students (*mathetai*) who were at table with Jesus. The text does not differentiate these terms from one another, but uses them alternately, or in a complementary way. The same can be seen in the Gospel of Matthew. While in Matt 26:20 (NIV), "Jesus was reclining at table with the twelve," in Matt 26:17, 19, 26 the text uses *mathetai* to designate the persons who were at table with Jesus.

> Luke 22:14: He took his place at the table, and the *apostoloi* with him.

Luke speaks here of apostles, not of the twelve; and Luke 22:11 and 39 refer to *mathetai*.

We are used to imagining "the twelve" to mean twelve named apostles. But this is not what the Gospels are doing: the names of the disciples—or of the *apostoloi*—are not mentioned at the Last Supper. In addition, only Luke speaks of *apostoloi*, and all three Synoptic Gospels of *mathetai*. Finally, only Mark and Matthew mention "the twelve" at the table with Jesus. How the three Synoptic Gospels handle these three terms shows that Jesus ate together with the twelve (Matt and Mark), as well as with the apostles (Luke), and with disciples/students (Matt, Mark, Luke) at the Last Supper.

The argument that "the twelve" were always the same twelve men suffers in that varying lists of names have been handed down. These lists are inconsistent, which shows that the tradition of that time did not place much value on the names of the twelve, who appear to a certain extent interchangeable. The order of names and the nicknames also vary in the tradition. But the symbolism of the number twelve appears indisputable in the Synoptic Gospels:

> Matt 10:2–4 and Mark 3:16–19 name: *Simon Peter, Andrew, James, John, Philip, Bartholomew, Thomas, Matthew, James son of Alphaeus, Thaddaeus, Simon the Cananaean, Judas Iscariot*
>
> Luke 6:14–15 names: *Simon Peter, Andrew, James, John, Philip, Bartholomew, Matthew, Thomas, James son of Alphaeus, Simon the Zealot, Judas son of James, Judas Iscariot*

It should also be noted that John's Gospel does not give a list of names at all.

10.3 How should we interpret the number twelve?

Paul's Letters are the oldest New Testament Scriptures and as such they are the closest in time to the Jesus movement. But Paul does not hand down any indications that there could have been a circle of twelve men around Jesus. He barely mentions the disciples, and when he does, his way of referring to them appears not to support the idea of twelve men.

> 5 [H]e appeared to Cephas, then to the twelve. 6 Then he appeared to more than five hundred brothers and sisters at one time, most of whom are still alive, though some have died. 7 Then he appeared to James, then to all the *apostoloi* (1 Cor 15:5–7).

Paul speaks here of the Messiah's appearances. He names Cephas (Peter) as the first to have seen the Messiah, and then the twelve. Does this mean that Peter should not be counted among the twelve? And James (v. 7), the brother of John, is he removing him as well? And equally the expression "all the apostles" makes it difficult to assume a twelve-apostle circle around Jesus.[443] However we might want to break down this list: Paul does not use *dodeka* to mean a limited, numbered group of apostles around Jesus.

It is notable that the Christian interpretation understands the number twelve to have a metaphoric character and be inextricably linked with the twelve tribes of Israel, a collective we can also refer to as Zion, Jerusalem, or the house of Israel (see Chapter 8, above). But as soon as we are talking about the twelve in the Gospels, a different measure is applied. Then we suppose it to mean individual persons. This interpretation is based on the doctrinal assumption that Jesus had in mind a new "people of God" made up of Jews and Gentiles, a new "Israel," detached from the people who lived in Palestine and the Diaspora under Roman rule. But the Gospels tell of the hope that GOD would not forget her people, that YHWH would one day gather his children from all the ends of the earth, from wherever the great powers had banished them. They tell of the hope of the Twelve, that the disoriented, impoverished masses will become one people, receiving bread and dignity, space to live, and a future.

It is not surprising that the hope of the Twelve gained strength under the difficult political circumstances of the first century. The number twelve connects the stricken people with their tumultuous history, and with the tradition of the Prophets and the Torah. In Roman Christianity, which in the fourth century was declared the Empire's state religion, these hopes and references faded. The Twelve turned into a powerful committee of men—even if their power was of a spiritual kind—and became a founding myth. Missionaries, bishops, doctors of the church, and royal court theologians began to shape these ideas in a lasting way: these named twelve men were the origin of the "conversion of the heathens," they were said to have founded the church that became the pillar of the Roman state.

10.4 The twelve in the book of Revelation

Dodeka also appears in places other than the Synoptic Gospels and Paul's Letters. Here, I am making a digression to Revelation, because the number twelve is important there as well. This excursus might illuminate the interconnectedness of *dodeka* with Israel's hope for space to live and for a future. I would like to show, using two interpreters of the book of Revelation, that this connection is indeed evident—provided it has nothing to do with the twelve individuals at Jesus' table.

The book of Revelation was written after the Gospels, towards the end of the first century. As in Paul, no reference to the idea of the Twelve as a named historical circle around Jesus is discernible. Karl H. Rengstorf interprets the woman in heaven crowned with stars (Rev 12:1) as an allegory of the daughter of Zion, because her crown consists of twelve stars.[444] In addition, where Revelation talks about the New Jerusalem, we also come across the number twelve, which Rengstorf understands as an expression for the whole people of Israel:

> If the number twelve occurs again in the measurements and arrangement of the new Jerusalem (21:12, 14, 16, 20f), this is connected with the fact that in the

> formula *dodeka phylai* it had become "the typical number of completeness, of the inviolable totality of the theocratic people, of the people of possession."[445]

So Rengstorf is reading the expression "twelve tribes" as a wide-ranging metaphor of hope for the completeness of a people who were at that time politically and economically devastated.

Equally, according to Rengstorf, the number 144,000 (Rev 7:4; 14:1) should in no way be taken literally. Out of each of the twelve tribes, it says, 12,000 will be chosen, which means that the new community will be enormous and complete: "The Jewish world expected that the time of the Messiah would bring with it a restoration of the Davidic kingdom of the twelve tribes without any restrictions, as we can see clearly from Josephus (*Ant* 11:133)."[446] Even if the twelve foundation stones of the newly built city bear the names of the twelve apostles of the Lamb (Rev 21:14), Rengstorf reads this metaphorically and refers to the idea of the New Israel gathered together out of all peoples.[447]

For Rengstorf, the imagery of the number twelve is embedded in the hope for Israel's salvation. But although he sees the significance of twelve for Israel, he rejects this connection as soon as it concerns the twelve apostles: "Essentially, the Twelve are far more than 'representatives of the twelve tribes of Israel' or part of the Messianic court of Jesus."[448]

Traugott Holtz, too, understands the Twelve metaphorically, and considers them to be closely linked to Israel—as long as we are not talking about the twelve around Jesus. He wants the names of the tribes in Rev 7:5–8 to be understood metaphorically, and points out that they differ from the passages in the Old Testament.[449] He emphasizes that in the first century, only Judah, Benjamin, and Levi were present as tribes, and there was already a belief that the lost tribes would one day return.[450] This hope was expressed, says Holtz, at the end of the book of Revelation, where the city is rebuilt. The number twelve is very prominent in the description of the new city:

> 10 And in the Spirit he carried me away to a great, high mountain and showed me the holy city Jerusalem coming down out of heaven from God. 11 It has the glory of God and a radiance like a very rare jewel, like jasper, clear as crystal. 12 It has a great, high wall with *twelve* gates, and at the gates *twelve* angels, and on the gates are inscribed the names of the *twelve* tribes of the Israelites; 13 on the east three gates, on the north three gates, on the south three gates, and on the west three gates. 14 And the wall of the city has *twelve* foundations, and on them are the *twelve* names of the *twelve* apostles of the Lamb (Rev 21:10–14; author's emphasis).

This repetition of *dodeka* in the building of the New Jerusalem is, for Holtz, a "conscious metaphorical indication that access to the eschatological community of the redeemed has been made possible for the people of God of the old covenant." Nevertheless, Holtz distinguishes this heavenly Jerusalem from Israel, in emphasizing that the foundations of the new city would bear the names of the twelve apostles.[451] Thus, in his interpretation, the twelve tribes are replaced by the twelve apostles, and Israel is superseded by the new people of God, i.e., the church.

Rev 21:10–14 speaks of rebuilding the city that was destroyed ca. 70 CE and remained in ruins for a long time, because, for political reasons, the Romans did not want it to rise again. But this vision allows the city to arise, and *dodeka* forms the principle of rebuilding or resurrection. The city stands upon these twelve, and is structured and aligned according to them. The number twelve is the measure for the future of Jerusalem. The vision uses this metaphorical hope-number to sketch a path into the future: if a community takes the traditions of the Torah, the Prophets and the Writings as a foundation, the future will open up.

10.5 *Dodeka* as a hope-body

An anti-Judaist interpretation divides the old and the new Israel from one another, with the traditions of the old covenant (twelve gates) and the vision of a Christian church (twelve apostles) as the new covenant. In this thinking, the "twelve apostles" can no longer be understood as the hope of Israel, and they lose their rootedness in the tradition of the Torah. But equally, anyone who wishes to hold fast to the historical interpretation of the Twelve in terms of missionaries or apostles must not forget the metaphor of the *dodeka*. This is the number out of which the future grows, a blueprint for hope so to speak, designing a space for living for the people who were stricken, scattered, and enslaved after the great war against Rome. This number also holds fast to the completeness, to the absolute integrity of the people. They are concerned not with numbers as such, but with not leaving anyone out. Together, they will create a new beginning. The number reminds them that a future is possible only if the people show solidarity and work together. If this is true for the book of Revelation, it could also apply to the twelve at Jesus' table.

Luise Schottroff highlights the hope-aspect of the number twelve, and understands it as a vision of a gathered, healed people, and thus as an inclusive collective term, which is not limited to twelve men.

> The designation "the Twelve" comes across primarily as an independent term, which does not need supplementing through *mathetai* or *apostoloi*. It creates a link between the disciples and the twelve tribes of Israel. According to biblical tradition, Israel consisted of twelve tribes. Ten of these (the northern kingdom) were expelled from their lands in the eighth century [BCE], and dispersed for good. In the sixth century, the two tribes of the southern kingdom suffered the exile of their ruling class to Babylon; after their return, a Jewish state arose once more. But the ten lost tribes remained alive in memory from then on. Hope thus arose for a return of all the dispersed tribes, and the reconstitution

> of the Israel of twelve tribes. At the same time, this hope expressed the longing for liberation from war and tyranny.[452]

Schottroff is reading "twelve" metaphorically, not abstractly or divorced from time, but against the political backdrop of the first century.

"The Twelve" encompasses everyone, all of Israel, including women and men, children and the elderly, the dead and the missing. When the twelve are going about with Jesus (e.g., Luke 8:1), this means: Those who were traveling with him all shared the same vision. Jesus was not traveling with a handful of students, nor with a faceless mass of people, but with a vision that encompassed the whole People. The group surrounding him revived the twelve, they embodied the healed People, the twelve tribes, which in terms of *Realpolitik* had not existed for a long time. This group formed the beginnings of a collective movement that was not a random crowd, but had the whole in view.

"The twelve" is also a key term from Jacob's family. Jacob had twelve sons with his wives and concubines (Gen 35:22–27), sons who would in tradition become linked to the tribes of Israel. In the story in the book of Genesis, the brothers had sufficient grain and sheep while they lived together. The world is perfect, so to speak, as long as they are all together. Yet after Joseph is sold by his brothers into Egypt, there is increasing mention of "years of famine" (Gen 41:50).

Jacob therefore sends his sons to Egypt to buy grain. But he sends only ten of them, because he wants to keep the youngest with him (Gen 42:4). This nearly brings disaster upon the brothers. They are presenting themselves as twelve brothers (Gen 42:13), yet they are only ten. Now an uphill struggle breaks out between Joseph, his brothers, and finally their father Jacob, concerning the youngest brother. Only if they appear in full will Joseph believe they are honest (Gen 42:20). At first, Jacob does not agree to send the youngest to Egypt with the rest. But famine continues to be severe in the land (Gen 43:1), until Jacob's family is forced to take action. They can fetch new grain only if all the sons appear together. Jacob finally agrees (Gen 43:11) and lets the youngest go. After a long time, Joseph reveals himself as the brother they had sold, and the twelve are once again gathered as a complete group. Even though the famine lasts for years more, it no longer affects Jacob's family. They move to Egypt to be with Joseph, who takes care of them.

This story of famine is an important background for the number twelve. The story of Joseph links the twelve with being well fed, with caring, solidarity, and the future of the next generation. If the brothers do not pull together, they lose their credibility. Joseph will not give them credit if they appear without the youngest. Who knows what they have done with him? After all, they had betrayed and sold Joseph. As long as their father fails to entrust them with the youngest son, Joseph distrusts his brothers. They will first have to earn his trust. Their spirited advocacy finally creates credibility in Joseph's eyes—and thus brings them access to grain.

We can understand the twelve in the Gospels as descendants of Jacob's family. Talk of the twelve appeals to memory, to hope, to imagination, and to solidarity: "We are more than just a disorganized bunch. We are the descendants of Jacob." The *dodeka* form the start of a solidarity-based people, which in times of scarcity or famine does not savage anyone, sell them or abandon them, and thus earns credibility.

We can therefore understand the twelve at Jesus' table as a collective term at a time in which the masses were neglected or crushed by the great political powers. Like the sons of Jacob, "the twelve at the table" do not stand for individuals, but for allied tribes, and for extended families, which always included women and children. Within the number twelve, even strangers had their place, people with a different origin and skin color.

Reference to the twelve in the New Testament should thus be understood as an attempt to embody solidarity in the tradition of Israel. The twelve is a metaphorical way of imagining a body, a form with its roots in tradition, without being exclusionary. Israel in its heterogeneous dimensions, scattered to the four winds, will come together with her GOD in the temple. This belief is evidenced by the twelve gemstones on the breastplates of the high priests.[453] "Twelve tribes" is a term also used in an inclusionary sense in Luke 22:30 and Jas 1:1. Although by Paul's time ten tribes had long since been wiped out, he too spoke of the twelve tribes, who "earnestly worship day and night" (Acts 26:7).

To disengage the twelve from the hope of Israel, and to transport them into the patriarchal Roman world as a community that excluded women and Jews, is both sexist and anti-Judaist. Instead, we should read "the twelve who were with him" as a vision of the healed people, recognizing this vision in the healings of the Gospels, in lived solidarity, and in work with the poor.

10.6 The calling of the twelve (Mark 3:13f)

Having extracted the twelve from anti-Judaism, we must now discuss a problem of translation. Many English translations insert subheadings:

> Jesus Appoints the Twelve (NRSV and NIV)
> Jesus Chooses the Twelve Apostles (GNB)
> The Twelve Apostles (NKJV)

However, such subheadings are not present in the Greek sources, which consist of continuous text without headings or paragraphs. Subheadings carve up the text into small portions, setting the course for our reading, and creating potential misunderstandings.

As an example, here is the New Revised Standard Version's rendition of this passage:

Jesus Appoints the Twelve

> 13 He went up the mountain and called to him those whom he wanted, and they came to him. 14 And he appointed twelve, whom he also named apostles, to be with him, and to be sent out to proclaim the message, 15 and to have authority to cast out demons. 16 So he appointed the twelve (Mark 3:13–16).

In verses 14 and 16, we search the Greek text in vain for a call or an appointment of the twelve. What we find both times is *epoiesen dodeka*, which means literally: "He made twelve."

So Jesus shaped, constructed, created the Twelve out of the multitude (Greek: *ochlos*), along the lines of his vision of a healed, unified People. Jesus was going about with a disorderly crowd of people from Judea, Jerusalem, Idumea, Transjordan, and the coastal cities of Tyre and Sidon (v. 8). These crowds were unsettled and rebellious, and thus posed a threat to the house of Herod. This is why, in verse 7, Jesus had to flee from Herod's police, who wanted to destroy him. But for Jesus it was precisely these restless, hungry people who should become *the* People; it was with them that he wanted to create a community of the righteous, not a nation, but an ethical-social-religious people. We see Jesus here working on his vision: he healed sick people, he drove out unclean spirits (v. 11), and this is how he made the twelve.

We should take this repeated phrase "he made the twelve" (vv. 14 and 16), as an opportunity to think about how one can *make* twelve. The translation "he appointed twelve" is based on an official theology, in which appointing dignitaries is familiar. Equally, the heading "Jesus Appoints the Twelve" assumes that the Jesus movement had members who were specially appointed. From the outset, therefore, the translation assumes what it is translating. This phrase is not evidence for the image of twelve appointed men: it assumes that Jesus' "making" is an appointment of officials or a nomination of dignitaries.

I read Jesus' "making" as a creative process of work, as building the house of Israel. Jesus joins together, binds stone upon stone. He teaches in the synagogue (vv. 1–5), he has to flee from the police (v. 6), but is always there, where the crowds are, and works with them:

> 7 Jesus departed with his disciples to the sea, and a great multitude from Galilee followed him; 8 hearing all that he was doing, they came to him in great numbers from Judea, Jerusalem, Idumea, beyond the Jordan, and the region around Tyre and Sidon (Mark 3:7–8).

Out of this "multitude" from all over—people who had been scattered to Judea, Jerusalem, Idumea, Transjordan, and the coastal cities—he built the house of Israel. He cured many (v. 10) and drove out their fears and compulsions (v. 11). In this way he "made twelve" (v. 14)—and in Mark's Gospel we can watch him at work. But how precisely did he do it? What did his work consist of?

10.7 For they had no bread (Mark 3:20)

In Mark 3, we see Jesus working intensively with the crowd, which has come from all around. We can only surmise what these people are seeking, since the text is silent on this. But verse 20 gives us an important hint: There was no bread to eat. Most of the English translations omit "bread," although the Greek text explicitly mentions it (*artos*):

> Then he went home; and the crowd came together again, so that they could not even eat. (NRSV)
>
> Then Jesus entered a house, and again a crowd gathered, so that he and his disciples were not even able to eat. (NIV)

Another weak point of some English translations is the phrase "he went home." The Greek text states "he went into a house." If we read that he went home, we have totally different images in our mind's eye. We imagine Jesus going home in the evening—hopefully, to a meal that someone has prepared for him. Yet the text does not say Jesus went home, merely that he went into a house. Whose house? Was it a private house at all? Or was it a public building? The house that Jesus entered in verse 20 may have been a meeting place for the community: Mark 3:1 mentions a synagogue, where Jesus is teaching the Torah and debating with "scribes who came down from Jerusalem" (v. 22f). The text gives no indication that Jesus leaves this context of teaching and debating. All the text tells us is: He went into a house.

Another problem arises where some translations of verse 20 suggest that the crowd kept the apostles from eating:

> And the multitude cometh together again, so that they could not so much as eat bread. (KJV)
>
> When he returned to the house where he was staying, the crowds began to gather again, and soon it was so full of visitors that he couldn't even find time to eat. (LB)
>
> Then Jesus went home. Again such a large crowd gathered that Jesus and his disciples had no time to eat. (GNB)

These translations assume that Jesus and his friends ("they," "Jesus and his disciples") and the multitude are two opposing groups. The crowd becomes an obstacle, preventing Jesus and his disciples from being able to eat properly. This assumption shapes our reading—the multitude is a different group from the twelve—so that we begin to perceive the multitude as a bothersome crowd, who has never had enough, from whom Jesus occasionally has to protect his people, and so on (cf. Mark 6:31; see Chapter 1, above).

It makes a difference whether Jesus and his disciples are part of the crowd or not: they are all really hungry, and lack their daily bread, the basic foodstuff. I consider this

EATING A TRANSFORMATION

to be something we should not ignore. Out of these hungry people from all around, who lack life's necessities, Jesus "makes the twelve." Out of this hungry crowd, Jesus builds the house of Israel. He works with them on the vision of a righteous People who will have bread in their hands. It takes until Mark 14:17–26, for the twelve to recline together at table and have bread to share and eat—a long-awaited, precious moment!

10.8 Where transformation takes place . . .

Bread is mentioned frequently in the Gospels, even if it is as a lack of bread, as here in Mark 3:20. In the feeding of the multitude stories, bread is mentioned together with fish.[454] Bread and wine, on the other hand, are never mentioned together, not even in connection with the Last Supper:

- 1 Cor 11:17–34: Bread and cup
- 1 Cor 10:16–17: Cup and bread
- Mark 14:12–26: Bread and cup, fruit of the vine
- Matt 26:17–30: Bread and cup, fruit of the vine
- Luke 22:7–38: Bread and cup, fruit of the vine
- Acts 2:42–47: Bread and food
- John 6:52–58: Eating flesh, drinking blood, eating the bread of heaven
- John 13: Bread

Of course our imaginations can fill this cup with wine, but the texts do not. Where they speak of the vine, wine is an obvious conclusion—but it could also be grape juice with very little or no alcohol content, or diluted wine, or water with a little juice. Mark 14:12's reference to the Passover meal, at which wine would certainly have been drunk—and still is—also suggests wine. But the New Testament Scriptures do not use the word "wine" at the Last Supper.[455]

These texts give readers the right to fill the cup with whatever they would drink at such an occasion. But the texts do not suggest an alcoholic beverage. This appears to me to be important, because the drinking of alcohol would exclude some people.[456]

Alcohol transports its drinkers into a different mood. When those who had gathered in Jerusalem were seized by the Holy Spirit and began to speak in other languages, outsiders commented on it like this:

> "What does this mean?" 13 But others sneered and said, "They are filled with new wine" (Acts 2:12–13).

Likewise, when Hannah was deeply distressed and praying in the temple, Eli took her to be drunk:

> 12 As she continued praying before the Lord, Eli observed her mouth. 13 Hannah was praying silently; only her lips moved, but her voice was not heard; therefore Eli thought she was drunk. 14 So Eli said to her, "How long will you make a drunken spectacle of yourself? Put away your wine" (1 Sam 1:12–14).

Perhaps the texts of the New Testament are avoiding the suggestion of alcohol, to avoid provoking such ridicule; perhaps they intend to emphasize that it is not wine, but God's Spirit that has brought about the perceived, visible change. In the table fellowships with Jesus, as the Gospels describe, changes take place in those who are present. János Bolyki refers to this in his investigations of Jesus' table fellowships.[457] Something takes place in the life of those who eat with Jesus, ranging from being filled right through to conversion. Some experience salvation, others were lost and are found (Luke 15; 19:1–6). At the wedding in Cana, the disciples achieve a deeper faith (John 2:11). The shared meals are places of refreshment and reconciliation, as well as places of conflicts that come up at the table and have to be resolved.

The table fellowship is not just a bright, pleasant place. Dark changes can also take place there. For example, the last meal that Jesus shares with his disciples sees great conflicts arise. The coming betrayal is an element that destroys fellowship (Matt 26:21–25; Mark 14:18–20). During the Lukan meal, further conflicts flare up when the betrayal is announced: the gathered disciples begin to compete as to which of them should be regarded as the greatest (Luke 22:24). Thereupon, Simon Peter is shocked to be warned that he will deny Jesus three times (vv. 31–34). Jesus even mentions the devil (v. 31), and the mood at the table certainly becomes even darker and more tense. At the end he calls upon the gathering to flee, and speaks of his death, so that the friends pull out two swords (vv. 35–38). Here, the table becomes a place of despair and outrage, as well as jealousy, betrayal and failure.

10.9 And all ate and were filled (Mark 6:34–40)

Let us concentrate once more on Mark's Gospel. Here, the hunger of Jesus (Mark 11:12f) is clearly documented and can be perceived in the text. Not until in Jerusalem, at the Passover feast, will Jesus hold bread and a full cup in his hands (Mark 14:22). Before the feeding of the multitude story, as we have seen, Jesus was battling many problems that paralyzed, ailed, and afflicted the people (Mark 3). And he began to "make" the Twelve. Hunger came into our view in this context (Mark 3:20). In Mark 3, Jesus is unable to chase hunger away. He works against it, by creating the vision of the Twelve, the righteous Israel. But the people continue to bustle about, aimless and panic-stricken, as we sketched out above (Chapter 1). "The times were not good for eating" (Mark 6:31)—times were bad because the political rule was hard on the hungry masses, and because they were times of famine, due perhaps to late-arriving winter rains or a lasting drought, which caused the rural population to suffer.

Mark 6:34 mentions the people's pitiful state: the crowds were like sheep who had been abandoned by their shepherd. No one was taking care of their needs, they had to pay numerous taxes—to Herod's royal house, to the Roman governor, and to their own overlords, so that many farmers became destitute and fell into debt slavery, while the Herodians gilded their palaces.

How must this have felt for the people in Nazareth and Magdala, when directly within their view, Herod Antipas, a son of Herod the Great, had the little city of Sepphoris (about 8 km north of Nazareth) converted into his own personal jewel? He made it into his flagship city, until in 19 CE he moved to Tiberias. The archaeological findings show that the roads in Sepphoris were laid out with precious broken marble, and a Roman theatre stood in the most beautiful spot. Richly colored mosaic floors are evidence of the luxury the wealthy enjoyed in this city, with its two markets, which presumably traded mostly in food (wheat, olives, grapes, vegetables, dried fish), as well as ceramics, jewelry, and textiles.

When the First Jewish Revolt against Rome began, Sepphoris distanced herself from it. While there was fierce resistance around neighboring Magdala for water and land, in 66 CE Sepphoris had already opened its gates to the Roman soldiers, annoying the surrounding towns.[458] Sepphoris was well fortified and armed, and could have led the Jewish Revolt. Its Rome-friendly attitude lay in the social structure of the city, where major landowners, traders, and tax collectors dominated city life. They owned country estates in the surrounding region, and also worked for the Herodian government. Some researchers suspect that Joseph, the father of Jesus, could also have worked as a craftsman in the construction of Sepphoris.[459]

Thus, in Mark 6:34, Jesus sees the people without a leader, following John's execution, and wandering about unprovided for. He begins to work with these crowds, and to teach them. This scene is followed by a beautiful narrative, which is for me the queen of all Gospel stories, and central to the understanding of the Last Supper in the hermeneutic of hunger.

> 34 As he went ashore, he saw a great crowd [ochlos]; and he had compassion for them, because they were like sheep without a shepherd; and he began to teach them many things. 35 When it grew late, his disciples came to him and said, "This is a deserted place, and the hour is now very late; 36 send them away so that they may go into the surrounding country and villages and buy something for themselves to eat." 37 But he answered them, "You give them something to eat." They said to him, "Are we to go and buy two hundred denarii worth of bread, and give it to them to eat?" 38 And he said to them, "How many loaves have you? Go and see." When they had found out, they said, "Five, and two fish." 39 Then he ordered them to get all the people to sit down in groups [symposia] on the green grass. 4 So they sat down in groups

[*prasiai*] of hundreds and of fifties. 41 Taking the five loaves and the two fish, he looked up to heaven, and blessed and broke the loaves, and gave them to his disciples to set before the people; and he divided the two fish among them all. 42 And all ate and were filled; 43 and they took up twelve baskets full of broken pieces and of the fish. 44 Those who had eaten the loaves numbered five thousand (Mark 6:34–44).

Being filled—the dream of all hungry people—and there is still some left over! This story holds a vision that hungry people could tell themselves over and over again.[460] The people's poverty is plain to see. They do not have any food with them; they first have to acquire some. The disciples, too, have only meager supplies. They assume that the people will still be able to find something in the fields, despite having realized in verse 35 that the place was *eremos*—"wild, uninhabited, uncivilized, empty, barren, devastated"—and thus would provide barely anything to eat. In Palestine, it was quite common to collect and eat wild plants.[461]

Angela Standhartinger[462] has examined the feeding miracle against the background of mass feedings documented in antiquity. There are inscriptions testifying that some rulers and rich men hosted great feasts. How many tables were set up, how many people were invited, how many barrels rolled out, and what untold wealth was served—these things show how potent the host was. Standhartinger establishes a few striking differences between these documents of imperial generosity and the New Testament's feeding of the multitude stories. For example, nowhere else is it clear who undertook distribution of the food. The Gospels, however, attach value to reporting that it was the disciples or apostles who took on this task. Equally, the statement that all ate and were filled is found only in the Gospels. No other ancient source makes this statement.

10.10 Leek beds in the desert

As previously in Mark 3:20, Mark 6:34 describes the hungry as *ochlos*: a disorderly bunch. Now the text does not relate that Jesus simply fed this bunch of people. There are a few thought-provoking steps in advance of this. First, teaching is mentioned: "he began to teach them many things" (v. 34). This is, so to speak, the heading over what follows. Jesus taught so well that, in the end, the people were satisfied. That is precisely what good teaching should be.

What did this teaching consist of? What did he teach? This is something we can reconstruct out of the verses that follow, if we look very carefully at what is actually said and done. Everything is part of this teaching in verse 34. We hear that his disciples came to him. They had realized that it was late and the people were hungry, i.e., they had been hungry for a long time, with a hunger that grew and grew, and tortured them. Perhaps this is why the crowds became all the more restless and irritated; perhaps some were on the point of fainting. This is the case in Mark's second feeding story (Mark 8:2–3).

Jesus' teaching thus consisted of approaching this problem of hunger. We should not imagine Jesus preaching over the heads of thousands of people and losing track of the time. The hunger mentioned here must have been greater than "it's time for supper!"—verse 35 points out twice that much time has already passed. So we could also understand this as "it's high time" for the people to receive bread.

Torah teachings had a practical focus. Specific questions were addressed to the teacher, for him to explain. Here the crowd demands bread, welfare, and guidance from a shepherd who would lead them to succulent pastures—Jesus recognized this at once (v. 34). The shepherd—the country's political leadership—had failed totally. After Jesus had taught them many things, the disciples registered that someone would now have to take on the shepherd's tasks, for the crowds needed "pasture" and out here it was *eremos* (v. 35, "uncultivated, stony, deserted"). The disciples had thus understood one key point of Jesus' teaching: awareness of the needs of the poor.

But who could undertake this task? How could it be achieved? With this question, they approach their teacher:

> 35 When it grew late, his disciples came to him and said, "This is a deserted place, and the hour is now very late; 36 send them away so that they may go into the surrounding country and villages and buy something for themselves to eat." 37 But he answered them, "You give them something to eat." They said to him, "Are we to go and buy two hundred denarii worth of bread, and give it to them to eat?" 38 And he said to them, "How many loaves have you? Go and see." When they had found out, they said, "Five, and two fish" (Mark 6:35–38).

The disciples have understood that it's all about eradicating hunger. This stony and deserted land is incapable of feeding the hungry masses. Who can help the hungry? Jesus asks about their stockpiles (v. 38). Do they have anything they can share? The text attaches importance to this process of clarification within the group of disciples. They must take counsel together, look around, find out what they actually have at hand. In this sense, the disciples are at the center of the story. The Torah teacher flips the perspective and hands the question back to those who are asking.

What do they have at hand? Five loaves and two fish. They have to decide whether that is enough, whether it will be sufficient. They bring this paltry offering before their teacher. Jesus does not utter a single word on what his disciples bring, but he does include what they bring in the solution to the problem.

> 39 Then he ordered them to get all the people to sit down in groups [*symposia*: table fellowships] on the green grass. 40 So they sat down in groups [*prasiai*] of hundreds and of fifties. 41 Taking the five loaves and the two fish, he looked up to heaven, and blessed and broke the loaves, and gave them to his disciples to set before the people; and he divided the two fish among them all. 42 And all ate and were filled; 43 and they took up twelve baskets full of broken pieces

and of the fish. 44 Those who had eaten the loaves numbered five thousand men (Mark 6:34–44).

So what does the teacher do now? Out of the disorderly crowd in verse 34 (*ochlos*), drinking groups (*symposia*) are to be formed. Etymologically, *symposium* means a drinking fellowship. In the Greek translation of the Old Testament (the Septuagint) the expression appears only once, in 3 Macc 5:36, where *symposium* means a merry table fellowship convened by the king. In the New Testament, *symposium* is used only here, in verse 39, but not in any other story of a banquet, i.e., it is a *hapax legomenon*, a word or phrase occurring only once.

I find it surprising that Jesus wants to divide the people into *symposia*, drinking fellowships. The disciples found bread and fish, but there is no talk of water or wine. So what should the people be drinking together? Was Jesus assuming that everyone would have brought a water bottle? In this region, which is described as a wilderness, we cannot simply assume there will be water sources. Consequently, the mention of *symposium* is a point that snags our attention.

The second snag follows immediately: the hungry *ochlos* do not do what Jesus suggested, and follow his instruction to form drinking fellowships. Instead, the crowds form up *prasiai prasiai* (v. 39). This means, literally, "leek bed by leek bed." The people sit or lie down in rows like beds of vegetables. The phrase *prasiai prasiai* "in garden beds" comes from *prason*, leek.[463] This phrase is also unique in the New Testament and therefore conspicuous. So here we have two striking *hapax legomena*, which have something to do with one another.

Now we have food for thought. First, why this mention of drinking fellowships? Second, why did people sit down on the green grass like rows of leeks? Further, the green grass surprises me. The place is described in verse 35 as *eremos*, an expression that in Palestine does not allow readers to envision green grass, but rather uncivilized, unirrigated land outside a settlement. The noun can also be translated as "desert." The people are located in no-man's-land, not in this or that village, but outside, where there are a lot of stones and rubble. Why is Jesus suddenly speaking of "green grass"?

It is interesting that, in the Hebrew Bible, the expression for "green fodder, green grass" (*châtsîyr*) is often rendered in the Septuagint's Greek as "leek" (*prason*).[464] The Hebrew word usually refers simply to something "green," something that grows quickly, "green fodder," which English translations therefore generally render as "grass."[465] On a linguistic level, this "green grass" of verse 39 points the way to *châtsîyr*: this Hebrew expression means green fodder, grass, green things. Jesus ordered them to lie on "the green grass" in drinking fellowships. The people surpassed his instruction, by not just lying down on the green, but ordering themselves into rows like vegetable beds. They themselves were forming the green, so to speak, because of the way they lined up in rows like leeks.

The English translations cannot make head or tail of the drinking fellowships or the vegetable beds and therefore just leave them out:

> 39 Then he ordered them to get all the people to sit down in groups on the green grass. 40 So they sat down in groups of hundreds and of fifties. (NRSV)

> 39 And he commanded them to make all sit down by companies upon the green grass.
> 40 And they sat down in ranks, by hundreds, and by fifties. (KJV)

> 39 Jesus then told his disciples to make all the people divide into groups and sit down on the green grass. 40 So the people sat down in rows, in groups of a hundred and groups of fifty. (GNB)

Without these beds of leeks the text lacks not only pictorial charm, but also the link to Exodus. For although in the majority of cases in the Old Testament, *châtsîyr* means "green grass," in one case it really does mean Egyptian leeks. When the Israelites suffered from hunger during the exodus, the rage grew in their bellies and they began to revolt. This provoked an intervention by GOD, who had food rain down from heaven for them, in the form of manna (Exod 16:2–4).

This manna saved the lives of the people in the desert. They collected it every day. But after they had eaten the manna for some time, they longed for the rich food they had eaten in Egypt:

> And the Israelites also wept again, and said, "If only we had meat to eat! 5 We remember the fish we used to eat in Egypt for nothing, the cucumbers, the melons, the leeks, the onions, and the garlic (Num 11:4–5).

In Num 11:5 "the leeks" (Greek: *prason*, Hebrew: *châtsîyr*) appear in the memories of the hungry, together with fish of the Nile, cucumbers, melons, onions, and garlic. The memory of the succulent green fodder of Egypt, which included both fish and vegetables, brought the people in the desert to tears.

In Mark 6:39, in addition to fish, the green grass appears—and in verse 40 the beds of leeks. The crowds lying down like this means they had understood the teaching of Jesus. They had therefore surpassed his instruction to lie on the green grass in *symposia*. Here, outside in the inhospitable region, they realized that they were on a new exodus. They, too, were in the desert, they too were hungry. They depended on GOD's allowing rain to fall—whether as manna, bread of heaven, or simply heavy rain so that the beds of leeks could grow and green. And so we have the miraculous result of the teaching: the crowd sat down, leek bed by leek bed, and formed drinking fellowships in expectation of divine rain.

The crowd's interpretive power impresses me. They heard the reference to the green grass—and responded in such a way that they arranged themselves as beds of leeks. Jesus' Torah lesson had borne fruit, and the people actualized the Torah's words in Exodus in their own present day. When Jesus spoke of the succulent green, he not only reminded them of their forebears' arduous journey through the desert, but also awakened in them a longing for a new exodus. Every exodus into freedom is arduous—but is accompanied by GOD. Those who have too little, because their political rulers leave them in the lurch, are in a similar situation to their ancestors on their path towards freedom. Back then, GOD had mercy, and made manna rain down. In their miraculous seating arrangement, the people manifest that they remember the exodus of their forebears, who got up out of their misery, and trusted GOD, so that he would make it rain from heaven, and they would turn into merry drinking fellowships.

10.11 Excursus: Like rain on fresh grass

Let us take a close look at the relationship between "teaching" and "learning" in this text. Jesus' teaching caused the hungry people to turn into beds of leeks, stretching up to heaven. The teachings of the Torah, which appear here in connection with the exodus—the people's hunger and their famine revolt—start to bear fruit as soon as attentive listeners react and ask questions. These listeners are Torah students in the sense that they are able to address the Torah with their actual needs. In verses 35–37, some listeners present a question to the teacher. Mark's text describes them as *mathetai*, from the Greek verb "to learn": *manthanein*). The text here does not suggest a particular group of disciples, as we are generally used to reading. It speaks of learners who have understood something, who as good pupils apply what they have learnt to their present situation, and develop the next question out of that. Devaluing the group of disciples by saying they are thinking too materialistically, that they are too petty and have no idea what this is about, is not appropriate. Some of this disorderly bunch of people have become pupils; they have begun to learn. And out of their learning grows the next question, which relates quite specifically to eradicating the great crowd's hunger.

I would like to direct our gaze once more to the teaching activity described here. As Christian readers, we are used to seeing the miracle of the multiplication of the loaves. And then, when we have seen it, we have to believe it: We believe in the miracles that Jesus performed, believe that they are possible. This way of reading Mark's text, however, is coarse and reductionist, for Mark describes how teaching and learning[466] take place. What is important is not whether we believe in the literal truth of a miracle—but drawing the readers into a culture of questioning, of being amazed, and questioning again, and provoking critical thinking and attentiveness.

This teaching and learning includes applying the exodus tradition to the present situation of the hungry, as we have seen above. For Torah readers, a few key words in Mark's brief text, such as *eremos* (desert, empty land), "green grass" and "beds of leeks," evoke Num 11:5, a memory the hungry have of succulent food on their journey through the desert. For the hungry crowd in Mark 6:34f, this memory also signifies that they understand themselves as Israel on the path to freedom. Teaching and learning have to do with this journey into freedom.

Later, in the rabbinic tradition, the phrase *prasiai prasiai* would become associated with a *beth midrash* situation (an assembly of Torah students). Strack and Billerbeck quote from the Talmud dictionary: "When students sit arranged like garden-beds (*prasiai prasiai*), and are engaged in studying the Torah, then I come down to them and hearken to their voice and hear them."[467] If we read Mark 6:39 in the light of this later Talmudic tradition, the Feeding of the Five Thousand could be compared to a *beth midrash*. Whenever rows of attentive Torah students are sitting together, the heavenly Spirit pours out like rain on a well-prepared garden. It will bring blossoming and greening.

It is precisely this part of the sentence that will escape readers, if they are no longer able to create a link to the exodus (Num 11:5). Jesus did not simply "perform magic"; he taught. And the people were not simply spectators at a magic show, but hungry crowds, hearing Torah and eagerly discussing it, and learning how to create a link between the Torah and their own miserable situation. Their own hunger was an important doorway to recognizing that their forebears had been crying for bread and green food on their path, just as they in Mark 6:34f had too little to eat.

On our passage, Strack and Billerbeck quote from the Talmud: "*p. Ber.* 4:7d, 15 Bar: This teaching R. Eleazar b. Azariah (ca. 100) expounded before the sages at the 'vineyard' (*kerem*) in Yavneh. But was there a vineyard there? Rather, these are the scholars who were arranged in rows (*shurot shurot*), as in a vineyard."[468] This passage also compares the Torah school with a plantation. The language concerning the vineyard is a metaphor, not the description of a locality. The rows of scholars form the vineyard of GOD, and out of them will flow wine—the teachings of the Torah. Good teaching is the product of the Torah vineyard, the Torah garden.

The rabbinical examples are relatively late (no earlier than the third century), but there are also biblical examples that support this reading. For one, it is GOD herself, GOD's Spirit and transformative power, that comes down and seizes the assembled people in Num 11:25 and Acts 2:2–4; 10:44 (cf. also Matt 18:20). If the multitude arrange themselves like a garden bed, they show clearly that they are begging for something from the heavenly Spirit. They need GOD's response now. They are assembled as Israel was at one time, on its arduous journey through the desert. Now GOD will have to listen and, as she did that time, help her people and open the heavens.

This rabbinical language and pattern of thought is prepared in the ancient Eastern and Jewish wisdom traditions. In the book of Sirach,[469] wisdom praises herself for how she has put down roots in Jerusalem, how she has grown like a cedar, like rose plants in Jericho, like a splendid olive tree on the plain. Thus she sings of how beautiful she has become in Israel, how rich, what a blessing she is for those who take pleasure in her. Wisdom has become like a budding vine, the fruits of which are desired by and satisfy those who eat them:

> 17 Like the vine I bud forth delights,
>
> and my blossoms become glorious and abundant fruit.
>
> 19 "Come to me, you who desire me,
>
> and eat your fill of my fruits.
>
> 20 For the memory of me is sweeter than honey,
>
> and the possession of me sweeter than the honeycomb."
>
> . . .
>
> 30 As for me, I was like a canal from a river,
>
> like a water channel into a garden.
>
> 31 I said, "I will water my garden
>
> and drench my flower-beds" (Sir 24:17–20, 30–31).

In verses 30–31, wisdom refers to herself as water that brings life and growth. The Markan feeding of the multitude story can therefore be read with the Jewish wisdom tradition as a backdrop. The people have understood that they need wisdom, if they wish to progress. Wisdom will water them and let them grow, so that they will find ways and means of approaching their vision. They themselves are a little bit wise, if they understand themselves as foodstuffs, just as wisdom in verses 16–21 offers herself up to be eaten.

We can also find a comparison of the Torah's words with enlivening water in the book of Deuteronomy, the fifth book of Moses. After Moses had written down the words of the Torah, he sang a song that begins with these words:

> 1 Give ear, O heavens, and I will speak;
>
> let the earth hear the words of my mouth.
>
> 2 May my teaching drop like the rain,
>
> my speech condense like the dew;
>
> like gentle rain on grass [*epi ta chorta*],
>
> like showers on new growth (Deut 32:1–2).

Moses compares the effects of the Torah, which he had written down, with that of reviving water. Anyone who listens to and practices the words of GOD will grow like fresh, succulent green. We find this green in Mark 6:39 too: *epi to chloro chorto* (on the green grass). If we draw Deut 32:1–2 alongside our passage in Mark, Jesus the teacher acquires Moses-like characteristics. His teaching enlivens the masses, falls on them like dew or a refreshing shower of rain. No wonder people sit down in rows like garden beds, so that they can receive the greatest possible refreshment, so that they can take root and stretch out under the Torah teachings of Jesus.

Early rabbinic literature related Deut 32:2 to study of the Torah. One example of this:

> *Sifre Devarim* 306 on Deut 32:2:[470]

17 "as the rain": Just as rain is life for the world, so, words of Torah.

But then (why not say:) Just as with rain, part of the world is happy (with it) and part, sad (e.g., One whose pit and vat is full of wine, and his vat and threshing floor is exposed to the rain, is grieved by it) so, words of Torah! It is, therefore, written (Ibid.) "My word shall flow as the dew": Just as with dew, all the world is happy with it, so, words of Torah.

18 "as winds upon the herbage": Just as winds raise the grass and make it flourish, so, words of Torah raise their disciples and make them flourish, viz. (Proverbs 4:8) "Caress it (Torah) and it will uplift you."

19 "and as showers upon the grass": Just as showers descend upon the grass and beautify and preen it, so, words of Torah beautify and preen their disciples. And thus is it written (Proverbs 1:9): "For they (words of Torah) are a chaplet of grace to your head," and (ibid. 4:9) "It (Torah) will set a chaplet of grace upon your head" (*Sifre Devarim* 306:17–19).

The words of GOD, his Torah, are like enlivening rain upon green grass or herbs, in the early rabbinic literature. The fact that English translations leave out *prasiai prasiai* makes it harder to remember the exodus, and renders its roots in the wisdom tradition—the background of Jewish teaching and learning—invisible.

10.12 Transformative power

Now we are able to read Mark's feeding of the multitude story in a new way. At its core are the scholars, the teacher, and the lesson itself. What distinguishes good teaching is the effect it has on people's lives. Jesus taught Torah, and indeed so well (Mark 6:34) that the people surpassed his instructions. He ordered them to come together in *symposia* (drinking fellowships), but they went one further: the scruffy "flock of sheep" became lively "vegetable beds." "Sitting in rows" suggests rows of scholars, and is a metaphorical expression for a Torah school in a *beth midrash*, preparing itself for study. Here in our text, which dates from some years earlier than rabbinic Judaism, the teaching transforms hungry people into "filled" ones, and even more astoundingly, it causes hungry people to become food—beds of leeks.

We could now discuss to what extent they really became filled. The question that arises here is: In what reality do these events take place? We certainly have before us a literary description, which uses metaphorical language and symbolic actions to sketch a successful teaching situation. Yet we could ask ourselves whether the 5,000 people really did arrange themselves into rows of 50 or 100. And did GOD's Spirit come down after they had formed up like this, and listen to their voice? This is what the text presupposes: GOD listens to her hungry children. This is why she sent manna and quails during their withdrawal from Egypt, this is why he repeatedly opened the heavens and let it rain. This is a fundamental conviction of biblical belief. GOD is on the side of the hungry, whether they are people hungry for Torah, or groups who have to find their way through a desert.

A second basic conviction of this text is that the Torah lesson supports the hungry and makes them strong. It is important for the hungry to form into a people who embark on a new exodus. The multitude (*ochlos*) were given support to set off on the arduous journey through the desert, away from the land of slavery that the Herodian kings had made of their own country, and into the land of milk and honey—towards the vision of the Twelve, who eat together at the table, as descendants of Jacob. The lesson of Torah offers the multitude the vision of a people, who are formed through their shared experience, through their shared journey and the hope of a nourishing table for all.

10.13 The abundance of hope

The wasteland becomes green grass, the lost sheep become lively beds of leeks, the disorderly crowd becomes the vision of the people of the exodus, the people of the twelve tribes, and the hungry are filled. The Torah lesson bears abundant fruit, as the people not only share foodstuffs but understand themselves to be nourishing, growing, and sprouting roots, like vegetable beds on the green grass. They themselves become refreshing green—nourishing each other.

> 42 And all ate and were filled; 43 and they took up twelve baskets full of broken pieces and of the fish (Mark 6:42–43).

Everyone receives food, and yet there is still something left over for tomorrow, for the long journey to freedom. In this sense, the narrative does not end with those present being filled (v. 42). The twelve baskets draw us towards the future. We have seen above that the biblical hope-number, *dodeka*, serves as a blueprint for re-assembling the whole people, for "Israel reunited." The hungry are filled, and given the necessary means to continue their journey. The narrative thus culminates in the hope-number twelve (v. 43) and the idea that there is still something left over for those who are no longer here or not yet present: the story refers to something beyond itself. The vision of the Twelve (Mark 3:14), which was being crafted while the bread was lacking (Mark 3:20), takes full shape here. Already five thousand people are filled—and twelve baskets are still left over. In Mark 14:22, the twelve sit together at table; now all are there, the number is complete. The credibility of these twelve is proven: they have learnt to share, have studied Torah, have come all the way up to Jerusalem.

Here, we could also remember Luke 24 (see Chapter 9, above), where momentous transformations took place while people were eating. The two walkers on their way to Emmaus were discussing the Torah and the things that had taken place in Jerusalem in those days (Luke 24:19). But only as they broke bread were their eyes opened (v. 31). They realized how their hearts were burning (v. 32), and so they got up at once

(v. 33) and hurried to their companions. In this circle of companions, they fitted into the body of the Resurrected, into the Messiah project (vv. 39–40). Now that they had perceived themselves to be the hands and feet of the Resurrected, they had something with which to counter hunger (v. 42). Just like this, the scholars in Mark's feeding story also have fish and bread to hand, much more than they had thought, which they are able to distribute to the hungry. Now they have something to give people; their hands are not empty and powerless in the face of widespread hunger. The transformation affects not just the hungry who are filled, but also the learners—the multitude—who begin to learn and to arrange themselves anew like beds of leeks.

Let us also remember another feeding story. In Caesarea, the Roman centurion Cornelius opened his house to the group from Joppa (see Chapters 5 and 6, above). In Joppa, death reigned (Acts 9:36), as well as hunger (Acts 10:10). In other parts of the East there was even talk of worldwide famine (Acts 11:28). Cornelius proved to be a righteous benefactor, by sending for the group from Joppa. The hungry and needy became guests in the centurion's house. But the transformation was also visible in those who had something with which to counter hunger: while Peter taught Torah, the Holy Spirit poured out upon the house of Cornelius, turning the soldiers into brothers who sang psalms and praised GOD (Acts 10:44).

10.14 "This is my body"

The unkempt, straying crowd (Mark 6:34) becomes, in Mark 6:42, a group of people who are sated, who sit in rows like beds of vegetables, or like Torah scholars. The downcast disciples in Jerusalem become, in Luke 24, the hands and feet of the Resurrected, who are able to conjure up fish (and honey). In Acts 10, the hungry from Joppa become welcome guests in the house of the Roman centurion, while his soldiers transform into singing comrades, and the poor in Corinth form a hope-body watered by the Spirit. Sharing food transforms people. But let us be clear: In none of these feeding stories is bread transformed, or wine. It is the people who are transformed—both those who receive bread and those who give it. Transformation encompasses those who are hungry and can now eat, and those who give them food, i.e., who work to counter hunger.

If we read the Last Supper (Mark 14:17f) in the context of hunger, we can situate it in the continuity of Jesus' working against this hunger. The table is finally laid for everyone. Jesus has bread in his hands, and eats it. He has bread to give, as well as a full cup. He has ample resources on which to draw. Those who recline at table with him have learned to make a connection between the Torah and their present distress, and this has mobilized energies, imagination, resources, and strategies to curb hunger. The Torah itself then becomes the bread of life, becomes spiced fish and honey, becomes rain that falls upon the green grass and brings blessings. How does Mark's Jesus in Mark 14:17f create a connection to the Torah? And what is it?

> 17 When it was evening, he came with the twelve. 18 And when they had taken their places and were eating, Jesus said, "Truly I tell you, one of you will betray me, one who is eating with me." 19 They began to be distressed and to say to him one after another, "Surely, not I?" 20 He said to them, "It is one of the twelve, one who is dipping bread into the bowl with me. 21 For the Son of Man goes as it is written of him, but woe to that one by whom the Son of Man is betrayed! It would have been better for that one not to have been born." 22 While they were eating, he took a loaf of bread, and after blessing it he broke it, gave it to them, and said, "Take; this is my body." 23 Then he took a cup, and after giving thanks he gave it to them, and all of them drank from it. 24 He said to them, "This is my blood of the covenant, which is poured out for many. 25 Truly I tell you, I will never again drink of the fruit of the vine until that day when I drink it new in the kingdom of God." 26 When they had sung the hymn, they went out to the Mount of Olives (Mark 14:17–26).

Jesus breaks the bread in order to pass it on. As a teacher he had always passed on the Torah like this, in precious little bites. He used the Torah to make the Twelve; the Torah formed them into a People, filled them with its sweetness and spice. They became the bread of life for the disciples. The words "This is my body" (v. 22)[471] can thus relate to the Torah, for it embodies the bread of life in the rabbinic tradition as well.[472] Above all, the power of the Torah to create and shape things is important here. It is the wisdom, the lesson, that the hope-body of the People is able to report, build up, create.

Anyone who eats it is part of the hope-body of the Twelve. Thus, the Torah is not over here with the people over there, on two different sides—eating the bread of life with one another brings the two together. Where the Twelve are, the healing of the people has begun (Mark 3:1f). If Mark's Gospel attaches importance to the presence of the twelve at the Last Supper (Mark 14:17), this means that gathering and healing the people has taken on a form. Those who are present transform into a collective hope-body—for the Twelve are a collective hope-body, just like the newly established house of Israel, the comforted Mother Zion, the house of Jacob, or as Paul puts it: the temple of GOD, the body of the Messiah (see Chapter 8, above).

Jesus' words enable the hope-body to appear in another way as well: Take this, you are the body of the Messiah. They, the Twelve, participate in this shared meal, they eat the same food, drink the same cup. The bread is distributed among them, and everyone has a piece. This interpretation is based on the idea of equality of all who recline together at the table and eat the same meal. The idea of equality is fundamental to the banquet tradition in antiquity.[473] At the table, a table fellowship takes shape—a body that is eating. The words of Jesus put this into Israel's language of hope: the Twelve are the messianic body, to whom a future will be opened up even after their defeat by Rome in the famine of the post-war years.

The biological, physical body of Jesus is in the hands of the Romans. But the body of the Messiah lives on in the Twelve, who have not gone under, through all the changing courses of history. The number twelve looks to the future, opening up space for living and new beginnings. When they are together, they are one body, they form the collective hope-body, which lies in God's hands—and not in the hands of the great political powers. Where people work against hunger, there, transformation takes place. The work transforms both those who hunger for bread and those who give bread. Out of the individuals it makes a collective hope-body, the hands and feet of the Messiah, this body that no one can kill, into which everyone can integrate if they want to learn how to counter hunger.

10.15 Conclusion: The Last Supper in the context of hunger

To what extent has our reading of the Last Supper changed? How can it be sketched in the context of hunger? I would like to try to answer these initial questions here.

Consistently embedding the Last Supper in experiences of hunger demands that we perceive it as a blissful moment: they all ate (Mark 14:18, 22, 23)—a longing fulfilled, a yearning for bread that is satisfied for once. This "all" is linked, using the collective metaphor *dodeka*, with the eventful history of Israel. The Twelve, all of them, the People in their "inviolable totality"[474] eat together at one table: what unimaginable joy! We have seen that "the Twelve" stands for the whole People, for a People that stands together. The metaphor does not make a quantitative statement, but a qualitative one. It was not twelve individuals who sat at the table, but everyone. This is a utopian statement, which should not be read from an exclusionary perspective. The hungry, who at last have bread in their hands, know about the need for everyone to have bread and a place at the table.

Mark's Gospel relates how, stone upon stone, the house of Israel was rebuilt after the war. The observation that Jesus "makes" the Twelve (Mark 3:14) sharpens the perception that this is about building a house. In the end, the house stands: the Twelve are in Jerusalem, at table together. As long as they hold together, they have a future before them. However, the "betrayal" by one of the twelve jeopardizes this future. It also shows that the twelve are not beyond all doubt, but have to work on their credibility, as did the sons of Jacob who sold Joseph. They presented themselves as twelve (Gen 42:13), even though they were only ten. This is how they remembered the missing ones, which ultimately opened up their path to becoming whole again.

Why has the last meal before Jesus' execution constituted church ritual, and not the feeding of the multitude in the open air? I do not want to leave this hanging as an either-or question. Mark's Gospel highlights these points consecutively; I would therefore like to read them consecutively and together. This means we should not isolate the Last Supper from the golden thread of hunger, nor from the making of the Twelve as the building of the house of Israel. Just as the metaphor of the Twelve was important in their post-war period, so we should not now cut ourselves off from the biblical language of hope. It is however surprising that there is a biblical blueprint for the future, and it is called *dodeka*, the hope-number: only together are we capable of survival. We do not need to become "one," but participating in a shared hope-body would be wonderful. The Last Supper in the hermeneutic of hunger focuses not on the death of Jesus, but on the Twelve, who are filled, and live.

The Feeding of the Five Thousand, too, culminates in the number of twelve baskets, in the surplus of bread, which is sufficient for everyone. The twelve baskets are a further variant of the hope-body of Israel. The twelve at the table and the twelve baskets full of bread are the foundation on which life and a future can be built. The hungry arrange themselves into beds of leeks, they form up in rows, indicating their ability to learn. They do not do what Jesus tells them, but go one step further. Thus, they insert themselves actively into the history of Israel. When the Israelites came out of Egypt, suffering from hunger, the rage grew in their belly and they attempted to revolt. This provoked God to intervene, and make bread rain down for them, manna (Exod 16:2–4).

A meal is a place of transformation; it contains transformative power and releases it. Thus, the five thousand hungry people, who were like a neglected flock of sheep, turned into joyful vegetable beds on the green grass. The hungry people develop a hunger for the Torah, they want to learn and are able to learn; for they have bread in their hands that brings them strength. This transformative power also comes into effect in the words "take, eat, this is my body." Jesus teaches his people one more time: They, the Twelve, are the hope-body, the messianic body, who have learned how to counter hunger.

Interpreting the words "this is my body" to mean the body of Jesus, who was executed, is the most common way of reading them in Christian exegetic practice, but today it is ultimately no longer plausible. For why should those present eat the body of Jesus? Exegetically this is difficult to justify. In Mark's Gospel the body of Jesus is never center stage. This issue is always other bodies, women and men and children who are healed. The issue is people who will become one People. In Mark 14:12f, Jesus has bread in his hands, the Twelve are here, he can eat, celebrate, pass on Torah and bread. Distributing his body as the quintessence of the meal makes no sense to me. On the other hand, his distributing bread does make sense, just as he divides the Torah into edible portions.

What I consider most likely is that Jesus sees those present as one body, the twelve-body, who will live, who will continue to fight against hunger. The rulers cannot destroy the collective body of the Messiah through acts of violence. The rulers can destroy individual bodies—but not hope-bodies. These will always grow back, they will never give up, will always stretch out anew towards the future and life. They lie in the hands of God.

Endnotes

1. Ziegler, *Wie kommt der Hunger*, 12. "Almost 1 billion people are currently starving, and at the same time more than 1 billion are experiencing overweight or obesity, so that we now call it Globesity" (Oltersdorf, "Lage der Welt," 21). According to the latest United Nations estimates (published in 2018 by the FAO), around 821 million people worldwide are undernourished, the majority of them in developing countries.
2. FAO, "Hunger and food insecurity."
3. 821 million people in the world do not have enough to eat. The number of undernourished people has fallen since 2005 by 124 million; however, this figure has been rising again since 2014. See: FAO, *The State of Food Security*.
4. Neidhart, "Vier von fünf Nordkoreanern," 3.
5. Focus Online, quoted by Cap Anamur, "Hunger in Nordkorea."
6. Chung, *Reis und Wasser*, 169.
7. Schönborn and Welten, "Hunger, Hungersnot," 268–269.
8. Luz, *Matthew 1-7*, 195–196.
9. Sölle, *Silent Cry*, 48–49.
10. Sölle, *Silent Cry*, 49.
11. Garnsey, *Famine and Food Supply*, 18.
12. St. John Chrysostom in his Matthew commentary (61:3), quoted in: Stegemann and Stegemann, *The Jesus Movement*, 90.
13. "The inscriptions, the other main source of evidence for subsistence crises, do not offer the terminological exactitude that is lacking in the literary sources. There is the additional striking fact that they systematically avoid the terms for hunger or starvation" (Garnsey, *Famine and Food Supply*, 19).
14. For example, Franz Jung states: "In narrative terms, as has already been described, verses 30-34 function as a transition: they do not present an independent, individual scene, but only prepare it. A glance at the verbs clarifies this once again. The passage is dominated by *verba movendi* (v. 30: to gather; v. 31: to come and go; v. 32: to go away; v. 33: to depart, to arrive; v. 34: to alight). These verbs reinforce the impression of unrest that lies upon this moment. Only in v. 34 does calm return, allowing Jesus to teach the crowds, and later to feed them" (Jung, *16. Sonntag*, 1).
15. Garnsey, *Famine and Food Supply*, 18.
16. Compare Peter's denial that he knew Jesus: Matt 26:69-74 and par. This is handed down in all four Gospels.
17. English translations render this as "Come away ... all by yourselves" and "they went away ... by themselves" or similar.
18. Queen Helena of Adiabene, during the great famine in the reign of Emperor Claudius, organized the shipping of grain from Egypt. See: Eusebius, *Ecclesiastical History*, vol. I, 135–136.
19. Peter Garnsey's investigation of food supply in the Graeco-Roman world shows how fear of famine led to protests, and how the rulers reacted with repression to subdue the people. "The standard reaction of the people of late Republican Rome to food shortage was hostile demonstration, for which the typical setting was the public meeting *(contio)* or the show. Such protest sometimes turned into

ENDNOTES

riot. . . . Hunger or fear of hunger had driven the plebs to protest long before the era of organized violence or orchestrated demonstration had arrived" (Garnsey, *Famine and Food Supply*, 206).

20   Kegler, "Hunger," 325.

21   In Matt 14:13–21; 15:32–39; Mark 6:35–44; 8:1–9, 19–21; Luke 9:10–17; John 6:1–13.

22   In her reading of the Psalms, Klara Butting shows how they open up experiential spaces into which the praying people can enter and thus can give and receive answer. Spirituality and political-ethical world-centeredness and responsibility thus go together. Butting, *Hier bin ich!*

23   Cf. Schroer and Staubli, *Körpersymbolik*, 75.

24   In Luke, compassion spreads for the weeping widow in Nain (Luke 7:13), in the parable of the Good Samaritan (Luke 10:33), and in the return of the Prodigal Son (Luke 15:20). In Matt 9:36 and 14:14, we find compassion parallel to Mark 6:34. It also appears in Matt 15:32 (parallel to Mark 8:2), in the parable of the unforgiving servant (Matt 18:27), and the healing of two blind men (Matt 20:34).

25   The protests began in June 2013. Their primary target was the organization of the 2014 soccer World Cup, as well as corruption and social injustice, raised prices for local public transport, and police brutality against demonstrators. See: https://en.wikipedia.org/wiki/2013_protests_in_Brazil.

26   Horst-Dieter Westerhoff sketches a nuanced definition of poverty, which assumes an average income and inequitable distribution of goods. See: Westerhoff, "Armut." He does not mention hunger, however. See: Westerhoff, "Wie sich eine Nation."

27   The United Nations defines poverty as "a denial of choices and opportunities, a violation of human dignity. It means lack of basic capacity to participate effectively in society. It means not having enough to feed and clothe a family, not having a school or clinic to go to, not having the land on which to grow one's food or a job to earn one's living, not having access to credit. It means insecurity, powerlessness and exclusion of individuals, households and communities. It means susceptibility to violence, and it often implies living on marginal or fragile environments, without access to clean water or sanitation." Economic poverty, strictly speaking, is divided into overall poverty and absolute poverty. The latter is defined as "a condition characterized by severe deprivation of basic human needs, including food, safe drinking water, sanitation facilities, health, shelter, education and information. It depends not only on income but also on access to services." (UN Declaration at the Word Summit on Social Development in Copenhagen, 1995. Both of these definitions quoted in Gordon, "Indicators").

28   *King James Dictionary*: "poor." https://av1611.com/kjbp/kjv-dictionary/poor.html.

29   Crüsemann and Schottroff, "*dal*."

30   Stegemann and Stegemann, *The Jesus Movement*, 89.

31   Stegemann and Stegemann, *The Jesus Movement*, 89.

32   St. John Chrysostom in his Matthew commentary (61:3), quoted in: Stegemann and Stegemann, *The Jesus Movement*, 90 [author's emphasis].

33   "Poverty took different forms, expressed in different terminology. Destitute people (*ptochoi, tapeinoi*) lived below the subsistence minimum: beggars, ill people, disabled people, widows, orphans, elderly people, anyone not attached to a patriarchal household which would care for them. Many peasant families who had lost their land through debt, unskilled workers, slaves no longer able to work: all were either rendered destitute or at least threatened with destitution. Many women and children worked to survive, yet often their efforts did not even cover their food needs. Alongside these were poor people (*penetes*), who maintained a stable existence on or above the poverty line. They worked as tradespeople on a wage, as slaves or in debt bondage, in craft workshops, on farms" (Schäfer-Lichtenberger and Schottroff, "Armut," 24).

34   Friesen, "Injustice."

35   Friesen, "Injustice," 243. The individual figures should be treated with some caution, although the extent of poverty is evident. The arguments for this kind of structuring have been published in: Friesen, "Poverty."

36   Which can still be interesting! See, for example, Ernst Bammel's article on "*ptochos*" in TDNT. He explains *ptochos* as a derivation of *ptossein*: to bow down timidly. Begging (*ptocheia*) should be understood analogously to bowing down. The Hebrew term *ani* is similar, expressing primarily a relationship of dependence and not social distress.

37   "Female poverty was long underestimated because women did not, for the most part, show

up in the ranks of the unemployed.... What is apparent from these modern studies is that the very indexes used to identify and measure poverty have been biased with respect to gender. That appears also to be in the case in biblical studies of the poor" (Bird, *Missing Persons*, 67).

38   For example, in J. David Pleins's study: "The poor constituted a diverse body of social actors: small farmers, day laborers, construction workers, beggars, debt slaves, village dwellers" (Pleins, "Poor, Poverty," 402). English does not differentiate these groups into men or women, so the question is whether the readers do so either.

39   Reicher and Stott, *Mad Mobs*.

40   On the riots in the Paris suburbs, see: Vogel, *"Aufstand."*

41   In Israel too, tens of thousands of people protested against the high cost of living; they demanded a reduction in prices and taxes, and a fairer distribution of wealth. According to police, more than 70,000 people took part in the demonstrations across the country; organizers claimed there were 100,000 participants. After 250,000 people had joined one of the largest social protests in Tel Aviv the previous week, this time people took to the streets in 15 smaller cities. The largest demonstration, with about 25,000 participants, was reported in Haifa, a port city north of Tel Aviv. People chanted: "We demand social justice." See: Avnery, "Wie fein."

42   RT Question More, "Feminists."

43   See: Kornder, "Früchte des Zorns."

44   Reycep Erdogan called the protesters on Taksim Square in Istanbul "looters." This showed his undemocratic point of view and considerably angered the protesting citizens. See: Calatayud, "'Just a few looters.'" The term "Çapuling" (modification of the Turkish word for "marauder" or "plunderer") arose during the 2013 protests in Turkey and refers to the President's choice of words; it has since been used by the demonstrators themselves. See: https://en.wikipedia.org/wiki/Chapulling.

45   This is the same problem as in "savages" or "natives." The savages are not to be taken seriously, they do not count—although the good Indians are transfigured, as wise and sustainably living role models. The poor are both demonized and romanticized, and to the same extent, both today and in biblical times.

46   "εὐαγγέλιον [euangelion] is a technical term for 'news of victory.'" Friedrich, "εὐαγγέλιον [euangelion]," *TDNT* 2:722.

47   Tahrir Square was the scene of the spontaneous and violent "Bread Riots" in 1977.

48   See: Emam, "Egypt's food subsidy system."

49   In 2008, the soccer European Championship was held in Switzerland. Extra potatoes had to be imported for this event: football was manifestly impossible without potato chips. These additional tons of potatoes came from Egypt, where prices rose on the domestic markets, because the potatoes were destined for export.

50   Beinin, "Egypt: Bread riots." It was also reported that laborers, white-collar workers, professors and doctors had demanded a rise in the minimum wage from 115 Egyptian pounds a month ($21), set in 1984, to 1,200 pounds (around $222). "Between 2005 and 2008, food prices rose by 33% for meat and as much as 146% for chicken, and this March inflation reached 15.8%."

51   In 2008, the World Bank estimated that there was a risk of famine in 33 countries, and associated unrest and uprisings. Three years later, crowds of people brought down the government in Egypt. While the Arab world is experiencing the greatest transformations for decades, the UN Food and Agriculture Organization warns of further famines. See also note 48, above.

52   Erman, *Life in Ancient Egypt*, 125–126. The German translation specifies "fish" rather than the generic "food" of the English version.

53   See: Kinealy, *Irish Famine*; Haines, *Charles Trevelyan*; O'Mahony, *Famine in Cork City*.

54   Shaw, *Man and Superman*, 482.

55   It is ultimately difficult to determine when the book of Judges was written, ca. eighth–sixth century BCE. The same applies to the even older Song of Deborah.

56   Kegler, "Das Zinsverbot"; Kegler, "Hunger."

57   *Strong's Concordance*, 1520.

58   "Man wählte neue Göttinnen und Götter; verschwunden war das Gerstenbrot. Schilde wurden nicht gesehen noch Speere unter 40.000 in Israel" (Judges 5:8, *Bibel in gerechter Sprache*).

ENDNOTES

59 The Old Testament contains numerous laws that regulate slavery and seek to mitigate it. Alongside enslavement brought about by being taken prisoner, it also assumes the need for impoverished people to sell themselves. Exod 21:2–11 and Deut 15:12–17 limit debt slavery to six years. Sabbath rest in the Decalogue explicitly also includes slaves. On debt slavery, see: Kreuzer and Schottroff, "Sklaverei."

60 The wealthy were able to prepare their food in different ways, using richer spices and other ingredients; but they ate fundamentally the same products. See: Garnsey, *Food and Society*, 119. Nathan MacDonald points out the lower nutritional value of barley, which made it less popular, and cheaper. See: MacDonald, *Ancient Israelites*, 20–21. See also: Josephus, *War* 5.427.

61 "If we describe the social crisis of the kings era using the word 'impoverishment,' we should now refer to 'destitution.' Increasingly, people appear who can be described as 'hungry' and 'naked' (Isa 58:7, 10; Ezek 18:7, 16; Job 24:5–8, 10; Matt 25:35–38, 42–44). They have no means, not even scarce ones, to look after themselves" (Kessler, "Armenfürsorge").

62 We should however note that the Gospels only bring us the view from Matthew's, Mark's or Luke's perspective, and not from the historical time of Jesus (ca. 30–35 CE). The Synoptic Gospels show us their view of recent history, not what really went on in recent history.

63 In his novel *L'Évangile selon Pilate*, Éric-Emmanuel Schmitt sketches the internal psychological state of Pilate and Jesus, but leaves behind the socio-political circumstances. This is in line with the great need for religion, as we currently understand it, to be a search for peace of mind, and harmony with oneself.

64 The Gospels know the reality of enslavement. Slaves are beaten in Luke 12:45, tortured in Matt 18:34, killed in Mark 12:1–12, and cut in pieces in Matt 24:51. In the heyday of the Roman Empire, slavery was essential to maintaining prosperity and affected whole peoples, urban and rural communities who were sold, as well as masses of people affected by debt slavery.

65 In antiquity as well, people protested together in public places. Whether these protests were peaceful or violent had much to do with the reaction of the authorities, as Peter Garnsey explains. "A discussion of protest in an urban setting can usefully embrace non-violent demonstration as well as riot. The distinction is made explicitly by Tacitus. In AD 32 when prices were high, the people raged for several days in the theatre against the emperor Tiberius 'with unusual insolence, almost crossing the border between demonstration and riot.' My impression is that peaceful protest was much more common than riot, and that only in the city of Rome itself in certain periods was the food riot a phenomenon of any significance" (Garnsey, *Famine and Food Supply*, 30 [Tacitus, *Ann.* 6.13]). Garnsey also points out that it was above all the fear of famine that set people on the rampage (*Famine and Food Supply*, 31).

66 The Gospels are sparing in giving figures. Only the feeding miracle mentions numbers: 5,000 in Matt 14:13–21; Mark 6:32–44; Luke 9:10–17; John 6:1–13; 4,000 in Mark 8:1–9; and Matt 15:32–39 refers to 4,000 men, not counting women and children.

67 Gerd Theissen assumes that the Jesus movement started with wandering radical preachers, characterized by a radical ethos of rootlessness, distance from family, criticism of property ownership, and non-violence (Theissen, *Soziologie der Jesusbewegung*). However, many New Testament texts refer to people having barely any property, fields, houses, etc. that they could "leave behind." Theissen's thesis does not take this into account. Further criticism of his theory can be found in: Stegemann, "Hinterm Horizont."

68 Warren Carter ("Matthew's People," in: Horsley, *Christian Origins*, 138–161) describes the living conditions for Matthew's community as being very hard. Hard work, disease and poverty characterized their daily life. "The life expectancy for nonelites was low: for men twenty-five to forty years, less for women" (146). Food shortage was common even in the great city of Antioch, reflected in deficiency diseases and contagion. Bladder stones, eye diseases, bone malformations, infectious diseases—the list of conditions is long (157).

69 In Matt 11:18–19, Jesus says that the people mocked John because he ate nothing, and that they call him, Jesus, "a glutton and a drunkard" because he ate and drank with tax collectors and sinners. Here, too, our minds can play a trick on us, so that we imagine Jesus at sumptuous banquets. But Matthew writes nothing of this. The text is about the accusation that Jesus sought bad company, that he went to places where the laws on food and fasting were not observed. But there is no indication of

whether Jesus did ever eat or drink in great quantities.

70   Mark 6:21f tells us nothing about the wine or the menu, and neither do Matt 26:6–13; Luke 7:36–50; John 2:1f; 12:1–8.

71   Only after the Passover meal in Matt 26:30 do the students and their teacher sing a hymn of praise.

72   The exception, or dramatic highlight, is in Luke 15:23–25, when the Prodigal Son comes home, the fatted calf is killed and there is music and dancing, i.e., a celebration.

73   "The accumulation of diseases and the all-encompassing nature of the emergency suggest that the situation of the Jewish population in the Roman province of Judea is a primary focus of the text" (Schottroff, "Heilungsgemeinschaften," 42).

74   Horsley, "Jesus Movements," 35.

75   Josephus speaks of 2,700,000 men (not including women and children), who had gathered for the Passover feast in Jerusalem in 65 CE (Josephus, *War* 6.420–427). Even if this figure ought to be regarded as an exaggeration, the number must have been very great.

76   The history of Judea and Galilee was driven by the persistent conflict between the peasantry and their rulers: the Maccabean revolt around 160 BCE, the upheavals that followed Herod's death around 4 BCE, the great revolt against Roman rule from 66 to 70 CE, and the Bar Kokhba revolt in 132–135 CE. Richard A. Horsley writes on this: "Peasants generally do not mount serious revolts, unless their backs are against the wall or they are utterly outraged at their treatment by their rulers" (Horsley, "Jesus Movements," 25). "That several such messianic movements emerged a generation before and a generation after the time of Jesus' mission is significant when we recognize that literature produced by the Judean scribal elite rarely mentions a messiah. This is in sharp contrast to previous Christian understanding, according to which the Jews were eagerly expecting *the* Messiah to lead them against foreign rule. . . . The Judean elite, of course, would not have been interested, since their positions of power and privilege depended on the Romans, who appointed oppressive kings such as Herod" (Horsley, "Jesus Movements," 28).

77   See: Sutter Rehmann, "Geschwister, Jünger und Frauen."

78   Luke makes this group even clearer: "A great number of the people followed him, and among them were women who were beating their breasts and wailing for him. But Jesus turned to them and said, 'Daughters of Jerusalem, do not weep for me, but weep for yourselves and for your children'" (Luke 23:27–28).

79   See: Schottroff, "Frauen in der Nachfolge," 114.

80   Jürgen Ebach presumes that the Hebrew differentiation between *am* (the people with an internal shared identity) and *goy* (the People in relation to other peoples) was continued in the Greek. In later Old Testament texts, *am* predominantly describes the People of Israel (Isa 19:25), whilst *goyim* describes other peoples. In the New Testament the words *laos* and *ethne* largely correspond to this differentiation. See: Ebach, "goj, am, mischpacha."

81   The Vulgate, i.e., the fourth-century Latin translation of Luke 7:22, does not put "the poor" into the dative, but leaves it in the nominative: "Et respondens dixit illis: Euntes nuntiate Joanni quae audistis et vidistis et audistis: quia *caeci* [the blind] vident, *claudi* [the lame] ambulant, *leprosi* [the lepers] mundantur, *surdi* [the deaf] audiunt, *mortui* [the dead] resurgunt, *pauperes* [the poor] evangelizantur" [author's emphasis].

82   On "the multitude, *polloi*" see the article by Joachim Jeremias in: *TDNT* 6:536–45. The article considers whether *polloi* has an inclusive or exclusive meaning. The "many" in Matt 24:12 and 2 Cor 2:17 have an exclusive sense ("most"). Otherwise it is always used with an inclusive meaning, i.e., "all," "all present," "the whole community." This certainly applies to our passage: Luke 7:21 does not intend to emphasize that only some, but not all, will be healed. Rather, this verse refers to the many whose healing has not yet begun, who will stand up and who are part of the whole community.

83   We find the same middle voice in the phrase concerning the dead. All English translations render it passively, as "the dead are raised" (or "raised up"). Some German translations do this too, but both Luther 1984 and BigS use an active verb. Luther 1984 translates the phrase as "die Toten stehen auf" (the dead rise), while BigS uses a reflexive form—"die Toten erheben sich"—(literally: the dead raise themselves)—to make the middle voice visible.

Endnotes

84 "The middle voice denotes that the subject is both an agent of an action and somehow concerned with the action" (Rydberg-Cox, *A Digital Tutorial*, Lesson 5.48).

85 Jensen, "The Greek Middle."

86 Wallace, *Greek Grammar*, and McKay, *A New Syntax*, both quoted in Pennington, "Setting Aside 'Deponency,'" 183.

87 Pennington, "Setting Aside 'Deponency,'" 185.

88 The words "gloom and darkness" make it clear that the eyes are unable to see, because they are in darkness. They are, so to speak, "night-blind." If despite that they begin to see, then because they discover the connection to their situation, they are able to read the words of the book themselves. It is therefore not a reference to healing of the blind in a medical sense, but to eyes that can see and understand without light. How far they can see through this gloomy situation would be another thing to consider.

89 That the verb encompasses more than just speaking and preaching has already been emphasized by Gerhard Friedrich: "εὐαγγελίζεδθαι [euangelizontai] is not just speaking and preaching; it is proclamation with full authority and power. Signs and wonders accompany the evangelical message. They belong together, for the Word is powerful and effective. The proclamation of the age of grace, of the rule of God, creates a healthy state in every respect. Bodily disorders are healed and man's relation to God is set right" (Friedrich, "εὐαγγελίζομαι [euangelizomai]," *TDNT* 2:720).

90 This relativizes my own translation of Luke 7:22 in BigS. There, I translated using the active form, in order to interrupt the long, unbroken tradition of translation that turns the poor into objects and sets them in the passive. And I do not consider the active voice to be wrong. But here I prefer to reproduce the middle voice, since it is richer in meaning.

91 *Mekhilta de-Rabbi Ishmael*, 267–268. Stemberger has dated this work in the second half of the third century. Stemberger, "Die Datierung."

92 John dared to criticize the divorce of Herod Antipas and his marriage to his half-brother's wife, Herodias. His criticism was based on the Torah's rules on marriage, which do not permit intermarriage between relatives (Lev 18:16). The king's power politics not only ignored the Torah, but secured more power through intermarriage, so that the power of Herodias was added to that of Herod Antipas. This should therefore be understood in the context of Herod's accumulation of power; John's condemnation was directed against this power grab as well (cf. Matt 14:10; Mark 6:17f, 27; Luke 3:20; 9:9).

93 What Jesus' messiahship represented for Matthew is evident in Matt 11:2–6, where Jesus explicitly refers to his deeds. Healing the injured members of the people shows that the Messiah is among us. Luise Schottroff refers to communities of healing arising, providing hope. This is why Jesus could be called "Son of David, Messiah, King, or God's son among many brothers and sisters." See: Schottroff, "Heilungsgemeinschaften," 30.

94 Lorde, *Sister Outsider*, 127.

95 His biography has been published (in German). See: Durnowo, *Mein Leben mit Daniil Charms*.

96 Kharms, "This is how hunger begins."

97 Näslund and Hellström, "Appetite Signaling."

98 Müller, *The Hunger Angel*, 18.

99 Voluntary starvation as religious fasting or a conscious hunger strike must be fundamentally differentiated from hunger in captivity or in poverty, because imposed starvation damages a person's autonomy. As long as people decide for themselves to take only very little food, or none at all, and as long as they interpret their fasting themselves, and apply meaning and message to it, they have a different sense of their body and of the world than if the hunger is imposed.

100 Müller, *The Hunger Angel*, 17–18.

101 Müller, *The Hunger Angel*, 76.

102 Müller, *The Hunger Angel*, 81.

103 Müller, *The Hunger Angel*, 105.

104 Cf. Petra Schulz's documentary for ZDF, "Hunger und Wut" (in German). And: "'The hungry man is an angry man' is what they say in Haiti. In May 2008, hunger drove not only angry men but

also angry women, first onto the streets, and then onto the barricades. If rice is twice as expensive, that doesn't mean that 80 percent of poor Haitians are paying twice as much. It means they only eat half as much" (Tagesschau.de, "Ein hungriger Mann").

In 1990, *Der Spiegel* reported: "Zambia—hungry and angry: unrest due to price rises, an attempted coup, protests against the one-party state—after 26 years, President Kaunda is starting to fear for his grip on power . . . The 3-hour airwaves coup was a temporary high point following days of unrest which plunged the country into its deepest crisis since gaining independence in 1964. Discontent, which had been smoldering for a long time, erupted when the government more than doubled the price for previously subsidized cornmeal—an essential component of the International Monetary Fund's (IMF) strictly regulated savings program. Poor people helped themselves to what they could no longer afford, and stormed shops and department stores. In the town of Kabwe, angry residents plundered the public mill, in Lusaka furious citizens cleared supermarket shelves and wrecked everything, likewise in Kabulonga Market where the 'apamwamba'—the elites—do their shopping. . . . The trades unions protested too: 'a hungry man is an angry man' were the words trade union leader Emanuel Lungu used to criticize government policy" (*Der Spiegel*, July 9, 1990, 117–118).

105 See: Goodwin et al., *Passionate Politics*; Foweraker, *Theorizing Social Movements* (on the connection between anger and social movements, see p. 67).

106 Lorde, "The Uses of Anger," 9.

107 Lorde, *Sister Outsider*, 127.

108 Schutzbach, "Reclaim Anger."

109 Patricia Purtschert makes this point in "Not Wanting To Be Governed Like That."

110 von Roten, *Frauen im Laufgitter*.

111 "Her inclusion of poetry, song, general knowledge and collective thinking joins together current issues of pop-feminism, analysis and anecdotes, everyday life and politics. The question is, how can criticism be made in a way that is productive, subversive, inspiring and galvanizing? Her stubborn mixture of analysis, powerful language, irony and rage continues to provoke and challenge, as does her 'everyday ethnology,' which is characterized by her continuous precise references to the realities and living conditions of women" (Joris et al., "Offene Worte," 6). In the same volume, Heidi Witzig broaches the subject of the author's suppressed anger being a problem or at least going against the grain. She maintains that Iris von Roten uses many diminutives out of anger, in order to point out oppression, but this relegates women to "a land of smiles." See: Witzig, "Poesie der Polemik."

112 "The 'politics of emotion' is a concept which highlights how emotion can be the driving ingredient binding collectives such as nations, kinship groups and religious communities through the shaping of memory and relationships" (Ahmed, *Cultural Politics*, 42–43).

113 "For an intertextual interpretation, revisions fundamentally have meaning in this respect, as recognized here: the dialogue of different texts and their association through similarities and/or repetition forms the basis for reading a text out of which a complex web becomes apparent" (Dieckmann, *Segen für Isaak*, 103).

114 Buber, "*Leitwort* Style." Translator Lawrence Rosenwald's notes explain: "The German term *Leitwort* is retained as a term of Buber and Rosenzweig's art, without any exact English equivalent" (114, footnote 1). And: "A *Leitwort* etymologically is a 'leadword,' a word that leads or guides the reader through the thickets of the text" (120, footnote 9).

115 Buber, "*Leitwort* Style," 120.

116 See Ernst, *Johannes der Täufer*, 284–86; Strecker, *Theology of the New Testament*, 222f.

117 Lev 16:29–30; 23:26–32; Num 29:7–11.

118 Dando, "Famine," 144 (figure 12).

119 "[L]ivestock not in ordinary circumstances destined for slaughter; 'inferior' cereals, either ranked low (for whatever reason) or damaged by pests or weather; regular animal food, such as vetch or acorns; 'last resort' natural products or non-foods such as roots, twigs, leaves, bark, leather; and finally, human flesh" (Garnsey, *Famine and Food Supply*, 28).

120 In the Septuagint, *akris* is often used to mean locust. Except in Lev 11:22, which expressly permits the eating of locusts, they do not appear in any other menu. Rather, they are the scavengers that strip crops bare, that eat all the plants in the land (Exod 10:4f; Deut 28:38; Judg 6:5; Ps 104:34;

ENDNOTES

Joel 1:4; 2:25; Amos 7:1). Armies are often compared to swarms of locusts, since they cover the land, cannot be counted, and destroy and eat up everything (Judg 7:2; Jer 46:23; Nah 3:17; Jdt 2:20).

[121] In Acts 11:28, we encounter a further prophet who is associated with locusts: Agabus (Hebrew for "locust"). Agabus predicts a famine all over the world.

[122] Josephus, *Ant.* 15.9.1–2, tells of a famine in ca. 25 BCE; Acts 11:26–29 of a worldwide famine in the time of Emperor Claudius (who reigned from 41 to 54 CE). See also: Drexhage et al., *Wirtschaft*, 99.

[123] "Years of drought and famine ran like a scarlet thread through the ancient history of Palestine" (Aharoni, *Land of the Bible*, 14).

[124] Cf. Rev 6:6, where a daily ration of wheat costs one denarius, i.e., the pay of a day laborer was barely enough for himself, so that he could not put anything aside for the Sabbath, or for times of underemployment. Women generally earned less than their male counterparts, so the work of a female day laborer would not even be enough to live on. See: Schottroff, *Lydia's Impatient Sisters*, 91–95.

[125] "For the majority of ancient Israelites severe food shortages or famines would probably have been episodic. Nevertheless an insufficient diet for a temporary period could have significant and disproportionate health implications, especially for certain sectors of the population, such as pregnant or lactating mothers, and children. Physical starvation would have been an unusual extreme, brought about by a combination of circumstances, but for a child or woman weakened by hunger, illness could bring an early death. Those who survived would have remained more susceptible to disease for the rest of their lives. For a much smaller number of Israelites, those who were very poor either because they were landless or socially dislocated, malnourishment would have been ever on the horizon" (MacDonald, *Ancient Israelites*, 59).

[126] "Pre-harvest hunger occurs most frequently among the poor. According to ancient chroniclers and modern records, every society has people who suffer from hunger. Hunger in any form damages the moral and economic base of society. Acute or chronic hunger produces a segment of a nation's population that is physically or psychologically damaged and creates a core of resentful people. Prolonged hunger can set an environment for social unrest and revolution; prolonged mass starvation and famine lead to submission, resignation and death" (Dando, "Famine," 139).

[127] William A. Dando's "modern starvation cycle" diagram differentiates the overt and covert signs of starvation. On the overt side of the cycle are: "food shortages—increased food prices—eating 'famine foods'—beggary—weight loss—*crime, riots, or revolution*—sale of possessions—moral degeneracy—migration—disease—starvation." On the covert side: "shock—disbelief—fear—*anger*—frustration—despondency—resignation" [author's emphasis]. It should be noted that the psychological side of this diagram accords with the poem by Daniil Kharms, which also starts with disbelief and ends with resignation. It should also be noted that Dando's anger phase is aligned precisely with the "crime, riots, or revolution" phase. See: Dando, "Famine," 144 (figure 12).

[128] See, for example: Garnsey, *Food and Society*, 34.

[129] "In Deuteronomy and the prophetic literature famine is often used as one of God's covenant curses. When the Israelites rebel and turn from their God, he will punish them by suspending the rain, thus bringing famine on the land" (MacDonald, *Ancient Israelites*, 57).

[130] Cf. Garnsey, *Famine and Food Supply*, 15 and 24 (see also the water libation ritual in *m. Sukkah* 4:9; the prayers for rain in *m. Ta'an.* 2a–b).

[131] Dov Ashbel, "Israel"; MacDonald, *Ancient Israelites*, 56.

[132] Matthew uses the expression "brood of vipers" twice as Jesus' invective against the crowd. Matt 12:34 is about the good or bad fruit of a tree; Matt 23:33 is about God's judgement of wrath against the people who behave like snakes: speaking wisely, but acting foolishly.

[133] Nakedness and hunger are often mentioned together as the sign of abject poverty: Matt 25:35 is about giving clothing to the naked, a drink to the thirsty, and food to the hungry. Cf. 1 Cor 4:11: "To the present hour we are hungry and thirsty, we are poorly clothed and beaten and homeless."

[134] John's clothing can be compared to that of Elijah, yet there are differences in terminology; on the precise terminology, see: Ernst, *Johannes der Täufer*, 284–86.

[135] On the significance of the number twelve and the gathering of the twelve in the Gospels, see Chapter 10.

[136] Ulrich Luz explains "raising up children" out of stones in Matt 3:9 as "the future call of the

Gentiles," just as the reference to the tree of Israel that will be cut off at its roots radically challenges Israel. Such metaphorical interpretations isolate the text from the experience of poor people, who were familiar with drought and famine, and place it in an anti-Judaist European text tradition, which identified with the church of Gentiles. This masks the link to 1 Kgs 18, since Elijah could not have been talking about a calling of the Gentiles. See: Luz, *Matthew 1–7*, 137.

137   Cf. "Then a voice came from heaven, 'I have glorified it, and I will glorify it again.' The crowd standing there heard it and said that it was thunder. Others said, 'An angel has spoken to him'" (John 12:28–29). In Revelation, heaven opens repeatedly and powerful voices are heard. Voices "like a trumpet" (1:10; 4:1) or "like the sound of many waters" (1:15), are loud and come from "myriads of myriads and thousands of thousands" (5:11), "a voice of thunder" (6:1). An angel comes "down from heaven, wrapped in a cloud, with a rainbow over his head" (10:1). We can certainly imagine mighty clouds gathering, thunder and lightning, and downpours of rain.

138   In Matthew, copious rain falls only in 7:25–27, where it threatens to tear down houses. But even if rain has fallen from the opened heavens, this has not suddenly done away with hunger First, things have to grow. But perhaps rain was only announced, and did not actually fall (cf. 1 Kgs 18:42–45)?

139   "Semitic thinking, as demonstrated in language and visual art alike, is never about the shape, look or perspective, but about the dynamics or the effect that something has. So when the Song of Songs says 'your eyes are doves', it's not about the shape of the eyes, rather about the quality of their look, about their beguiling effect" (Schroer and Staubli, *Körpersymbolik*, 27).

140   The Greek word *diabolos* means "slanderer, calumniator, vilifier"; *satanas*, from the Hebrew, means "adversary."

141   "The specific evil of violence is its speechlessness" (Hannah Arendt, *Denktagebuch*, 345).

142   Müller, *The Hunger Angel*, 17–18.

143   This does not mean I am interpreting the encounter described here psychologically, as Jesus wrestling internally about his mission, or his identity as the Son of God, or as a confrontation with his shadow, with unconscious evil. Mythical language narrates in a way that keeps the internal and external perspectives permeable, that criss-crosses logical categories, makes the invisible visible, and includes the material, outside world in the interpretation.

144   Mark 1:13 and Luke 4:2 refer only to forty days. Only Matthew explicitly includes nights in Jesus' fast. Ulrich Luz, too, considers Jesus' fast to be extraordinary, even though he ignores hunger as a real experience of violence: "Matthew puts special emphasis on Jesus' fasting. Jesus fasts not only forty days but also at night, as Moses (Exod 24:18; 34:28; Deut 9:9, 11, 18, 25; 10:10), and Elijah (1 Kgs 19:8) did. However, he does not do so in life-sustaining closeness to God on Horeb, nor is he miraculously fed with divine food. The reminiscence of Moses and Elijah makes clear that Jesus' fasting is an extraordinary fasting" (Luz, *Matthew 1–7*, 151).

145   This is mentioned explicitly in Exod 24:9–11: "Then Moses and Aaron, Nadab, and Abihu, and seventy of the elders of Israel went up, and they saw the God of Israel. . . . also they beheld God, and they ate and drank."

146   Müller, *The Hunger Angel*, 133.

147   Müller, *The Hunger Angel*, 154.

148   Müller, *The Hunger Angel*, 242.

149   Müller, *The Hunger Angel*, 149–150.

150   Müller, *The Hunger Angel*, 142–143.

151   Kegler, "Hunger," 325.

152   Some translations of the Bible give Mark 11:15–17 the heading "Jesus cleanses the Temple" (NRSV) or similar.

153   Martin Albertz coined the term *Streitgespräche* ("disputes") for pericopae in the Gospels, in which Jesus debates with his "opponents." See: Albertz, *Streitgespräche*.

154   See Bovon, *Luke 1*, 148–49, and the literature he cites there.

155   Anti-Judaism is a term describing—mainly Christian—animosity towards Jews that has a religious and theological basis. As a broad stream of Christian theology, anti-Judaism was long viewed in a positive light as an essential part of Christianity, Judaism being a superseded religion, since the

ENDNOTES

salvation of Israel had been passed on to the church. In contrast, criticism of anti-Judaism starts from the view that the God of both Old and New Testaments is the same GOD, who has never renounced his faithfulness towards Israel. Attempts must therefore be made to determine afresh the relationship between Christianity and Judaism without devaluing Judaism in the process. Cf.: Ruether, *Faith and Fratricide*; Crüsemann and Theissmann, *Ich glaube*.

156   See: Arnhold, "Entjudung," 25.
157   Presented in a critical light by Schottroff, *Parables*, 81.
158   For example, Lieu, *Neither Jew nor Greek*; Boyarin, *Border Lines*; Goodman, *Judaism*; Becker and Yoshiko Reed, *Ways That Never Parted*.
159   See also: Strecker, "Judentum."
160   Schottroff, "Der Hunger Jesu," 150.
161   Donahue and Harrington, *Mark*, 327.
162   Dschulnigg, *Das Markusevangelium*, 298.
163   "Only Jesus himself says that he is hungry, which is the motivation for his search for figs on the fig tree in leaf in v. 13" (Dschulnigg, *Das Markusevangelium*, 301).
164   Eckey, *Das Markusevangelium*, 286.
165   Ernst, *Markus*, 325.
166   Ernst, *Markus*, 324.
167   Donahue and Harrington, *Mark*, 331.
168   Kertelge, *Markusevangelium*, 109.
169   Bayer, *Markus*, 397.
170   Cf. also the widow of Zarephath's empty house, 1 Kgs 17:12.
171   "We should not expect that, just after leaving Bethany in the morning, Jesus is already hungry again. What is being narrated must have a symbolic meaning" (Lentzen-Deis, *Das Markus-Evangelium*, 254).
172   Schottroff, "Jesus' Hunger," 74–77.
173   "On no level of the narrative is Jesus' action found puzzling. There is no indication in the text that shares the alienation of today's reader. The incomprehension about Jesus' action is that of today. The hungry are destroying the last of their own basic needs" (Schottroff, "Der Hunger Jesu," 152).
174   Luise Schottroff reads the fact that the story does not mention the hunger of Jesus' companions as an indication that "it is taken for granted as a normal circumstance of life" (Schottroff, "Jesus' Hunger," 75).
175   "But what does the withered fig tree symbolize? At this point scholars tend to speak with great confidence but with little agreement. The fig tree has been said to symbolize the Jewish crowds, the Jewish religious leaders, the Temple, the sacrificial worship enacted in the Temple, Israel as God's people, Judaism as a religious system, or even the Markan community" (Donahue and Harrington, *Mark*, 331).
176   "Perhaps the best explanation is that the withered fig tree represents the failure by many in Israel to accept Jesus as God's messenger and Jesus' message of the kingdom of God" (Donahue and Harrington, *Mark*, 331).
177   "Israel, which is compared to the fig tree, has closed itself off to God's offer of salvation and has not used the time given—the season for harvesting figs . . . Israel, which misjudged its purpose and did not bring forth fruit at the intended time, has now ceased to be God's chosen people" (Ernst, *Markus*, 326).—"The fig tree serves as an example and a symbol for something else. Given the context, it is about the temple as the center and the epitome of traditional worship and thus also about Jerusalem as the place of traditional hope of salvation. The city and the temple do not offer Jesus the fruit that he seeks there. . . . Readers familiar with the Old Testament prophecies know that the fig tree and its fruits can occasionally serve as a symbol and allegory for the fruitfulness or barrenness of God's People, Israel (cf. Jer 8:13; 24:1–10; Hos 9:10)" (Eckey, *Das Markusevangelium*, 287).—"The fig tree serves in the Old Testament as a metaphor for Israel and its position before God (cf. Jer 8:13; Hos 9:10, 16; Joel 1:7; Mic 7:1–6; cf. Jer 24:1–10). When the fig tree is destroyed here, this indicates 'God's judgement over Israel'" (Bayer, *Markus*, 398).

178 Ebner, *Das Markusevangelium*, 119.
179 Dschulnigg, *Das Markusevangelium*, 300.
180 "The narrator is scrupulous in associating negative statements about Jesus, and the plans to kill him, exclusively with the official representatives of religion and politics" (Ebner, *Das Markusevangelium*, 120).
181 "In connection with Jesus' previous appearance in the temple, the image of the fig tree that has withered right down to its roots allows us to perceive his meaning as criticism of Jerusalem or Israel. Judgement is made over Israel, which is refusing the demands of the approaching theocracy that Jesus has announced" (Kertelge, *Markusevangelium*, 112).
182 "The symbol is followed by the action that reveals Israel's unworthiness" (Grundmann, *Markus*, 308). Grundmann wrote *völkische Theologie* in the 1930s and '40s. I am quoting him here to make visible how even more modern interpreters participate in the old anti-Judaist patterns.
183 Grundmann, *Markus*, 312.
184 "Jerusalem has played out its role as the center of God's People" (Eckey, *Das Markusevangelium*, 290).
185 Josef Ernst puts it similarly: "The temple, as an external expression of Israel's role in mediating salvation, is from now on insignificant . . . The worldwide perspective expressed by the opening up 'to all peoples' can be understood as a mark of the new spiritual temple of the Christian community" (Ernst, *Markus*, 329).
186 Kertelge, *Markusevangelium*, 109.
187 Ernst, *Markus*, 332.
188 Dschulnigg, *Das Markusevangelium*, 295.
189 Eckey, *Das Markusevangelium*, 288.
190 Ernst, *Markus*, 328.
191 Grundmann, *Markus*, 308.
192 Grundmann, *Markus*, 311.
193 Eckey, *Das Markusevangelium*, 281.
194 Ernst, *Markus*, 329.
195 Metzdorf's study, too, confirms that despite differing arguments and starting from different textual bases, the interpreters do not reflect on Jesus' anger. See: Metzdorf, *Tempelaktion Jesu*.
196 Ancient temples were treasuries, collection points for taxes and levies, so that the financial sector found its place within the sanctuaries: "Thus loan and deposit operations grew up in the sanctuaries; the temples were 'sacred banks.' Probably the most important was the temple of Apollo at Delos, which in addition to its main business of providing loans to private individuals and communities, also leased property and rented houses" (Speck, *Handelsgeschichte*, 505). This also applied to the temple in Jerusalem, which Hengel calls "one of the richest in antiquity" (Hengel, *Hellenization*, 22).
197 The money changers in the inner courtyard were responsible for allowing people to exchange their small copper coins into half-shekels. They charged a fee for this exchange. A half-shekel, or tetradrachm, was a valuable, heavy silver coin. The Jewish temple tax of the time required every male Jew over the age of 20 to pay a half-shekel to the temple every year. This silver coin bore the Tyrian stamp, i.e., an image of the Tyrian god on one side. As the tetradrachm was effectively the most stable currency in Palestine, the temple—in this case the temple bank—accepted only these silver coins. See: Reiser, "Numismatik."
198 Schottroff describes v. 23 as being "aggressively phrased," a view I also share. Schottroff, "Der Hunger Jesu," 160.
199 Millman and Kates, "Towards Understanding Hunger," 15.
200 Luise Schottroff distinguishes four apocalyptic conceptions of time: The Time of Alarm over Losing One's Security, The Time of Growing and Ripening, The Time of Watching in the Night, and The Time of Festive Rejoicing. Schottroff, *Lydia's Impatient Sisters*, 156–62.
201 On the parable of the greening fig tree in Mark 13:28–33 see: Sutter Rehmann, *Geh, frage die Gebärerin*, 32–68.
202 The Greek word *hosanna*, a call for rescue and aid, cf. Ps 118:25, is often wrongly understood to be the same as "*hallelujah*" (sing to Yhwh!).

ENDNOTES

203   As the *Sitz im Leben* (which roughly translates as "setting in life"), Luise Schottroff describes the apocalyptic hopes, however diverse they may be, the indignation of oppressed people at the injustice and arbitrariness to which they are exposed in their economic and political life. See: Schottroff, *Der erste Brief*, 329, footnote 925.

204   Henze et al., *Antijudaismus*, 39. See also note 153, above.

205   "No perfectly accurate parallels . . . Jesus consciously tailored the Old Testament text to the new situation" (Ernst, *Markus*, 103).

206   "Jesus' answer uses 1 Sam 21:2–10 with a slightly modification: instead of . . . Ahimelech it names his son Abiathar. . . . Jesus' use of this passage goes further, however, and emphasizes the greater power of Jesus, which entitles him to break the Pharisees' Sabbath rules" (Lentzen-Deis, *Das Markus-Evangelium*, 104).

207   Eckey, *Das Markusevangelium*, 108.

208   Kertelge, *Markusevangelium*, 37.

209   John R. Donahue and Daniel J. Harrington state: "The Markan Jesus never questions the sacredness of the Sabbath. . . . The issue is never the abrogation or disparagement of the biblical Sabbath but how 'work' is to be interpreted" (Donahue and Harrington, *Mark*, 113), while Fritzleo Lentzen-Deis does not see a breach of laws in Jesus' answer, but a new interpretation: "He does not repeal the sabbath law, but releases it from an overcharged, legalistic interpretation" (Lentzen-Deis, *Das Markus-Evangelium*, 105).

210   However, Donahue and Harrington do take this view, first listing the deviations from 1 Sam 21:1–6: "1) David has no companions with him; 2) there is no mention of hunger; 3) David does not enter the house of God; 4) the priest (not high priest) is Ahimelech, not Abiathar; and 5) neither David nor his companions eat the bread of presence"—and then adding "Mark . . . freely rewrote the OT narrative to fit the controversy" (Donahue and Harrington, *Mark*, 111).

211   In 1 Sam 22:9–10 Doeg answers Saul's query about David: "I saw the son of Jesse coming to Nob, to Ahimelech son of Ahitub; he inquired of the Lord for him, gave him provisions, and gave him the sword of Goliath the Philistine." These verses relate to 1 Sam 21:2–6, but add the part about asking Yнwн.

212   By contrast, Donahue and Harrington consider Jesus' question to be purely ironic: "Have you never read (the question, which is slightly ironic)" (Donahue and Harrington, *Mark*, 111).

213   On the exegesis of Mark 12:18–27, see: Sutter Rehmann, "Wenn die Toten sich ausruhen," 74–88.

214   Schiffner, *Lukas liest Exodus*, 45.

215   "The substance of this controversy concerns Sabbath observance" (Donahue and Harrington, *Mark*, 113). Wilfried Eckey, too, says: "On their way, the disciples pluck ears of grain from their stalks by the wayside, to still their hunger. Although Deut 23:26 allows this, the Pharisees and rabbinic casuistry view it as harvest-like activity, which is accordingly forbidden on the Sabbath" (Eckey, *Das Markusevangelium*, 107). Cf. also Karl Kertelge: "Plucking the ears of grain breaches the Sabbath commandment, at least if the law is interpreted strictly (Exod 20:8–11; Deut 5:12–15). This is what is being emphasized here. An excuse such as hunger comes into view only in retrospect and only directly with the example of David (v. 25)" (Kertelge, *Markusevangelium*, 37); "His opponents' question focuses exclusively on the plucking of grain, which if one splits hairs in interpreting the law can be understood as prohibited harvesting, despite Deut 23:26" (Ernst, *Markus*, 102).

216   Schmithals, *Lukas*, 174.

217   Bovon, *Luke 1*, 152.

218   Schmithals, *Lukas*, 62.

219   KJV, the Geneva Bible, NIV and NRSV all render this as "where he had been brought up"; The Living Bible translation is "his boyhood home."

220   Garnsey, "Responses to Food Crisis," 141.

221   "In contrast to the impression of need on the part of the woman, which Jesus' brief description evokes, triggered by catchwords such as 'widow' and 'famine,' the real emphasis in the telling of the scripture lies with Elijah's need. In his escape from Jezebel he needed assistance and care from others" (Schiffner, *Lukas liest Exodus*, 315–16).

222   Jas 5:17 also gives the length of the drought as three years and six months. 1 Kgs 18:1, however, gives different information: "After many days the word of the Lord came to Elijah, in the third year of the drought, saying, 'Go, present yourself to Ahab; I will send rain on the earth.'" Three years and six months are significantly longer than "in the third year."

223   Schönborn and Welten, "Hunger, Hungersnot," 268–69.

224   Baneth, *Mischnajot*, 412.

225   *M. Ta'anit*, translated by Joshua Kulp.

226   The Jubilee Year takes its name from the ram's horn (Hebrew: $yōḇhel$), which was blown to mark its beginning. For more background to the meaning of Jubilee, see: Atwater, *Debt cancellation*.

227   See: Albertz, "Die Tora Gottes."

228   Ernst, *Lukas*, 172.

229   Ulrike Schorn understands that the number twelve in the tradition of Israel functions primarily in a literary and theological way, and is not based on a historical organization of tribes. Rather, it emphasizes how much the different tribes belong together, by listing time-honored names. "This can be made out particularly convincingly in the figure of Joseph: obviously not a tribe, but a representative of the central region of the northern kingdom" (Schorn, *Ruben*, 82).

230   Cf. Ezek 37:16–19, which refers to Joseph's "stick of wood" (NIV), representing the house, i.e., the tribes. And in dividing up the land west of the Jordan, Josh 17:17 refers to Joseph not as a tribe but as a house.

231   "As a wisdom narrative the Joseph stories can be recognized as the development of Joseph from a thoughtless and vain intellectual within his family into a patient, farsighted and magnanimous vizier of the mightiest ruler" (Staubli, *Begleiter*, 163). The mention of Joseph's name here could also have something to do with Jesus' education, which is shown in his reading from the Torah. This son of Joseph is an intellectual, a scribe, whose education has made him somewhat conceited.

232   "The citation agrees verbatim with the LXX; Luke only skips over the words, 'to heal those who are downcast in their hearts,' and adds the phrase, 'to let the oppressed go free,' from Isa 58:6. Did Luke intend to avoid connecting Jesus' miraculous healings to the Spirit, or to concentrate only on the messianic interpretation, thus omitting, in opposition to Jewish trends of interpretation, the words of consolation? Neither is convincing, but I have no better suggestion" (Bovon, *Luke 1*, 153). Other interpreters also puzzle as to what this collage could mean. See, for example: Kremer, *Lukasevangelium*, 55; Ernst, *Lukas*, 171; Eckey, *Das Lukasevangelium*, 222–23.

233   Schiffner, *Lukas liest Exodus*, 302.

234   Schiffner, *Lukas liest Exodus*, 306.

235   Schiffner, *Lukas liest Exodus*, 305.

236   Schiffner, *Lukas liest Exodus*, 308.

237   Interpreters have repeatedly asserted that Nazareth is not up a mountain and that there is no cliff nearby (see, for example: Ernst, *Lukas*, 174; Bovon, *Luke 1*, 156; Petzke, *Das Sondergut*, 81). There are hills, however. Galilee is anything but a flat plain! According to Kerstin Schiffner, Luke is working with the topographical term "hill" to connect the story to that of the exodus. In addition to specific hills such as Mount Sinai (Acts 7:30, 38) and the Mount of Olives (Luke 19:29, 37; 21:37; 22:39; Acts 1:12), which have key significance, Luke also refers to mountains without giving a specific name (for example, Luke 6:12 and 9:28–36). "As in scripture the mountain is *the* place for encounters between humans and God, this particularity is retained by Luke's narration" (Schiffner, *Lukas liest Exodus*, 241). She does not, however, mention our passage, Luke 4:29. The attempt to throw Jesus off the cliff can therefore be read as an attempt to bring him down to the city that lives at the foot of the cliff and waits for help from its God.

238   Final verse added for the ending of the 1931 film of *The Threepenny Opera* by G. W. Pabst, based on Brecht's play, *Die Dreigroschenoper*, 497. An English version might be:

> So there's some who stand in darkness
> And the others in the light.
> And we see those in the brightness
> Those in dark escape our sight.

239   See notes 120 and 121, above.

ENDNOTES

²⁴⁰ See also: Drexhage et al., *Wirtschaft*, 99; Eusebius, *Ecclesiastical History*, 127; Tacitus, *Ann.* 12.43; Josephus, *Ant.* 20.51 and 20.101.

²⁴¹ Queen Helena had ships sail to Egypt and Cyprus, to fetch dried figs and grain for Jerusalem (Josephus, *Ant.* 20.51). This did bring momentary relief, but was unable to reach broad sections of the population.

²⁴² "The verbs *anistemi* (to stand up, to rise up) and *egeirein* (to rouse, to awaken, to set upright) play a key role regarding resurrection. They are verbs of movement, used in Greek as everyday verbs without religious overtones. It is only via the connection to divine power that arising becomes a resurrection. This divine power finds its way into language in the guise of the angel, the messenger from a different world, that of God's power, who imparts 'his' closeness" (Sutter Rehmann, "Auf der Spur des Unsichtbaren," 166; see also Ulrike Metternich, "Auf-er-stehen," in the same volume, 176).

²⁴³ Garnsey, *Famine and Food Supply*, 18.

²⁴⁴ Josephus, *War*, 2.426–27.

²⁴⁵ Whether Blastus was Jewish or whether he just had strong links with the Jewish congregation is not clear. A number of Scriptures, however, mention Jewish officials occupying senior positions, such as Daniel, who was a royal official in the court of Nebuchadnezzar (Dan 2:48); Shadrach, Meshach and Abednego, Daniel's companions, also held similarly high positions (Dan 3:30); Ahikar, under King Sennacherib, held the positions of senior cupbearer, keeper of the signet, public finance administrator and accounting executive (Tob 1:21); Tobit was a purchasing agent at the royal court of Shalmaneser (Tob 1:13); Mordecai worked at the gate of King Ahasuerus (Esth 2:19); Esther became the king's wife and as such was an advocate for her people (Esth 8:3); a eunuch was put in charge of the treasury of Candace, Queen of the Ethiopians (Acts 8:27).

²⁴⁶ Cf. Richter Reimer, *Women*, 31f.

²⁴⁷ Angela Standhartinger points out that women's work was poorly remunerated in antiquity. Groups of widows in Acts 9:39–41 and 1 Tim 5:16 are evidence that women in communities for living and working formed part of the congregation in Joppa, yet the Pastoral Epistles situate them outside the congregation. See: Standhartinger, "Die verehrteste Judith," 105.

²⁴⁸ Cf. Chapter 4: the synagogue congregation in Nazareth that was hoping for help from Jesus (Luke 4:16–30).

²⁴⁹ Mussner, *Apostelgeschichte*, 62.

²⁵⁰ These discourses swirl unswervingly around the relationship between Jews and Gentiles. For example: "Peter is the primary figure of the narrative; even though resisting it, he is led to cross over the separation barrier between Jews and Gentiles—and that is the chief theme of the text" (Pesch, *Die Apostelgeschichte*, 333).—Or: "10:34–35 not only justifies the association of the Jewish Peter with the Gentile Cornelius, but opens the way for the mission to Gentiles, allowing any Jewish believer to receive hospitality and share meal fellowship with any God-fearing and upright Gentile" (Heil, *Meal Scenes*, 254).—Or: "that God himself forced the mission to the Gentiles and their acceptance into the church against a reluctant Peter and a resisting community in Jerusalem" (Jervell, *Die Apostelgeschichte*, 316).—Cf. Eckey, *Die Apostelgeschichte*, 235f; Malina and Pilch, *Social-Science Commentary*; Bock, *Acts*, 380f.

²⁵¹ In this context, exegetes also reflect on the polluting contact with Gentiles and connect it with table fellowship, even though table fellowship is not described in the text. For example, Jacob Jervell notes that, although there was no prohibition against Jews associating with Gentiles, it was still quite customary. The nature of the relationship is expressed here as *kollasthai*; a close relationship, a close attachment to someone: "As 11:3 puts it, Peter eats together with an uncircumcised man, that is, shares table fellowship with him, which strictly speaking was seen to be polluting" (Jervell, *Die Apostelgeschichte*, 308).

²⁵² Pesch, *Die Apostelgeschichte*, 335.

²⁵³ Cf. Lieu, *Image and Reality*, 11.

²⁵⁴ Ben Witherington also concludes that we do not have technical terminology here: Luke uses "proselytes," "God-fearers," and "God-worshippers" to describe Gentiles who worship the God of Israel and belong to the synagogue; but he does not use these terms unambiguously. See: Witherington, *Acts*, 344.

255 Cohen, *Beginnings of Jewishness*.
256 Fredriksen, "What 'Parting.'"
257 Tomson, "The Wars against Rome."
258 Cf. Boyarin, *Border Lines*, 6.
259 Garnsey, *Famine and Food Supply*, 28.
260 Josephus, *War* 5.571.
261 "Hunger brings humiliation. The hungry person thinks of bread and nothing else. Hunger fills his or her universe. His prayer, his aspiration, his hope, his ideal are not lofty: they are a piece of bread. To accept another person's hunger is to condone his or her tragic condition of helplessness, despair and death" (Wiesel, "The Hunger Crisis").
262 For a critique of this concept, see Schottroff, "'Gesetzesfreies Heidenchristentum.'"
263 Witherington, *Acts*, 353.
264 Contracting ritual impurity was not necessarily problematical. If one were obliged to be ritually pure, one could submit to an appropriate purification bath or sacrifice (Num 5:57; Matt 5:23f). Moral impurity, however, was less easy to wash off. Murderers, adulterers, and idolaters could not just take a bath and become "clean." They needed to seek genuine forgiveness, to appeal to the people whom they had harmed, and to GOD, i.e., to seek change and a new start. Cf. Klawans, *Impurity*, 137.
265 M. *Yoma* 8:6.
266 The Romans had destroyed the famous temple; now the Jews would have to rebuild it, as they did with other relics. In addition, the emperors up to 66 CE also respected the Jewish cult in Rome. Only after 135 CE, with the defeat of the Bar Kokhba revolt, did hope fade for a rebuilding of the temple. See: Goodman, *Judaism*, 53.
267 Jürgen Kegler refers to starvation as a tactic of war. See: Kegler, "Hunger," 326.
268 Ezek 6:11–12; 7:15; 13:16. Compare also Isa 51:19; Jer 14:12; 21:9; 24:10; 27:8, 13; 29:17, 18; 32:24, 36; 38:2; 42:17, 22; 44:13.
269 Cf. Kern, *Ancient Siege Warfare*, 54–56.
270 Reports of sieges always include these cannibalistic stories of mothers or parents who are so hungry that they eat their own children. Flavius Josephus, too, writes of Mary Bat Eleazar, who served up a "roast" of her own infant (*War* 6.205). Luise Schottroff has analyzed Josephus' story to understand the viewpoint from which he is narrating. She believes it is not enough to read the text in the tradition of descriptions of distress that show how terribly famine was raging in the city. "Mothers eating their own children is seen, as it is here, as a destruction of human order that cannot get any worse. There are texts which suggest that fathers are even more susceptible to cannibalism than mothers" (Schottroff, *Lydia's Impatient Sisters*, 165). Schottroff points out contradictions in Josephus' text, such as Mary not killing her child to secure her own survival. "She wants to die herself and kills the child because he has no future. She speaks of sacrifice and that the child is to be an avenging spirit against the plundering Jewish soldiers. . . . In her eyes, it is they who have brought the greater guilt on themselves" (*Lydia's Impatient Sisters*, 165–66).
271 Josephus, *War*, 4.106f.
272 Cf. the night-time break-out as described in Jer 52:6–7 and 2 Kgs 25:3–4. The men of Gischala did what those from Jerusalem had also done: Every man for himself! Should slower or weaker individuals be left behind, that is the price to pay.
273 Josephus, *War*, 4.107.
274 Josephus, *War*, 4.109–111.
275 Josephus, *War*, 4.116.
276 "Woe to those who are pregnant and to those who are nursing infants in those days! Pray that it may not be in winter. For in those days there will be suffering" (Mark 13:17–19).
277 Schottroff, *Lydia's Impatient Sisters*, 163.
278 Josephus, *War*, 5.342–346. Quotes from Josephus in this section are all taken from William Whiston's translation.
279 Josephus, *War*, 5.344.
280 Josephus, *War*, 5.345.
281 Josephus, *War*, 5.424–25.

ENDNOTES

282 Josephus, *War*, 5.428.
283 Josephus, *War*, 5.429–30.
284 Josephus, *War*, 5.432–33.
285 Josephus, *War*, 5.435–36.
286 Josephus, *War*, 5.438.
287 Kegler, "Hunger," 326.
288 Oppenheim, "Siege-Documents," 69–89.
289 Oppenheim, "Siege-Documents," 81, footnote 42.
290 Oppenheim, "Siege-Documents," 71.
291 Oppenheim, "Siege-Documents," 76.
292 Oppenheim, "Siege-Documents," 72.
293 "Herod spared nothing in his elaborate designs for the port facilities—a major engineering feat at the time—as well as for the city, which included palaces, temples, a theater, a marketplace, a hippodrome, and water and sewage systems. When it was completed 12 years later, only Jerusalem outshone the splendor of Caesarea. Its population under Herod grew to around 100,000, larger than that of Jerusalem; the city was spread over some 164 acres" (Haberfeld, *Fodor's Israel*, 199). It is certainly significant that such information is available in travel guides. However, they lack the reflection about who bore the costs of Herod's city expansion.
294 "The Romans annexed Judaea in 6 B.C., and made Caesarea the headquarters of the provincial governor and his administration. Of these governors Pontius Pilate was one. At first the province was known as Judaea, later Palestina" (Freeman-Grenville, *The Holy Land*, 135). See also: Avi-Yonah, *Historical Geography*.
295 The presence of Peter and Agabus locates the story in the late 40s, perhaps close to 50 CE.
296 Josephus, *War*, 2.305–306.
297 Josephus, *War*, 2.285–286.
298 Josephus, *War*, 2.457.
299 Josephus, *War*, 7.37.
300 See also: Sutter Rehmann, "What Happened in Caesarea?"
301 See: Reinbold, *Propaganda*, 57.
302 See note 250, above.
303 J. Julius Scott, "The Cornelius Incident," 477. Scott also attacks the Jewish Christians as being completely misguided: "What place were contemporary (first-century) Jewish traditions, attitudes and observances to have in the new faith? These were issues rooted in a second commonwealth Judaism that resulted in deficiencies in at least three areas: its doctrine of God, its doctrine of Christ, its eschatology. It held to an aberration of the true nature and work of God that promoted and sustained a blatant ethnocentricity" (483). This is an example of anti-Judaist hermeneutics.
304 Cohen, *Beginnings of Jewishness*, 156.
305 See, for example: Cohen, *Beginnings of Jewishness*, 209–17. The rabbinic conversion ceremony is described in the Babylonian Talmud: *Yebamot* 47a–b (Cohen dates this in the second or third century) and in the thirteenth-century post-Talmudic tractate *Gerim* 1.1. For the period in which Cornelius lived, Cohen identifies various terms for closeness to and membership of the synagogue, which are not unambiguous in the sense of "really Jewish" or "only a little bit Jewish."
306 In addition to Cornelius, the New Testament describes Joseph (Matt 1:19), Zacharias and Elizabeth (Luke 1:6), Simeon (Luke 2:25), Jesus on the Cross (Luke 23:47), Joseph of Arimathea (Luke 23:50), Lot (2 Pet 2:7) and Abel (Heb 11:4) as being righteous (Greek: *dikaios*).
307 There were Jews in the Roman army. For example, at the same time as our story, a certain Julius Tiberius Alexander held high military rank in Judea (46–48 CE). He came from a Jewish family, but appears to have distanced himself from his religion (Josephus, *Ant.* 20.5.100). Josephus also reports that under the Procurator Alexander a great famine arose in Judea, which led to revolts. Alexander had their leaders Simon and James crucified (Josephus, *Ant.* 20.5.102).
308 Acts 10:30 refers to: "a man in bright clothing" (KJV). Some translators turn this into a supernatural apparition: an angel. *Lampros*, however, can also mean bright in the sense of "in a natural state, unbleached, untinted," and thus indicate the untreated, rough material of the common people.

Acts 10:3 refers to a "messenger from God"—which all English translations render as "angel." This shows how concepts from a later period can easily creep in. We can imagine a messenger of God to be a prophet, or simply a man sent by the synagogue to bear a message.

309 At that time, the Jewish way of counting hours started at sunrise, at 6 a.m. "At the 9th hour" indicates about 3 p.m. This was the time that Jesus died on the cross: "44 And it was about the sixth hour, and there was a darkness over all the earth until the ninth hour. 45 And the sun was darkened, and the veil of the temple was rent in the midst. 46 And when Jesus had cried with a loud voice, he said, Father, into thy hands I commend my spirit: and having said thus, he gave up the ghost. 47 Now when the centurion saw what was done, he glorified God, saying, Certainly this was a righteous man" (Luke 23:44–47, KJV). This timing is all the more interesting since the same author (of Acts and Luke) assigns words to a Roman centurion at explictly the same time of day.

310 "Pliny the Younger gave money for the support of needy children. [Pliny the Younger, *Epistulae* VII.18; I.8.10; IX.30. See also: Hans Kloft, *Liberalitas principis*. Cologne: Böhlau, 1970, 65]. In doing so, he was acting within the tradition of aristocratic *liberalitas* ('liberality'). This liberality primarily serves one's own social and political interests. In the Gospel of Luke this liberality of lordly 'benefactors' is explicitly criticized (Luke 22:25)" (Schottroff, *Parables*, 210–11).

311 Standhartinger, "And all ate."

312 Plutarch, *Caes.* 57.8. And: A ruler who is not generous enough is at risk of being hounded out of office. Q. Maximus was not re-elected because the banquet he had laid on to honor his late uncle was not considered splendid enough. Cicero, *Mur.* 75.

313 Garnsey, *Famine and Food Supply*, 236–39. This changed the idea of equality, which had characterized the Greek tradition of the symposium. In the Greek *polis* the city fed its free citizens with equal measures as an expression of equality and community.

314 "An incident in a food shortage at Antioch in AD 362–3 is sometimes discussed in this connection. The emperor Julian sent for large quantities of wheat from Chalcis and Hierapolis, 50 and 100 km away by land, respectively. Why hadn't the wheat been sent for earlier? To say that the operation was too expensive is misleading.... The brute fact is that men in authority in the city were themselves capable of relieving the crisis, by releasing their own grain or bringing it in from elsewhere, but were either cashing in on the high prices for food or unable or unwilling to prevent such profiteering.... My guess is that there were usually sufficient local stocks to keep a community from going over the brink—the problem was how to extract them from profiteering landlords and merchants" (Garnsey, *Famine and Food Supply*, 22–23).

315 Garnsey, *Famine and Food Supply*, 27.

316 "What appears desirable, they seize and render their own, and transform their will and pleasure into their law, as arbitrarily as victors in a conquered city" (Sallust, *Rep.* 1:3).

317 The wise foresight of the victors, their efforts to care for the inferior masses, who for their part are indolent and ungrateful—"[T]hese well-rehearsed themes are the foundations of an ideology of benefaction by which rulers, ancient and modern, represent to themselves the fundamental justice of their position" (Elliott, "Disciplining the Hope," 180).

318 Elliott, "Disciplining the Hope," 181.

319 Livy 4.13; 6.17.

320 Peter Garnsey notes that "Spurius Maelius is the only private benefactor to figure in the narratives of food crisis in early Rome [fifth century BCE]. According to the tradition an equestrian and therefore not a member of the 'political class,' he was spectacularly successful in bringing in grain from all sides. He did this, moreover, at a time when the official in charge of the grain supply could only produce a trickle of grain from Etruria—not the only implausibility in this fantastic story. Maelius proceeded to sell his grain cheap or ... to give it away to the very poor. He was put to death on the grounds that he was aiming at tyranny" (Garnsey, *Famine and Food Supply*, 177).

321 Cicero, *Dom.* 38; *Mil.* 27.

322 "Marco Sulpicio, Marci filio, Felici, domo Roma, tribu Quirina, liberatori et patrono, praefecto cohortis primae Germanorum, tribuno militum legionis sextae decimae Flaviae Firmae Fidelis, tribuno militum cohortis tertiae Ulpiae mil[l]iariae Petraeorum, electo et retento ad census excipiendos in partem provinciae Armeniae, item Cappadociae, praefecto equitum alae secundae Syrorum

civium Romanorum, amici ob adfectionem municpii Salensium et innocentiam dedicaverunt decretumque ordinis subiecerunt." The inscription has been published with a commentary and translation (into French) by Stéphane Gsell and Jérôme Carcopino. See: Gsell and Carcopino, "La base," 3. Ulpius was Trajan's *nomen gentilicium*. Gsell and Carcopino suggest reading the word after it as *milliarius*; it is barely legible in the inscription on the stone.

323   "[M]urorum opere, minimo sumtu ambiendo, seu annonae avaris difficultatibus ex copi[i]s armaturae suae plurima ad nostram utilitatem, nihil at militum damnum commodando." Quoted in Gsell and Carcopino, "La base," 16.

324   Gsell and Carcopino, "La base," 19.

325   Flavius Josephus reports the massacre of the Jewish people before the outbreak of the Jewish-Roman War in 66 CE. He refers to the killing of 20,000 Jewish people (*War* 2.18.1; see Chapter 5).

326   We can see this discretion earlier in the text as well, when the brethren from Joppa sought out Peter in Lydda. They did not tell him exactly why he should come or what they hoped for. The two men just said: "Please come to us without delay" (Acts 9:38). It was only when Peter had arrived in Joppa and was led into the upper room that it became clear all was not well in Joppa, where grief and despair reigned. In the case of the disciples from Joppa, it was a request that Peter could not refuse. He surely felt a strong bond with them.

327   It was essential to accept an invitation to a banquet given by a ruler, so as not to cause offence. This was less about hospitality and more about submission, or the politics of banquets. See: Friedländer, *Darstellungen*, 10; Schottroff, *Parables*, 49–56.

328   See note 308, above.

329   Cf. Kessler, "Armenfürsorge," 93.

330   "Almsgiving, acts of charity, good works" were practiced as something that were part of justice, and mean the same thing. See: Richter Reimer, *Women*, 36.

331   Mark 10:42–44 clearly criticizes Roman *liberalitas*, which was only practiced by the great in society as a system-affirming principle of governance. Consider the differences between Jewish charitableness and Graeco-Roman charitableness; see: Bolkestein, *Wohltätigkeit*, 264, 270, 338f.

332   See note 306, above.

333   Helen Schüngel-Straumann points out that the noun *eleemosyne* and other terms related to *eleos* are among the commonest *Leitworte* in the book of Tobit. They describe individual good deeds, as well as a basic attitude of solidarity. "The verb used for practicing righteousness in Tob 4:5 is constructed the same way as in *eleemosyne poeien*; righteousness is thus almost synonymous with *eleemosyne*" (Schüngel-Straumann, *Tobit*, 101).

334   Ps 107 forms the frame of reference for the shadow of hunger and poverty in Matt 4:16 as well; see Chapter 3.

335   Peter Garnsey (*Famine and Food Supply*, 28) lists a sequence of disgusting foods; see Chapter 5.

336   See Chapter 3, and especially note 140.

337   See Chapter 4 and note 224, above, on *m. Ta'anit* and praying for rain; as well as Chapter 3. John also sharply criticized the regime and appealed to everyone, including soldiers, for social responsibility, so that the prevailing situation would turn to the better and GOD would bring reconciliation (Matt 3:5; Mark 1:5).

338   Only 1 Tim 6:2 uses the expression *euergesia*, uncritically, in the power imbalance between masters and slaves (treating slaves well).

339   "Come, let us return to the Lord. He has torn us to pieces but he will heal us; he has injured us but he will bind up our wounds. After two days he will revive us; on the third day he will restore us, that we may live in his presence. Let us acknowledge the Lord; let us press on to acknowledge him. As surely as the sun rises, he will appear; he will come to us like the winter rains, like the spring rains that water the earth" (Hos 6:1–3); see also Chapter 9.

340   The King James Version inserts the phrase "and wild beasts" here, anticipating Acts 11:5–6.

341   "By the end of the Roman Republic and indeed during the imperial era, when practically the whole world was subject to Roman dominion and the Mediterranean had, to an extent, become a '*mare Romanum*,' the state held exclusive fishing rights for the sea coast, for rivers, lakes and ponds, in Italy as well as within each individual province. But there were, . . . often enough, disputes and

ambiguities, particularly in the East of the empire" (Bohlen, *Fischerei*, 44).

342 "Give us 5 nets and we will deliver to you 500 fish of a good quality *(Tukkunu)* by the 15th of Tishri," Contract dating from 419 BCE, which Ribat, servant and steward of the banker Rimut-Ninurta, concluded with five Aramaic fishermen. (Bohlen, *Fischerei*, 13).

343 This is often claimed, e.g., "God commands Peter to kill any of the creatures and eat it . . . of course, the reference is to Israel's Torah rules of prohibited foods [Leviticus 11]" (Malina and Pilch, *Social-Science Commentary*, 77). Even the passages Darrell L. Bock cites do not substantiate this: They do not fit into these four categories of animal. Lev 10:10 does not list animals at all; Lev 20:25 does not name *ta tetrapoda* or *ta theria*. "[T]o eat all these unclean things would be a violation of the law [Lev 10:10; 20:25; Ezek 4:14; Dan 1:8–12; 2 Macc 5:27; 6:18–25; Tob 1:10–11; Jdt 10:5; 12:2]" (Bock, *Acts*, 389).

344 "For in his anger he put to death many Israelites; but I would secretly remove the bodies and bury them. So when Sennacherib looked for them he could not find them. Then one of the Ninevites went and informed the king about me, that I was burying them; so I hid myself. But when I realized that the king knew about me and that I was being searched for to be put to death, I was afraid and ran away. Then all my property was confiscated; nothing was left to me that was not taken into the royal treasury" (Tob 1:18–20).

345 See the introduction by Martin Leutzsch to the Greek book of Daniel in *Bibel in gerechter Sprache*, 1710. This (German) translation has twelve chapters and is followed directly by Susanna and Bel and the Dragon.

346 In ancient literature, the image was fueled by the extravagant Persians and their luxurious cuisine: "The more common picture of Persian eating habits in Greek literature, however, is one of luxury and extravagance. . . . Persian dinner, according to the same comic fragment [Antiphanes in Athenaeus 4,130e-f], included whole oxen, swine, deer and lambs and a whole roasted camel" (Sancisi-Weerdenburg, "Persian Food," 292–93). See also: MacDonald, "The Eyes of All," 7–8.

347 Up to 332 BCE Judea was under Persian rule. By this time the Greeks were already rising to supremacy in the East, their customs and goods increasingly reaching as far as Persian Palestine. See: Schwartz, *Imperialism*, 24. This is illustrated by Persian coins, which were all minted in the Greek fashion. Alexander the Great finally supplanted the Persians in Palestine, and after his death Ptolemy took over the rule of Palestine and Syria until around 200 CE. "Although coastal Palestine and Phoenicia in this century witnessed nearly constant warfare between the two dynasties, Judaea, which was a poor hill country district off the main roads and of little strategic interest, remained at peace" (Schwartz, *Imperialism*, 26).

348 Seth Schwartz refers to Jewish society in ca. 200 BCE and later (i.e., the period when the Septuagint and the Greek book of Daniel were written) as a "loosely integrated Palestinian Jewish society" (Schwartz, *Imperialism*, 19), since the many foreign powers passing through it had turned it into a corridor. The Hasmonean royal family needed strong symbols in their fight for national unity. Queen Shelamzion (Salome Alexandra) promoted the books of Judith and Esther in an attempt to shore up her power base. "If Judaean society in the Second Temple period was characterized by a constant tension between inner and external integration—between separatism and assimilation—then the reformist high priests of the 170s and 160s tried to resolve the tension by downgrading the Jews' separatism, if not eliminating it" (Schwartz, *Imperialism*, 32). The ruler Antiochus IV Epiphanes tried to resolve the tension by dissolving Jewish separatism entirely, in that he prohibited observation of the Torah (including circumcision).

349 Flavius Josephus describes several mass executions under Roman leadership. See, e.g., *War* 2.76; 5.449f; *Ant.* 17.296.

350 On the significance of Caesarea for the Jewish-Roman War, see Chapter 5.

351 Seth Schwartz thus refers to them as interventionist. Cyrus was celebrated as a liberator and restorer of the old gods. "In some cases, . . . Persian interventionism practically created the nations the Persians ruled" (Schwartz, *Imperialism*, 21). The Persian influence can be seen in Esther, Daniel, and Judith.

352 *Bel* was revered throughout the Orient, not just between the Euphrates and the Tigris. In Akkadian, *Bel* denotes "Lord" and can indicate different gods. The name of the Babylonian deity

Marduk was considered so potent during the first millennium BCE that it could not be said out loud. His name was replaced with the honorary title *Bel* ("Lord"). See: Bible Study Tools, "Bel".

353 See: Plonz, "Vom Bel zu Babel."

354 Little figures and statues of gods are not worth the flour sacrificed to them: they are not alive, but are made of clay or wood. On this, see the story "Abraham and the Idol Shop," which appears in *Genesis Rabbah* chapter 38 and is a biblical commentary on the prohibition of making images in Exod 20:2–7 and Deut 5:6–10. See also: Breitmaier, "Von Terachs Götzenbilderladen."

355 Maul, "Tor der Götter," 24.

356 The Greek word *drakon* comes from the verb "to stare." Snakes and crocodiles have the special staring gaze of reptiles, which fixes their prey in an almost hypnotized state. This staring gave the Greek dragon its name, and says something about its character.

357 In Revelation, the serpent spews water like a river (Rev 12:15).

358 *Mushkhushshu*, the "king of all dragons," was also named Bel (Lord), and is as much the fire-red dragon of the Sumerians as the later Akkadian-Babylonian dragon, created by the dragon goddess Tiamat. *Mushkhushshu* is a hybrid creature with a horned snake head and a scaly body, a scorpion sting at the tail. His front feet are lion's paws and the back are eagle's feet. On the Ishtar gate of Babylon are representations of lions, bulls, and dragons, the symbols of the main Babylonian deities. This gate was brought in crates to Germany in 1930 and reassembled in Berlin's Pergamon Museum. The dragon remained a favorite heraldic creature, threatening to stare down, scare off, or devour one's enemies.

359 See: Veyne, *Brot und Spiele*. Domination was underpinned by switching off compassion towards the vanquished, and subduing nature. See also: Kahl, *Galatians Re-Imagined*, 152: "Exotic and savage beasts such as lions, panthers, and elephants, as well as domesticated bulls shown and killed in the *venationes* of the morning exemplify the other of raw nature as such and the power to subdue it. Since ancient times in the Near East the king's prowess as hunter had signified his social and military power. At the same time, these wild beast fights also proclaim the triumphant message of victory over faraway lands like Africa, where these animals were caught, to be subsequently transported over long distances in costly and complicated transactions." Kahl also states that "on a single day, five thousand animals were killed in a hunt [Suetonius, *Tit.* 7.3; Cassius Dio 66.25]. Over a period of no less than one hundred days, Emperor Titus presented thousands of animals and humans to fight to the death" (*Galatians Re-Imagined*, 150).

360 "Salva nos 2," in: Domin, *Sämtliche Gedichte*, 118.

361 Bieler and Schottroff, *The Eucharist*, 19f.

362 The delay of the Parousia is a theory according to which, writes Luise Schottroff, "the eschatology of the Gospels arose out of the attempt to resolve the problem of the immediate return of Christ not having taken place. I consider this model—which constructs this problem out of a so-called immediate expectation on the part of the first Christian generations in order to furnish a foundation for the eschatology of the New Testament—to be an invention of biblical scholarship that is urgently in need of hermeneutical critique. It is based on linear conceptions of time and on a religious dualism that contrasts 'the time of this world' with 'the kingdom of that world/of God' (*basilea tou theou*)" (Schottroff, *Parables*, 2).

363 Townes, *Blaze of Glory*; Martin, "Sacred Hope."

364 On the sociology of food, see: Douglas, *Food in the Social Order*; Barlösius, *Soziologie des Essens*.

365 Zingerle, "Identitätsbildung," especially 80f.

366 "The shortest definition of religion: interruption" (Metz, *Faith in History*, 171).

367 Of the 755 instances of the Hebrew word *nephesh*, the Septuagint (dating from the third century BCE) translates 600 as *psyche*. It is unclear whether this translation is already a reference to Greek philosophical concepts making their way into the Old Testament, or whether it is simply a traditional usage of the word *psyche*. See: Schroer and Staubli, *Körpersymbolik*, 68.

368 Schroer and Staubli, *Körpersymbolik*, 68–72.

369 Compare Friesen, "Poverty."

370 Schottroff, *Der erste Brief*, 42–43.

371 Sölle, *The Mystery of Death*, 62.

372 Sutter Rehmann et al., *Sich dem Leben in die Arme werfen*.

373 In German, "auferstehen" is a theologically constructed verb not in use in daily language. Its central "-er-" fundamentally demarcates the verb "to stand up, get on your feet, get up" from the holy or divine. This is not the case in English, which uses the same verb "to rise" for getting up in the morning, rising from the dead, and rising up in political revolt. Greek also uses ordinary verbs that mean getting up in all its dimensions: *anistemi, egeirein*. These verbs also appear in the Septuagint (the Greek translation of the Old Testament). See also: Sutter Rehmann, "Manchmal stehen wir auf."

374 The book of Wisdom was written in the first century CE in Alexandria, Egypt, and is addressed to educated Jewish people who would fully understand the Torah and Greek literature. As it is written in Greek, it does not belong to the Hebrew Bible but is in the Apocrypha. Creation contains a secret that only the wise can name; see also Sir 1:1–7; Job 38:1f.

375 For example, Janssen, *Anders*, 29. Claudia Janssen refers to eschatological language—for speaking of the miracle of transformation—as the language of the secret. It does not get lost in poetry, but is a language of relationship, depending on practice, on managing daily life, on doing things collectively. This is why Paul also adds ethical pleas, reminding people of the dimension of responsibility in shaping the world (*Anders*, 319).

376 In the history of exegesis, the death of the seed is generally compared to human dying. People will experience new life only after their death. Luise Schottroff rightly criticizes the insertion of a dualistic interpretive framework into this observation of nature. God and the world are not two separate areas. New creation, new life, and transformation belong to this one world of God. See: Schottroff, *Der erste Brief*, 313–14.

377 "Greening power" is a term that goes back to Hildegard of Bingen. For her, *viriditas* exists in animals, fish, and birds, in herbs, flowers, and trees. The dew of the Holy Spirit—the gift of wisdom—is what awakens this greening in all creatures. See: Schipperges, *Hildegard of Bingen*; Schipperges, *The World of Hildegard*.

378 Compare the speech by Menenius Agrippa (494 BCE), who uses the metaphor of a body made up of different parts to convince the plebs that they must work hard, while the social elite do not (Livy 2.32.7—33.1, in: Schottroff, *Der erste Brief*, 252–53).

379 Paul does give us a detailed picture of the network of relationships in the congregation in Rome. But his description lacks all mention of hierarchies or social order (Rom 16:1 16).

380 See: Crüsemann, "Trost"; Ehrensperger, *Paul*, 63–80.

381 Schottroff, *Der erste Brief*, 246–48.

382 Paul calls the work of the congregation in Achaia *diakonia*; similarly also the work of the different body parts in 12:5. *Diakonein* refers to menial service, almost exclusively performed by women and slaves (see: Schottroff, *Lydia's Impatient Sisters*, 205).—In Rom 16:3, 6, 12, Paul speaks of *kopian* (toiling) and *synergein* (working together). The verbs in Rom 16:1–16 refer to shared, common need and responsibility (working together, making an effort, standing up for one another, taking the rap for one another, being captured, proving oneself, being rewarded, becoming someone's mother, belonging to one another). The repeated occurrence of these verbs shows clearly what a great effort the community members made, and how hard the living and working conditions were for the lower social classes. However, the commitment of the women and men who stood up for one another in the congregations shows no socially defined roles, but is in line with the Apostle Paul's way of living in 2 Cor 11:23–28.

383 See: Schottroff, *Der erste Brief*, 245.

384 Burkert, "Oriental Symposia," 8.

385 *Hen* poma *epotisthaimen*: "the one *drink* was given us to drink" [author's emphasis]. Minuscules 630, 1505, 1881 (dated 1350), 2495 and al sy^h; see also: Stein, *Frühchristliche Mahlfeiern*, 130.

386 A second text variant in the fifth-century *Codex Alexandrinus* reflects once again that v. 13b seemed to require further clarification. *Hen soma esmen*: "we are one body" considerably simplifies the matter. This variant leaves out being watered by the Spirit, and emphasizes the result of drinking: We are one body, that is what is important.

387 In many groups, drinking is a way to cement bonds. See: Jellinek, "Symbolism," 864. Oswyn Murray underscores the significance of drinking in groups, especially when drinking alcoholic beverages. Drinking together enables people to identify with one another. See: Murray, "War and the Symposium," 84.

388 "[F]ood has symbolic meanings. At the macro-social level, various forms of feasting serve to

Endnotes

link individuals to the wider social fabric through shared understandings of cultural conventions.... food can be a form of currency either in a literal sense whereby animals are exchanged for goods and services, or the giving of food as a gift is intended to elicit some reciprocal gift, service, or obligation to behave in particular ways or to repay some social debt" (Wood, *Sociology of the Meal*, 47).

389 Meals are associated with eating utensils, particular seating arrangements, order of courses, etc. They are very complex, in terms of both their material structure and their social arrangements. Drinks, by contrast, are much simpler. They can be shared unproblematically with friends, acquaintances, family, work colleagues, strangers, and others. Sharing a meal is not possible with all these people. While meals tend to encompass friendship, solidarity, and closeness, it is easier and less binding to drink together. Sociological research therefore describes drinks as being more democratic and having wider social applications. Cf. Wood, *Sociology of the Meal*, 50.

390 Douglas, *Constructive Drinking*, 8 (Introduction).

391 One exception is 1 Cor 3:2, where Paul gives milk to the young congregation in Corinth—he gave them milk, not solid food, which they were not yet ready to digest. By nursing the infant congregation, like watering the ploughed earth (1 Cor 3:6), Paul is supporting the child's growth process.

392 Dio Chrysostom, *Ven.* (*Or. 7*), 105–106.

393 *Sifre Devarim* 48:7.

394 In Acts, Paul mostly teaches in synagogues. He certainly knew the synagogues in Damascus (Acts 9:1), Thessalonica (17:3), Antioch (13:14), Iconium (14:1), Philippi (16:16), Beroea (17:10), Athens (17:17), Corinth (18:4), and Ephesus (18:19).

395 To see the images: https://commons.wikimedia.org/wiki/Category:Dura-Europos_synagogue_painting. The synagogue was destroyed in 256 CE, a short time after it was remodeled. The unique frescoes, which decorated the whole synagogue, presumably date from this period. See also: Schottroff, *Der erste Brief*, 320–21.

396 Ezekiel lived in the sixth century BCE. After the first wave of Babylonian conquests in 594 BCE, he was deported to Babylon, together with others. The second conquest in 574 BCE brought about the destruction of the temple in Jerusalem.

397 Ausländer, *Gedichte*, 339.

398 "The reality of their lives is sketched in Psalm 1: It is marked by outside control, which encompasses all of life. In this situation the Messiah is a figure of hope, guarantor of the checks that God places on the unleashed power of unchecked growth, symbol of the liberation of the destitute people. This messianic figure acquires form in the congregation" (Butting, *Hier bin ich*, 71).

399 See: Kahl, *Galatians Re-Imagined*, 148–64.

400 Recent scholarship has relinquished the concept of a single author in favor of a group. On the text passages in Luke's Gospel that have traditionally been considered Lukan special materials, Claudia Janssen and Regene Lamb say: "We assume, however, that the texts of the special material represent ideas and theological foundations of Lukan communities and originated in their circles.... Furthermore, we assume that the Lukan materials are to be located in Jewish-Christian circles, based on their re-working of First Testament traditions and their creative interaction with them" (Janssen and Lamb, "Gospel of Luke," 645–46).—I agree with those who situate Luke in the Jewish context, such as: "The texts ... are Jewish texts, written by people who do not describe themselves at any point as 'no-longer-Jewish', who are differentiated from the majority of Jews through their trust in the Messiah Jesus, but share their history and their belief in God's advocacy with other Jewish brothers and sisters" (Schiffner, *Lukas liest Exodus*, 53).

401 Many English translations, including NRSV, end verse 3 after "did not find the body." Only some, e.g., KJV and NASB, add "of the Lord Jesus."

402 The Roman general Varus is reported to have crucified masses of Jewish rebels after the death of Herod in 4 BCE, see: Josephus, *War* 2.75; *Ant.* 17.296. Later, in 70 CE, during the siege of Jerusalem, Emperor Titus ordered 500 and more Jews who were fleeing from famine to be tortured and crucified daily before the city walls, to weaken the besieged population's resistance. The great number of crosses even caused a shortage of timber (*War* 5.449f).

403 Bovon refers to Rembrandt's drawings and engravings, which have a kind of shimmer about them, fitting with Luke: "There the artist tries to represent what cannot be pictured, the resurrection.

He hesitates, trying something, then correcting or retracting it. Sometimes he shows the human but radiant face of the Risen One; sometimes he prefers to see him as disappearing; and sometimes he emphasizes the vivid, luminous streak Christ leaves when he departs. Never have I so keenly felt the truth of this presence–absence, this vanishing spiritual presence as I do with Rembrandt" (Bovon, *Luke 3*, 380).

404 "The supernatural nature of what is happening, and presumably also of Jesus' appearance, shakes them. They therefore believe him to be a ghost" (Petzke, *Das Sondergut*, 204). I do not believe that the "supernatural" level leads us anywhere. This binary division into natural and supernatural does not correspond to Lukan thinking.

405 We should retain this openness despite the exegetes, e.g., "Jesus appears before the eleven disciples" (Petzke, *Das Sondergut*, 203); "The joy of recognizing Jesus" (Bovon, *Luke 3*, 386); "The risen Jesus appears before all the disciples" (Eckey, *Das Lukasevangelium*, 988).

406 See note 373, above.

407 Compare the lines by Dorothee Sölle from her poem "Gott, du Freundin der Menschen":

> We set off in pairs,
> but because of you
> we are always at least three,
> on the path to the bread
> that is edible, the water
> that no one has poisoned.

408 Wolff, *Anthropologie*, 12.

409 Margareta Gruber and Andreas Michel point out that the most intensive texts about bodies can be found in the Song of Songs and the Lamentations, including the book of Job. But the body as a whole is seldom mentioned: reference is almost always to individual body parts. "In this sense, the guiding concepts *basar*, *oesoem* and *se'er* are synecdoche for the living flesh and skeleton. The text is referring not to outward appearance, but to the abilities and feelings associated with the parts of the body, which sometimes differ greatly in their biblical sense from today's metaphors or scientific thinking" (Gruber and Michel, "Körper," 308).

410 Schroer and Staubli, *Körpersymbolik*, 128.

411 Schroer and Staubli, *Körpersymbolik*, 128.

412 According to Deut 29:4, a person has eyes to see, ears to hear, and a heart to perceive (at least, in the King James Version; other translations use "mind"). It is the heart that organizes impressions that come from outside. When Hos 7:11 states that Ephraim is like a silly dove without heart (KJV) this means Israel has taken leave of its senses, has become irrational and foolish like a dove. Cf. Schroer and Staubli, *Körpersymbolik*, 47 and 49.

413 Schroer and Staubli, *Körpersymbolik*, 171.

414 Navarro Puerto, "Female Disciples," 145.

415 Schroer and Staubli, *Körpersymbolik*, 205.

416 Fernando Belo refers to the Jesuan practice of the eyes, hands, and feet. See: Belo, *Das Markusevangelium*, 205f, 306–18.

417 Schroer and Staubli, *Körpersymbolik*, 240.

418 When François Bovon comments on these verses: "There the evangelist somehow established a transition between two originally independent stories" (Bovon, *Luke 3*, 385) he is not recognizing their significance in the process of resurrection!

419 François Bovon, on the other hand, views Luke and John as being very close when he states: "In the episode of the doubting Thomas, the fourth evangelist dots the 'i.' By looking and touching, the disciple wants to find the prints of the nails (John 20:25). Without explicitly saying so, Luke wants to achieve the same result. The feet and hands must bear the marks that reveal an identity" (Bovon, *Luke 3*, 391). And later: "What the double imperative had demanded is realized in v. 40. While he is still talking, the Risen One shows his wounds" (392). See also: Petzke, *Das Sondergut*, 204; and Eckey, *Das Lukasevangelium*, 989.

420 For a long time it was believed that fish were rarely eaten in Israel/Palestine. There were hardly fish in the highlands, the seacoast was not controlled by Israel, and natural ports were scarce.

ENDNOTES

The sacrificial rites do not feature fish. But archaeological discoveries have shown that fish were eaten in great quantities in Palestine throughout the centuries. "The discovery of fish remains from almost every recent excavation requires that these conclusions be abandoned. . . . The remains indicate that some of the inhabitants of Palestine had access to a variety of freshwater and saltwater fish" (Mac Donald, *Ancient Israelites*, 37).

421   On the significance and the preparation of pickled fish, see: Bohlen, *Fischerei*.—"[Magdala] has been identified with the ancient city of Migdal Nunia which means *fish tower*. It was also known as Taricheae with a related meaning of *the place of salted fish*" (Magdala.org, "History I"). See also: Pahlitzsch and Kühne, "Magdala."

422   Gerd Petzke says: "Jesus eats before the very eyes of the disciples, thus proving his corporeality definitively" (Petzke, *Das Sondergut*, 205). And Wilfried Eckey: "The meal of fish proves unequivocally that he is physically alive. With his resurrection into God's sovereign life he has not been transformed into a heavenly being, an angel, but—although he has not returned to mortal existence on earth like Nain's little boy ([Luke] 7:11–16) and the daughter of Jairus ([Luke] 8:49–56)—the same who was there before" (Eckey, *Das Lukasevangelium*, 990). Both Petzke and Eckey refer to this supernatural Jesus-related resurrection, which does not encompass the bodies present. It is not the reanimated body of Jesus that must prove its aliveness in the text, but the collective body of his followers. Are they alive or are they dreaming?

423   See critical apparatus in NA^{28}; as well as Bovon, *Luke 3*, 392. Bovon lists all the manuscripts and concludes: "These lists are impressive. They prove how vital the biblical writing was in its variety in the patristic era" (*Luke 3*, 393). But he leaves open the question of why these manuscripts mentioned honey.

424   Num 11:7–9 describes manna as a natural phenomenon, which appears like dew, or together with the dew. Exod 16:16f tells of collecting manna. Ps 78:24 describes manna as "the grain of heaven," and v. 25 as "the bread of angels"; cf. also Ps 105:40 and Neh 9:6f.

425   Brenner, "Song of Songs," 289.

426   "Is it not ridiculous to hold fast to a belief in God in the face of scorn from one's environment about how primitive and useless such convictions are . . . and faced with the opacity of God's work in the world?" (Scoralick, "Das Buch der Weisheit").

427   Ambrose was bishop of Milan in the fourth century, and was later canonized. There is a legend that as an infant, a swarm of bees settled on his face while he lay in his cradle, leaving behind a drop of honey. This was considered a sign of his future eloquence and honeyed tongue. He was in any case beloved of the people; he was said to be a good pastor, who cared for the poor, as well as a gifted preacher. He forced the Roman Emperor Theodosius to repent publicly for having 7,000 insurgents killed in the circus. St. Ambrose is revered as the patron saint of beekeepers, candlemakers, peddlers, and gingerbread bakers, swarms of bees and domestic animals, and—learning. For this reason, beehives often appear in the saint's symbology. See: Dassmann, *Ambrosius von Mailand*.

428   On the text and the problem of the two available texts, one short and one long, see: Burchard and Burfeind, *Josef und Aseneth*.

429   Dennis E. Smith understands that the motif of sacred foods and the messianic banquet are connected. "For the Greeks the 'food of the gods' was ambrosia and the 'drink of the gods' was nectar. . . . In the Jewish work *Joseph and Aseneth*, a honeycomb is identified as the food of the angels . . . the miraculous bread from heaven, or manna . . . is also associated with the miraculous water from the rock. . . . Philo interprets manna and rock to be types of the *logos*, or word and wisdom of God, which nourish the soul" (Smith, *From Symposium to Eucharist*, 167–68).

430   Verses 4–8 translated by David Cook, in: Sparks, *The Apocryphal Old Testament*, 489–90. Sparks lacks the subsequent verses, so they have been quoted from the translation by Eugene Mason, 7.

431   As in Jeremiah and Isaiah, Aseneth's mouth is touched (Isa 6:7f; Jer 1:9; *Jos. Asen.* 16:5, 9). The bread of life, manna, the bread of heaven, and the honeycomb are synonyms for ambrosia, which can bring about transformation. Together with the angel, Aseneth eats heavenly food, like other angels or the righteous in Old Testament Pseudepigrapha (cf. *1 En.* 24:4—25:7; *4 Ezra* 7:123; 8:52; *Apoc. Mos.* 28:4; *T. Levi* 18:11; *Sib. Or.* III 741–50). See also: Standhartinger, *Das Frauenbild*, 119–20.

432   The book of Hosea dates from the eighth century BCE and reflects the drama and cruelty

of its period, in which the great power Assyria threatened the northern kingdom of Israel and finally conquered it.

433   The exegesis tends to understand verse 11 to mean that the apostles did not believe the women's report (e.g., Bovon, *Luke 3*, 345). But the question is really what we should take "report" to mean. Are they reports of what the women did and what they found? Or is it the prophetic words from the Torah that apply now? Do the men not believe that the women saw two shining men in the tomb? Or are they unable to link this to the yearning expectation from Hos 6:2?

434   On the different denominational interpretations see, for example: Luz, *Matthew 21-28*, 374-78.

435   See, for example: Altmann, *Festive Meals*.

436   Klinghardt and Staubli, "Essen, gemeinsames," 117.

437   In Mark 14:3-9, a woman comes to the house of Simon the leper with costly ointment. One or two English versions translate Jesus' position as "reclining at table" (most even as "sat at table" or "sat at meat"), giving the impression that the woman has burst into a banquet for men. But both these assumptions are hasty. The expression *katakeimenos* (v. 3) means, first and foremost, "lying exhausted, collapsing with sickness or weakness." This verb is suited to the location of the story, which is described as a kind of hospital. For another thing, the text does not speak of men who were in the house, but of "some" (*tines*, v. 4). This expression is gender-neutral, which fits with a hostel in which poor, sick or homeless people found a roof over their heads. This anointing scene in Mark has nothing to do with eating; it does not yet interrupt the explicitly mentioned hunger of Jesus in Mark 11:12. Cf. Sutter Rehmann, "Olivenöl als Zündstoff."

438   Leonardo painted *L'ultima cena* between 1495 and 1498 for the refectory in the Dominican Convent of Santa Maria delle Grazie in Milan, Italy. By placing the table transversely, he collected all those eating on one side of the table, while the observers are seated on the side opposite Jesus. Leonardo thus opened up the circle of table fellowship for all who ate with one another in the refectory. Cf. Sutter Rehmann, "Verräterische Konflikte," 301.

439   According to Mary Douglas, food can be interpreted as a code from which we can decipher the social structures dominating at the meal (Douglas, "Deciphering a Meal"). The Jewish dietary laws (*kashrut*) are very important in this regard. Their function in defining Jewish identity is indisputable, as is their contribution to hindering social intercourse between Jews and non-Jews (Sanders, "Jewish Associations"). Yet research has often focused too much on tensions and conflicts between communities and the *polis*—the Empire—while in reality, Jewish communities did find many ways to interact with their non-Jewish surroundings (Harland, *Associations*).

440   Renee Cox, *Yo Mama's Last Supper*, 1999; Susan D. White, *The First Supper*, 1988; Bohdan Piasecki, *The Last Supper*, 1998. On the use of Leonardo da Vinci's painting in popular culture and advertising, see: https://en.wikipedia.org/wiki/The_Last_Supper_(Leonardo).

441   Quentin Quesnell was the first to attempt to show that women were also at Jesus' table. See: Quesnell, "Women."

442   Luise Schottroff has already drawn our attention to these exegetic observations; see: "Sind die 'Zwölf' zwölf Männer?"

443   Paul is familiar with both expressions—*apostoloi* and *dodeka*—but does not link them together. In Rom 16:6 Paul refers to the Apostles Andronicus and Junia—thus he clearly does not understand *apostoloi* as a limited number of men.

444   Rengstorf, "*Dodeka*," 323.

445   Rengstorf, "*Dodeka*," 323.

446   Rengstorf, "*Dodeka*," 324.

447   Rengstorf, "*Dodeka*," 326.

448   Rengstorf, "*Dodeka*," 328.

449   Following Traugott Holtz we could ask whether the listing of the twelve names in the Gospels (Matt 10:2; Mark 3:16; Luke 6:13) should not also be understood metaphorically—related to the Hope of Israel—and whether the inconsistencies in the lists of names can be seen in parallel to the deviating lists of tribes. That the twelve are preserved in metaphor, but not the precise names, makes much more sense than assuming that there were twelve individuals who within a short time had different names. See: Holtz, *Offenbarung*, 70.

ENDNOTES

450 Holtz, *Offenbarung*, 139.

451 "The number twelve dominates the account. Twelve angels guard the twelves city gates, which bear the names of the twelve tribes of Israel (see Ezek 48:30–34 [which lists the names of the tribes]). This could be a conscious metaphorical indication that access to the eschatological community of the redeemed has been made possible for the People of God of the Old Covenant, through the Lamb (v. 22f), who is the Lion of the Tribe of Judah, the Root of David (5:5; 22:16). The foundation underpinning the wall that defines the city, however, is formed by the twelve foundations on which the twelve names of the twelve apostles stand" (Holtz, *Offenbarung*, 138).

452 Schottroff, "*dodeka*."

453 Traugott Holtz also says: "Rather, the (high) priest Aaron's breastplate, which was set with twelve gemstones, in Exod 28:17–21; 39:10–14 must have been of significance, with its explicit link to the names of the twelve sons of Israel" (Holtz, *Offenbarung*, 139).

454 The synoptic narratives about Jesus' table fellowships with sinners never mention the food itself. Bread was the basic foodstuff, and only in parables are meat dishes mentioned at all.

455 Only in John 2:3, 9ff is *oinos* (wine) mentioned explicitly for a banquet. But here the wine has run out; it is a situation of scarcity.

456 Women and children, invalids, and people under oath might be excluded from drinking alcohol. It is also interesting that groups of warriors often drank alcohol together (Murray, "War and the Symposium"; see also: Jellinek, "Symbolism," 864). Walter Burkert links the shared drinking of alcoholic beverages with the ancient culture of symposia: "[T]he symposium is an organization of all-male groups, aristocratic and egalitarian at the same time, which affirm their identity through ceremonialized drinking" (Burkert, "Oriental Symposia," 7).

457 János Bolyki has differentiated six groups of motifs in the table fellowships of the Gospels. They appear in various categories and subthemes: Situation, Invitation, Socializing, Participation (the foods and their consumption), Communication, and Transformation (what changes the table fellowship brings about in the lives of those who take part). See: Bolyki, *Jesu Tischgemeinschaften*, 23.

458 Sepphoris is not mentioned at all in the Gospels. Ulrike Metternich has suggested to me that this silence could be deliberate—a late revenge against the Rome-friendly town.

459 Since Mark 6:3 and Matt 13:55 refer to Jesus and his father as *tekton* (craftsmen), there are some researchers who suspect that they took part in the construction of Sepphoris. See: Rousseau and Arav, *Jesus and His World*, 251; Meyers, "Jesus and His World."

460 See Matt 14:13–21; 15:32–39; Mark 6:35–44; 8:16–21; Luke 9:10–17; John 6:1–13.

461 MacDonald, *Ancient Israelites*, 109. For the Roman period, see: Broshi, "The Diet of Palestine."

462 Standhartinger, "And all ate."

463 On *prasia*, see: LSJ, 1460.

464 Leek, *Allium porrum*, was very popular in the Orient, as well as Egyptian leek, or kurrat (*Allium ampeloprasum kurrat*). Cf. Germer, *Altägyptischen Heilpflanzen*, 198–99.

465 *Châtsîyr* is generally translated as "grass" or "green grass," or "tender grass" (1 Kgs 18:5; 2 Kgs 19:26; Job 40:15; Ps 37:2; 90:5; 103:15; 104:14; 129:6; 147:8; Isa 15:6; 35:7; 37:27; 40:6, 7, 8; 51:12). On one occasion it is also rendered as "hay" (Prov 27:25 KJV).

466 The most well thought-out presentation of Jesus can be found in Matthew's Gospel, where he is called teacher twelve times. Jesus' teaching corresponds in form and content to that of Jewish teachers in that period. See: Taschner, "Lehren/Lernen." And also: Breitmaier, *Lehren und Lernen*.

467 Strack and Billerbeck, *Kommentar*, 13.

468 Strack and Billerbeck, *Kommentar*, 13.

469 The Hebrew version was written in the second century BCE, the Greek translation around 60–80 years later. The Wisdom of Sirach is one of the deuterocanonical books, and is considered the most comprehensive wisdom book from the ancient Orient. Sirach focuses on wisdom as a fascinating figure that speaks and teaches with divine authority. See: Strotmann, "Die göttliche Weisheit."

470 *Sifre Devarim* 306:17. *Sifre Devarim* is one of the halakic midrashim from the third and fourth centuries.

471 "This" in the Greek text is neuter. However, if "this" really did refer to the bread, it would

ENDNOTES

have to be masculine, since bread in Greek is masculine (unlike German, where *das Brot* is neuter; or English, where nouns do not have genders). "This" can therefore allow many interpretations.

[472] Strack and Billerbeck refer to *Genesis Rabbah* 70 (44d, 44), in: Strack and Billerbeck, *Kommentar*, 483.

[473] "Those who dine together were to be treated equally. This was a standard feature of ancient dining protocol. It functioned as an elaboration of the concept of social bonding at the meal and was a strong feature of banquet ideology at all levels of the data" (Smith, *From Symposium to Eucharist*, 11). See also: Klinghardt, *Gemeinschaftsmahl*, 24–25.

[474] Rengstorf, "*Dodeka*," 323.

Bibliography

Aharoni, Yohanan. *The Land of the Bible: A Historical* Geography. London: Burns & Oates, 1979.

Ahmed, Sara. *The Cultural Politics of Emotion*. Edinburgh: Edinburgh University Press, 2004.

Aland, Barbara, et al., eds. *Novum Testamentum Graece*. Nestle-Aland, 28th revised ed. Stuttgart: Deutsche Bibelgesellschaft, 2012.

Albertz, Martin. *Die synoptischen Streitgespräche: Ein Beitrag zur Formengeschichte des Urchristentums*. Berlin: Trowitzsch 1921.

Albertz, Rainer. "Die Tora Gottes gegen die wirtschaftlichen Sachzwänge: Die Sabbat- und Jobeljahrgesetzgebung Lev 25 in ihrer Geschichte." *Ökumenische Rundschau* 44 (1995) 290–310.

Altmann, Peter. *Festive Meals in Ancient Israel: Deuteronomy's Identity Politics in their Near Eastern Context*. Berlin: De Gruyter, 2011.

Anchor Bible Dictionary. 6 vols. Edited by David Noel Freedman. New York: Doubleday, 1992.

Arendt, Hannah. *Denktagebuch 1950–1973*. Munich: Piper, 2003.

Arnhold, Oliver. *"Entjudung"—Kirche im Abgrund: Das "Institut zur Erforschung und Beseitigung des jüdischen Einflusses auf das deutsche kirchliche Leben" 1939–1945*. Studien zu Kirche und Israel, vol. 25/2. Berlin: Institut Kirche und Judentum an der Humboldt-Universität, 2010.

Ashbel, Dov. "Israel, Land of (Geographical Survey): Climate." In *EncJud*, vol. 9, 181–94. Jerusalem: Keter 1971.

Atwater, Tim. *Debt Cancellation: Biblical Norm, not Exception*. https://www.jubileeusa.org/faith/faith-and-worship-resources/debt-cancellation-a-biblical-norm.html.

Ausländer, Rose. "Wieder II." In *Gedichte*, 339. Frankfurt: S. Fischer, 2001.

Avi-Yonah, Michael. *A Historical Geography from the Persian to the Arab Conquest 536 B.C. to 640 A.D.* Grand Rapids: Baker, 1966. Revised edition Jerusalem: Carta, 2002.

Avnery, Uri. "Wie fein sind deine Zelte." http://www.uri-avnery.de/news/149/33/Wie-fein-sind-deine-Zelte.

Bammel, Ernst. *"ptochos."* In *TDNT* 6:885–915.

Baneth, Eduard. Introduction to *m. Ta'anit*. In *Mischnajot: Die sechs Ordnungen der Mischna*, edited by Eduard Baneth et al. Basel: Victor Goldschmidt, 1968.

Barlösius, Eva. *Soziologie des Essens: Eine Sozial- und kulturwissenschaftliche Einführung in die Ernährungsforschung*. Weinheim/Munich: Juventa, 1999.

Barnett, Victoria J., ed. "*After Ten Years*": *Dietrich Bonhoeffer and Our Times*. Translation of Bonhoeffer's text by Barbara and Martin Rumscheidt. Minneapolis: Fortress, 2017.

Bayer, Hans F. *Das Evangelium des Markus*. Witten: Brockhaus, 2008.

Becker, Adam H., and Annette Yoshiko Reed, eds. *The Ways That Never Parted: Jews and Christians in Late Antiquity and the Early Middle Ages*. Minneapolis: Fortress, 2007.

Beinin, Joel. "Egypt: bread riots and mill strikes." *Le Monde diplomatique* (May 2008). https://mondediplo.com/2008/05/08egypt.

Belo, Fernando. *Das Markusevangelium materialistisch gelesen*. Stuttgart: Alektor, 1980.

Bibel in gerechter Sprache. 3rd ed. Edited by Ulrike Bail et al. Gütersloh: Gütersloher Verlagshaus, 2007.

Bible Study Tools. "Bel and the Dragon." https://www.biblestudytools.com/encyclopedias/isbe/bel-and-the-dragon-2.html.

Bieler, Andrea, and Luise Schottroff. *The Eucharist: Bodies, Bread, and Resurrection*. Minneapolis: Fortress, 2007.

Bird, Phyllis. *Missing Persons and Mistaken Identities: Women and Gender in Ancient Israel*. Minneapolis: Fortress, 1994.

Bock, Darrell L. *The Acts of the Apostles*. Grand Rapids: Baker Academic, 2007.

Bohlen, Diedrich. *Die Bedeutung der Fischerei für die antike Wirtschaft*. Hamburg: H. Christian, 1937.

Bolkestein, Hendrik. *Wohltätigkeit und Armenpflege im vorchristlichen Altertum*. 1939. Reprint, Groningen: Bouma's Boekhuis, 1967.

Bolyki, János. *Jesu Tischgemeinschaften*. Wissenschaftliche Untersuchungen zum Neuen Testament II 96. Tübingen: Mohr Siebeck, 1998.

Bovon, François. *Luke 1: A Commentary on the Gospel of Luke 1:1—9:50*. Translated by Christine M. Thomas, edited by Helmut Koester. Minneapolis: Fortress, 2002.

———. *Luke 3: A Commentary on the Gospel of Luke 19:28—24:53*. Translated by James Crouch, edited by Helmut Koester. Minneapolis: Fortress, 2012.

Boyarin, Daniel. *Border Lines: The Partition of Judaeo-Christianity*. Philadelphia: University of Pennsylvania Press, 2004.

Brecht, Bertolt. *Gesammelte Werke*, vol. 2. Zurich: Ex Libris, 1976.

Breitmaier, Isa. *Lehren und Lernen in der Spur des Ersten Testaments: Exegetische Studien zum 5. Buch Mose und dem Sprüchebuch aus religionspädagogischer Perspektive*. Münster: LIT, 2004.

———. "Von Terachs Götzenbilderladen zum 'Iconoclash.' Gedanken zum religionspädagogischen Umgang mit den Bildern von Gott." In *Welt, Bilder, Welten: Beiträge zum Dialog zwischen Kunst und Theologie*, edited by Peter Müller, 73–84. Karlsruhe: karlsruher pädagogische beiträge, special vol. 1, 2003.

Brenner, Athalya. "Song of Songs: Polyphony of Love." In *Feminist Biblical Interpretation: A Compendium of Critical Commentary on the Books of the Bible and Related Literature*, edited by Luise Schottroff et al., 288–302. Translated by Lisa E. Dahill et al. American edition edited by Martin Rumscheidt. Grand Rapids: Eerdmans, 2012.

Broshi, Magen. "The Diet of Palestine in the Roman Period: Introductory Notes." In *Bread, Wine, Walls, and Scrolls*. JSPSup 36, 121–43. Sheffield: Sheffield Academic Press, 2001.

Buber, Martin. "*Leitwort* Style in Pentateuch Narrative." In *Scripture and Translation*, by Martin Buber and Franz Rosenzweig, 114–28. Translated by Lawrence Rosenwald with Everett Fox. Bloomington, Indiana University Press, 1994.

Burchard, Christoph, and Carsten Burfeind, eds. *Gesammelte Studien zu Josef und Aseneth.* Leiden: Brill, 1996.

Burkert, Walter. "Oriental Symposia: Contrasts and Parallels." In *Dining in a Classical Context,* edited by William J. Slater, 7–24. Ann Arbor: University of Michigan Press, 1991.

Butting, Klara. *Hier bin ich! Unterwegs zu einer biblischen Spiritualität.* Uelzen: Erev-Rav, 2011.

Calatayud, Jose Miguel. "'Just a few looters': Turkish PM Erdogan dismisses protests as thousands occupy Istanbul's Taksim Square." *The Independent* (June 3, 2013). https://www.independent.co.uk/news/world/europe/just-a-few-looters-turkish-pm-erdogan-dismisses-protests-as-thousands-occupy-istanbuls-taksim-square-8641336.html.

Cap Anamur. "Hunger in Nordkorea" (August 3, 2011). https://www.cap-anamur.org/pressespiegel/hunger-in-nordkorea/.

Carter, Warren. "Matthew's People." In *Christian Origins: A People's History of Christianity,* edited by Richard A. Horsley, 138–61.

Chung, Meehyun. *Reis und Wasser: Eine feministische Theologie in Korea.* Berlin: Frank & Timme, 2012.

Cicero. *De Domo Sua.* In *Pro Archia. Post Reditum in Senatu. Post Reditum ad Quirites. De Domo Sua. De Haruspicum Responsis. Pro Plancio,* 132–311. Translated by N. H. Watts. Loeb Classical Library 158. Cambridge, MA: Harvard University Press, 1923.

———. *Pro Milone.* In *Pro Milone. In Pisonem. Pro Scauro. Pro Fonteio. Pro Rabirio Postumo. Pro Marcello. Pro Ligario. Pro Rege Deiotaro,* 6–123. Translated by N. H. Watts. Loeb Classical Library 252. Cambridge, MA: Harvard University Press, 1931.

———. *Pro Murena.* In *In Catilinam 1–4. Pro Murena. Pro Sulla. Pro Flacco,* 186–301. Translated by C. Macdonald. Loeb Classical Library 324. Cambridge, MA: Harvard University Press, 1976.

Cohen, Shaye J. D. *The Beginnings of Jewishness: Boundaries, Varieties, Uncertainties.* Berkeley: University of California Press, 1999.

Crüsemann, Frank, and Luise Schottroff. "*dal, dal* (hebr.)—schwach, elend, arm; *ani* (hebr.)—geduckt, gedemütigt, elend, arm; *evjon* (hebr.)—arm, verarmt; *tapeinos* (griech.)—demütig, gering; *tapeinosis* (griech.)—Erniedrigung." In *Bibel in gerechter Sprache,* Glossary, 2340–41. Gütersloh: Gütersloher Verlagshaus, 2007.

Crüsemann, Frank, and Udo Theissmann, eds. *Ich glaube an den Gott Israels: Fragen und Antworten zu einem Thema, das im christlichen Glaubensbekenntnis fehlt.* Gütersloh: Gütersloher Verlagshaus, 1998.

Crüsemann, Frank, et al. *Sozialgeschichtliches Wörterbuch zur Bibel.* Gütersloh: Gütersloher Verlagshaus, 2009.

Crüsemann, Marlene. "Trost, *charis* und Kraft der Schwachen: Eine Christologie der Beziehung nach dem zweiten Brief an die Gemeinde in Korinth." In *Christus und seine Geschwister: Christologie im Umfeld der Bibel in gerechter Sprache,* edited by Marlene Crüsemann and Carsten Jochum-Bortfeld, 111–37. Gütersloh: Gütersloher Verlagshaus, 2009.

Dando, William A. "Famine." In *Food and Famine in the 21st Century,* edited by William A. Dando. Santa Barbara: ABC-CLIO 2012.

Dassmann, Ernst. *Ambrosius von Mailand: Leben und Werk.* Stuttgart: Kohlhammer, 2004.

Dieckmann, Detlef. *Segen für Isaak: Eine rezeptionsästhetische Auslegung von Genesis 26 und Kotexten.* Berlin: De Gruyter, 2003.

Dio Chrysostom. *Venator (Discourse VII)*. Translated by J.W. Cohoon. Loeb Classical Library, Cambridge, MA: Harvard University Press, 1932.

Domin, Hilde. "Salva nos." In *Sämtliche Gedichte*, 118. Frankfurt: S. Fischer, 2009.

Donahue, John R., and Daniel J. Harrington. *The Gospel of Mark*. Collegeville: Liturgical Press, 2002.

Douglas, Mary, ed. *Constructive Drinking: Perspectives on Drink from Anthropology*. New York: Cambridge University Press, 1989.

———. "Deciphering a Meal." In *Myth, Symbol and Culture*, edited by Clifford Geertz, 61–81. New York: Norton, 1971.

———. *Food in the Social Order: Studies of Food and Festivities in the Three American Communities*. New York: Russell Sage Foundation, 1984.

Drexhage, Hans-Joachim, et al. *Die Wirtschaft des römischen Reiches (1.-3. Jahrhundert): Eine Einführung*. Berlin: De Gruyter, 2002.

Dschulnigg, Peter. *Das Markusevangelium*. Stuttgart: Kohlhammer, 2007.

Durnowo, Marina. *Mein Leben mit Daniil Charms: Erinnerungen*. Berlin: Galiani, 2010.

Ebach, Jürgen. "*goj, am, mischpacha* (hebr.), *ethnos, laos* (griech.)—Volk, Nation, Leute." In *Bibel in gerechter Sprache*, Glossary, 2355–56. Gütersloh: Gütersloher Verlagshaus, 2007.

Ebner, Martin. *Das Markusevangelium: Neu übersetzt und kommentiert*. 2nd ed. Stuttgart: Katholisches Bücherwerk, 2009.

Eckey, Wilfried. *Die Apostelgeschichte: Der Weg des Evangeliums von Jerusalem nach Rom*, vol. 1. Neukirchen-Vluyn: Neukirchener, 2000.

———. *Das Lukasevangelium: Unter Berücksichtigung seiner Parallelen. Band 1: Lk 1:1–10:42*. Neukirchen-Vluyn: Neukirchener, 2004.

———. *Das Markusevangelium: Orientierung am Weg Jesu. Ein Kommentar*. Neukirchen-Vluyn: Neukirchener, 1998.

Ehrensperger, Kathy. *Paul and the Dynamics of Power*. London: T&T Clark, 2007.

Elliott, Neil. "Disciplining the Hope of the Poor in Ancient Rome." In *Christian Origins: A People's History of Christianity*, edited by Richard A. Horsley, 177–200. Minneapolis: Fortress, 2005.

Emam, Amr. "Egypt's food subsidy system reform faces opposition." *The Arab Weekly* (March 3, 2019). https://thearabweekly.com/egypts-food-subsidy-system-reform-faces-opposition.

Encyclopaedia Judaica. 16 vols. Edited by Cecil Roth. Jerusalem: Keter, 1972.

Erman, Adolf. *Life in Ancient Egypt*. Translated by Helen M. Tirard. London: Macmillan, 1984.

Ernst, Josef. *Das Evangelium nach Lukas*. Regensburger Neues Testament. Supplementary vol. D. Regensburg: Pustet, 1976.

———. *Das Evangelium nach Markus*. Regensburger Neues Testament. Supplementary vol. E. Regensburg: Pustet, 1981.

———. *Johannes der Täufer: Interpretation, Geschichte, Wirkungsgeschichte*. Berlin: De Gruyter, 1989.

Eusebius. *Ecclesiastical History*, vol. I, Book 2.12. Translated by Kirsopp Lake, Loeb Classical Library 153. Cambridge, MA: Harvard University Press, 1926.

Food and Agriculture Organization of the United Nations. "Hunger and food insecurity." http://www.fao.org/hunger/en/.

———. *The State of Food Security and Nutrition in the World*, 2018. http://www.fao.org/publications/sofi/en/.

Foweraker, Joe. *Theorizing Social Movements*. Critical Studies on Latin America. London: Pluto, 1995.

Fredriksen, Paula. "What 'Parting of the Ways'? Jews, Gentiles, and the Ancient Mediterranean City." In *The Ways That Never Parted: Jews and Christians in Late Antiquity and the Early Middle Ages*, edited by Adam H. Becker and Annette Yoshiko Reed, 35–64. Minneapolis: Fortress, 2007.

Freeman-Grenville, Greville Stuart Parker. *The Holy Land: A Pilgrim's Guide to Israel, Jordan and the Sinai*. Peabody, MA: Hendrickson Publishers, 1996.

Friedländer, Ludwig. *Darstellungen aus der Sittengeschichte Roms in der Zeit des Augustus bis zum Ausgang der Antonine*. 4 vols., 10th edition. Aalen: Scientia, 1964.

Friedman, Thomas L. "WikiLeaks, Drought and Syria." *New York Times* (January 21, 2014). https://www.nytimes.com/2014/01/22/opinion/friedman-wikileaks-drought-and-syria.html.

Friedrich, Gerhard. " εὐαγγέλιον [euangelion]." In *TDNT* 2: 721–36.

———. "εὐαγγελίζομαι [euangelizomai]." In *TDNT* 2: 707–21.

Friesen, Steven J. "Injustice or God's Will: Explanations of Poverty in Proto-Christian Communities." In *Christian Origins: A People's History of Christianity*, edited by Richard A. Horsley, 240–60. Minneapolis: Fortress, 2005.

———. "Poverty in Pauline Studies: Beyond the So-called New Consensus." *JSNT* 26 (2004) 323–61.

Garnsey, Peter. *Famine and Food Supply in the Graeco-Roman World: Responses to Risk and Crisis*. Cambridge, UK: Cambridge University Press, 1988.

———. *Food and Society in Classical Antiquity*. Cambridge, UK: Cambridge University Press, 1999.

———. "Responses to Food Crisis in the Ancient Mediterranean World." In *Hunger in History: Food Shortage, Poverty, and Deprivation*, edited by Lucile F. Newman, 126–46. Oxford: Blackwell, 1990.

Germer, Renate. *Handbuch der Altägyptischen Heilpflanzen*. Wiesbaden: Harrassowitz, 2008.

Goodman, Martin. *Judaism in the Roman World: Collected Essays*. Leiden: Brill, 2007.

Goodwin, Jeff, et al., eds. *Passionate Politics: Emotions and Social Movements*. Chicago: University of Chicago Press, 2001.

Gordon, David. "Indicators of Poverty and Hunger." Presentation at the UN, New York, December 12–14, 1995. https://www.un.org/esa/socdev/unyin/documents/ydiDavidGordon_poverty.pdf.

Gruber, Margareta, and Andreas Michel, "Körper." In *Sozialgeschichtliches Wörterbuch zur Bibel*, edited by Frank Crüsemann et al., 307–12. Gütersloh: Gütersloher Verlagshaus, 2009.

Grundmann, Walter. *Das Evangelium nach Markus*. 10th ed. Berlin: Evangelische Verlagsanstalt, 1989.

Gsell, Stéphane, and Jérôme Carcopino. "La base de M. Sulpicius Félix et le décret des décurions de Sala." *Mélanges d'archéologie et d'histoire* 48 (1931) 1–39.

Günther, Inge. "Der Fluch der Sonne: In Israel wächst die Angst vor einer Dürre." *Frankfurter Rundschau* 38 (February 14, 2014).

Haberfeld, Caroline. *Fodor's Israel*. 3rd ed. New York: Fodor's Travel Publications, 1997.

Haines, Robert F. *Charles Trevelyan and the Great Irish Famine*. Dublin: Four Courts, 2004.

Harland, Philip. *Associations, Synagogues, and Congregations: Claiming a Place in Ancient Mediterranean Society*. Minneapolis: Fortress, 2003.

Heil, John Paul. *The Meal Scenes in Luke-Acts: An Audience-Oriented Approach.* Atlanta: Society of Biblical Literature, 1999.

Hengel, Martin. *The "Hellenization" of Judaea in the First Century after Christ.* Translated by John Bowden. London: SCM, 1989.

Henze, Dagmar et al., eds. *Antijudaismus im Neuen Testament? Grundlagen für die Arbeit mit biblischen Texten.* Gütersloh: Gütersloher Verlagshaus, 1997.

Holtz, Traugott. *Die Offenbarung des Johannes.* Göttingen: Vandenhoeck & Ruprecht, 2008.

Horsley, Richard A. "Jesus Movements and the Renewal of Israel." In *Christian Origins: A People's History of Christianity,* edited by Richard A. Horsley, 23–46. Minneapolis: Fortress, 2005.

Janssen, Claudia. *Anders ist die Schönheit der Körper: Paulus und die Auferstehung in 1 Kor 15.* Gütersloh: Gütersloher Verlagshaus, 2005.

Janssen, Claudia, and Regene Lamb, "Gospel of Luke: The Humbled Will Be Lifted Up." In *Feminist Biblical Interpretation: A Compendium of Critical Commentary on the Books of the Bible and Related Literature,* edited by Luise Schottroff et al., 645–61. Translated by Lisa E. Dahill et al. American edition edited by Martin Rumscheidt. Grand Rapids/Cambridge UK: Eerdmans, 2012.

Jellinek, E. M. "The Symbolism of Drinking: A Cultural-Historical Approach." *Journal of Studies on Alcohol* 3 (1977) 849–66.

Jensen, Aaron Michael. "The Greek Middle." *Wisconsin Lutheran Quarterly* 115 (2018) 101–3.

Jeremias, Joachim. "The multitude, *polloi.*" In *TDNT* 6:536–45.

Jervell, Jacob. *Die Apostelgeschichte.* Göttingen: Vandenhoeck und Ruprecht 1998.

Joris, Elisabeth, et al. "Offene Worte. Zur Aktualität von Iris von Rotens 'Frauen im Laufgitter,'" Foreword to *Olympe: Feministische Arbeitshefte zu Politik* 28 (2009) 5–7.

Joseph and Aseneth, translated by David Cook. In *The Apocryphal Old Testament,* edited by H. F. D. Sparks, 473–503. Oxford: Clarendon, 1984.

Joseph and Aseneth, translated by Eugene Mason. Cambridge, Ontario: In Parentheses, 2001.

Josephus. *Antiquities of the Jews.* Translated by William Whiston. http://penelope.uchicago.edu/josephus/.

———. *Wars of the Jews.* Translated by William Whiston. http://penelope.uchicago.edu/josephus/.

Jung, Franz. *16. Sonntag im Jahreskreis (B): Mk 6,30–34. Die grosse Sammlung.* http://www.perikopen.de/Lesejahr_B/16_iJ_B_Mk6_30-34_Jung.pdf.

Kahl, Brigitte. *Galatians Re-Imagined: Reading with the Eyes of the Vanquished.* Minneapolis: Fortress, 2010.

Kegler, Jürgen. "Das Zinsverbot in der Hebräischen Bibel." In *Schuld und Schulden: Biblische Traditionen in gegenwärtigen Konflikten,* edited by Marlene Crüsemann and Willy Schottroff, 17–39. Munich, 1992.

———. "Hunger." In *Essen und Trinken in der Bibel: Ein literarisches Festmahl für Rainer Kessler zum 65. Geburtstag,* edited by Michaela Geiger et al., 319–29. Gütersloh: Gütersloher Verlagshaus, 2009.

Kern, Paul Bentley. *Ancient Siege Warfare.* Bloomington: Indiana University Press, 1999.

Kertelge, Karl. *Markusevangelium.* Würzburg: Echter, 1994.

Kessler, Rainer. "Armenfürsorge als Aufgabe der Gemeinde." In *Dem Tod nicht glauben: Sozialgeschichte der Bibel. Festschrift für Luise Schottroff zum 70. Geburtstag,* edited by Frank Crüsemann et al., 91–102. Gütersloh: Gütersloher Verlagshaus, 2004.

Kharms, Daniil. "This is how hunger begins." 1937. Translated by Robert Chandler. In *The Penguin Book of Russian Poetry*, edited by Robert Chandler et al., 380–81. London: Penguin UK, 2015.

Kinealy, Christine. *The Great Irish Famine: Impact, Ideology and Rebellion*. Basingstoke: Palgrave Macmillan, 2002.

KJV Dictionary. https://av1611.com/kjbp/kjv-dictionary/kjv-dictionary-index.html.

Klawans, Jonathan. *Impurity and Sin in Ancient Judaism*. Oxford: Oxford University Press, 2000.

Klinghardt, Matthias. *Gemeinschaftsmahl und Mahlgemeinschaft: Soziologie und Liturgie frühchristlicher Mahlfeiern*. Tübingen: Francke, 1996.

Klinghardt, Matthias, and Thomas Staubli, "Essen, gemeinsames." In *Sozialgeschichtliches Wörterbuch zur Bibel*, edited by Frank Crüsemann et al., 116–23. Gütersloh: Gütersloher Verlagshaus, 2009.

Kloft, Hans. *Liberalitas principis—Herkunft und Bedeutung: Studien zur Prinzipatsideologie*. Cologne: Böhlau, 1970.

Kornder, Johan. "Früchte des Zorns." *Amnesty Journal*, July 20, 2010. http://www.amnesty.de/journal/2010/august/fruechte-des-zorns.

Kremer, Jacob. *Lukasevangelium*. Würzburg: Echter Verlag, 1989.

Kreuzer, Siegfried, and Luise Schottroff. "Sklaverei." In *Sozialgeschichtliches Wörterbuch zur Bibel*, edited by Frank Crüsemann et al., 524–30. Gütersloh: Gütersloher Verlagshaus, 2009.

Lentzen-Deis, Fritzleo. *Das Markus-Evangelium: Ein Kommentar für die Praxis*. 2nd ed. Edited by Eleonore Beck and Gabriele Miller. Stuttgart: Katholisches Bibelwerk, 1998.

Leutzsch, Martin. Introduction to the Greek Book of Daniel in *Bibel in gerechter Sprache*, 1710. Gütersloh: Gütersloher Verlagshaus, 2011.

Liddell, Henry George, and Robert Scott. *A Greek-English Lexicon*. 9th ed. Oxford: Clarendon, 1968.

Lieu, Judith. *Image and Reality: The Jews in the World of the Christians in the Second Century*. London: T&T Clark 1996.

———. *Neither Jew nor Greek?* London: T&T Clark, 2002.

Livy. *History of Rome, Book 4*. In *History of Rome, Volume II: Books 3–4*, 255–457. Translated by B. O. Foster. Loeb Classical Library 133. Cambridge, MA: Harvard University Press, 1922.

———. *History of Rome, Book 6*. In *History of Rome, Volume III: Books 5–7*, 193–351. Translated by B. O. Foster. Loeb Classical Library 133. Cambridge, MA: Harvard University Press, 1922.

Lorde, Audre. "The Uses of Anger." Keynote address to the NWSA. *Women's Studies Quarterly* 9 (Fall 1981) 7–10.

———. *Sister Outsider: Essays and Speeches*. Berkeley: Crossing, 1984/2007.

Luz, Ulrich. *Matthew 1–7: A Commentary*. Translated by James E. Crouch, edited by Helmut Koes. Minneapolis: Fortress, 2007.

———. *Matthew 21–28: A Commentary*. Translated by James E. Crouch, edited by Helmut Koes. Minneapolis: Fortress, 2005.

MacDonald, Nathan. "'The Eyes of All Look to You': The Generosity of the Divine King." In *Decisive Meals: Table Politics in Biblical Literature*, edited by Nathan MacDonald et al., 1–14. London: T&T Clark 2012.

BIBLIOGRAPHY

———. *What did the Ancient Israelites eat? Diet in Biblical Times*. Grand Rapids: Eerdmans, 2008.

Magdala.org. "History I." https://www.magdala.org/about-magdala-2/.

Malina, Bruce J., and John J. Pilch. *Social-Science Commentary on the Book of Acts*. Minneapolis: Fortress, 2008.

Martin, Joan M. "A Sacred Hope and a Social Goal: Womanist Eschatology." In *Liberating Eschatology: Essays in Honor of Letty M. Russell*, edited by Margaret Farley and Serene Jones, 209–26. Louisville: Westminster John Knox, 1999.

Maul, Stefan. "Tor der Götter." *Antike Welt* (2008) 21–29.

McKay, Kenneth L. *A New Syntax of the Verb in New Testament Greek: An Aspectual Approach*. New York: Peter Lang, 1994.

Mekhilta de-Rabbi Ishmael. Translated by Jacob Z. Lauterbach, vol. 2. Philadelphia: Jewish Publication Society, 1933.

Metternich, Ulrike. "Auf-er-stehen." In *Sich dem Leben in die Arme werfen*, edited by Luzia Sutter Rehmann et al., 176. Gütersloh: Gütersloher Verlagshaus, 2002.

Metz, Johann Baptist. *Faith in History and Society: Toward a Practical Fundamental Theology*. Translated by David Smith. London: Burns & Oates, 1980.

Metzdorf, Christina. *Die Tempelaktion Jesu: Patristische und historisch-kritische Exegese im Vergleich*. Wissenschaftliche Untersuchungen zum Neuen Testament II 168. Tübingen: Mohr Siebeck, 2003.

Meyers, Eric. "Jesus and His World: Sepphoris and the Quest for the Historical Jesus." In *Saxa Loquentur: Studien zur Archäologie Palästinas/Israels. Festschrift für Volkmar Fritz zum 65. Geburtstag (AOAT 302)*, edited by Cornelis G. den Hertog et al., 185–97. Münster: Ugarit 2003.

Millman, Sara, and Robert W. Kates. "Towards Understanding Hunger." In *Hunger in History: Food Shortage, Poverty, and Deprivation*, edited by Lucile F. Newman, 3–24. Oxford: Blackwell, 1990.

Mishnah Sukkah. Translated by Joshua Kulp. https://www.sefaria.org/Mishnah_Sukkah.4.9?lang=bi.

Mishnah Ta'anit. Translated by Joshua Kulp. https://www.sefaria.org/Mishnah_Taanit.3.8?lang=bi.

Mishnah Yoma 8:6. Translated by Joshua Kulp. https://www.sefaria.org/Mishnah_Yoma.8.6?lang=bi.

Müller, Herta. *The Hunger Angel*. Translated by Philip Boehm. New York: Henry Holt, 2012.

Murray, Oswyn. "War and the Symposium." In *Dining in a Classical Context*, edited by William J. Slater, 83–104. Ann Arbor: University of Michigan Press, 1991.

Mussner, Franz. *Apostelgeschichte*. Würzburg: Echter, 1984.

Näslund, Erik, and Per M. Hellström. "Appetite Signaling: From Gut Peptides and Enteric Nerves to Brain." *Physiology & Behavior* 92 (2007) 256–62.

Navarro Puerto, Mercedes. "Female Disciples in Mark? The 'Problematizing' of a Concept." In *Gospels: Narrative and History*, edited by Mercedes Navarro Puerto and Marinella Perroni, 145–72. English edition edited by Amy-Jill Levine. Atlanta: SBL, 2015.

Neidhart, Christoph. "Vier von fünf Nordkoreanern sind unterernährt." *Tages-Anzeiger* (October 1, 2013) 3.

O'Mahony, Michelle. *Famine in Cork City: Famine Life at Cork Union Workhouse*. Cork: Mercier, 2005.

Oltersdorf, Ulrich. "Lage der Welt: globale Probleme und deren Vernetzung." In *Ernährungsökologie: Komplexen Herausforderungen integrativ begegnen*, edited by Ingrid Hoffmann et al., 18–23. Munich: Oekom, 2011.

Oppenheim, A. L. "'Siege-Documents' from Nippur." *Iraq* 17 (1955) 69–89. https://doi.org/10.2307/4241717.

Pahlitzsch, Johannes, and Hartmut Kühne, "Magdala." In *Brill's New Pauly*, edited by Hubert Cancik and Helmuth Schneider. English edition by Christine F. Salazar. https://referenceworks.brillonline.com/entries/brill-s-new-pauly/magdala-e12223720.

Pennington, Jonathan T. "Setting Aside 'Deponency': Rediscovering the Greek Middle Voice in New Testament Studies." In *The Linguist as Pedagogue: Trends in the Teaching and Linguistic Analysis of the Greek New Testament*, edited by Stanley E. Porter and Matthew Brook O'Donnell, 181–203. Sheffield: Sheffield Phoenix, 2009.

Pesch, Rudolf. *Die Apostelgeschichte: Evangelisch-katholischer Kommentar zum Neuen Testament*. Neukirchen-Vluyn: Neukirchener, 1986.

Petzke, Gerd. *Das Sondergut des Evangeliums nach Lukas*. Zurich: Theologischer Verlag, 1990.

Pleins, J. David. "Poor, Poverty (Old Testament)." *ABD* 5:402–14.

Plonz, Sabine. "Vom Bel zu Babel. Populäre Götzenkritik: Auslegung und Kommentar zu Dan 14." In *Die besten Nebenrollen. 50 Porträts biblischer Randfiguren*, edited by Marion Keuchen et al., 178–82. Leipzig: Evangelische Verlagsanstalt, 2006.

Plutarch, *Caesar*. In *Lives, Volume VII: Demosthenes and Cicero. Alexander and Caesar*, 411–609. Translated by Bernadotte Perrin. Loeb Classical Library 99. Cambridge, MA: Harvard University Press, 1919.

Purtschert, Patricia. "Not Wanting To Be Governed Like That: On the Relationship between Anger and Critique." Translated by Erika Doucette. Transversal Texts, April 2008. http://eipcp.net/transversal/0808/purtschert/en.

Quesnell, Quentin. "The Women at Luke's Supper." In *Political Issues in Luke-Acts*, edited by Richard J. Cassidy and Philip J. Scharper, 59–79. Maryknoll: Orbis, 1983.

Reicher, Steve, and Clifford Stott. *Mad Mobs and Englishmen? Myths and Realities of the 2011 Riots*. London: Constable & Robinson, 2011.

Reinbold, Wolfgang. *Propaganda und Mission im ältesten Christentum: Eine Untersuchung zu den Modalitäten der Ausbreitung der frühen Kirche*. Göttingen: Vandenhoeck & Ruprecht, 2000.

Reiser, Marius. "Numismatik im Neuen Testament." *Biblica* 81 (2000) 457–88. https://www.bsw.org/biblica/vol-81-2000/numismatik-und-neues-testament/302/.

Rengstorf, Karl H. "*Dodeka*." In *TDNT* 2:321–28.

Richter Reimer, Ivoni. *Women in the Acts of the Apostles: A Feminist Liberation Perspective*. Translated by Linda Maloney. Minneapolis: Fortress, 1995.

Rousseau, John J., and Rami Arav. *Jesus and His World: An Archeological and Cultural Dictionary*. Minneapolis: Fortress, 1995.

RT Question More. "Feminists call for sex boycott against Ukrainian premier." March 23, 2010. https://www.rt.com/news/ukraine-premier-feminist-protest/.

Ruether, Rosemary Radford. *Faith and Fratricide: The Theological Roots of Anti-Semitism*. New York: Seabury, 1974.

Rydberg-Cox, Jeff. *A Digital Tutorial for Ancient Greek*, based on John William White: *First Greek Book*. https://daedalus.umkc.edu/FirstGreekBook/JWW_FGB5.html.

BIBLIOGRAPHY

Sallust. *First Letter to Caesar*. In *Fragments of the Histories. Letters to Caesar*, 478–95. Edited and translated by John T. Ramsey. Loeb Classical Library 522. Cambridge, MA: Harvard University Press, 2015.

Sancisi-Weerdenburg, Heleen. "Persian Food: Stereotypes and Political Identity." In *Food in Antiquity*, edited by John Wilkins et al., 286–302. Exeter: Exeter University Press, 1995.

Sanders, E. P. "Jewish Associations with Gentiles and Galatians 2:11–14." In *The Conversation Continues: Studies in Paul and John*, edited by Robert T. Fortna and Beverly R. Gaventa, 170–88. Nashville: Abingdon, 1990.

Schäfer-Lichtenberger, Christa, and Luise Schottroff. "Armut." In *Sozialgeschichtliches Wörterbuch zur Bibel*, edited by Frank Crüsemann et al., 22–26. Gütersloh: Gütersloher Verlagshaus, 2009.

Schiffner, Kerstin. *Lukas liest Exodus: Eine Untersuchung zur Aufnahme ersttestamentlicher Befreiungsgeschichte im lukanischen Werk als Schrift-Lektüre*. Stuttgart: Kohlhammer, 2008.

Schipperges, Heinrich. *Hildegard of Bingen: Healing and the Nature of the Cosmos*. Translated by John A. Broadwin. Princeton: M. Wiener, 1996.

———. *The World of Hildegard of Bingen: Her Life, Times and Visions*. Translated by John Cumming. Collegeville: Liturgical, 1998.

Schmithals, Walter. *Das Evangelium nach Lukas*. Zürcher Bibelkommentare: Neues Testament. Zurich: Theologischer Verlag, 1980.

Schmitt, Éric-Emmanuel. *L'Évangile selon Pilate*. Paris: Albin Michel, 2000.

Schönborn, Ulrich, and Peter Welten. "Hunger, Hungersnot." In *Sozialgeschichtliches Wörterbuch zur Bibel*, edited by Frank Crüsemann et al., 268–69. Gütersloh: Gütersloher Verlagshaus, 2009.

Schorn, Ulrike. *Ruben und das System der zwölf Stämme Israels*. Berlin: De Gruyter, 1997.

Schottroff, Luisa. "Come, Read with My Eyes." Dorothee Soelle's Biblical Hermeneutics of Liberation. In *The Theology of Dorothee Soelle*, edited by Sarah K. Pinnock, 45–53. Harrisburg, PA: Trinity, 2003.

———. "dodeka." In *Bibel in gerechter Sprache*, Glossary. Gütersloh: Gütersloher Verlagshaus, 2011, 1795–96.

———. *Der erste Brief an die Gemeinde in Korinth*. Stuttgart: Kohlhammer, 2013.

———. "Frauen in der Nachfolge Jesu in neutestamentlicher Zeit." In *Befreiungserfahrungen: Studien zur Sozialgeschichte des Neuen Testaments*, edited by Luise Schottroff, 96–133. Munich: Christian Kaiser, 1990.

———. "'Gesetzesfreies Heidenchristentum'—und die Frauen?" In *Von der Wurzel getragen: Christlich-feministische Exegese in Auseinandersetzung mit Antijudaismus*, edited by Luise Schottroff and Marie-Therese Wacker, 227–45. Leiden: Brill, 1996.

———. "Heilungsgemeinschaften: Christus und seine Geschwister im Matthäusevangelium." In *Christus und seine Geschwister: Christologie im Umfeld der Bibel in gerechter Sprache*, edited by Marlene Crüsemann and Carsten Jochum-Bortfeld, 23–44. Gütersloh: Gütersloher Verlagshaus, 2009.

———. "Der Hunger Jesu. Mk 11,11–25; Mt 21,10–22." In *Kultur, Politik, Religion, Sprache: Text. Wolfgang Stegemann zum 60. Geburtstag*, edited by Christian Strecker, 150–60. Kontexte der Schrift, vol. II. Stuttgart: Kohlhammer, 2005.

———. "Jesus' Hunger." In *The Eucharist: Bodies, Bread, and Resurrection*, edited by Andrea Bieler and Luise Schottroff, 74–77. Minneapolis: Fortress, 2007.

———. *Lydia's Impatient Sisters: A Feminist Social History of Early Christianity.* Translated by Barbara and Martin Rumscheidt. Louisville: Westminster John Knox, 1995.

———. *The Parables of Jesus.* Translated by Linda Maloney. Minneapolis: Fortress, 2006.

———. "Sind die 'Zwölf' zwölf Männer?" http://www.bibel-in-gerechter-sprache.de/wp-content/uploads/Die_Zwoelf.pdf.

Schottroff, Luisa, and Marie-Theres Wacker. *Feminist Biblical Interpretation: A Compendium of Critical Commentary on the Books of the Bible and Related Literature.* Translated by Martin Rumscheidt. Grand Rapids: Eerdmans, 2012.

Schroer, Silvia, and Thomas Staubli. *Die Körpersymbolik der Bibel.* Darmstadt: Wissenschaftliche Buchgesellschaft, 1998.

Schulz, Petra. *Hunger und Wut: Warum die Welternährungskrise kein Zufall ist.* Documentary film. Mainz: ZDF, 2008.

Schüngel-Straumann, Helen. *Tobit: Herders Theologischer Kommentar zum Alten Testament.* Freiburg: Herder, 2000.

Schutzbach, Franziska. "Reclaim Anger." Speech given at the QueerFeministischer Stadtspaziergang, March 9, 2012 in Berlin-Kreuzberg. https://fuckermothers.wordpress.com/2012/03/15/reclaim-anger/.

Schwartz, Seth. *Imperialism and Jewish Society 200 B.C.E. to 640 C.E.* Princeton: Princeton University Press, 2001.

Scoralick, Ruth. "Das Buch der Weisheit." In *Bibel in gerechter Sprache*, 1599. Gütersloh: Gütersloher Verlagshaus, 2007.

Scott, J. Julius. "The Cornelius Incident in the Light of its Jewish Setting." *Journal of the Evangelical Theological Society* 34 (1991) 475–84.

Shaw, George Bernard. *Man and Superman and Three Other Plays.* New York: Barnes and Noble Classics, 2004.

Sifre Devarim 48:7. Translated by Marty Jaffee. https://jewishstudies.washington.edu/book/sifre-devarim/chapter/pisqa-48/.

Sifre Devarim 306:17. Translated by Shraga Silverstein. https://www.sefaria.org/Sifrei_Devarim.306.17?lang=bi.

Smith, Dennis E. *From Symposium to Eucharist: The Banquet in the Early Christian World.* Minneapolis: Fortress, 2003.

Sölle, Dorothee. "At a peace gathering." In *The Mystery of Death*, translated by Nancy Lukens-Rumscheidt and Martin Lukens-Rumscheidt, 62. Minneapolis: Fortress, 2007.

———. "Gott, du Freundin der Menschen." In *Träume mich, Gott: Geistliche Texte mit lästigen politischen Fragen*, 57–58. Wuppertal: Hammer, 1994.

———. *The Silent Cry: Mysticism and Resistance.* Translated by Barbara and Martin Rumscheidt. Minneapolis: Fortress, 2001.

Sparks, H. F. D., ed. *The Apocryphal Old Testament.* Oxford: Clarendon, 1984.

Speck, Ernst. *Handelsgeschichte des Altertums. Band 2: Die Griechen.* 1901. Reprint, Paderborn: Salzwasser, 2012.

Spiegel, Der. "Sambia: Hungrig und wütend." *Der Spiegel* 28/1990 (July 9, 1990), 117–118. https://www.spiegel.de/spiegel/print/d-13500583.html.

Standhartinger, Angela. "'And All Ate and Were Filled' (Mark 6:42 and par): The Feeding Narratives in the Context of Hellenistic-Roman Banquet Cultures." In *Decisive Meals: Table Politics in Biblical Literature*, edited by Nathan MacDonald et al., 62–82. London: T&T Clark, 2012.

BIBLIOGRAPHY

———. *Das Frauenbild im Judentum der hellenistischen Zeit: Ein Beitrag anhand von "Joseph und Aseneth."* Arbeiten zur Geschichte des antiken Judentums und des Urchristentums 26. Leiden: Brill, 1995.

———. "Wie die verehrteste Judith und die besonnenste Hanna." In *Dem Tod nicht glauben: Sozialgeschichte der Bibel. Festschrift für Luise Schottroff zum 70. Geburtstag*, edited by Frank Crüsemann et al., 103–26. Gütersloh: Gütersloher Verlagshaus, 2004.

Staubli, Thomas. *Begleiter durch das Erste Testament.* Düsseldorf: Patmos, 1999.

Stegemann, Ekkehard W., and Wolfgang Stegemann. *The Jesus Movement: A Social History of its First Century.* Minneapolis: Fortress, 1999.

Stegemann, Wolfgang. "Hinterm Horizont geht's weiter: Erneute Betrachtung von Gerd Theissens These zum Wanderradikalismus der Jesusbewegung." In *Grenzgänge: Symposium zur kritischen Rezeption der Arbeiten Gerd Theissens*, edited by Peter Lampe and Helmut Schwier, 76–93. Göttingen: Vandenhoeck & Ruprecht, 2010.

Stein, Hans Joachim. *Frühchristliche Mahlfeiern: Ihre Gestalt und Bedeutung nach der neutestamentlichen Briefliteratur und der Johannesoffenbarung.* Wissenschaftliche Untersuchungen zum Neuen Testament II 255. Tübingen: Mohr Siebeck, 2008.

Stemberger, Günther. "Die Datierung der Mekhilta." *Kairos* 21 (1979) 81–118.

Strack, Hermann L., and Paul Billerbeck. *Kommentar zum Neuen Testament aus Talmud und Midrasch.* 6 vols, 10th edition. Vol. 2: *Das Evangelium nach Markus, Lukas und Johannes und die Apostelgeschichte.* Munich: C.H. Beck, 2009.

Strecker, Christian. "Judentum." In *Sozialgeschichtliches Wörterbuch zur Bibel*, edited by Frank Crüsemann et al., 279–83. Gütersloh: Gütersloher Verlagshaus, 2009.

Strecker, Georg. *Theology of the New Testament.* German edition edited and completed by Friedrich Wilhelm Horn; translated by M. Eugene Boring. New York: De Gruyter; Louisville: Westminster John Knox, 2000.

Strong, James. *Strong's Exhaustive Concordance of the Bible: Updated and Expanded Edition.* Peabody, MA: Hendrickson 2007.

Strotmann, Angelika. "Die göttliche Weisheit als Nahrungsspenderin, Gastgeberin und sich selbst anbietende Speise: Mit einem Ausblick auf Joh 6." In *"Eine gewöhnliche und harmlose Speise?" Von den Entwicklungen frühchristlicher Abendmahlstraditionen*, edited by Judith Hartenstein et al., 131–56. Gütersloh: Gütersloher Verlagshaus, 2008.

Sutter Rehmann, Luzia. "Auf der Spur des Unsichtbaren." In *Sich dem Leben in die Arme werfen*, edited by Luzia Sutter Rehmann et al., 156–71. Gütersloh: Gütersloher Verlagshaus, 2002.

———. *Geh, frage die Gebärerin: Feministisch-befreiungstheologische Untersuchungen zum Gebärmotiv in der Apokalyptik.* Gütersloh: Gütersloher Verlagshaus, 1995.

———. "Geschwister, Jünger und Frauen: Warum finden sich keine 'Männer' um Jesus?" *Bibel heute* 195 (2013) 10–13.

———. "Manchmal stehen wir auf: Eine Annäherung an eine apokalyptische Spiritualität." In *Vom Mut genau hinzusehen. Feministisch-befreiungstheologische Interpretationen zur Apokalyptik*, edited by Luzia Sutter Rehmann, 140–60. Lucerne: Exodus, 1998.

———. "Olivenöl als Zündstoff: Die vier Salbungsgeschichten der Evangelien im Kontext des Judentums des Zweiten Tempels." *Lectio difficilior* (1/2013). http://www.lectio.unibe.ch/13_1/sutter_rehmann_luzia_olivenoel_als_zuendstoff.html.

———. "Verräterische Konflikte: Abendmahlsdarstellungen im Gespräch mit neutestamentlichen Traditionen." In *"Eine gewöhnliche und harmlose Speise?" Von den Entwicklungen frühchristlicher Abendmahlstraditionen*, edited by Judith Hartenstein et al., 296–319. Gütersloh: Gütersloher Verlagshaus, 2008.

———. "Wenn die Toten sich ausruhen vom Totsein: Eine widerständige Spiritualität." *Sich dem Leben in die Arme werfen: Auferstehungserfahrungen*, edited by Luzia Sutter Rehmann et al., 74–88. Gütersloh: Gütersloher Verlagshaus, 2002.

———. "What Happened in Caesarea? Symphagein as Bonding Experience (Acts 10–11:18)." In *Decisive Meals: Table Politics in Biblical Literature*, edited by Nathan MacDonald et al., 99–113. London: T&T Clark, 2012.

———. *Wut im Bauch: Hunger im Neuen Testament*. 2nd ed. Gütersloh: Gütersloher Verlagshaus, 2016.

Sutter Rehmann, Luzia, Sabine Bieberstein, and Ulrike Metternich. *Sich dem Leben in die Arme werfen: Auferstehungserfahrungen*. Gütersloh: Gütersloher Verlagshaus, 2002.

Tacitus. *Annals, Book 12*. In *Annals: 4–6, 11–12*, 316–417. Translated by John Jackson. Loeb Classical Library 312. Cambridge, MA: Harvard University Press, 1937.

Tagesschau.de. "Ein hungriger Mann ist ein wütender Mann." April 14, 2008. https://tsarchive.wordpress.com/2008/04/14/haiti54/.

Taschner, Johannes. "Lehren/Lernen." In *Sozialgeschichtliches Wörterbuch zur Bibel*, edited by Frank Crüsemann et al., 348–53. Gütersloh: Gütersloher Verlagshaus, 2009.

Theissen, Gerd. *Soziologie der Jesusbewegung: Ein Beitrag zur Entstehungsgeschichte des Urchristentums*. 7th ed. Gütersloh: Gütersloher Verlagshaus, 1997.

Theological Dictionary of the New Testament. 10 vols. Edited by Gerhard Kittel and Gerhard Friedrich. Translated by Geoffrey W. Bromiley. Grand Rapids: Eerdmans, 1977.

Tomson, Peter J. "The Wars against Rome, the Rise of Rabbinic Judaism and of Apostolic Gentile Christianity, and the Judaeo-Christians: Elements for a Synthesis." In *The Image of the Judaeo-Christians in Ancient Jewish and Christian Literature*, edited by Peter J. Tomson and Doris Lambers-Petry, 1–31. Wissenschaftliche Untersuchungen zum Neuen Testament 158. Tübingen: Mohr Siebeck, 2003.

Townes, Emily. *In a Blaze of Glory: Womanist Spirituality as Social Witness*. Nashville, TN: Abingdon, 1995.

Veyne, Paul. *Brot und Spiele: Gesellschaftliche Macht und politische Herrschaft in der Antike*. Frankfurt: Campus, 1988.

Vogel, Friedemann. *"Aufstand"—"Revolte"—"Widerstand": Linguistische Mediendiskursanalyse der Ereignisse in den Pariser Vorstädten, 2005*. Frankfurt: Peter Lang, 2009.

von Roten, Iris. *Frauen im Laufgitter: Offene Worte zur Stellung der Frau*. Dortmund: eFeF, 1991.

Wallace, Daniel B. *Greek Grammar Beyond the Basics: An Exegetical Syntax of the New Testament*. Grand Rapids: Zondervan, 1996.

Westerhoff, Horst-Dieter. "Armut." Konrad Adenauer Stiftung, *Lexikon der Sozialen Marktwirtschaft*. http://www.kas.de/wf/de/71.10457.

———. "Wie sich eine Nation arm rechnet." Universität Potsdam, Volkswirtschaftliche Diskussionsbeiträge, No. 72, 2004.

Wiesel, Elie. "The Hunger Crisis: Securing the World's Food." Speech given at Petra IV: Reaching for New Economic, Scientific and Educational Horizons, June 17–19, 2008. https://eliewieselfoundation.org/conferences/petra-conferences/.

Witherington, Ben. *The Acts of the Apostles: A Socio-Rhetorical Commentary*. Grand Rapids: Eerdmans 1998.

Witzig, Heidi. "Die Poesie der Polemik: Lektüreerfahrungen mit Iris von Rotens 'Frauen im Laufgitter.'" *Olympe: Feministische Arbeitshefte zu Politik* 28 (2009) 18–20.

Wolff, Hans Walter. *Anthropologie des Alten Testaments*. 3rd ed. Munich: Kaiser, 1977.

Wood, Roy C. *The Sociology of the Meal*. Edinburgh: Edinburgh University Press, 1995.

Ziegler, Jean. *Wie kommt der Hunger in die Welt? Ein Gespräch mit meinem Sohn*. 6th ed. Translated from French to German by Hanna van Laak. Munich: Bertelsmann, 2002.

Zingerle, Arnold. "Identitätsbildung bei Tische: Theoretische Vorüberlegungen aus kultursoziologischer Sicht." In *Essen und kulturelle Identität: Europäische Perspektiven*, edited by Hans Jürgen Teuteberg et al., 69–86. Berlin: Akademie, 1997.

www.ingramcontent.com/pod-product-compliance
Lightning Source LLC
Chambersburg PA
CBHW081824230426
43668CB00017B/2372